Understanding the Digital Economy

Data, Tools, and Research

edited by Erik Brynjolfsson and Brian Kahin

The MIT Press, Cambridge, Massachusetts, and London, England

This book was printed and bound in the United States of America.

Library of Congress Cataloging-in-Publication Data

Understanding the digital economy : data, tools, and research / edited by Erik Brynjolfsson and Brian Kahin.
    p. cm.
Includes bibliographical references and index.
ISBN 0-262-02474-8 (hc : alk. paper)
1. Electronic commerce—Congresses. I. Brynjolfsson, Erik. II. Kahin, Brian.

HF5548.32 .U53 2000
330.9—dc21   00-033947

Contents

Introduction

Erik Brynjolfsson and Brian Kahin

"The digital economy—defined by the changing characteristics of information, computing, and communications—is now the preeminent driver of economic growth and social change. With a better understanding of these fundamental transformations, we can make wiser decisions—whether we are investing in research, products, or services, or are adapting our laws and policies to the realities of a new age."—Neal Lane, Assistant to the President for Science and Technology, April 1999

Although there is now a substantial body of literature on the role of information technology in the economy, much of it is inconclusive. The context is now changing as the success of the Internet and electronic commerce ("e-commerce") introduces new issues of influence and measurement. Computers created a platform for the commercial Internet; the Internet provided the platform for the Web; the Web, in turn, provided an enabling platform for e-commerce. The Internet and the Web have also enabled profound changes in the organization of firms and in processes within firms.

The Internet links information to locations, real and virtual. It links the logic of numbers to the expressive power and authority of words and images. Internet technology offers new forms for social and economic enterprise, new versatility for business relationships and partnerships, and new scope and efficiency for markets.

The commercial Internet has only had about six years to play out in earnest, but the numbers show a remarkable acceleration—a doubling of Internet connections year after year and, more recently, a variety of figures on e-commerce showing even faster growth. Web transaction costs are as much as 50–99 percent less than conventional transaction costs.[1] It is this chain of drivers and its implications for the economy and society as a whole that leads us to speak of a *digital economy*.

The term "information economy" has come to mean the broad, long-term trend toward the expansion of information- and knowledge-based assets and value relative to the tangible assets and products associated with agriculture, mining, and manufacturing. The term "digital economy" refers specifically to the recent and still largely unrealized transformation of all sectors of the economy by the computer-enabled digitization of information.

Because of its mandate in matters of interstate commerce and foreign trade, the federal government has primary responsibility for evaluating the health and direction of the economy. The emerging digital economy makes commerce less local, more interstate, and, especially, more global, in line with a long-term trend toward market liberalization and reduced trade barriers. At the same time, the picture presented by public information sources is becoming less and less complete. What we know about e-commerce comes from proprietary sources that use inconsistent methodologies. Economic monitoring, like policy development, is challenged by quickly evolving technologies and market practices.

The nature and scope of the digital economy are matters of concern to nations at all levels of development. Like consistent legal ground rules, an open, testable platform of public economic information is essential to investment and business decisions. It is also essential to sound monetary policy and to setting taxes and spending budgets. Ultimately, understanding the digital economy is relevant to a wide range of policies: R&D investment, intellectual property, education, antitrust, government operations, accounting standards, trade, and so on.

All countries must confront the unfettered flow of information on the Internet and the ease with which international transactions and investments can take place. While the digital economy is known as a generator of new business models and new wealth, it is also undermining old business models and threatening investments and jobs in certain established businesses. With the excitement comes anxiety and concern about the how the ingredients of the digital economy should be configured for optimal advantage.

Outside the United States, it is sometimes viewed as a suspect phenomenon, deriving in part from American strengths in computer technology and software, flat-rate phone service, and the scale advantages of the English language. For all these reasons, it begs investigation.

In April 1998, the U.S. Department of Commerce issued *The Emerging Digital Economy*, a landmark report that recognized the accelerating importance of the Internet and e-commerce in the national economy. Bearing the imprimatur of the federal government, the report offered new perspective on the role of information technology in productivity, inflation, economic growth, and capital investment. It has been cited frequently and succeeded by a number of reports assessing these and other developments.[2]

In November 1998, as part of the second phase of an initiative on global electronic commerce, President Clinton charged the assistant to the president for economic policy to undertake an assessment of the digital economy. In addition to asking the Department of Commerce to update *The Emerging Digital Economy*, the president asked that experts be convened to assess the implications of the digital economy and to consider how it might best be measured and evaluated in the future. Accordingly, an interagency working group on the digital economy planned a public conference, which took place on May 25–26, 1999, at the Department of Commerce (www.digitaleconomy. gov). The conference was sponsored by the Department of Commerce, the National Science Foundation, the National Economic Council, the Office of Science and Technology Policy, and the Electronic Commerce Working Group, the umbrella interagency group for the administration's global e-commerce initiative.

The conference sought a common baseline for understanding the digital economy and considered how a clearer and more useful picture of that economy might be developed. While recognizing the convergence of communications, computing, and information, the conference looked beyond those sectors to focus on the transformation of business and commerce, processes and transactions, throughout the economy.

This book's four parts mirror the four basic topics considered at the conference:

- *The macroeconomic perspective:* How do we measure and assess "the digital economy" and its implications for the economy as a whole?

- *The texture of the digital economy:* How do firms compete and how do markets function, and how is this different from traditional competition? What are the opportunities for and impediments to the participation of individuals and small businesses?

- *The impacts on labor demand and participation:* Do the new technologies exacerbate inequality? What skills, technologies, and institutions are needed to support broader access to the benefits of the digital economy by different individuals and groups?

- *Organizational change:* How does the digital environment affect the structure and operation of firms and institutions?

The Macroeconomic Perspective

Information technology is playing an increasing role in growth, capital investment, and other aspects of the economy. The scope and significance of these transformations remain open to question, however, in large part because underlying measurement and methodology problems have not been resolved.

- How should we identify and measure the key drivers of the digital economy?

- What are the industry-level and economy-wide investments related to e-commerce, including investments in information technology equipment and workers?

- What are the implications for growth, employment, productivity, and inflation?

- How should we account for intangible consumer benefits and burdens?

There are three chapters in this part. In "Measuring the Digital Economy," John Haltiwanger and Ron Jarmin note that the emergence of e-commerce is part of a broad spectrum of changes over several decades related to advances in information technology and the growth of the broader digital economy. After reviewing the current activities of federal statistical agencies, they conclude that current data collection activities are inadequate and provide some practical advice on how to improve measurement of the digital economy.

In "GDP and the Digital Economy: Keeping up with the Changes," Brent Moulton argues that inadequate measurement of the true output of the digital economy has contributed to past difficulties economists have had in identifying the productivity benefits of the IT revolution. He shows that despite these measurement difficulties, the measured contribution of computers to GDP has grown substantially in the late 1990s, and he outlines an agenda for improving research in this area.

In a seminal paper a decade ago, Paul David noted that new technologies such as electric motors or computers require enormous complementary investments, such as changes in organizational structure, in order to reach their full productive potential.[3] In his chapter, "Understanding Digital Technology's Evolution and the Path of Measured Productivity Growth: Present and Future in the Mirror of the Past," David provides a detailed review of the subsequent literature and shows how much of the micro and macro evidence on IT and productivity affirms the importance of organizational complements.

Market Structure, Competition, and the Role of Small Business

The digital economy includes information and communications technology, e-commerce, and digitally delivered services, software, and information. The characteristics of these goods and services (including factors such as economies of scale, network effects, public good characteristics, and transaction costs) can lead to different market structures and competitive conditions. Unfortunately, such characteristics are difficult to measure, technologies are changing rapidly, and relevant market boundaries are fluid and difficult to define. Some have speculated that the Internet and e-commerce hold great promise for small firms, by liberating them from proprietary value chains, diminishing transaction costs, and providing access to global markets, but without adequate data it is difficult to test this speculation.

• What are the relationships and interactions between the economic characteristics of digital technologies, products, and services and the structure and competitiveness of markets?

• What are the key determinants of prices (overall price levels, price flexibility, price dispersion, etc.), market structure and efficiency (competitive, noncompetitive, segmented, etc.), and competition (price based, market share based, etc.)?

• What roles do startups and small firms play in different segments of the digital economy? What are the barriers to launching and growing small firms?

• How and to what extent do the Internet and e-commerce either benefit or handicap entrepreneurs and small- to medium-sized firms?

The five chapters in this part review the empirical evidence on how competition and strategy differ in the digital economy. Two of the chapters specifically look at the changing role of smaller firms.

In "Understanding Digital Markets: Review and Assessment," Michael Smith, Joseph Bailey, and Erik Brynjolfsson summarize the recent literature on how the Internet is affecting competition and market efficiency. They start with findings for several dimensions of market efficiency and then focus on the puzzling finding of unusually high price dispersion on the Internet. They conclude with a set of developments to watch and provide an annotated appendix of research on the Internet and competition.

In "Market Structure in the Network Age," Hal Varian shows how several fundamental principles of economics can be used to increase understanding of how e-commerce changes competition. He analyzes versioning, loyalty programs, and promotions, in each case illustrating his points with examples from e-commerce and outlining the research issues raised.

Shane Greenstein admirably demonstrates the value of developing new data sources in his chapter, "The Evolving Structure of Commercial Internet Markets." He focuses on the commercialization of a key link in the e-commerce value chain: the Internet Service Providers (ISPs) who supply access to the Internet for millions of consumers and businesses. Using this example, he analyzes a set of broader questions that are important for researchers, policymakers and managers.

In "Small Companies in the Digital Economy," Sulin Ba, Andrew Whinston, and Han Zhang outline some of the Internet's special opportunities and challenges for smaller enterprises. They focus on the way information asymmetries on the Internet enhance the importance of branding and of trusted third parties, and they describe some significant technologies that are likely to help with these issues.

In "Small Business, Innovation, and Public Policy in the Information Technology Industry," Josh Lerner documents the ambiguous overall role of small business in innovation but shows that a particular subset of small businesses—firms that are venture backed—have been particularly strong innovators. He focuses on the concentration of venture financing in IT industries and concludes by discussing recent changes in intellectual property laws that appear to favor larger firms, drawing some implications for policy makers.

Employment, Workforce, and Access

As information and communications technologies transform the global economy, they are changing the U.S. workforce in terms of size, composition, and the knowledge and skills required for success. Indeed, the competitiveness of nations and companies appears increasingly dependent on the ability to develop, recruit, and retain technologically sophisticated workers. There are concerns that the U.S. workforce is already unable to meet the market demand for skilled and knowledgeable workers and that this gap is growing. Furthermore, there is growing concern that the benefits of the digital economy are not equitably shared, giving rise to a "digital divide." There are a variety of options for overcoming barriers to participation, and it is important to understand the extent to which such options are available, utilized, and cost-effective.

• How reliable are current models for projecting the size and composition of labor markets in occupations where technologies are changing rapidly? How can they be improved?

• How does the growth of e-commerce and investment in the Internet and related technologies affect the level and composition of labor market demand? How can these influences be untangled from other factors?

• What can be learned from firm-level or industry-level studies as compared to aggregate labor market models?

• What barriers impede the diffusion of e-commerce across the society?

• To what extent and in what ways does e-commerce enhance, preserve, or diminish diversity? To what extent does e-commerce work to increase or lessen opportunities for economic progress for disadvantaged individuals, groups, and regions?

The three chapters in this part raise troubling questions about growing inequality and underscore that the benefits of the digital economy are not necessarily evenly spread among different groups in society.

In "Technological Change, Computerization, and the Wage Structure," Larry Katz discusses one of the most troubling economic phenomena of the past two decades. Wage inequality has expanded dramatically, making the rich even richer relative to the poor. Katz notes that this widening inequality has coincided with growing use of IT and is particularly closely linked to increased relative demand for more educated and skilled workers. He reviews the existing literature and suggests some new empirical approaches that might help us identify the relationships among computerization, demand for skilled labor, and income inequality.

Donna Hoffman and Thomas Novak summarize a range of statistical evidence in "The Growing Digital Divide: Implications for an Open Research Agenda." They highlight the differential levels of computer adoption and Internet usage among various demographic groups. The provocative facts they review raise important questions for researchers and policy makers who are concerned about the potential gap between information "haves" and "have-nots."

In "Extending Access to the Digital Economy to Rural and Developing Regions," Heather Hudson examines opportunities for extending Internet access to disadvantaged groups in industrial nations and also to populations in developing nations. She documents some striking disparities in basic measures of access, such as telephone lines, and provides a useful guide to future research in this area as well as an appendix summarizing some of the available technological options.

Organizational Change

While information technology is routinely deployed in organizations to reengineer processes, gain strategic new advantages, or network across boundaries, it may also produce unintended outcomes. With the rise in interorganizational systems, e-commerce, and new organizational forms, questions arise about how new relationships among suppliers, customers, competitors, and providers will be crafted and what these new configurations imply for existing organizations.

• How will a digital economy affect structure and relationships within and among firms?

• To what extent and under what conditions will a digital economy lead to new organizational cultures?

• How will a digital economy affect stratification within and across firms?

The three chapters in this part look at the question of IT and organizational change from three different perspectives. In "IT and Organizational Change in Digital Economies: A Sociotechnical Approach," Rob Kling and Roberta Lamb argue that information systems require substantial organizational changes before they become fully effective. Through a series of insightful case studies, they highlight how this perspective diverges from the alternative view that treats IT largely as a tool. They call for a program of longitudinal research on the interaction of IT, organizations, and outcomes.

Kathleen Carley draws on research from Carnegie Mellon and elsewhere in her chapter, "Organizational Change and the Digital Economy: A Computational Organization Science Perspective." She characterizes the emerging "intelligence spaces" from the perspective of computational organizational science and shows how simulations can help us understand the nature of social and economic interactions as commerce becomes electronic, agents become artificial, and more and more of the world becomes digital.

This part and the book conclude with a cautionary perspective from Wanda Orlikowski and Suzanne Iacono. In "The Truth Is Not Out There: An Enacted View of the 'Digital Economy,'" they stress that the digital economy is not an immutable and inevitable object, subject to dispassionate analysis, but rather an ever-changing social construction. This has important implications for researchers, who need to be cognizant of the complex and often nonlinear relationships they are studying. It also serves as an essential reminder to us all that we have not just the opportunity but the responsibility to shape the digital economy in ways that reflect our values and goals.

Notes

1. OECD, *The Social and Economic Implications of Electronic Commerce* (1998), p. 63 (Table 2.4).

2. Lynn Margherio et al., *The Emerging Digital Economy* (Department of Commerce, April 1998); *Fostering Research on the Economic and Social Impacts of Information Technology* (Washington, DC: National Academy Press, 1998); "Economic and Social Significance of Information Technologies," in National Science Foundation, *1998 Science And Engineering Indicators*; *The Economic and Social Impacts of Electronic Commerce* (OECD, September 1998); David Henry et al., *The Emerging Digital Economy II* (Department of Commerce, June 1999).

3. "Computer and Dynamo: The Modern Productivity Paradox in a Not-Too-Distant Mirror," in *Technology and Productivity: The Challenge for Economic Policy*, Paris: Organization for Economic Co-operation and Development (1991), pp. 315–348.

The Macroeconomic Perspective

Measuring the Digital Economy

John Haltiwanger and Ron S. Jarmin

Introduction

This chapter focuses on the data needs and measurement challenges associated with the emerging digital economy. We must start, however, by defining what we mean by the digital economy. The dramatic growth of what is being called electronic commerce (e-commerce) has been facilitated by the expansion of access to computers and the Internet in workplaces, homes, and schools. There is a broad consensus that computers and the Internet are producing rapid changes in how goods and services are produced, the nature of the goods and services being offered, and the means by which goods and services are brought to market. We view the emergence of e-commerce, however, as part of a broad spectrum of changes in the structure of the economy related to developments extending over several decades in information technology (IT). U.S. statistical agencies are still addressing the challenges of measuring the changes brought on by the IT revolution. For measurement purposes, the challenges brought on by the growth of e-commerce are closely linked to those brought on by advances in IT.

The banking sector provides a good example of the problems confronting statistical agencies. The IT revolution has led to the introduction of new services such as electronic banking and ATMs. Statistical agencies have struggled with how to define and measure output in banking for years, and the IT revolution has done nothing to ease the struggle. For example, ATMs allow customers to access their accounts 24 hours a day 7 days a week while reducing or eliminating the time they spend in teller lines. This clearly represents an increased level of customer service. Yet the value of such services is not directly measured in any official statistics, whereas the cost of installing ATM networks is. Because of measurement problems of this sort, government statistics understate the productivity increases in banking that come from investments in IT.

There is widespread belief that we need to make significant changes to the U.S. statistical system in order to track the growth and impact of the digital economy. The 1997 Department of Commerce report on *The Emerging Digital Economy* provides examples of aspects of the digital economy that we should be measuring:

1. The shape and size of the key components of the evolving digital economy, such as e-commerce and, more generally, the introduction of computers and related technology in the workplace.

2. The process by which firms develop and apply advances in IT and e-commerce.

3. Changes in the structure and functioning of markets, including changes in the distribution of goods and services and changes in the nature of international and domestic competition.

4. The social and economic implications of the IT revolution, such as the effects of IT investments on productivity.

5. Demographic characteristics of user populations.

After presenting what we believe are the data needs for assessments of the digital economy, we will summarize the current activities of federal statistical agencies. Not surprisingly, we will argue that current data collection activities are inadequate and that a number of difficult issues need to be resolved to improve the situation. We will offer some practical and feasible examples of what statistical agencies can do to improve measurement, but we stop short of providing specific suggestions and instead describe a framework in which discussions about changes to the measurement system can take place. This process needs to begin soon because of the considerable lag that often occurs between identifying a data need, finding a way to address it, implementing a collection program, and getting data to users.

Data Needs for the Information Economy

We will restrict our attention to the types of data that are required for public policy and general economic research and that are typically collected by government statistical agencies through nationally representative surveys of individual, household, and business units. We recognize that there is a large data-using constituency that requires types of data different from those collected by the statistical agencies. This constituency has traditionally been served by private-sector sources, and we believe that this will continue to be the case.

Given the pace of change in IT and the myriad new ways in which businesses, households, and others exploit IT, it is understandable that the institutions that collect economic and demographic data are behind in measuring the magnitude and scope of IT's impact on the economy. But before discussing measurement issues directly related to IT and the digital economy, we need to stress that improved measurement of many "traditional" items is crucial if we are to understand fully IT's impact. It is only by relating changes in the quality and use of IT to changes in traditional measures such as productivity and wages that we can assess IT's impact on the economy. For example, if we cannot measure and value output in the service-sector industries where IT is important, it will be difficult to say anything about its impact. Thus, as part of the attempt to improve measurement of the digital economy, we also need better ways to measure the activities of firms in the so-called unmeasured sectors of the economy (e.g., services) and to improve the quality of statistics for the measured (i.e., the goods-producing) sectors.

Three broad areas of research and policy interest related to the digital economy require high-quality data. First, there is the investigation of the impact of IT on key indicators of aggregate activity, such as productivity and living standards. Aggregate productivity growth slowed over much of the period in which large investments in IT occurred, especially in service industries, such as banking, that had particularly large IT investments. A number of studies, at various levels of aggregation, failed to find a link between IT investments and productivity, leading to the identification of a "productivity paradox" (Solow 1987; Berndt and Morrison 1995; for a review of the literature on the link between IT investments and productivity see Brynolfsson and Yang 1996).

Several explanations have been offered for this paradox. One is that official statistics do not capture all the changes in output, quality, and cost savings associated with IT and therefore understate its impact (Siegel and Griliches 1994). Another compares IT to previous innovations in the economy, such as electrification, and notes that there can be a considerable lag between investments in such innovations and related productivity increases (David 1990; Greenwood and Yorgulu 1997).

Recent studies using data from a variety of sources have in fact reported a link between IT and productivity (e.g., Jorgenson and Stiroh 1995; Greenan and Mairesse 1996; Brynjolfsson and Hitt 1995, 1996; Dunne et al. 1999). These, combined with improved aggregate productivity performance, have led some to speculate that productivity is no longer a paradox (Anonymous 1999). While it is undoubtedly the case that several firms and industries have finally seen returns on investments in IT, the empirical evidence for an economy-wide impact is limited. A large part of this limitation, though, may be due to the inadequacy of available data.

With the growth of e-commerce, particularly in business-to-business transactions, we are no longer interested only in measuring the impact of computers and IT on productivity within organizations. We now want to assess whether there have been measurable increases in productivity related to improvements in information flows and reduced transaction costs between organizations that do business electronically. We want to see whether e-commerce is associated with measurable productivity gains in sectors and firms that rely heavily on e-commerce with respect to those that employ e-commerce less extensively.

Of related interest are the implications of IT and e-commerce for the measurement of the capital stock—particularly equipment. For accuracy we need measurements of equipment investment by

detailed asset category, quality-adjusted deflators for such investment that take into account advances in technology, and appropriate measures of the depreciation rates of the assets in question. In
the case of IT, the measurement of depreciation rates has become
much more difficult due to the rapid pace of the changes involved
(e.g., the rate at which the speeds of successive generations of
processors increase) and the associated rapid turnover of computer hardware and software. Storage closets, attics, and junkyards
are increasingly cluttered with PCs that were on the cutting edge
just a few years ago! While it is important to measure the national
capital stock, we must also understand where—in what industries,
geographic locations, and types of firms—IT is being applied. This
will provide a basis for evaluating the impact of IT on productivity
because, in principle, we should observe the greatest gains in
productivity in those sectors that apply IT most effectively. This
suggests that using accounting methods to estimate IT (or other
types of) investment is insufficient, since these analyses require
micro-level data. For this reason, data on IT investment must be
collected from businesses and other organizations in every major
sector of the economy.

The second area of research and policy interest that requires
high-quality data is the impact of IT on labor markets and income
distribution (for broader discussions of these issues see OECD 1999
and DOC 1999). Of particular interest here is the issue of whether
IT is increasing wage and income dispersion by creating groups of
haves and have-nots based on whether people have the skills and/
or are employed in the appropriate sectors to take advantage of IT
advances (Autor, Katz, and Krueger 1997; Dunne et al. 1999).
Answering this question requires measuring the use of computers
and other IT equipment in the workplace and relating it to wages.
It would also be useful to assess whether or not the educational
system is providing the next generation of workers with the skills
needed to succeed in the digital economy.

Third, many people would like to assess the impact of IT on the
way production is organized. They want to understand how firm
and industry structures have changed as IT has become a more
important input to production in every sector of the economy (Hitt
and Byrnolfsson 1997). And, most importantly, they want to under-

stand the impact of the digital economy on market structure. There is a growing sense that e-commerce is dramatically changing the ways in which buyers and sellers find and interact with each other. Electronic networks in the form of Electronic Data Interchanges (EDIs) have existed for some time, allowing companies to communicate with major suppliers and customers. Until recently, however, EDIs were limited primarily to large firms with mainframe computers that communicated across expensive proprietary lines. The Internet allows anyone with a PC and modem to communicate with millions of computers worldwide. This has important implications for the nature and location of businesses—particularly those involved in the distribution of goods and services—and for how markets work.

The availability of inexpensive yet powerful computer hardware and software reduces the costs of setting up an e-business and expands the possibilities for siting businesses. The open structure of the Internet now allows small firms to download specifications and bid on jobs previously available only to a select few who had access to EDIs. This is likely to have significant market structure implications for a wide array of goods and services.

At the same time, the Internet is giving consumers more power in the marketplace by making information on the prices and qualities of a wide range of goods and services more accessible. Price competition could be substantially enhanced when buyers can easily search for alternative suppliers of goods and services.

It is also important to get a handle on the degree of substitution occurring between goods and services purchased through e-commerce (e.g., from Amazon.com) and similar goods and services purchased through traditional channels (e.g., from a neighborhood bookstore). This substitution may be particularly important for "digital" goods and services. Digital goods, which will eventually include books, movies, and music, are goods that can be delivered to customers in digital form over the Internet. Such goods can theoretically bypass traditional distribution channels. This obviously has major implications for the wholesalers, retailers, and transporters of this class of products. Researchers will want to keep track of changes in how these products are delivered as the bandwidth of the Internet expands.

We can now summarize the general data requirements for the digital economy. We need statistics on inputs and outputs that will allow us to construct measures of productivity at several levels of aggregation, to maintain the National Income and Product Accounts, to conduct cross-region and industry studies, and to perform micro-level data analyses. This includes the construction of appropriate quality-adjusted price deflators. We are interested in understanding not only the implications for consumer and producer prices but also whether market competition (as reflected, for example, in price-cost markups) has changed as a result of e-commerce. We also need to understand the organization and location of production and where workers of different types work. This requires collecting at least some data at the subfirm, or establishment, level. We also need data on the human capital embodied in workers and on the occupations and industries they work in and the wages they receive. Finally, we need detailed demographic data on the U.S. population, and in particular on individuals and households that participate in the digital economy.

Assuming that we will continue to collect and improve our traditional menu of economic and demographic data, and given the three broad research areas in which we would like to assess the impact of IT, what are some of the specific data items we should be measuring in order to keep track of the digital economy? We believe that there are five areas where good data are needed. These are: (1) measures of the IT infrastructure, (2) measures of e-commerce, (3) measures of firm and industry organization, (4) demographic and labor market characteristics of individuals using IT, and (5) price behavior. Boxes 1–5 give examples of specific data items of interest to policymakers and researchers in each of these five areas.

How Well Are We Measuring the Digital Economy?

Because we cannot survey all data sources, we will focus on data collected by the Census Bureau and other federal statistical agencies. (In several cases, data relevant to the digital economy are available from sources outside the federal statistical system. These data sets tend to be specialized, are often based on nonrepresenta-

---

Box 1
Data Needs for the Digital Economy: Information Technology Infrastructure

We should measure the physical and software infrastructure of the information economy. In particular, data collection efforts should focus on investments in physical infrastructure (e.g., IT equipment including computers, phone lines, switches, fiber optic and cable lines, satellites, wireless networks, and LAN equipment). We should also measure investments in software infrastructure. We should collect data on the capacity of the Internet and other networks as well as the actual traffic on these systems. It is crucial that we measure depreciation in infrastructure (both equipment and software) and how investments and depreciation act to change the capacity of the digital infrastructure. And we need to have some idea of the IT and software components of "non-IT" equipment such as numerically controlled machines.

---

tive surveys, and are rarely available to the wider research and policy communities.) Even though our survey is incomplete, it should be apparent that current data collection for the items outlined in the last section is spotty and inconsistent.

Infrastructure

Our estimates of the impact of computers and related information technologies are based on relatively limited data sets. As with most equipment investment, we measure the magnitude of aggregate investment in computers by examining the output of sectors producing such equipment and adjusting for exports and imports (i.e., the statistics are generated from Current Industrial Reports and export and import statistics, as well as annual surveys of businesses). This accounting methodology provides reasonable national totals of investment in computers and related technologies on a nominal basis. Much work has been done to generate quality-adjusted deflators for computers, and to the extent that these deflators are reliable, a reasonable estimate of the national real investment in computers emerges. However, we know very little about what types of firms and industries are implementing computers and other advanced technologies. In the past, the Annual Survey of Manufactures (ASM) asked about computer investment in economic census years (in 1977, 1982, 1987, and

---

Box 2

Data Needs for the Digital Economy: E-Commerce

We should measure e-commerce by the magnitude and type of both business-to-business and business-to-consumer electronic transactions. We should also try to measure separately digital and nondigital goods and services. Nondigital products must be physically delivered to consumers. Digital products can bypass the wholesale, retail, and transport network. Also, digital products may have very different (nonlinear) pricing structures due to their high fixed costs and low marginal costs (Shapiro and Varian 1999). This may be important for computing valid price deflators and may make it difficult to use revenue-based measures of activity levels. We should also measure the use of e-commerce for both transactions and nontransaction purposes (e.g., customer service, general information, and bid posting).

1992). This question was not asked in 1997 but will probably be asked again in the future. The ASM also asks about purchased communication services and software purchases. Every five years, as part of the economic census, the Census Bureau conducts the Business Expenditure Survey (formerly known as the Assets and Expenditures Survey) for businesses in Retail, Services, and Wholesale. This survey contains a question about spending on computers, peripherals, and software. For multiunit companies, the unit of analysis in this survey is not necessarily either the firm or the establishment. Rather, data are collected roughly at the level of a legal entity (as defined by Employer Identification Numbers) or line of business. (An example would be the drugstore operations of a company that operates in several retail markets.)

In the past, the Annual Capital Expenditure Survey (ACES) did not break out equipment investment by type of capital, but it will soon begin to do so. Because this survey is at the firm level and many large, multiunit firms span several industries and regions, it will be difficult to use the results to construct accurate statistics for investments in IT and other types of capital by industry and geographic region. (The 1998 survey asked companies to break out equipment by both type of equipment and industry—roughly at a 2-digit level.) The Bureau of Economic Analysis (BEA) produces data on capital expenditures and stocks by asset type by industry. However, the allocation of assets by industry are derived from Capital Flow allocation tables that are based on strong assumptions and limited

---

Box 3

Data Needs for the Digital Economy: Firm and Industry Structure

We should measure the impact of improvements in IT, software, and the Internet on firm and market structures. More generally, we should quantify the changes in the location, industry, size, and organizational structure of businesses, as well as changes in their input mix (e.g., capital, labor, inventories) and their relationships with other businesses (e.g., outsourcing).

---

data (e.g., the asset allocations by industry are based in part on the occupational mix within industries). In short, while we may have a reasonable national estimate of investment in computers, we know little about investment in computers by industry, geographic area, or firm type.

There is little official data on the investments in and the capacity of the telecommunications networks that support the Internet. There is also little information outside of the ASM about investments in software. It is especially important to get a handle on the differential pricing and depreciation of software. Without this information, it will be virtually impossible to get an accurate measure of the service flow of software investments.

E-Commerce

There is even less information collected on e-commerce. It is important to emphasize that e-commerce sales should be covered by economic censuses and surveys since the Census Bureau maintains representative samples of all businesses, including those engaged in e-commerce. In the past, however, there has been no systematic attempt to break out sales by method of selling. Thus, we know how much firms engaged in e-commerce sell, but not how much they sell via e-commerce.

The Census Bureau has begun to inquire about e-commerce sales on many of its monthly and annual business surveys. While there is considerable interest in separately measuring business-to-consumer and business-to-business e-commerce transactions, currently no Census Bureau survey elicits such information. As for digital goods and services, there is currently no way to estimate the value of sales in which the good or service being transacted is delivered to the purchaser electronically.

> **Box 4**
> **Data Needs for the Digital Economy: Demographic and Worker Characteristics**
> We should measure the demographic and labor market characteristics of individuals and workers and compare those participating in the digital economy to those not participating. In particular, we should measure computer use at school, work, and the home and relate these to measures of economic outcomes such as wages and assets and to demographic characteristics such as education, occupation, gender, race, age, and place of residence.

Firm and Industry Structure

The ingredients for characterizing the changing structure of markets in terms of the location of businesses, the industries in which businesses operate, and the size distribution of businesses are available in business lists maintained by federal statistical agencies. For example, the Census Bureau maintains the Standard Statistical Establishment List (SSEL), which is constructed from administrative data, economic censuses, and surveys. The SSEL follows the universe of all establishments in the United States and is a very useful resource for keeping track of the changing demography (in terms of size, location, and industry) of U.S. businesses. It is an underutilized resource for this type of analysis. For example, there is some sense that e-commerce has reduced entry barriers substantially, allowing small businesses to compete in an unprecedented manner. Because the SSEL offers a comprehensive dynamic picture of all businesses (large and small), it is a superb resource for tracking the impact of the digital economy on small businesses. There is also an ongoing collaborative project between the Small Business Administration and the Census Bureau to develop and use a longitudinal version of the SSEL to track the dynamics of small vs. large businesses.

There are some challenges in the use of the SSEL for these types of analyses. First, the quality of the analyses depends critically on the quality of the industry and location codes in the SSEL. While the quality of such codes is relatively high for most businesses, the quality for new and small businesses is lower. This could prove to be problematic for tracking the impact of the digital economy because of its dynamic nature and purportedly large number of small start-

---

Box 5

Data Needs for the Digital Economy: Price Behavior

Price deflators for goods and services must be adjusted to reflect changes in quality induced by IT. This will allow us to do more accurate measurements of changes in key aggregate statistics such as productivity. Measures of price differentials across goods and services sold by different methods (e.g., e-commerce vs. traditional methods) as well as measures of price dispersion across producers using the same method are of critical importance to understanding the changing nature of competition in the digital economy.

---

ups. In addition, while the new North American Industrial Classification System (NAICS) offers much greater detail in terms of industries in the information and service sectors, it is unclear how easy it will be to track key aspects of the digital economy without additional modifications to our industry codes. For example, there are no current plans to classify businesses that primarily sell by e-commerce in a separate category. Instead they are grouped with mail-order houses.

Demographic and Worker Characteristics

The Current Population Survey (October supplement every three years) looks at household computer use. This information has enabled analysis of the impact of computer use on labor market outcomes, such as wages, and better understanding of the connection between computer use and worker characteristics such as age, gender, and education. The most recent supplement includes a substantial set of questions about the use of computers and the Internet at home, work, and school. The CPS and the BLS Occupational Establishment Survey offer opportunities to assess how the mix of occupations and, thus, skill types is changing in response to the emerging digital economy. An open question is whether the occupation codes need to be revised to reflect the changing nature of skills and tasks involved in the digital economy.

Price Behavior

Quality-adjusted deflators for computers have been in use for a number of years, and this has greatly helped in quantifying the impact of the IT revolution. Clearly this program must continue since the performance of computers continues to increase while their nominal prices continue to fall. Furthermore, as computer technology becomes embedded in a growing number of other products, we must ensure that the appropriate quality-adjusted deflators are constructed for these as well.

Little thought or effort has been devoted to the impact of e-commerce on output price behavior. The ability of purchasers to use the Internet to search for the best price and other changes in distribution channels that have the potential to eliminate whole-sale and retail markups may have important implications for both the CPI and PPI programs.

What Can the Census Bureau and Other Statistical Agencies Do to Improve Our Understanding of the Digital Economy?

It is clear from the discussion so far that there are many holes in the data collection efforts of the federal statistical system that need filling before a clear understanding of the digital economy can emerge. There are many difficult and longstanding measurement and data collection issues that arise again in the context of measuring the digital economy. Important examples include defining and measuring output in the non-goods-producing sectors, collecting establishment-level data from multiestablishment companies, and issues surrounding industry, commodity, and occupation classification systems. The digital economy has exacerbated many of these problems by spawning new products and services, new delivery methods and forms of communication, and improved data-processing capabilities. The result is a rapidly changing business environment that poses many challenges to agencies not known for rapid change. We are optimistic, however, that there are several practical and feasible steps that agencies can take to fill some of these data holes. Below are some examples.

Infrastructure

We should consider improving how we measure investment and depreciation of IT and software. This would go beyond current efforts with the ACES to break out equipment investment by type of equipment. In particular, plant- (or some other subfirm-) level measures are preferable if we are to assess the effects of these investments on productivity, employment, and firm and industry structure. (This is because many large firms span several industries, sectors, and geographic regions, and these firms account for a large share of investment in IT. Thus, it is not possible to get accurate measures of IT investment by industry or by geographic area with firm-level surveys.) Some of this could be accomplished by augmenting current data collection efforts. For example, questions on IT investment could be added to the Economic Censuses. Annual plant-level data could be collected for manufacturing via the Annual Survey of Manufactures. Outside of manufacturing, other annual business surveys could be used to collect I 𝖳 ꞏ investment data. (The ASM is a plant-level survey. The annual surveys outside of manufacturing are establishment-based for single-unit firms. In the case of multiunit firms, however, these surveys typically use a unit of observation based on business unit—that is, EI-line of business—and, therefore, are not exactly plant- or firm-level surveys.) While we should try to improve measures of the IT infrastructure for all sectors of the economy, the manufacturing, services, wholesale, and retail sectors should get the highest priority.

Unfortunately, many large multiestablishment firms find it difficult to report investment and other items at the establishment level. This is especially true outside of manufacturing. The Census Bureau and other statistical agencies need to work with businesses to get data at the lowest level of aggregation that firms can provide, so that agencies can provide the richest possible data for research and policy analysis at a reasonable cost to the taxpayer.

E-Commerce

To get a handle on the extent and magnitude of e-commerce, we suggest that the Census Bureau include class-of-customer and method-of-selling questions on all Economic Censuses and Annual Surveys. These questions ask respondents to break out revenue by type of buyer (e.g., consumers, businesses, government) and by transaction method (e.g., in-store, mail order, Internet). Simple cross tabs could then provide estimates of business-to-business and business-to-consumer e-commerce alongside traditional commerce.

Questions of this type are typically asked only in the retail, whole-sale, and service sectors and are used primarily for classification purposes. The Internet and other direct-marketing channels have increased the need for such questions in the goods-producing sectors as well.

Classification efforts are particularly important for examining e-commerce. Under NAICS, businesses engaged primarily in Internet commerce are classified separately from traditional retailers. This is consistent with maintaining a "production"-oriented classification system. However, we still want to know how many books are sold. Thus, survey forms for Internet retailers should break out revenues by commodity types. Currently, statistical agencies in the United States, Canada, and Mexico are developing a North American Product Classification System (NAPCS) as the product classification companion to NAICS. This system should be designed with e-commerce and the digital economy in mind.

We expect that the impact of e-commerce on the markets for digital goods (e.g., books, CDs, stock quotes) and services will be much larger than for goods and services that must be physically delivered (e.g., furniture, haircuts, pizza). Digital products are characterized by high fixed costs (e.g., writing a "book") and low marginal costs (e.g., emailing a PDF file of a "book"; see Shapiro and Varian 1999). This has important implications for the operation and structure of the markets for these goods and services, for intellectual property rights, for local tax authorities, and for international trade (the Internet has no customs posts). Thus, it is important that we try to track the sales of digital goods and services by method of delivery. Currently, the limited bandwidth of the Internet limits this area of e-commerce., but improved technology will allow for increased electronic delivery of such goods.

Finally, we might consider undertaking an occasional survey that examines e-commerce practices in the economy. This would include asking firms how they use IT to communicate with suppliers and customers, whether they purchase or sell goods and services electronically, and whether they use the Internet or other telecommunication networks for customer service and related tasks. The 1999 ASM contained questions that address some of these issues. If the Bureau is successful in collecting this information, it should consider expanding inquiries of this type to surveys for other sectors. This might also include surveying consumers on their electronic buying habits, perhaps through the Consumer Expenditure Survey. An important goal for such a consumer survey would be to compare prices paid for similar goods and services purchased electronically and through traditional retail outlets.

Firm and Industry Structure

The Census Bureau and the Bureau of Labor Statistics already have much of what is required to examine the impact of investments in IT and the growth of e-commerce on the structure of firms and industries. In particular, the Bureau's Standard Statistical Establishment List has basic data on employment, payroll, industry, and location for the universe of employer business establishments in the United States. The data can be linked to other Census Bureau establishment-level and firm-level surveys. In this way, one could compare how the structure of IT-intensive firms changes over time relative to less IT-intensive firms. An important question in this area is whether lower transaction costs associated with business-to-business e-commerce are leading to flatter firm organizational structures. For example, instead of relying of internal sources of supply and support, firms that exploit e-commerce, with its associated lower transaction costs, may now outsource these functions to other firms. If we combine data collected following our suggestions above with the SSEL, we expect to see firms that use e-commerce extensively shedding establishments that are outside the firm's main line of business.

Another important issue is how the different marketing channels made available by electronic networks are changing the structure of markets. Not only can firms set up an electronic storefront on the Internet and serve customers all over the world, but goods producers can market directly to consumers and avoid traditional distribution channels (e.g., manufacturer to wholesaler to retailer to consumer). Thus, traditional boundaries defined by geography and industry are being blurred. The SSEL linked to surveys asking about class of customer and method of selling is the best way to see how the structure of the economy is shifting from the traditional model to the digital model.

Demographic and Worker Characteristics

We need to understand how both consumers and workers in the digital economy differ from those in the traditional economy. The Consumer Expenditure Survey should be modified to describe the digital consumer better. First, household spending on computers and IT equipment and related expenditures (e.g., fees for Internet access) should be broken out separately. Next, the CES should ask about the magnitude and nature of household e-commerce purchases (how much was spent, and on what goods and services). In a similar vein, special supplements to the Current Population Survey should continue to ask questions about computer and Internet use at home, school, and work. The precise nature of these questions should evolve so that they track the evolving role of computers and the Internet in our activities.

Also, just as industry coding requires further consideration, occupation codes should be examined to determine whether they need to be modified to reflect the changing structure and tasks of the workforce. Modified occupation coding and related workforce composition change questions are relevant not only for household surveys but also for business surveys such as the BLS Occupation Establishment Survey that measure and characterize changes in the structure of the workforce.

Price Behavior

It will be important to quantify the impact the IT revolution and e-commerce are having on the prices businesses charge for goods and services, many of which have been undergoing, and will continue to undergo, major quality changes. We are also interested in whether e-commerce is changing price-cost margins and the nature of competition. For capturing quality change, we must collect information about the characteristics of goods and services sold. Understanding changes in the nature of competition requires collection of information about the pricing of goods sold over the Internet and that of the same goods sold through more traditional methods. In this regard, it would be useful to quantify how price-cost markups have changed and how price dispersion across sellers of the same product varies by method of selling and, in the case of digital products, by method of delivery to the consumer. Since prices are traditionally collected by the BLS for the CPI and PPI programs, coordination between BLS and Census about method of selling and pricing behavior seems essential.

Other Areas

There are some more general ways in which we can modify the federal statistical system to improve measurement of the digital economy. First, we can improve our ability to measure output and productivity in the non-goods-producing sectors. Second, we can continue to refine our industry, product, and input classification systems and increase the resources devoted to assigning establishments and businesses to appropriate categories. Third, we can increase the resources devoted to developing and maintaining a master list of business establishments, such as the SSEL, with high-quality industry, location, business age, and size information. This would be an invaluable tool for providing a comprehensive perspective on the changing landscape of business activity. Fourth, we can increase the collection of micro-level data on businesses and households. Such data would allow us to control for relevant worker and business characteristics and to compare businesses and workers that have differentially adopted new processes and differentially produced new products and services. Moreover, as discussed above, linking comprehensive files, such as the SSEL, to micro data from specific targeted surveys allows us to shed light on how changing business practices have influenced firm and industry structure. The newly developed (and proposed) databases linking employer-employee data will also be valuable for examining the impact that the digital economy is having on both businesses and the workers within those businesses.

Discussion and Conclusions

While the ubiquity of IT is self-evident, our ability to quantify its impact on the economy is limited by the nature and types of data currently being collected by federal statistical agencies and other sources. There are a number of unresolved conceptual questions that exacerbate the measurement difficulties. For instance, the IT revolution is closely connected to the growth of sectors of the economy (e.g., services) that we have traditionally struggled to measure.

The digital economy is forcing statistical agencies to rethink how they measure the basic building blocks of our national accounts: outputs, inputs, and prices. Some progress has is being made on refining the measurement of individual components (e.g., national investment in computers and the fraction of retail sales attributable to e-commerce). Clearly, policy and research needs require further efforts by statistical agencies to improve data collection and measurement of the digital economy.

It is not likely that all the suggestions that we and others have offered can be implemented. We recognize that while policymakers and researchers have an insatiable appetite for data, concerns about respondent burden and the resource costs of collecting data cannot be ignored. Realistic priorities must therefore be set by the data-using community. We suggest that suggestions for changes to the data collection programs at U.S. federal statistical agencies be made within the following framework:

• Plans to measure the digital economy should complement the basic and longstanding programs of the U.S. statistical system that measure the characteristics, inputs, outputs, and prices of businesses and the characteristics and activities of individuals and households. The focus should be on measuring changes in the quality and use of IT and its impact on all sectors of the economy. There should be a special focus on improving measurement in sectors such as services where measurement has traditionally been difficult but there have been large investments in IT.

• Plans to measure the digital economy should leverage existing data resources in a variety of ways including: development and use of underutilized administrative data sources, such as the SSEL; addition of supplementary questions to existing surveys and censuses; and encouragement of micro-level data development, including linking data from different sources and sharing data across different U.S. federal statistical agencies.

In short, we suggest an incremental approach that modifies and keeps intact our basic system for economic and demographic measurement.

In spite of this apparent caution, it is also important to recognize that making changes in the basic data collection plans of the U.S. statistical agencies is a very slow process. For example, the new industrial classification system, NAICS, is being implemented by the statistical agencies over a 7-year horizon, and even though it is a great advance over the prior system, it does not adequately capture the changes emerging from the growth of e-commerce. Moreover, plans are being made now for the next Economic Census in 2002. The inherently slow process of altering the course of U.S. data collection activities implies that, unless we make progress in our thinking and plans now, we may find ourselves with relatively little information about the magnitude, scope, and impact of e-commerce for another decade or more.

Put differently, U.S. statistical agencies need to set priorities now in order to implement specific data collection plans. This paper intentionally stops short of setting these priorities. Instead, we have sought to provide a menu of measurement concerns and have stressed some general considerations that should be taken into account in planning how to improve measurement of the digital economy.

Acknowledgments

Opinions, findings, or conclusions expressed here are those of the authors and do not necessarily reflect the views of the Census Bureau or the Department of Commerce. We thank B. K. Atrostic, Erik Brynjolfsson, Frederick T. Knickerbocker, and Thomas Mesenbourg for very helpful comments on earlier drafts of this paper. This paper was written while John Haltiwanger served as Chief Economist of the Census Bureau.

References

Anonymous, 1999. "Computer Age Gains Respect of Economists," *New York Times*, April 19.

Autor, D. H., L. F. Katz, and A. B. Krueger, 1997. "Computing Inequality: Have Computers Changed the Labor Market?" NBER Working Paper No. 5956.

Berndt, E., and C. Morrison, 1995. "High-tech Capital Formation and Economic Performance in U.S. Manufacturing Industries: An Exploratory Analysis." *Journal of Econometrics* 65: 9–43.

Brynolfsson, E., and L. Hitt, 1995. "Computers as a Factor of Production: The Role of Differences Among Firms." *Economics of Innovation and New Technology* 3 (May): 183–199.

Brynolfsson, E., and L. Hitt, 1996. "Paradox Lost? Firm-level Evidence on the Returns to Information Systems Spending." *Management Science* 42(4): 541–558.

Brynolfsson, E., and S. Yang, 1996. "Information Technology and Productivity: A Review of the Literature." *Advances in Computers* 43: 179–214.

David, P., 1990. "The Dynamo and the Computer: A Historical Perspective on the Modern Productivity Paradox." *American Economic Review Papers and Proceedings* 80(2): 355–361

Dunne, T., L. Foster, J. Haltiwanger, and K. Troske, 1999. "Wage and Productivity Dispersion in U.S. Manufacturing: The Role of Computer Investment." Mimeo, Center for Economic Studies, U.S. Bureau of the Census, Washington, DC.

Greenan, N., and J. Mairesse, 1996. "Computers and Productivity in France: Some Evidence." NBER Working Paper No. 5836.

Greenwood, J., and M. Yorgulu, 1997. "1974." *Carnegie-Rochester Conference Series on Public Policy* 46: 49–96.

Hitt, L., and E. Byrnolfsson, 1997. "Information Technology and Internal Firm Organization: An Exploratory Analysis." *Journal of Management Information Systems* 14(2): 81–101.

Jorgenson, D., and K. Stiroh, 1995. "Computers and Growth." *Economics of Innovation and New Technology* 3 (May): 295–316.

OECD, 1999. *The Economic and Social Impacts of Electronic Commerce: Preliminary Findings and Research Agenda.* Paris: OECD.

Shapiro, C., and H. Varian, 1999. *Information Rules: A Strategic Guide to the Network Economy.* Boston: Harvard Business School Press.

Siegel, D., and Z. Griliches, 1994. "Purchased Services, Outsourcing, Computers, and Productivity in Manufacturing." In Z. Griliches et al., eds., *Output Measurement in the Services Sectors*, NBER Studies in Wealth, vol. 56 (Chicago: University of Chicago Press).

Solow, R., 1997. *New York Times Book Review*, July 12.

U.S. Department of Commerce, 1997. *The Emerging Digital Economy*. Washington, DC: Government Printing Office.

GDP and the Digital Economy: Keeping up with the Changes

Brent R. Moulton

The perception is widely held that the growth of the digital economy[1] is unprecedented and has been a major contributor to recent economic growth, the booming stock market, and the revival of productivity. What do we know about the growth of the digital economy? What would we like to know that the data currently do not reveal? And what does the federal statistical system need to do to provide that information? Because the economic data do not tell an unambiguous story about the digital economy, knowledgeable observers disagree about the importance of information technology (IT) and electronic commerce in the economy.

Economists have been engaged in a debate over the so-called productivity paradox, which asks how productivity growth could have slowed during the 1970s and 1980s in the face of phenomenal technological improvements, price declines, and real growth in computers and related IT equipment.[2] Much of this debate has revolved around questions of measurement—for example, are the output and growth of industries that use IT equipment being adequately measured? There are reasons to think that they are not, that is, that the measures of output for the banking, insurance, and several other industries are particularly problematic, and the measured productivity of these industries appears to be implausibly low. If productivity in IT-using industries is not being measured adequately, can the measurement errors explain the productivity paradox?[3] Several economists think that measurement may be an important piece of the solution to the puzzle.

In addition, the IT revolution has raised questions about the ability of the federal statistical system to keep up with a changing economy. The availability of inexpensive IT equipment and services has enabled businesses to do their work in new ways and has led to the creation of new firms and even entire industries. Are these new forms of business and production being adequately counted in our gross domestic product (GDP)? Have our economic statistics kept up with electronic commerce, new kinds of financial services, and new methods of inventory and product distribution?

The economic data produced by the Department of Commerce are critically valuable to our nation's economic information infrastructure. The monthly releases of GDP are meticulously followed by policymakers and financial analysts, serving as a barometer of the economy's health. These economic data provide information for understanding major policy issues, for forecasting the economy's potential for future growth, for conducting monetary policy, for understanding the tradeoffs between inflation and full employment, for projecting tax revenues and conducting fiscal policy, and for studying long-term issues such as the future of the social security system. While these data serve as very good indicators of overall economic activity, they must constantly be improved and refined to keep up with our rapidly evolving economy.

What Is Measured Well?

There are many aspects of IT and electronic commerce that are measured well in the official statistics. Some features of the digital economy are captured perfectly well by the same data collections that regularly provide information about the rest of the economy. The U.S. economic statistics for product and income are benchmarked to input-output tables that are painstakingly constructed from data collected in the economic censuses. The incomes earned from production are benchmarked to tax and administrative data. Adjustments are made to remove any sources of bias that are known and measurable. Because the IT and electronic commerce sectors, like most other sectors, are covered by the economic censuses, tax statistics, and unemployment insurance programs, data on the digital economy enter into the overall measure of how the economy is doing in general. The GDP and other basic economic statistics have been shown to provide very good information about the movements over the business cycle of production, aggregate demand and its components, income, and prices.[4]

Because the digital economy is not a standard classification for economic data, there may be some disagreement on what it entails. However it is defined, though, as a share of total GDP it is still fairly small. (For example, private investment in information-processing equipment and software, a component of nonresidential fixed investment, was $407 billion in 1999, or 4.4 percent of GDP. At this point, Census Bureau estimates of the magnitude of electronic commerce are more speculative but are still quite small as a percentage of all retail and wholesale sales.) Furthermore, at least so far, movements in IT investment have not been highly correlated with the ups and downs of the business cycle. Consequently, the measurement problems that are central to the debate about the effects of IT on long-term growth and productivity are not questions about the usefulness of the national economic accounts for measuring the short-term movements of the business cycle. Rather they are questions about small biases or omissions that amount to perhaps tenths of a percent per year, but that cumulatively affect the measurement of long-term trends in growth and productivity.

The Bureau of Economic Analysis (BEA) within the Department of Commerce has tracked the direct effect of computers on measured GDP growth using its "contributions to percent change" methodology.[5] The contribution to the percent change of GDP can be approximated by simply excluding the computer components in the various sectors of GDP (e.g., private fixed investment, personal consumption expenditures, government gross investment) in its calculation, and comparing the growth rate of real GDP less computers to the growth rate of real GDP. These data are now regularly published in the GDP news release and are also available from the BEA's web site. As shown in table 1, the direct contribution of final sales of computers to real GDP growth averaged about 0.1–0.2 percentage point per year from 1987 to 1994, then accelerated to 0.3–0.4 percentage point per year from 1995 to 1999. The acceleration reflected both increases in current-dollar final sales and more rapid declines in computer prices, and sug-

Table 1 Real GDP, Final Sales of Computers, and GDP Less Final Sales of Computers

	GDP (% change)	GDP less final sales of computers (%change)[1]	Difference	Final sales of computers (% change)
1987	3.4	3.2	.2	23.4
1988	4.2	4.0	.2	20.3
1989	3.5	3.4	.1	13.4
1990	1.8	1.7	.1	5.6
1991	-.5	-.6	.1	12.0
1992	3.0	2.9	.1	24.8
1993	2.7	2.5	.2	22.1
1994	4.0	3.9	.1	20.1
1995	2.7	2.3	.4	53.7
1996	3.6	3.2	.4	55.3
1997	4.2	3.9	.3	45.4
1998	4.3	3.9	.4	53.9
1999	4.2	3.8	.4	44.1

gests that computers have recently become more important to the business cycle.

The measurement of real growth of computers in the national accounts is an example of a major statistical success—an important aspect of information technology that is now being more accurately measured and better understood than it was a decade or two ago.

Fifteen years ago there was no adequate official price index for computers. Nearly everyone recognized that the price of computing had been falling dramatically, but the methods used by the Bureau of Labor Statistics (BLS) and the BEA for estimating price indexes could not adequately account for quality changes of the magnitude that were occurring in computers.

The computer price problem was resolved through an exceptional collaboration between a government agency (BEA) and industry (in the form of a team of researchers from IBM). The research group included people with technological and engineering knowledge as well as economists and statisticians. The quality-adjusted computer price index, which was introduced in the national accounts in December 1985, helped rewrite economic history. The price index showed a remarkable multidecade decline in prices and growth in output of computers and peripheral equipment.[6] Application of the new index resulted in significantly higher real economic growth. The method that was used to adjust for quality improvements in the BEA computer price index has also been adapted by the BLS for the computer components of its producer, consumer, export, and import price indexes.

Since 1985, the work on quality-adjusted price indexes has been extended to several other IT products, such as semiconductors and telephone switching equipment.[7] The BEA introduced improved price indexes for some types of software as part of the comprehensive revision of the national economic accounts released in fall 1999. I must acknowledge, however, that progress on improved measures of output and prices for high-tech products has been slow and difficult. Developing the statistical estimates that are required for state-of-the-art quality adjustment is a resource-intensive activity, and the necessary data and other resources have not always been available.

Another success story in measuring the economic effects of information technology was the elimination of *substitution bias* (that is, the tendency of indexes with fixed weights to overstate growth). Prior to 1996, the national accounts measured changes in "real" (that is, inflation-adjusted) product by holding prices constant at their levels during a particular base year. It was known that this method led to a distortion or bias as prices moved away from the levels of the base year, but it was generally assumed that changes in relative prices tended to be modest and that this bias could therefore be ignored. Once the improved price index for computers was introduced, however, it became clear that its extreme and sustained downward trend wreaked havoc on the constant-price measures of real GDP. The substitution bias caused the estimates of real GDP growth to be overstated by as much as a percentage point. Furthermore, because the bias was not constant over time, it led to significant distortions in measuring the long-term trends in growth.

The BEA embarked on a research program that eventually led to the adoption in January 1996 of *chain-type* quantity and price indexes (that is, indexes in which the weights are continually updated, rather than held fixed). In other words, the prices used for measuring year-to-year changes in quantities are now the prices occurring during the two adjacent years that are being compared. These new indexes corrected an *upward* bias in GDP growth—that is, the effect of the change was in the opposite direction from the effect of incorporating the new computer price indexes. Users of the national accounts data have had to become accustomed to these new measures, because the chained-dollar measures are not additive, and some changes were required in the methods used to analyze these measures. These changes have been worth making, however, because a significant and major source of bias was eliminated, using the best available statistical methods.[8]

Agenda for Improvements and Future Research

If the digital economy were more accurately measured, would the long-term rate of real GDP growth be higher? There are good reasons to think that improved measures would raise the long-term growth rate of GDP, and there are several specific areas on which we can focus. More work is needed on price indexes. Better concepts and measures of output are needed for financial and insurance services and other "hard-to-measure" services. Our measures of capital stock need to be strengthened, especially for high-tech equipment. Also, economic surveys need to be expanded and updated to do a better job of capturing electronic commerce and its consequences.

Separating Quality Change from Price Change

Besides computers and peripheral equipment, semiconductors, and telephone switching equipment, there are other high-tech or IT products and services that have achieved major improvements in quality that have not been adequately adjusted for in our price and quantity measures.[9] As mentioned before, I view this as largely a problem of data and resource limitations. More cooperation and collaboration with the private sector, such as occurred between BEA and IBM, would be a major step forward. The private sector is often the only source for the detailed data needed to measure quality changes. Without such assistance, we would need to devote significant resources to collecting the data needed to make quality adjustments. The resulting improved price measures for IT equipment and services would very likely raise the real rate of growth.

Measuring Output of Services

At least as serious are the problems of measuring changes in real output and prices of the industries that intensively use computer services.[10] If the output of these industries cannot be measured adequately, then it will be impossible to determine the extent to which computers contribute to producing that output. Among the industries that are the most intensive users of computers are wholesale trade, finance, banking, insurance, and business services. For some of these industries, the output cannot be measured directly—for example, in the case of banks, many services are paid for implicitly by the difference between the interest rates paid by borrowers and those received by depositors. The national accounts presently make an imputation for these services, but it is not clear whether some of these imputed services should be assigned to borrowers (presently it is assumed that all go to depositors). In fall 1999 BEA introduced an improved measure of real banking services that resulted in a substantially higher measured growth rate (Moulton and Seskin 1999). BEA's strategic plan acknowledges that the outputs of these industries are difficult to measure, and that further conceptual and statistical improvements are needed.[11]

To the extent that industries produce intermediate services that are purchased by other businesses, mismeasurement of their output leads to a misstatement of the allocation of GDP and productivity changes by industry, but would not affect growth in overall GDP. In 1992 about 63 percent of the output of depository and nondepository institutions was sold to final consumers and therefore included in GDP. For business and professional services, about 17 percent was included in GDP.

To measure the real growth of an industry's output accurately, it is necessary to have either an accurate price index or a quantity index. The private service industries for which accurate price indexes are either not available or have only recently become available include depository and nondepository institutions, parts of real estate, holding and investment offices, business and professional services, social services and membership organizations, water transportation, and transportation services. The gross product originating (GPO) of these industries collectively accounted for nearly 15 percent of GDP in 1997, up from 8.5 percent in 1977. Among these industries, the most significant in terms of both nominal GPO growth and investment in information technology are depository and nondepository institutions (which includes banking) and business and professional services (which includes computer services and management consulting services). These two broad industry groups together accounted for 11 percent of GDP in 1997, up from 5 percent in 1977. Lacking adequate price indexes, real output for many of these industries has either been extrapolated using trends in inputs—in particular, labor inputs— or else deflation has been based on indexes of input costs. Use of these methods makes it virtually impossible to identify any growth in labor productivity and may lead to negative estimates of changes in multifactor productivity.[12] It would undoubtedly be more realistic to assume that labor productivity has grown as these industries have invested in IT, and for this reason it is likely that improved measures of services output would raise the real growth rate.

Furthermore, to calculate either an industry's real GPO (that is, value added) or its multifactor productivity accurately, we also need accurate price and quantity indexes for inputs. Because many service industries also consume services as intermediate inputs, it is seldom possible to measure their real GPO or multifactor productivity accurately.

Economists have debated for decades about the appropriate definition of output for some of these industries. In several cases the output is not directly priced and sold, but takes the form of implicit services that must be indirectly measured and valued. The BEA and its sister statistical agencies are committing resources to improving measurement of the output of these industries, but the conceptual issues are extraordinarily deep and complex, and progress will likely be measured in a series of modest steps.

Measurement of the digital economy presents some additional challenges.[13] Services such as information provision are more commonly provided for free on the web than elsewhere. There may therefore be less of a connection between information provision and business sales on the web than there is elsewhere. The dividing line between goods and services becomes fuzzier with E-commerce. If you receive a newspaper on-line, is it a good or a service? E-commerce prices and goods and services quality are frequently different from brick-and-mortar outlet prices and goods and services quality. Do we need price indexes for E-commerce goods and services that are different from price indexes for brick-and-mortar outlet goods and services? On the household side, notably, E-commerce may be bringing about a significant change in distribution methods. For households, the effect of E- commerce on distribution is similar to that of the mail-order business, but the size of the effect is expected to be significantly larger. In addition, the digital economy may be bringing about a significant growth in Business-to-Consumer (B-to-C) sales, in new business formation, and in cross-border trade. Because existing surveys may not fully capture these phenomena, private-sector data might be useful supplements to government surveys.[14] Meanwhile, the nature of the products provided by these industries continues to evolve very rapidly, driven in part by the availability of powerful IT equipment and software and the appearance of many new products, including new investment goods.

Accounting for Capital Stock

One reason for our difficulty in measuring the effects of information technology on the economy is that it often enters the production process in the form of capital equipment.[15] The BEA publishes data on the nation's wealth held in the form of capital structures, equipment, and software as well as on consumer durable goods, and the BLS publishes data on the productive services provided by the capital stock. The two agencies have gone to considerable lengths to develop information on investment flows, service lives, and depreciation patterns. Sophisticated perpetual inventory methods and user-cost formulas are used to estimate capital inputs, but some of the data entering these formulas (for example, service lives and industry breakdowns) are rather meager. Further progress in replacing assumptions with validated observations is one of BEA's goals for improving the capital stock estimates.

Another weakness of the capital stock estimates is that important components of capital may not be adequately captured in the measures. Intellectual property (for example, software, inventions, patents, and other forms of knowledge) has been an important omission. In the 1999 revision, the BEA changed the treatment of software in the economic accounts and began counting the development or purchase of software as a capital investment that enters the capital stock and brings returns for a number of years.

Research and development and other intellectual property are presently not treated as capital investment in the national accounts, though in principle they probably should be. Considerable measurement difficulties remain in developing such estimates, though the BEA has done some promising work in developing a satellite account for research and development.[16]

Expanding and Updating Surveys

The Census Bureau is working to expand and modernize its surveys to improve its tracking of businesses involved in electronic commerce and its measurement of transactions conducted via the Internet, to track new firms that enter electronic business, and to measure the increased spending on equipment and services that support Web-based commerce. To measure GDP, it is critical to know whether output is being consumed by final users (so that it enters GDP) or is consumed by business as intermediate inputs (so that it is not directly added to GDP). The rapid developments in the Internet may change some of the assumptions that have historically supported the BEA's estimates and the Census Bureau's surveys. For example, there have been substantial increases in direct sales by manufacturers to households, to other businesses, and to foreigners.

Electronic commerce has contributed to changes in transportation and distribution services because it relies heavily on the increased availability of air and courier services and local trucking to get products to consumers. Eventually we may even expect the occupational structure and geographic location of the labor force to shift in response to the reduced cost of communication and the availability of electronic transactions.

The Census Bureau has been developing and planning initiatives to capture better growth and innovation in electronic commerce in its surveys. Similarly, the BLS has been rapidly extending its coverage of service industries in the producer price index program, to capture better the growth of business, financial, and high-tech services.

Using New Electronic Sources of Data

Accompanying the growth of the digital economy has been a simultaneous growth in the availability of new types of digitally recorded data. Almost every trip to the grocery store or the mall leaves an electronic track of items scanned through cash registers. Several private companies collect and market these data. Other private sources collect data on particular industries—for example, on motor vehicles, financial services, and information technology. In several cases, the BEA selectively purchases these trade source data to supplement the survey and administrative data collected by the federal statistical system. In other cases, important data are freely available on the Internet.

The BLS has been researching the use of scanner data to estimate its price indexes. Scanner data, at least in principle, should allow for expanded and improved collection of price and quantity information and should permit the capture of new products and services nearly instantaneously. The downside of some of these new forms of data is the sheer volume of data collected. One recent study of coffee prices in two metropolitan markets reported weekly observations of prices and quantities for about 1,200 distinct products.[17] If this level of detail were to be used in constructing official price indexes, significant resources would clearly be needed to track changing product characteristics and quality changes.

Looking to the Future

The digital economy continues to grow, and measuring it well will continue to be a concern. Serious measurement problems must be faced as we endeavor to understand its impact. More and better source data are needed for developing and carrying back in time new quality adjustments or definitions of output. We must undertake fundamental research, both to develop better price indexes and to develop conceptual and statistical improvements in measuring service-sector real and nominal output. This work will enable BEA to continue to improve its measurement of macroeconomic activity in general, while also answering specific questions about the impact of the digital economy.

While it is not clear to me how much of the productivity paradox can be explained by measurement problems, I am confident that these problems are an important contributing factor. Solving them is important not only for assessing the role of the digital economy in the macroeconomy, but also for producing economic data that provide the best possible measure of our long-term growth and productivity. BEA's successful experience with measuring computer prices and converting to the chain-type measures of real GDP, as well as the current efforts to improve the measurement of software, all suggest that further progress is indeed possible.

Acknowledgments

I thank Barbara Fraumeni for extensive comments and suggestions. I also thank Erik Brynjolfsson, Steven Landefeld, Rosemary Marcuss, Sumiye Okubo, Robert Parker, and Eugene Seskin for comments on an earlier draft.

Notes

1. The terms "digital economy," "information technology," and "electronic commerce" do not have standard definitions. When I refer to information technology, I will be referring to information processing and related equipment, software, semiconductors, and telecommunications equipment. References to electronic commerce will mean the use of the Internet to sell goods and services. I interpret the digital economy as including both information technology and electronic commerce.

2. There are two measures of productivity. Labor productivity measures output per hour worked. Multifactor productivity measures output per combined unit of inputs, where inputs are broadly defined to include capital and labor inputs and intermediate goods and services. Both measures slowed beginning in the early 1970s.

3. The productivity paradox was first articulated by Solow (1987). Recent discussions of the productivity paradox include Diewert and Fox (1999), Gordon

(1998), Jorgenson and Stiroh (1999), Sichel (1999), and Triplett (1999). Note that the productivity slowdown was not limited to the United States, but was seen broadly across industrialized countries.

4. See Grimm and Parker (1998).

5. See Landefeld and Parker (1997).

6. The joint BEA-IBM research is described by Cole et al. (1986).

7. See Grimm (1998) and Parker and Seskin (1997).

8. See Landefeld and Parker (1995, 1997).

9. For recent discussion of problems in making appropriate quality adjustments in the consumer price index, see the report of the Advisory Commission to Study the Consumer Price Index, which was chaired by Michael Boskin (U.S. Senate, 1996), and Moulton and Moses (1997).

10. See Griliches (1994), Dean (1999), and Gullickson and Harper (1999).

11. The BEA's strategic plan commits the agency to improving hard-to-measure services (U.S. Department of Commerce, 1995).

12. See Gullickson and Harper (1999).

13. See Fraumeni, Lawson, and Ehemann (1999).

14. Hitt and Brynjolfsson (1998) describe how the digital economy has changed the way businesses conduct business with reference to case studies and firm-level studies.

15. For discussion of computer capital inputs, see Sichel (1999).

16. See Carson, Grimm, and Moylan (1994).

17. See Reinsdorf (1999).

References

Carson, C. S., B. T. Grimm, and C. E. Moylan, 1994. "A Satellite Account for Research and Development," *Survey of Current Business* 74(11): 37–71.

Cole, R., Y. C. Chen, J. A. Barquin-Stolleman, E. Dulberger, N. Helvacian, and J. H. Hodge, 1986. "Quality-Adjusted Price Indexes for Computer Processors and Selected Peripheral Equipment," *Survey of Current Business* 66(1): 41–50.

Dean, E. R., 1999. "The Accuracy of the BLS Productivity Measures," *Monthly Labor Review* 122(2): 24–34.

Diewert, W. E. and K. J. Fox, 1999. "Can Measurement Error Explain the Productivity Paradox?" *Canadian Journal of Economics* 32(2): 251–280..

Fraumeni, B. M., A. M. Lawson, and G. C. Ehemann, 1999. "The National Accounts in a Changing Economy: How BEA Measures E-Commerce," paper presented at the Workshop on Measuring E-Commerce, Brookings Institution, September 24.

Gordon, R. J., 1998. "Monetary Policy in the Age of Information Technology: Computers and the Solow Paradox," Northwestern University, paper prepared for the conference "Monetary Policy in a World of Knowledge-based Growth, Quality Change, and Uncertain Measurement," Bank of Japan, June 18–19.

Griliches, Z., 1994. "Productivity, R&D, and the Data Constraint," *American Economic Review* 84(1): 1–23.

Grimm, B. T., 1998. "Price Indexes for Selected Semiconductors, 1974–96," *Survey of Current Business* 78(2): 8–24.

Grimm, B. T., and R. P. Parker, 1998. "Reliability of the Quarterly and Annual Estimates of GDP and Gross Domestic Income," *Survey of Current Business* 78(12): 12–21.

Gullickson, W., and M. J. Harper, 1999. "Possible Measurement Bias in Aggregate Productivity Growth," *Monthly Labor Review* 122(2): 47–67.

Hitt, L. M., and Brynjolfsson, E., "Beyond Computation: Information Technology, Organizational Transformation and Business Performance," working paper, September 1998, available at http://ccs.mit.edu/erik/

Jorgenson, D. W., and K. J. Stiroh, 1999. "Information Technology and Growth," *American Economic Review* 88(2).

Landefeld, J. S., and R. P. Parker, 1995. "Preview of the Comprehensive Revision of the National Income and Product Accounts: BEA's New Featured Measures of Output and Prices," *Survey of Current Business* 75(7): 31–38.

Landefeld, J. S., and R. P. Parker, 1997. "BEA's Chain Indexes, Time Series, and Measures of Long-Term Economic Growth," *Survey of Current Business* 77(5): 58–68.

Moulton, B. R., and K. E. Moses, 1997. "Addressing the Quality Change Issue in the Consumer Price Index," *Brookings Papers on Economic Activity*, no. 1: 305–349.

Moulton, B. R., and E. P. Seskin, 1999. "A Preview of the 1999 Comprehensive Revision of the National Income and Product Accounts: Statistical Changes," *Survey of Current Business* 79(10): 6–17.

Parker, R. P., and E. P. Seskin, 1997. "Annual Revision of the National Income and Product Accounts: Annual Estimates, 1993–96; Quarterly Estimates, 1993:I–1997:I," *Survey of Current Business* 77(8): 6–35.

Reinsdorf, M. B., 1999. "Using Scanner Data to Construct CPI Basic Component Indexes," *Journal of Business and Economic Statistics* 17(2): 152–160.

Sichel, D. E., 1999. "Computers and Aggregate Economic Growth," *Business Economics* 34(2): 18–24.

Solow, R. M., 1987. "We'd Better Watch Out," *New York Times Book Review,* July 12, p. 36.

Triplett, J. E., 1999. "Economic Statistics, the New Economy and the Productivity Slowdown," *Business Economics* 34(2): 13–17.

U.S. Department of Commerce, Economic and Statistics Administration, Bureau of Economic Analysis, 1995. "Mid-Decade Strategic Review of BEA's Economic

Accounts: Maintaining and Improving Their Performance," *Survey of Current Business* 75(2): 36–66.

U.S. Senate, Committee on Finance, 1996. *Final Report of the Advisory Commission to Study the Consumer Price Index,* S. Prt. 104-72, 104 Cong., 2 sess., Washington, DC: U.S. Government Printing Office.

Understanding Digital Technology's Evolution and the Path of Measured Productivity Growth: Present and Future in the Mirror of the Past

Paul A. David

1 The Computer Revolution and the Productivity Paradox

Over the past forty years, computers have evolved from specialized and limited information-processing and communication machines into ubiquitous general-purpose tools. Whereas once computers were large machines surrounded by peripheral equipment and tended by technical staff working in specially constructed and air-conditioned centers, today computing equipment can be found on the desktops and in the work areas of secretaries, factory workers, and shipping clerks, often alongside the telecommunication equipment that links home offices to suppliers and customers. In the course of this evolution, computers and networks of computers have become an integral part of the research and design operations of most enterprises and, increasingly, an essential tool supporting control and decision-making at both middle and top management levels. In the last two decades, moreover, microprocessors have allowed computers to escape from their boxes, embedding information processing in a growing array of artifacts as diverse as greeting cards and automobiles, thereby extending the reach of this technology into new territory.

Although this novel technology is not being used everywhere to the same extent, the changes attributed to it are far-reaching. These include new patterns of work organization and worker productivity, job creation and loss, corporate profits and losses, and, ultimately, national prospects for economic growth, security, and the quality of life. Not since the opening of the so-called atomic age, with its promises of power too cheap to meter and threats of nuclear incineration, has a technology so deeply captured the imagination of the public. Nor since that era have hopes and doubts about the social usefulness of a technology been so closely coupled as has been the case with computing since the late 1980s.

It was at that point, in the midst of the "personal computer (PC) revolution," that mounting concerns about the absence of a clear link between progress in digital information technologies and the productivity performance of the economy at large crystallized around the perception that the United States, along with other advanced industrial economies, was confronted with a disturbing "productivity paradox." The precipitating event in the formation of this troublesome view of the digital information technology was an offhand pithy remark made in the summer of 1987 by Robert Solow, Institute Professor at MIT and Nobel Laureate in Economics: "You can see the computer age everywhere but in the productivity statistics."[1]

Almost overnight this comment was elevated into the leading economic puzzle of the late twentieth century. The divergence of opinion on this issue that eventually emerged within the economics profession has persisted, and has evolved recently into disagreements over the claim that in the United States information and communications technologies have given rise during the latter 1990s to a "new economy" or "new paradigm" of macroeconomic behavior.

It should not be surprising, therefore, that shifting understandings about the nature of the information revolution and the productivity implications of digital technologies are continuing to shape business expectations and public policies in areas as diverse as education and macroeconomic management. One indication of the wide importance of the subject matter of this volume can be read in its connection with the rhetoric and, arguably, the substance of U.S. monetary policy responses to the remarkable economic expansion of the 1990s. For a number of years in mid-decade, Alan Greenspan, the Chairman of the Federal Reserve Board, subscribed publicly to a strongly optimistic reading of the American economy's prospects for sustaining rapid expansion and rising real incomes without generating unhealthy inflationary pressures. Like many other observers, Greenspan viewed the rising volume of expenditures by corporations for electronic office and telecommunications equipment since the late 1980s as part of a far-reaching technological and economic transformation in which the U.S. economy was taking the lead:

We are living through one of those rare, perhaps once-in-a-century events. . . . The advent of the transistor and the integrated circuit and, as a consequence, the emergence of modern computer, telecommunication and satellite technologies have fundamentally changed the structure of the American economy.[2]

Yet, many economists continue to demur from this view, and there has been no lack of skepticism regarding the potential of the new information and communications technologies to deliver a sustained surge of productivity growth. According to Alan Blinder and Richard Quandt (1997: 14–15), even if information technology has the potential to raise the rate of growth of total factor productivity (TFP) significantly in the long run, the long run is uncomfortably vague as a time scale in matters of macroeconomic management. Instead, in their view, "we may be condemned to an extended period of transition in which the growing pains change in nature, but don't go away."

Some diminution of skepticism of this variety has accompanied the quickening of labor productivity growth in the United States since 1997, and especially the very recent return of the rate of increase in real GDP per man-hour to the neighborhood of 2 percent per annum. Among academic economists the consensus of optimistic opinion now holds a wait-and-see attitude, on the argument that it remains premature to try reading structural causes in what may well be transient or cyclical movements that, in any case, have yet to reverse materially the profound "slowdown" in the economy's productivity growth trend since the mid-1970s. The long-run perspective on U.S. productivity performance provided by Abramovitz and David (1999) shows a refined measure of the TFP growth rate (adjusting for composition-related quality changes in labor and capital inputs) having been maintained in the near neighborhood of 1.4 percent per annum throughout the era from

1890 to 1966.[3] From its 1.45 percent level over the 1929–1966 trend interval, the average annual growth rate plummeted to 0.04 percent during 1966–1989. The "slowdown" was so pronounced that it brought the TFP growth rate all the way back down to the very low historical levels indicated by statistical reconstructions of the performance of the American economy of the mid-nineteenth century (Abramovitz and David 1973, 1999).

More worrisome still, the post-1966 retardation was extended and intensified until the very end of the 1990s. Estimates of real gross output and inputs from the Bureau of Labor Statistics (USDL News Release 98-187, May 6, 1998) enable us to follow the path of measured productivity gains in the U.S. economy well into the 1990s. The figures relating to the private *nonfarm business* economy are generally regarded as providing a more accurate picture of recent movements, because the deflation of the current value of output has been carried out by using price indexes that reweight the prices of component goods and services in accord with the changing composition of the aggregate.[4] These "chain-weighted" output measures lead to productivity growth estimates that reveal two notable things about the "slowdown."

The first point is that the productivity growth rate's deviation below the trend that had prevailed during the 1950–1972 "golden age" of post–World War II growth became even more pronounced during the late 1980s and early 1990s, instead of becoming less marked as the oil shock and inflationary disturbances of the 1970s and the recession of the early 1980s passed into history. Measured labor productivity rose during 1988–1996 at only 0.83 percent per annum, half a percentage point *less* rapidly than the average pace maintained during 1972–1988, and thus fully 2.25 percentage points below the average pace during 1950–1972. Second, concerning the magnitude of the slowdown, the TFP growth rate estimate of the Bureau of Labor Statistics for 1988–1996 sank to 0.11 percent per annum, which represented a further drop of 0.24 percentage point from the 1972–1988 pace and brought it nearly a full 2 percentage points below the pace of TFP advance that had been achieved during the post–World War II golden age.

That having been said, it is worth remarking that the conjuncture of high rates of innovation and slow measured growth of total factor productivity is not a wholly new, anomalous phenomenon in the history of U.S. economic growth. Indeed, most of the labor productivity growth during the period from the 1830s through the 1880s was accounted for by the increasing capital-labor input ratio, leaving residual rates of TFP growth that were quite small by the standards of the early twentieth century and, a fortiori, by those of the post–World War II era. During the nineteenth century the emergence of technological changes that were biased strongly in the direction of tangible capital-deepening, involving the substitution of new forms of productive plant and equipment that carried heavy fixed costs and commensurately expanded scales of production, induced a high rate of capital accumulation. The capital-output ratio rose without markedly forcing down the real rate of return, and the substitution of increasing volumes of the services of reproducible tangible capital for those of other inputs (dispensing increasingly with the sweat and craft skills of workers in fields and shops along with the brute force of horses and mules) worked to increase real output per man-hour.[5]

Seen in longer historical perspective, therefore, recent developments hardly appear unprecedented and paradoxical. It could be maintained that there is little that is really novel or surprising in the way in which the rise of computer capital and OCAM (office, computing, and accounting machinery) capital more generally contributed to economic growth in the closing quarter of the twentieth century, except for the fact that this particular category of capital equipment only recently has begun to bulk large in the economy's total stock of reproducible capital. Indeed, Daniel Sichel (1997) has proposed a "resolution" of the productivity paradox in just the latter terms, arguing that the imputed gross earnings on hardware and software stocks amount to such a small fraction of GDP that the rapid growth of real computer assets per se can hardly be expected to be making a very significant contribution to the real GDP growth rate.[6] However valid an observation that might be, though, it fails to dispel the surprise and mystery surrounding the collapse of the TFP growth rate.[7]

Economists' reactions to questions concerning the anomalous slowdown of TFP growth and its perplexing conjuncture with the wave of investments involving information and communications technology (ICT) in the United States have continued to be couched in terms one or another of the three following explanatory claims:

1. The productivity slowdown is an artifact of inadequate statistical measurement of the economy's true performance.

2. There has been a vast overselling of the productivity-enhancing potential of investments in computers and related information equipment and software—due in part to misplaced technological enthusiasm, and also to exaggeration of the relative scale of those capital expenditures.

3. The promise of a profound impact upon productivity has not been mere hype, but optimism on that score has to be tempered by acknowledging that the transition to the techno-economic regime in which that potential will be realized is likely to be a much more arduous, costly, and drawn-out affair than was initially supposed.

It is only reasonable to ask whether what we have learned in the past decade allows us to evaluate this array of hypotheses and so better understand their bearing upon the future productivity performance of the digital economy. Having persisted since 1989 in advancing the "regime transition" interpretation of the productivity paradox, and therefore holding to a cautiously optimistic position on the computer revolution's potential economic impact, I should make it clear from the outset that I have yet to see evidence that persuades me to alter that stance. My approach to understanding the implications of the emerging digital economy continues to rest upon the idea that we are in the midst of a complex, contingent, and temporally extended process of transition to a new, information-intensive techno-economic regime, and that useful insights into the dynamics of this process can be gained by examining analogous historical episodes involving the elaboration and diffusion of other general-purpose technologies.[8]

Just as the systematic economic exploitation of the electric dynamo beginning in the last quarter of the nineteenth century eventually brought an end to the "steam engine age," the present process seems destined to accomplish the abandonment or extensive transformation of many features and concomitants of the technological regime identified with "Fordism." Fordism assumed full-blown form in the United States in the second quarter of the twentieth century, coincident with final stages in the electrification of industry. It was the mature form of the Fordist regime that underlay the prosperity and rapid growth of the post–World War II era—not only in the United States but in Western Europe and Japan, where its full elaboration had been delayed by the economic and political dislocations of the 1920s and 1930s, as well as by World War II itself.

The supplanting of an entrenched techno-economic regime involves profound changes whose revolutionary nature is better revealed by the breadth and depth of the clusters of innovation that emerge than by the pace at which they occur. Exactly because of the breadth and depth of the changes entailed, successful elaboration of a new general-purpose technology requires the development and coordination of a vast array of complementary tangible and intangible elements: new physical plant and equipment, new kinds of workforce skills, new organizational forms, new forms of legal property, new regulatory frameworks, new habits of mind and patterns of taste.

For these changes to be set in place typically requires decades rather than years. Moreover, while they are in process, there is no guarantee that their dominant effects upon macroeconomic performance will be positive. The emergence of positive productivity effects is neither assured nor free from the possibility that these will be overwhelmed by the deleterious consequences of devoting resources to the exploration of blind alleys—or, more formally described, technological and organizational trajectories that prove to be economically nonviable and, therefore, are eventually abandoned. The rise of a new techno-economic paradigm may, in addition, have transient, dislocating, backwash effects on the performance of surviving elements of the previous economic order.

It should not be so surprising, therefore, that the supplanting of the Fordist regime by one developed around digital information processing has produced clear disruptions as well as improvements in productive efficiency. We should have anticipated from the outset that this transition would entail some diminution in the productivity of old assets, and much new investment being allocated to ventures that are experimental and adaptive in nature—

more akin to learning than the implementation of chosen routines. In short, the productivity paradox may simply be a reflection of real phenomena whose nature is paradoxical only to those who suppose that the progress of technology is autonomous, continuous, and, being "hitchless and glitchless," bound to yield immediate cost savings and measurable economic welfare gains.

Those who are found, along with me, in the "cautious optimist" camp share the view that it is unlikely that the slow trend rates of TFP growth experienced in the U.S. economy over the past two decades will persist. Instead, we would argue that—with appropriate attention to problems of coordinating technological and organizational change with labor force training—the future may well bring a strong resurgence of the measured TFP residual that could be reasonably attributed to the exploitation of digital information technologies. Although intent to divine the early harbingers of a more widespread recovery in productivity growth, we acknowledge that such a renaissance is not guaranteed by any automatic market mechanism and maintain that it is foolish to adopt a passive public policy stance and simply await its arrival.

The development and exploitation of digital information, like previous profound historical transformations based on new general-purpose engines, turns out to entail a complicated regime transition whose success is contingent upon the coordination and completion of many complementary changes in methods of production, work modes, business organization, and institutional infrastructures. Transformations of this sort, however, involve not only the obsolescence of skills, capital assets, and business models; they are marked also by an accelerated rate of appearance of new goods and products. For a time, the latter developments are of a sort that will seriously challenge the ability of inherited statistical indicators to track and measure the performance of the economy. Thus, endogenous measurement biases may well be expected to add to the underlying "real" developments that tend to drag down the observed pace of productivity improvement, at least during the transition.

Furthermore, it is understandable enough that observers whose attention becomes focused at an early stage of such an extended process upon its most dynamic features may fail to appreciate how slow may be the progress toward fulfillment of the new technology's promise. In reaction to the disappointment of excessively optimistic expectations, or of initial misperceptions by business enthusiasts about the direction and speed of the product and process innovation that will have the greatest impact on measured productivity, there are likely to arise charges of "hype," accompanied by dismissal of the new technology as merely a snare and delusion. In other words, the disposition to embrace a cynical and pessimistic stance about a technology's long-run impact may be regarded as the flip side of the tendency toward "technological presbyopia," in which a bright distant future state of the world is clearly envisaged while enthusiasm blurs and dims vision of the likely obstacles, blind alleys, and pitfalls that bestrew the path immediately ahead.[9]

Consequently, it seems misleading for economists to have approached the three explanatory themes noted above as though they were independent, mutually incompatible, and hence competing. Rather than building a case for according one greater favor than the others, I think that we shall come closer to the truth of the matter by recognizing that there is empirical support—from both historical and contemporary evidence—for treating each of them as a significant facet of the larger phenomenon with which we must be concerned.

In the remainder of this chapter I shall examine (in section 2) some of the evidence relating to the more straightforward measurement problems that have been indicted as contributory factors in the slowdown of measured TFP growth, and point out the respects in which some of these are not independent and coincidental, but actually are sequelae of the ICT revolution itself. This point is pursued at a deeper conceptual level in section 3, where I consider the implications of the limited way in which a national income accounting system devised to deal with ordinary goods and services can cope with the shift toward integrating such commodities with the services of information. These considerations suggest the possibility that the past two decades have been marked by a more pronounced bias toward underestimation of the growth of aggregate real output and, consequently, of measured productivity.

Section 4 addresses some of the technological realities that underlie disappointment with the impact of computers upon the more readily measurable forms of task productivity. The argument here is that the historical course of the development of the PC as a general-purpose machine has not been conducive to enhancing "productivity" of the sort that can be gauged by conventional measurement approaches. Section 5 returns to the regime transition hypothesis and indicates the ways in which historical experience, particularly that of the diffusion of the electric dynamo, can be used as a source of insights into the dynamics and productivity performance of the digital economy. Section 6 concludes by looking to the future from the vantage point afforded us by an understanding of the past.

2 Measurement Problems

Those who contend that the slowdown puzzle and productivity paradox are mainly consequences of a mismeasurement problem must produce a consistent account of the timing and magnitude of the suspected errors in measurement. Estimating productivity growth requires a consistent method for estimating the growth rates of inputs and outputs. With a few notable exceptions (e.g., electricity generation), the lack of homogeneity in industry output frustrates direct measures of physical output and makes it necessary to use a price deflator to estimate output. Similar challenges arise, of course, in measuring the heterogeneous bundles of labor and capital services, but we are interested here mainly in problems in the measurement of real product growth. Systematic overstatement of price increases will introduce a persistent downward bias in estimated output growth and, therefore, an understatement of both partial and total factor productivity improvements.

Such overstatement can arise in several distinct ways. There are some industries, especially services, in which the concept of a unit of output itself is not well defined and, consequently, it is difficult if not impossible to obtain meaningful price indexes. In other cases, such as the construction industry, the output is so heterogeneous that it requires special effort to obtain price quotations for comparable "products" both at any one point in time and over time. The introduction of new commodities again raises the problem of comparability in forming the price deflators for an industry whose output mix is changing radically, and the techniques that statistical agencies have adopted to cope with the temporal replacement of old staples by new items in the consumer's shopping basket have been found to introduce systematic biases. These are only the simpler and more straightforward worries about mismeasurement, but before we tackle less tractable conceptual questions, we should briefly review their bearing on the puzzle of the slowdown and the computer productivity paradox.

2.1 Does Overdeflation of Output Account for the Productivity Slowdown?

That there is a tendency for official price indexes to overstate the true rate of inflation (and understate the pace of price declines) is a point on which there seems to be broad agreement among economists. The magnitude of that bias, however, is another question. The Advisory Commission to Study the Consumer Price Index concluded that the statistical procedures used by the BLS in preparing the CPI resulted in an average overstatement of the annual rate of increase in "the real cost of living" amounting to 1.1 percentage points (Boskin Commission Report, 1997). This might well be twice the magnitude of the error introduced by mismeasurement of the price deflators applied in estimating the real gross output of the private domestic economy over the period 1966–1989.[10] Were we to allow for this by making an upward correction of the real output growth rate by as much as 0.6–1.1 percentage points, the level of the Abramovitz-David (1999) estimates for the TFP growth rate during 1966–1989 would be pushed back up to essentially that range (0.64–1.14 percent per annum). Even so, that correction—which entertains the extremely dubious assumption that the conjectured measurement biases in the output price deflators existed only after 1966 and not before—would still have us believe that between 1929 and 1966 and between 1966 and 1989 there was a very appreciable slowdown in multifactor productivity growth.[11] Moreover, there is nothing in the findings of the Boskin Commission (1997) to indicate that the causes of the putative current upward bias in the price changes registered by the CPI have been operating only since the end of the 1960s.[12]

Thus, the simplest formulation of a mismeasurement explanation for the productivity slowdown falls quantitatively short of the mark. This does not mean that there is presently no underestimation of the growth rates of labor productivity or the TFP. Perhaps the paradox of the conjunction of unprecedentedly sluggish productivity growth with an explosive pace of technological innovation can be resolved in those terms, without, however, accounting for the slowdown itself. Plainly, what is needed to give the mismeasurement thesis greater bearing on the latter puzzle, and thereby help us to resolve the information technology paradox, is quantitative evidence that the suspected upward bias in the aggregate output deflators has been getting proportionally larger over time. Bailey and Gordon (1988) looked into this and came away without any conclusive answer; subsequently, Gordon (1996, 1998a) has moved toward a somewhat less dismissive position on the idea of slowdown being attributable to a worsening of price index mismeasurement errors. But we need some further efforts at quantification before dismissing the possibility.

2.2 Has the Relative Growth of "Hard-to-Measure" Activities Enlarged the Underestimation Bias?

A reasonable point of departure is the question of whether structural changes in the U.S. economy have exacerbated the problem of output underestimation and thereby contributed to the appearance of a productivity slowdown. In this connection Griliches's (1994) observation that there has been relative growth of output and employment in the "hard-to-measure" sectors of the economy is immediately pertinent. The bloc of the U.S. private domestic economy comprising Construction, Trade, Finance, Insurance, and Real Estate (FIRE), and miscellaneous other services has indeed been growing in relative importance, and this trend has been especially pronounced in recent decades.[13] There is certainly a gap in the man-hour productivity growth rates favoring the better-measured commodity-producing sectors. But the impact of the economy's structural drift toward "unmeasurability" is not big enough to account for the appearance of a productivity slowdown between the pre- and post-1969 periods. A simple reweighting of the trend growth rates lowers the aggregate labor productivity growth rate by 0.13 percentage points between 1947 and 1969 and between 1969 and 1990, yet that represents less than 12 percent of the actual slowdown that Griliches was seeking to explain.[14]

A somewhat different illustrative calculation supporting the same conclusion has been carried out by Abramovitz and David (1999). They make the following extreme assumptions: (1) that an upward bias of 1.6 percent per annum was present in the price deflator for the U.S. gross private domestic product, (2) that this bias arose entirely from deficiencies in the price deflators used to derive real gross product (and productivity) originating in the group of hard-to-measure sectors identified by Griliches, (3) that this condition has prevailed since the early post–World War II era in the hard-to-measure sectors, whereas prices and real output growth were properly measured for the rest of the economy. Taking account of the increasing relative weight of the hard-to-measure sectors in the value of current gross product for the private domestic economy, the implied measurement bias for the whole economy—under the conditions assumed—must have become more pronounced between the periods 1948–1966 and 1966–1989. But, once again, the effect is quantitatively minor: only 12 percent of the slowdown in the observed labor productivity growth rate could be accounted for in this way. Moreover, because the assumptions underlying this illustrative calculation are extreme, the implication is that even the comparatively minor mismeasurement effect found represents an upper-bound estimate. It seems that we need to look elsewhere.

2.3 The Role of New Goods in Unmeasured Quality Change

The literature devoted to the thesis that real output and productivity growth are being systematically mismeasured has hitherto not directed sufficient attention to the possibility that there has been a growing bias due to underestimation of output quality improvements associated with new goods and services. The problem arises from the practice (by those constructing price deflators) of waiting to "chain in" new products' prices until those new goods have acquired a substantial share of the market for the class of commodities for which they can be regarded as substitutes. During the early "market penetration" period, however, it is usually the case that the absolute and relative rates of decline in the new product's price are much more rapid than is the case subsequently. The aggregate price index therefore understates the true rate of price decline.

The difficulties created for price index statisticians by the turn-over of the commodity basket due to the introduction of new goods (before the old staples disappear) are quite ubiquitous across industries, and there is some basis for believing that during the past two decades these may have become more pronounced in their effect on the accuracy of the official price deflators. This line of speculation is attractive to explore because the mechanism that is hypothesized as the cause of an enlarged understatement of the productivity growth rate—namely, the higher rate of appearance of new goods in the basket of commodities available to consumers—is one that can be linked to the effects of the emerging information revolution. In that way it might turn out that the technological regime shift itself has been contributing to the appearance of a slowdown in measured productivity, and hence to the creation of its own paradoxically weak impact upon macroeconomic growth.

New information technologies and improved access to marketing data are indeed enabling faster, less costly product innovation and manufacturing process redesign, and shorter product life cycles. This development has been a central theme in the business and economics literature on "modern manufacturing" at least since the 1980s.[15] The increasing proliferation of new goods and its connection with the application of computers, electronic networks, and other new technologies has been identified as "forging a whole new paradigm that makes possible the delivery of custom-designed products to the masses—at ever lower prices"—a phenomenon for which the accepted descriptive phase is *mass customization*.[16] Leaving aside wholly new types of goods (e.g., PC models, which currently number over 400, or computer software titles, the count of which is in the neighborhood of a quarter of a million), the multiplication of the number of models available for consumers to chose among within preexisting product classes is a striking manifestation of this phenomenon. In the U.S. market between the early 1970s and the late 1990s the number of automobile vehicle models increased from 140 to 260, sports utility vehicle models increased from 8 to 38, and varieties of running shoes rose from 5 to 285, outstripping the rate of expansion in breakfast cereal products (160 to 340) but less impressive than the growth in types of contact lenses (1 to 36).[17]

While the absolute increase in the sheer variety of goods is staggering, that is not quite relevant to the issue at hand. Just how much welfare gain is attributable to the availability of each nominally "new" product is difficult to establish, and must vary widely, but there is some basis for suspecting that as the number of novel brands and styles has multiplied, the average value of the quality gain has been reduced. Beyond that consideration, what matters is whether the share of aggregate output (consumption) represented by newly introduced products has risen above its historical levels, that is, whether the rate of *turnover* of the economy's output mix has increased.[18]

Diewert and Fox (1997) present evidence from Nakamura (1997) on the fourfold acceleration of the rate of introduction of new products in U.S. supermarkets during the period 1975–1992, compared with the preceding period, 1964–1975. By combining this with data from Bailey and Gordon (1988) on the rising number of products stocked by the average U.S. supermarket, it is possible to gauge the movement in the ratio between these flow and stock measures, and thus the direction and magnitude of changes in the relative importance of new products (and the mean turnover rate). What this reveals is that a marked rise occurred in the new product fraction of the stock between 1975 and 1992, in contrast with the essential stability of the ratio between the mid-1960s and the mid-1970s. If only half of new products were stocked by the average supermarket, the share they represented in the stock as a whole would have risen from about .09 to .46. This fivefold rise in the relative number of new products in the total is certainly big enough to create the potential for a substantial growth in the relative downward bias in the measured real output growth rate, as a result of the standard delay in linking the prices of new goods to old ones.[19]

There is a further implication that runs in the same direction. The broadening of the product line by competitors may be likened to a common-pool/overfishing problem, causing crowding of the product space,[20] with the result that even the reduced fixed costs of research and product development must be spread over fewer units of sales. Moreover, to the extent that congestion in the product space raises the expected failure rate in new product launches, this reinforces the implication that initial margins are likely to be high when these products first appear, but will fall rapidly in the cases of the fortunate few that succeed in becoming standard items. Such a change would make the practice of delayed chaining-in of new products even more problematic than was previously the case, thereby helping to enlarge the underestimation bias in measured output and productivity growth in a manner quite independent of the rising rate of product turnover.

The mechanism of product proliferation involves innovations in both marketing and the utilization of distribution networks. Although in the United States the mass market distribution system was well established early in this century, utilizing it for product and brand proliferation was frustrated by the high costs of tracking and appropriately distributing (and redistributing) inventory. Traditionally, new product introduction involved the high fixed costs of major marketing campaigns and thereby required high unit sales. Recently, these costs have been lowered by application of information and communication technologies, and by the adoption of marketing strategies in which the existing mass market distribution system is configured under umbrellas of "brand name" recognition for particular classes of products (e.g., designer labels, "lifestyle" brands, and products related to films or other cultural icons), or for high-reputation retailers and service providers (e.g., prominent department store brands or financial services provided by large retail banks). The latter developments have been part of the proliferation of within-brand variety in "styles" that has characterized the rise of mass customization. It should not be surprising that the accuracy of a statistical system designed to record productivity in mass production and distribution should be challenged during the period when the "business models" of the system are changing as the result of marketing innovation and the use of information and communication technologies.

Some progress has been made in resolving the computer productivity paradox through the introduction of so-called hedonic price indexes for the output of the computer and electronic business equipment industries themselves. These indexes reflect the spectacularly rapid decline in the price-performance ratios of such forms of capital. Thus, the hedonic correction of computer and related equipment prices has done wonders in boosting the growth rate of output and multifactor productivity in the producing industry and, through that effect, has contributed to the revival of the manufacturing sector's productivity—simply as a result of the growing weight carried by that branch of industry in the sector as a whole.[21] By the same token, the hedonic deflation of investment expenditures on computer equipment contributes to raising the measured growth of computer capital services, which are intensively used as inputs in a number of sectors, including banking, financial services, and wholesale trade within the service sector. The implied rise in computer-capital intensity, and therefore in overall tangible-capital intensity, appears as a source of the growth of labor productivity in those sectors. But, in itself, the substitution of this rapidly rising input for others does nothing to lift the sectoral or economy-wide measured growth rates of TFP.

3 Conceptual Challenges: What Are We Supposed to Be Measuring?

Beyond the technical problems of the way in which national income accountants are coping with accelerating product innovation and quality change lie several deeper conceptual issues. These have always been with us, in a sense. But the nature of the changes in the organization and conduct of production activities, and particularly the heightened role of information—and changes in the information state—in modern economic life, seems to be bringing these problematic questions to the surface in a way that forces reconsideration of what measures are intended to measure, and how they actually relate to those goals.

The increasing application of IT to enhance the customized "service components" of a widening array of differentiated tangible products delivered to members of a heterogeneous population of users is vitiating the economic rationale for the statistician's use of relative product prices to aggregate these products. It is becoming more and more misleading to suppose, under the emerging conditions, that there is a "typical," representative consumer whose relative marginal utilities are revealed by the ratios of commodity prices in the market, or that those price ratios correspond to relative marginal costs of production. This is just one of the ways in which the conventional measurement scales that were developed for a regime producing tangible goods are being rendered obsolete by the economy's increasing "weightlessness." In the following, two other sets of conceptual problems are identified as equally deserving of further attention.

3.1 Micro-level Evidence on Payoffs from IT Investment: The Excess-Returns Puzzle

The first issue involves the surprising appearance of "excess rates of return on computer capital." These appeared when economists sought to illuminate the macro-level puzzle through statistical studies of the impact of IT at the microeconomic level, using observations on individual enterprise performance.[22] This phenomenon points to the conceptual gap between *task productivity* measures, on the one hand, and *profitability* and *revenue productivity* measurements, on the other. The former are closer in spirit to measuring the productive efficiency of the economy by calculating TFP as the ratio of aggregate real output to the aggregate inputs of labor and capital services, whereas, in comparing organizational departments and firms engaged in quite different production activities, the micro-level performance measure moves away from any physical, engineering notion of productivity and toward dimensions (revenue units per unit of real input cost) in which outputs can be rendered commensurable.

Not only is there an important difference between the measures, but the relationship between the two measures may itself be undergoing a transformation as a result of the way IT is being applied in businesses. The contrast between the strong (cross-section) revenue productivity impacts of observed computer investments and the weaker (time-series) effects gauged in terms of task productivity might indicate simply that very high gross private rates of return are associated with such capital expenditures. In view of the rapid rate of anticipated depreciation of capital value due to the high rate at which the price-performance ratio of new computer equipment has been falling (circa 20 percent per annum), these seemingly "excess" private returns would be needed in order to equalize net private rates of return on various assets held by the company.

Subsequent investigations along the same lines have found that other intangible investments were correlatives of high IT capital intensity. Much of the evidence for this is reasonably direct, being indicated by the presence of workers with high formal educational attainment and skill qualification, company-run training programs, and programs of company reorganization linked with computerization and retraining. Taking these factors into account statistically leads to substantial elimination of the apparent excess of the estimated returns on IT capital as compared to the returns on capital of other kinds.[23] But there is also some indirect support, from the relationship between the reproduction value of company tangibles and the market valuation of computer-intensive firms, for concluding that the diffusion of information technologies among large business firms has entailed substantial levels of intangible asset formation.[24] The latter, of course, is not reckoned on the output side (among the firms' revenue-generating products), nor are the service flows from those intangibles measured among the inputs in production-function studies and growth-accounting exercises. The broader significance of this situation, which is becoming increasingly widespread as digital information technologies diffuse throughout the economy, deserves further consideration.

3.2 Leaving out Investments in Organizational Change: The Narrow Scope of the NIPA

How should the investments made by organizations and individuals in learning to utilize a new technology be treated for purposes of national income accounting? The factor-payment side of the official National Income and Product Accounts (NIPA) include the expenditures that this may entail for labor time and the use of facilities, but the intangible assets formed in the process do not appear on the output side, among the final goods and services produced. This definition of the scope of GNP and GDP is not problematic so long as the relationship between marketed output and nonmarket investments in learning remains more or less unchanged. But that has not been the case.

A major technological discontinuity, involving the advent of a new general-purpose technology, is likely to induce more than the usual relative level of incremental learning activity; and the advent of digital information-processing technologies in particular, having stimulated the creation of new software assets within the learning organizations, has been marked by a relative rise in the production of intangible assets that have gone unrecorded in the national income and product accounts. This suggests the possibility that conventional statistical indicators could seriously distort our macroeconomic picture of what is being produced and how resources are being used.

The problem of nonmarket production of intangibles in the form of computer software was relatively more serious in the mainframe era than it has subsequently become, but the same would not appear to be true of intangible investments in retraining workers and reorganizing business operations, which, as has been noted, are generally required if firms are to exploit the enhanced capabilities of new information technologies. Thus, the narrow scope of conventional output measures may cause them to fail to register the relative rise of this form of asset production for some time, and so may contribute to a downward drag on the measured productivity growth rate.

4 Troubles with Computers: Effects of General-Purpose Machines on Task Productivity

Laying the whole burden of explanation on the notion that existing concepts and methods are inadequate in accounting for the effects of the computer revolution is not satisfactory. Even if a large share of these effects vanish into territory that is inadequately mapped by conventional statistical measurement approaches, it is puzzling why indexes of productivity in branches of industry that previously were not regarded to be "unmeasurable," or subject to unrecorded high rates of quality improvement, have not been more positively affected by the advent of new information technologies. Here, I believe, there is a case to be made that the customary link between innovation in the development of technological artifacts and improvements in productivity for the users of those tools has indeed frayed; that is, there have been real problems in delivering on the "task productivity" promises of the computer revolution.

4.1 Component Performance and System Performance

A common focus of attention in the computer revolution is the rapidity with which the performance of microelectronic components has been enhanced. The widespread acceptance of Moore's Law shapes user expectations and technological planning, not only in the integrated circuit industry, but in all of the information and communication technology industries. For software designers, Moore's Law promises that new computational resources will continue to grow at a high exponential rate and encourages the development of products embodying more features so that the diverse needs of an ever-growing user community can be fulfilled. It need not follow that any particular user will experience performance improvement as a result of component improvement. As has been pointed out, even if the user adopts the new technology, the learning time for mastering new software, the greater number of choices required to navigate the expanding array of options, and the longer time it takes for the more complex software to be executed will offset part or all of the gains from increasing component performance.

It is now widely recognized that the cost of PC ownership to the business organization may be tenfold the size of the acquisition costs of the computer itself.[25] Much of this cost is unrelated to the performance of microprocessor components, and for many applications the use of PCs is therefore relatively unaffected by microprocessor performance improvements. From a productivity measurement standpoint, the relatively constant unit cost of PC ownership has been further compounded by the cost of the continuing spread of the technology throughout the organization. To be sure, employees are being given general-purpose tools that may be and often are useful for devising new ways to perform their work.

At the same time, however, it is apparent to most sophisticated users of computers that the extension of these capabilities also creates a vast new array of problems that must be solved to achieve desired aims. Most organizations believe that learning to solve these problems will eventually create a greater range of organizational and individual capabilities that will improve profitability. In any case, it is now expected that a modern organization will provide reasonably sophisticated information technology as part of the office equipment to which every employee is entitled.

From a business process or activity accounting viewpoint, however, the spread of personal information and communication technologies has enormously complicated the task of maintaining coherence and functionality within the organization. A task such as the creation of a business letter involves a considerable range of choices, and it will seldom happen that efforts to define an efficient means of carrying out this operation will be confined to the individual who executes the task. Company formats and style sheets, equipment maintenance and troubleshooting, file server support and standards for archiving and backup of electronic documents all now enter into the task of producing a business letter. The existence of new capabilities suggests a potential for creating greater order and precision, whereas the reality of deploying these capabilities may substantially raise the unit cost of executing the letter-writing task.

These observations are not intended as a call for a return to the days of smudged typescripts and hand-addressed envelopes. The point is that most organizations have neither the capability nor the interest in performing detailed activity accounting for the new business processes arising from the use of information and communication technologies. Without attention to these issues, it is not surprising that they may often follow a version of Parkinson's Law ("work expands to fill the time available for its completion"); the ancillary complications of preparing to perform a computer-assisted task may fill the time previously allotted for its completion. Surely this is not the average experience, but we would be paying more careful attention to the management of information and communication resources if their costs were more fully recognized.[26]

Was this state of affairs a necessary, inescapable burden imposed by the very nature of the new information technology, and so destined to perpetuate itself as that technology becomes more and more elaborate? Those seeking an answer to this question may find it helpful to begin by stepping back and conceptualizing the recent and still unfolding trajectory along which the microelectronics-based digital computer has been developed and deployed, seeing it as a particular, contextualized instance of a more general class of historical processes.[27] Such an approach gives us a view of the path taken so far as not the only one conceivable but, on the contrary, a contingently selected course of development among a number of alternatives that were available. The actual path of computerization, seen in retrospect, led away from a tight coupling between the new technological artifacts and the task productivity of the individuals and groups to whom those microelectronics-based tools were offered.

4.2 The Trajectory of General-Purpose Computing: From Mainframes to PCs

The widespread diffusion of the stored-program digital computer is intimately related to the popularization of the PC as a general-purpose technology for information processing and the incremental transformation of this "information appliance" into the dominant technology of information processing. The historical process by which this was achieved has had major implications, not only for the success of PC technology and the hardware and software industries based upon it, but also for the economic functionality of the business organizations that have sought to utilize it profitably. For the PC, as for its parent the mainframe and its cousin the minicomputer, much adaptation and specialization has been required to apply a general-purpose machine to *particular* purposes or tasks. Such adaptations tend to be costly, and this has been especially true in the case of the PC. It is something of a historical irony that the core elements of the adaptation problems attending the diffusion of the semiconductor-based microprocessor (a general-purpose technology) into widespread business application derive from the historical selection of a trajectory of innovation that emphasized the "general purpose" character of the paradigmatic IT hardware and software components.

The development of the PC followed the invention of the microprocessor, which was a technical solution to the problem of creating a more general-purpose integrated circuit to serve a specific purpose, namely, creating a more flexible portable calculator—a foundational application that ultimately proved uneconomic due to the lower relative costs of more specialized integrated circuits. During the 1970s it was recognized that the microprocessor provided a general solution to the problem of the electronic system designer confronted by an ever-growing array of application demands. During the same period, efforts to downscale mainframe computers for use in specialized control and computation applications led to the birth of the minicomputer industry. These two developments provided the key trajectories for the birth of the PC. As microprocessors became cheaper and more sophisticated, and applications for dedicated information processing continued to expand, a variety of task-specific computers came into existence.

One of the largest markets for such task-specific computers created during the 1970s was for dedicated word-processing systems that could quickly modify and customize documents that were repetitive in content or format—such as contracts, purchase orders, legal briefs, and insurance forms—based upon stored formats and texts. Dedicated word processors appeared as an incremental step in office automation, but were rapidly displaced in the mid-1980s by PCs, which were perceived to be more "flexible" and more easily "upgradeable" as new generations of software were offered by sources other than the computer vendors.[28] The dedicated word processor's demise was mirrored in many other markets where task-specific data-processing systems had begun to develop. Digital Equipment Corporation, the leading minicomputer manufacturer, retreated from its vertical marketing strategy of offering computer systems specifically designed for newspapers, manufacturing enterprises, and service companies; it specialized instead in hardware production, leaving the software market to independent software vendors.[29] This process, which had begun in the late 1970s as an effort to focus corporate strategy, greatly accelerated during the 1980s with the advent of the large-scale personal computer platforms united under the IBM PC standard or utilizing that of Apple's Macintosh. The general-purpose software produced for these two platforms not only discouraged task-specific software, but also created a new collection of tasks and outputs specifically driven by the new capabilities such as "desktop publishing" (typeset-quality documents), "presentation graphics" (graphic-artist-quality illustrations for speeches and reports), and "advanced word processing" (the incorporation of graphics and tables into reports). All of these changes improved the "look and feel" of information communication, its quality and style, the capability for an individual to express ideas, and the quantity of such communications. But singly and severally they made very little progress in changing the structure of work organization or the collective productivity of the work groups employing these techniques.

The disappearance of task-based computing in favor of general-purpose PCs and general-purpose (or multipurpose) packaged software was largely completed during the 1980s.[30] Thus the early evolution of the PC can be seen as cutting across the path of development of an entire family of technically feasible information-processing systems focused on the improvement of "task productivity" in applications ranging from word processing to manufacturing operations control. In many cases, it has also precluded the effective development of collective "work group" processes whose synergies would support multifactor productivity improvement. Instead of breaking free from the mainframe, these general-purpose engines often wound up enslaved to the mainframe, using a small fraction of their capabilities to emulate the operations of their less expensive (and less intelligent) cousins, the "intelligent" display terminals.

By 1990, then, the PC revolution had seized control of the future of information processing but had left carnage in its wake, as many such movements do. The revolutionaries had kept their promise that the PC would match the computing performance of mainframes. What was not achieved, and could not be achieved, was a wholesale reconstruction of the information-processing activities of organizations.[31] Rather than contributing to a rethinking of organizational routines, the spread of partially networked PCs supported the development of new database and data entry tasks, new analytical and reporting tasks, and new demands for "user support" to ensure that the general-purpose technology delivered its potential.

This is not to claim that the process should be regarded as socially suboptimal, or mistaken from the private business perspective. A quantitative basis for such judgments, one way or the other, does not yet exist. It appears that what was easiest organizationally tended to be the most attractive task to undertake first. The local activities within the organization that were identified as candidates for PC applications often could and did improve the flexibility and variety of services offered within the company, as well as to customers who through the intermediation of personnel with appropriate information system access received an array of service quality improvements.

Arguably, many of these improvements are part of the productivity measurement problem examined above because they are not captured in the real output statistics, even though they could enhance the revenue-generating capacity of the firms in which they are deployed. The availability of 24-hour telephone reservation desks for airlines, or the construction of worldwide networks for securing hotel, automobile, or entertainment reservations, represent welfare improvements for the customer that do not appear in the measured real GDP originating in those sectors, nor in the real value expenditures on final goods and services.

There is a more evident downside to the process by which general-purpose PCs came to be furnished with general-purpose software. It may be accepted that general-purpose hardware and software in combination did "empower" users to think of "insanely great" new applications—to use the rhetoric of Steve Jobs, one of Apple Computer's co-founders. Relentless innovation, however, is inimical to the stabilization of routine and to the improvement in the efficiency of routine performance that such stability brings. Moreover, at best only a very small number of innovative software programs address the sort of mundane tasks that make a difference to the performance of a large number of users. But the ubiquity and complementarity of these dual "general-purpose engines"—PC hardware and packaged software—has the side effect of foreclosing the apparent need for more specialized task-oriented software development.[32]

Worse still, by the mid-1990s, the competition among packaged software vendors for extending the generality of their offerings became a syndrome with its own name: "creeping featurism" or "featuritis." Making light of these developments in 1995, Nathan Myrvhold of Microsoft suggested that software is a gas that "expands to fill its container. . . . After all, if we hadn't brought your processor to its knees, why else would you get a new one?"[33] Although offered in jest, this comment reflects the serious belief of many in the technological community that the continuous upgrading of PC capabilities, with which they are centrally preoccupied, ultimately redounds to the benefit of the user. From their perspective, the key to future success lies in establishing increasingly powerful platforms for new generations of software, whereas among users these developments may be welcomed by some while loathed by others. What can be reliably predicted is that the costs of adjustment, learning, and sheer "futzing around" with the new systems on the part of less skilled users will continue to constrain their contributions to improving overall task productivity.

5 The Regime Transition Hypothesis: Dark Journey toward a Brighter Future?

The "regime transition" hypothesis owes much in its general conception to the work of Freeman and Perez (1986), who emphasized the many incremental technological, institutional, and social adjustments that are required to realize the potential of any radical technological departure and pointed out that, typically, those adaptations are neither instantaneous nor costless.

At the same time, recent work in the spirit of the new growth theory has generalized the idea formulated by Bresnahan and Trajtenberg (1995) in terms of GPTs (general-purpose technologies) that transform an economy by finding new applications and fusing with existing technologies to rejuvenate other, preexisting sectors of the economy. While the positive, long-run growth-igniting ramifications of fundamental technological breakthroughs are stressed in the formalization of this idea in the growth theory literature, the downside of the process has also been recognized. Mathematical models of multisector learning and technology diffusion processes indicate that the resources absorbed in the increasing roundaboutness of the transition phase may result in slower growth of productivity and real wages.[34]

The GPT-regime transition hypothesis seems a natural framework for examining the computer productivity paradox. By drawing an explicit analogy between "the dynamo and the computer," David (1990, 1991a,b) sought to use the U.S. historical experience with such transformative technologies as the vertical watermill, the steam engine, the electrical dynamo, and the internal combustion engine to ground the argument that an extended phase of adjustment would be required to accommodate and elaborate the new technological and organizational regime that is emerging around the digital computer. The story of how the transmission of electric power came to revolutionize industrial production processes shows clearly that far more is involved in the transition to a new GPT than the simple substitution of a new form of productive input for an older alternative. The overall speed at which the transformation proceeds is governed, in both the past and current regime transitions, by the ease or difficulty of altering many other technologically and organizationally related features of the production systems involved.

The early formulation of the regime transition argument focused specifically on the economic aspects of the initial phases of the transition dynamics that could contribute to *slowing* the measured growth of industrial productivity. There are two distinct parts to the "extended transition" explanation of the productivity paradox. The first part argues that lags in the diffusion process involving a general-purpose technology can result in long delays in the acceleration of productivity growth in the economy at large. The underlying idea is that productivity advances stem from the substitution of new (IT-intensive) production methods for older ones, as well as from improvements to and enhancements of the new technologies themselves; and that because those improvements and the diffusion of the innovations are interdependent processes, it is possible for this dynamic process to be quite long and drawn out. The second part argues that in the earlier phases of the transition process resources tend to be directed to applying the innovation to provide new, qualitatively superior goods and services, and so yield welfare gains that escape being properly reflected in the measured output and productivity indexes of the economy. Because the latter theme already has been well aired (in sections 2 and 3), what is called for here is another, closer look at the first part of the argument.

5.1 Diffusion, Dynamos, and Computers

Although central generating stations for electric lighting systems were introduced by Thomas Edison in 1881, electric motors still constituted well under one-half of one percent of the mechanical horsepower capacity of the U.S. manufacturing sector at the end of that decade. Electrification was proceeding rapidly at this time, however, especially in the substitution of dynamos for other prime movers such as waterpower and steam engines. Between 1899 and 1904 the electrified portion of total mechanical drive for manufacturing rose from roughly 5 percent to 11 percent (see David 1991a, Table 3). Yet, it was not until the decade of the 1920s that this measure of diffusion, and the more significant measure of the penetration of secondary electric motors in manufacturing, moved above the 50 percent mark. It was the transition to the use of secondary electric motors (the unit drive system) in industry that my analysis found to be strongly associated with the surge of total factor productivity in manufacturing during the decade 1919–1929.

Recent estimates of the growth of computer stocks and the flow of services therefrom are consistent with the view that when the productivity paradox debate began to attract attention the U.S. economy was still in the early phase of IT deployment. Jorgenson and Stiroh (1995) found that in 1979, when computers had not yet evolved far beyond their role in information-processing machinery, computer equipment and the larger category of office, accounting and computing machinery (OCAM) were providing only 0.56 percent and 1.5 percent, respectively, of the total flow of real services from the (nonresidential) stock of producers' durable equipment.[35] These measures rose to 4.9 percent in 1985, ballooned further to 13.8 percent by 1990, and stood at 18.4 percent two years after that.[36] Thus, by this measure, the extent of "computerization" that had been achieved in the whole economy by the late

1980s was roughly comparable with the degree to which the American manufacturing sector had become electrified at the beginning of the twentieth century.

Does the parallel carry over to the pace of the transition in its early stages? The answer is yes, but the route to it is a bit tortuous, as may be seen from the following: If we consider just the overall measure of industrial electrification referred to above, the pace of diffusion appears to have been rather slower during the dynamo revolution than what was experienced during the 1979–1997 phase of the computer revolution. It took 25 years for the electrified part of mechanical drive in manufacturing to rise from 0.5 percent to 38 percent, whereas, according to the diffusion measure just presented, the same quantitative change was accomplished for the computer within a span of only 18 years. But that is not quite the right comparison to make in this connection.

When the historical comparison is narrowed more appropriately to the diffusion of secondary motors, a proxy for the spread of the unit drive system of electrification, the growth rate for 1899–1914 is almost precisely the same as that for the ratio of computer equipment services to all producers' durable equipment services in the United States. The index of the computerization of capital services that we can derive from the work of Jorgenson and Stiroh (1995) rises in part because the underlying estimates take into account the changing quality of the computer stock, whereas the electrification diffusion index simply compares horsepower rating of the stock of electric motors with total mechanical power sources in manufacturing. The latter index neglects the significance for industrial productivity of the growth of "secondary" electric motors, which were used to drive tools and machinery on the factory floor (and mechanical hoists between floors), and which actually had far greater impact on measured TFP growth in manufacturing than prime movers.[37] Between 1899 and 1914 the ratio of secondary motor horsepower to the horsepower rating of all mechanical drive in U.S. manufacturing was rising at an average compound rate of 26.2 percent per annum. It is therefore striking to observe that, over the period from 1979 to 1997, the estimated average rate of growth of the ratio of computer equipment services to all producers' durable equipment services in the United States was 26.4 percent per annum.

Such considerations should, at very least, serve as a constructive reply to commentators who have casually supposed that the computerization of the U.S. capital stock has been proceeding so much faster than the electrification of industry as to render illegitimate any attempt to gain insight into the dynamics of the computer revolution by examining the economic history of the dynamo revolution. But the latter is only one among several arguments that are advanced for dismissing historical GPT experience as quantitatively so different as to be irrelevant. Triplett (1998) has suggested that the pace at which the price-performance ratio of computer equipment has been plummeting so far exceeds the rate of fall in the real unit costs of electric energy that little if anything can be inferred from the time scale of the transition to the application of the unit drive system in manufacturing. What can be said in response to this contention?

The first point is to notice that the real price of computer equipment (quality-adjusted) has been declining much more rapidly than that of the bundle of "computer services" that forms the relevant input into production processes in the economy. Sichel (1997, Table 5-2) estimates the rate of decline in real prices of computer services for 1987–1993 to have been 7.9 percent per annum, and compares that to the 7.0 percent per annum rate of decline in the real price of electric power over the period 1899–1948. One might object to the foregoing comparison between the rates of change for two such disparate time spans, but one can put the estimated rate of price decline in the case of electricity on a more appropriate footing, by focusing on a 6–10-year interval that is equivalently early in the evolution of the dynamo's evolution. Taking electrification to have commenced with the introduction of the Edison filament lamp and the central power station in 1876–1881, and noting that the 1987–1993 interval came 16–22 years after the introduction of the microprocessor and magnetic memory, the corresponding temporal interval would be 1892–1903.[38]

The real prices of electric power declined at the rate of 1.3 percent per annum during 1892–1902, though it must be noted that the early evolution of electrical technology progressed at a pace more leisurely than that of modern computer technology. It was only around 1902–1903 that the main technical components for the implementation of universal electrical supply systems (based on central generating stations and extended distribution networks bringing power to factories and transport systems) could be said to have been put in place. Over the decade that followed, the rate of decline in the price of electric power accelerated to 6.8 percent per annum, and from 1912 to 1920 it was falling at an average rate of 10 percent per annum. This would seem sufficient to establish the following, very limited, negative point: the differing movements of the prices of electricity and quality-adjusted computer services hardly warrants dismissing the idea that insight into the dynamics of the current transition may be gained by looking back at the dynamo revolution.

In arguing for the opposite view, Triplett (1998) suggests that Sichel's (1997) estimates of the price of computer services—and, by implication, the comparison just reported—may be misleading. He contends that the hedonic price indexes for computers that come bundled with software actually would have fallen faster than the (unbundled) price-performance ratios that have been used as deflators for investment in computer hardware. If so, Sichel's (1997) price indexes of quality-adjusted "computer services"(from hardware and software) would seriously underestimate the relevant rate of decline. But Triplett's argument seems to suppose that operationally relevant "computer speed" is appropriately indexed by the speed of the central processing unit (CPU), whereas many industry observers have pointed out that the bundled PC operating system has grown so large that more processing power does not translate into more "effective operating power." In other words, one should be thinking about the movements in the *ratio* TEL/WIN, instead of their *product:* WIN × TEL.

Furthermore, the slower rate of fall in computer services prices estimated by Sichel (1997) is more in accord with the observation that applications software packages have also ballooned in size through the addition of many features that remain unutilized; that CPU speed may be too heavily weighted in the hedonic indexes for hardware, inasmuch as the utility of (net) computer power remains constrained by the slower speed of input-output functions; and that throughout much of the period since the 1960s the stock of "legacy software" running on mainframes continued to grow, without being rewritten to exploit the capacity available on the new and faster hardware.

Finally, I would argue, more fundamentally, that the dismissal of the regime transition hypothesis on the basis of a (putative) discrepancy in the rates of decline of prices reflects a misuse of historical analogies. As noted above, far more is involved in these transitions than a simple substitution of a new form of productive input for an older alternative. The pace of the transformation is governed by the ease or difficulty of altering many technologically and organizationally related features of the production systems. To focus on the decline of prices in such complex situations is therefore to miss a large part of the argument.

5.2 The Proper Limits of Historical Analogy: Computer and Dynamo Again

While there seems to be considerable heuristic value in the historical analogy between the computer and the dynamo, a cautious, even skeptical attitude is warranted in regard to predictions for the future based on the analogy. For one thing, statistical coincidences in economic performance are more likely than not to be just matters of coincidence, rather than indications that the underlying causal mechanisms really are identical. Nonetheless, one can show merely as a matter of algebra that only after the 50 percent mark in diffusion of a cost-saving technology will it have its maximum impact on the rate of TFP growth.[39] It then becomes pertinent to notice that in the case of U.S. factory electrification a surge of multifactor productivity growth occurred throughout the manufacturing sector during the 1920s, coincident with the attainment of the 50+ percent stage in that diffusion process. This observation is useful primarily to underscore the point that the biggest productivity payoffs should not be expected to come at the beginning phase of the regime transition, even though it is then that the pace of the new technology's diffusion is likely to be fastest.

This sort of historical anecdote also may be used quite legitimately in arguing, from the perspective of an observer in 1989–1990, that it was too soon to be disappointed that the computer revolution had failed to unleash a sustained surge of readily discernible productivity growth throughout the economy. To say that, however, was not at all the same thing as predicting that the continuing relative growth of computerized equipment with respect to the rest of the capital stock eventually and necessarily would cause a surge of productivity growth to materialize; nor does it imply anything specific about the future temporal pace of the computer's diffusion.

Least of all can the analogy tell us that the detailed shape of the diffusion path that lies ahead will mirror the curve that was traced out by the electrical dynamo during the early decades of the twentieth century. There is nothing foreordained about the dynamic process through which a new general-purpose technology permeates and transforms the organization of production in many branches of an economy. One cannot simply infer the detailed future shape of the diffusion path in the case of the digital information revolution from the experience of analogous episodes; the very nature of the underlying process renders that path contingent upon events flowing from private actions and public policy decisions, as well as upon the expectations that are thereby engendered—all of which still lie before us in time. To gain some reasonably well-grounded perception of the future, we must also take notice of the specific new technological and organizational developments that have already begun to emerge in regard to "the digital economy."

6 Historical Perspectives on the Growth of Measured Productivity in the Digital Economy

The historical trajectory of computer technology development appears to be on the verge of a profound shift in direction.[40] At least three new directions are emerging strongly enough in commercial applications to warrant notice here. None of these is likely to lead to the displacement of PCs in the production and distribution of highly customized information or of information that arises from the research processes for which the general-purpose computer was originally invented. What they do promise are greater and more systematic efforts to integrate information collection, distribution, and processing. To take advantage of these opportunities, enterprises and other institutions must re-examine workflow and develop new methods for designing information systems. This will have beneficial consequences in terms of improving measures of productivity.

First, a growing range of information technologies has become available that are purpose-built and task-specific. Devices such as supermarket scanners have been applied to a wide range of inventory and item tracking tasks, and related "data logging" devices are now found in the hands of maintenance, restaurant, and factory workers. The niches in which these devices have been able to achieve a foothold are ones where the mass-produced PC is neither appropriate nor robust. These more specialized devices have become sufficiently ubiquitous to provide the infrastructure for task-oriented data acquisition and display systems in which up-to-date and precise overviews of the material flows through manufacturing and service delivery processes.

Second, the capabilities of advanced PCs as "network servers" have become sufficiently well developed that it is possible for companies to eliminate the chasm between the PC and the mainframe environment by developing the intermediate solution of client-server data-processing systems. This development is still very much in progress and reflects a more complete utilization of the local area networks devised for information and resource sharing during the PC era. In this new networked environment, the reconfiguration of work organization becomes a central issue. Strategic and practical issues surrounding the ownership and maintenance of critical company data resources must be resolved, and these often are compelling enough to force redesign of the organizational structure.

Third, the development of Internet technology has opened the door to an entirely new class of organization-wide data-processing applications and has enormously enhanced the potential for collective and cooperative forms of work organization. Applications and their maintenance can be controlled by the technical support team who would previously have been responsible for the company's centralized data resources. The common standards defining Internet technology have the fortuitous feature that virtually all PCs can be similarly configured, facilitating not only intracompany network but also *inter*company networking.

The "general purpose" trajectory followed by PC technology has greatly reduced the price-performance ratio of the hardware without effecting commensurate savings in the resource costs of carrying out many specific computerized tasks. Some part of the limited resource savings clearly has been transitional, because PCs were added to existing mainframe capacity rather than substituted for it and, indeed, were underutilized by being allocated the role of intelligent terminals. This aspect of the story bears some striking similarities to the early progress of factory electrification, where the use of the group drive system supplemented without replacing the distribution of power within factories by means of shafts and belts. This added capital to an already highly capital-intensive industrial power technology without instigating any reorganization of factory layout and routines for materials handling. It was not until the dynamo was effectively integrated into individual tools under the unit drive system that major capital-saving contributions to multi-factor productivity growth from thoroughgoing factory redesign could be realized.

An analogous structural change has been envisaged on the basis of digital "information appliances"—hand-held devices or other robust specialized tools that are carried on belts, sewn into garments, and worn as head-gear—in which are embedded advanced microprocessors and telecommunications components that allow them to be linked through sophisticated networks to other such appliances, mainframe computers, and distributed databases, thereby creating complex and interactive intelligent systems. This may well be an emerging trajectory of convergent information and communications technology developments that will impinge directly upon the specific task performance of workers equipped with such devices, and hence upon conventional measures of productivity improvement.[41]

Other portents for the future, involving what eventually would amount to major structural transformations, may be seen in the expansion of interorganizational computing for the mass of transactions involving purchasing, invoicing, shipment tracking, and payments, all of which otherwise will continue to absorb much specialist white-collar labor time. Such service occupations might be viewed as the modern-day counterparts of the ubiquitous materials-handling tasks in the manufacturing sector that became the target of dynamo-based mechanization innovations during the 1920s.[42]

But, beyond these prospective sources of labor productivity gain in service activities, it is relevant that "teleworking" in the United

States remains far from fully deployed: only about 20 percent of large service-sector firms provide data and communication links to employees' homes, and many of those are trying out mixed systems of central office and "outside" work. As was the case with the group drive system of factory electrification, substantial duplication of fixed facilities characterizes this stage in the new GPT's diffusion. Significant capital savings through reductions in required commercial office space and transport infrastructures are therefore likely to result for the whole service sector as teleworking becomes more widely and completely deployed.

Major organizational reconfigurations of this kind have a potential to yield capital savings that do not come at the expense of labor productivity gains. Coupled with the widespread diffusion of "information appliances," they appear to hold out a realistic prospect for the older branches of an increasingly digitalized economy to enjoy a pervasive quickening in the pace of conventionally measured multifactor productivity improvements, alongside the continuing proliferation of new branches of industry offering novel and qualitatively enhanced goods and services. Rather than a distinct "new economy," the United States, then, may look forward to "a digitally renewed economy."

Acknowledgments

This essay represents an abridgement and recasting of my paper "Digital Technology and the Productivity Paradox: After Ten Years, What Has Been Learned?," prepared for the White House Conference on *Understanding the Digital Economy: Data, Tools and Research*, held at the U.S. Department of Commerce, Washington, D.C., 25–26 May 1999. It draws on joint work with Moses Abramovitz, Edward Steinmueller, and Gavin Wright, all of whom have contributed much more to shaping my views of this subject than the bibliographic references below will convey. In the revision process I have also had the benefit of excellent editorial comments from Erik Brynjolfsson.

Notes

1. Solow (1987), p. 36.

2. Testimony of Alan Greenspan before the U.S. House of Representatives Committee on Banking and Financial Services, July 23, 1996.

3. See Abramovitz and David (1999), esp., Part One, Table 1:IV. The estimates for

the endpoints of the indicated intervals are averages over 1888–1892 for "1890" and over 1965–1967 for "1966." The input-quality-adjusted TFP growth rate for 1929–1966 was 1.43 percent per annum, only slightly above the 1890–1929 rate.

4. Moving from the private domestic economy to the private business economy concept also eliminates the distortions in the picture of productivity that arise from the inclusion of the imputed gross rents on the stock of dwellings in the real output series and in the estimated flow of capital input services.

5. See Abramovitz and David (1973), David (1977), Abramovitz (1989). Thus, most of the labor productivity growth rate was accounted for by the increasing capital-labor input ratio, leaving residual rates of TFP growth that were quite small by the standards of the early twentieth century and, a fortiori, by those of the post–World War II era. See Abramovitz and David (1997, 1999) for further discussion.

6. See Sichel (1997), esp. Table 4-2. Sichel puts the 1987–1993 growth rates of inputs of computer hardware and software (allowing for quality improvements) at approximately 17 and 15 percent per annum, respectively; and he estimates the gross returns to these inputs at 0.9 and 0.7 percentage points on the assumption that the assets earn a "normal" net rate of return. The combined contribution to the annual real output growth is about 0.26 percentage points.

7. The growth accounting calculations, moreover, assume that investments embodying information technology earn only a normal private rate of return and do not yield significantly higher "social rates of return" due to externalities and other spillover effects. Were this really the case, it would reconstitute the productivity paradox in the form of the puzzle of why there was not a large positive gap between the social and the private rates of return on this the new information technology and all of its networked applications.

8. On the concept of a "general-purpose technology" and its historical and current relevance, see the remarks immediately below and in section 5 (with references to the literature).

9. See David (1991)for further discussion of the condition I have labeled "technological presbyopia" (sharp vision of the distant technological future, coupled with inability to see clearly the nearer portion of the transition path toward that state)—particularly the illustrative case of early-twentieth-century electrical engineers' views on factory electrification.

10. The Boskin Commission was charged with examining the CPI, rather than the GNP and GDP deflators prepared by the U.S. Commerce Department Bureau of Economic Analysis, and some substantial part (perhaps 0.7 percentage points) of the estimated upward bias of the former is ascribed to the use of a fixed-weight scheme for aggregating the constituent price series to create the overall (Laspeyres type) price index. This criticism does not apply in the case of the national product deflators, and consequently the 1.1 percent per annum figure could be regarded a generous allowance for the biases due to other, technical problems affecting those deflators.

11. On that calculation, the post-1966 reduction in the average annual TFP growth rate would amount to something between 0.3 and 0.8 percentage points, rather than the 1.4 percentage point slowdown discussed in section 1.

12. The Boskin Commission's findings have met with some criticism from BLS staff, who have pointed out that the published CPI reflects corrections that already are regularly made to counteract some of the most prominent among the suspected procedural sources of overstatement—the methods of "splicing in" price series for new goods and services. It is claimed that on this account, the magnitude of the continuing upward bias projected by the Boskin Commission may be too large (see Madrick 1997). The latter controversy does not affect the present illustrative use of the 1.1 percentage point per annum estimate, because it is being applied as a correction of the *past* trend in measured real output; furthermore, in the nature of the argument, an upper-bound figure for the measurement bias is what is wanted here.

13. Gross product originating in Griliches's "hard-to-measure" bloc averaged 49.6 percent of the total over the years 1947–1969, but its average share was 59.7 percent in the years 1969–1990. See Griliches (1995), Table 2, for the underlying NIPA figures from which the shares in the total private (nongovernment) product were obtained. These averages were calculated as geometric means of the terminal-year values in each of the two intervals. Given the observed trend difference (over the whole period 1947–1990) between the labor productivity growth rates of the "hard-to-measure" and the "measurable" sectors identified by Griliches (1994, 1995), the hypothetical effect on the weighted average rate of labor productivity of shifting the output shares can be calculated readily.

14. The gap between the measured and the hard-to-measure sector's long-term average rates of real output per man-hour amounted to about 1.40 percentage points per annum, but it was smaller than that during 1947–1969 period and widened thereafter. The more pronounced post-1969 retardation of the average labor productivity growth rate found for the hard-to-measure sector as a whole was thus responsible in a statistical sense for a large part of the retarded growth of the aggregate labor productivity. It would be quite misleading, though, to suggest that every branch of activity within the major sectors labeled "hard to measure" by Griliches participated in the slowdown, while the industries comprising the "measured" sectors did not; Gordon (1998b) presents more finely disaggregated data on labor productivity that reveals the pervasiveness of the slowdown.

15. See, e.g., Milgrom and Roberts (1990, 1992), Milgrom, Qian, and Roberts (1991).

16. The phrase quoted is from Federal Reserve Bank of Dallas (1998), p. 7. See also Cox and Ruffin (1998) and Schonfeld (1998). On the emergence of "mass customization" see Pine (1993).

17. See Federal Research Bank of Dallas (1998), Exhibit 1, p. 4.

18. Triplett (1999), p. 14, correctly points out that "a greater number of new things is not necessarily a greater rate of new things," and notes that if the relative

number of new products is to grow by additions to the product line, then the total number of products must grow faster and faster. He then dismisses the hypothesis of increasing underestimation of the contribution to productivity growth due to new product introductions on the ground that the actual rate of growth of the number of new products in U.S. supermarkets during 1972–1994 was substantially slower than was the case during 1948–1972. But the latter statistic is not relevant if the mean product life (the inverse of the turnover rate) also can be raised by *replacing* old products with new ones. From the turnover rate figures discussed in the text, below, it is apparent that the assumption (in Triplett's illustrative calculations) of an infinite product life is quite inappropriate.

19. Using these estimates as the basis for gauging the increased relative revenue share of newly introduced products in the "stock" of products carried by supermarkets between the periods 1965–74 and 1975–92, an illustrative set of calculations shows that the *increased* underestimation bias could quite plausibly be as large as 1 percentage point per annum when the later and earlier intervals are compared. Carried up to the GDP level, this might well account for an apparent 0.5 percentage point per annum "slowdown" in 1975–92. See David and Steinmueller (2000).

20. During the 1970s, the Federal Trade Commission was actively interested in whether such product proliferation was a new form of anticompetitive behavior and investigated the ready-to-eat breakfast cereal industry; see Schmalensee (1978) and Hausman (1997) on measuring economic welfare improvement from product innovations in the same industry.

21. The difference between the measured TFP performance of the "computer-producing" and the "computer-using" sectors of the economy, which emerges starkly from the growth accounting studies by Stiroh (1998), may be in some part an artifact of the distorting influence of the Bureau of Economic Analysis's use of hedonic price deflators just for the output of the industry producing computer equipment. See, e.g., Wykoff (1995) for an evaluation of other dimensions of the distortions this has created in comparisons of productivity performance.

22. See Brynolfsson and Hitt (1995, 1996), Lichtenberg (1995), and Lehr and Lichtenberg (1998). The early studies used cross-section observations from samples of large corporations.

23. See, e.g., Brynolfsson and Hitt (1997, 1998), Bresnahan, Brynolfsson, and Hitt (1999a,b). Greenan and Mairesse (1996, 1997), in a pioneering study of French manufacturing firms, found that controlling for the quality of the workforce eliminated the appearance of statistically significant "excess" returns in establishments that were making use of IT equipment.

24. Brynolfsson and Yang (1999) report that computer usage is associated with very high calculated values of Tobin's "q," which they assume reflects the presence of large accumulations of intangible assets.

25. Some of these costs are recorded directly, while others are part of the learning investments being made by firms in formal and informal "on-the-job" knowledge acquisition about information technology.

26. Much greater attention should therefore be devoted to the "task productivity" of information and technology use. Tasks that are repetitively performed using information and communication technologies are likely to be worthy of the same amount of analysis that is currently devoted to approval paths, logistics, and other features of the organization that are the focus of quality assurance and business process reengineering activities. From the productivity measurement viewpoint, it will not be possible to gather meaningful statistics about these aspects of productivity until organizations are performing these sorts of measurements themselves. Only when work processes are monitored and recorded are they likely to find their way into the adjunct studies that are performed to test the accuracy of more abstract productivity measurement systems.

27. The following draws upon the more detailed treatment of the productivity implications of the general-purpose computer technology that has characterized the PC revolution in David and Steinmueller (2000), Section 7.

28. Outside sourcing of applications software represented a significant departure from the proprietary software strategy that the suppliers of dedicated word-processing systems sought to implement during the 1970s, which left them unable to meet the rapidly rising demands for new, specialized applications software. Moreover, PCs could use many of the same peripherals, such as printers; because the widespread adoption of the new technology raised the demand for compatible printers, the dedicated word processors found themselves unprotected by any persisting special advantages in printing technology.

29. Similar decisions were made by all of the U.S. computer manufacturers.

30. In the medium and large enterprises of 1990, what remained was a deep chasm between the "mission-critical" application sembedded in mainframe computers and the growing proliferation of PCs. The primary bridge between these application environments was the widespread use of the IBM 3270, the DEC VT-100, and other standards for "intelligent" data display terminals, the basis for interactive data display and entry to mainframe and minicomputer systems. From their introduction, PCs had software enabling the emulation of these terminals, providing further justification for their adoption.

31. For an historical account of a potential alternative path of user-driven technological development, a path that entailed the reorganization of businesses as an integral aspect of the computerization of their activities, see Caminer et al. (1996).

32. For a recent development of this theme, see Norman (1998), esp. chapters 2–4, 12.

33. As quoted in Gibbs (1997).

34. See, e.g., Helpman and Trajtenberg (1998), Aghion and Howitt (1998), and the discussion of the GPT literature in David and Wright (2000).

35. The capital service flows in question are measured gross of depreciation, corresponding to the gross output concept used in the measurement of labor and multifactor productivity. Some economists who have voiced skepticism about the

ability of computer capital formation to make a substantial contribution to raising output growth in the economy point to the rapid technological obsolescence in this kind of producer durable equipment, and argue that the consequent high depreciation rate prevents the stock from growing rapidly in relationship to the overall stock of producer capital in the economy. This argument would be relevant were one focusing on the impact on real net output, whereas the entire discussion of the productivity slowdown has been concerned with gross output measures. See Sichel (1997), pp. 101–103, for a useful comparison of alternative estimates of net and gross basis computer service "contributions to growth."

36. If we extrapolate from the (slowed) rate at which it was rising during 1990–1992, the value of this index for 1997 would stand somewhat under the 38 percent level.

37. See the industry cross-section regression results and the discussion of the multifactor productivity growth rate estimates relating to Table 5 in David (1991a).

38. Fortuitously, these dates bound the period in which the possibility of a universal electrical supply system emerged in the United States as a practical reality, based upon polyphase AC generators, AC motors, rotary converters, electric (DC) trams, and the principle of factory electrification based on the "unit drive" system. See David (1991a) for further discussion.

39. See David (1991a), Technical Appendix, for this demonstration.

40. See David and Steinmueller (1999) and the formulation in David and Wright (1999), upon which the remainder of this section draws.

41. See Gibbs (1997) and especially Norman (1998), chapter 11.

42. See David and Wright (1999), for fuller discussion of the interrelatedness of mechanization of materials handling and factory electrification in the United States during the 1920s and 1930s.

References

Abramovitz, Moses, 1989. "Notes on Postwar Productivity Growth: The Play of Potential and Realization," Center for Economic Policy Research Publication No. 156, Stanford University, March.

Abramovitz, Moses, and Paul A. David, 1973. "Reinterpreting Economic Growth: Parables and Realities," *American Economic Review* 63(2).

Abramovitz, Moses, and Paul A. David, 1996. "The Rise of Intangible Investment: the U.S. Economy's Growth Path in the Twentieth Century," in D. Foray and B. A. Lundvall, eds., *Employment and Growth in the Knowledge-Based Economy* (OECD Documents), Paris: OECD.

Abramovitz, Moses, and Paul A. David, 1999. "American Macroeconomic Growth in the Era of Knowledge-Based Progress: The Long-Run Perspective," Stanford

Institute for Economic Policy Research, Discussion Paper Series, Stanford University, December.

Aghion, Philippe, and Peter Howitt, 1998. "On the Macroeconomic Effects of Major Technological Change," in Helpman, ed., *General Purpose Technologies and Economic Growth*, Cambridge, MA: MIT Press, 1998.

Bailey, Martin, and Robert J. Gordon, 1965. "The Productivity Slowdown, Measurement Issues, and the Explosion of Computer Power." *Brookings Papers on Economic Activity* 2: 347–420.

Beckett, Samuel, 1965. *Waiting for Godot: A Tragicomedy in Two Acts*, 2nd ed., London: Faber and Faber.

Blinder, Alan S., and Richard E. Quandt, 1997. "Waiting for Godot: Information Technology and the Productivity Miracle," Princeton University Department of Economics Working Paper, May.

Boskin, M.J., 1996. *Toward a More Accurate Measure of the Cost of Living*, Final Report to the Senator Finance Committee from the Advisory Commission to Study the Consumer Price Index.

Bresnahan, Timothy F., Erik Brynjolfsson, and Lorin Hitt, 1999a. "Information Technology and Recent Changes in Work Organization Increase the Demand for Skilled Labor," in M. Blair and T. Kochan, eds., *The New Relationship: Human Capital in the American Corporation*, Washington, DC: Brookings Institution.

Bresnahan, Timothy F., Erik Brynjolfsson, and Lorin Hitt, 1999b. "Information Technology, Workplace Organization and the Demand for Skilled Labor: Firm-level Evidence," *National Bureau of Economic Research Working Paper Series*, No. 7136 (May).

Bresnahan, Timothy F., and Manuel Trajtenberg, 1995. "General Purpose Technologies: Engines of Growth," *Journal of Econometrics* 65: 83–108.

Brynjolfsson, Erik, and Lorin Hitt, 1995. "Information Technology as a Factor of Production: The Role of Differences Among Firms," *Economics of Innovation and New Technology* 3(3–4): 183–199.

Brynjolfsson, Erik, and Lorin Hitt, 1996. "Paradox Lost? Firm-Level Evidence of High Returns to Information Systems Spending," *Management Science*, April.

Brynjolfsson, Erik, and Lorin Hitt, 1997. "Information Technology, Organization, and Productivity: Evidence from Firm-level," MIT Sloan School of Management Working Paper.

Brynjolfsson, Erik, and Lorin Hitt, 1998. "Beyond Computation: Information Technology, Organizational Transformation and Business Performance," MIT Sloan School of Management Working Paper, September.

Brynolfsson, Erik, and S. Yang, 1999. "The Intangible Costs and Benefits of Computer Investments: Evidence from Financial Markets," Proceedings of the International Conference on Informational Systems, Atlanta, Georgia, December 1997 (Revised April 1999).

Caminer, D. T., J. B. B. Aris, P. M. R. Hermon, and F. F. Land, 1996. *User-Driven Innovation: The World's First Business Computer*, London: McGraw-Hill.

Cox, W. Michael, and Roy J. Ruffin, 1998. "What Should Economists Measure? The Implications of Mass Production vs. Mass Customization," Federal Reserve Bank of Dallas, Working Paper no. 98-03, July.

David, Paul A., 1977. "Invention and Accumulation in America's Economic Growth: A Nineteenth Century Parable," in K. Brunner and A.H. Meltzer, eds., *International Organization, National Policies and Economic Development*, a supplement to the *Journal of Monetary Economics* 6: 179–228.

David, Paul A., 1990. "The Dynamo and the Computer: An Historical Perspective on the Productivity Paradox," *American Economic Review* 80(2): 355–361.

David, Paul A., 1991a. "Computer and Dynamo: The Modern Productivity Paradox in a Not-Too-Distant Mirror," in *Technology and Productivity: The Challenge for Economic Policy*, Paris: Organization for Economic Co-operation and Development, pp. 315–348.

David, Paul A., 1991b. "General Purpose Engines, Investment, and Productivity Growth: From the Dynamo Revolution to the Computer Revolution," in E. Deiaco, E. Hörner and G. Vickery, eds., *Technology and Investment: Crucial Issues for the 90s*, London: Pinter.

David, Paul A., 1999. "Digital Technology and the Productivity Paradox: After Ten Years, What Has Been Learned and What Do We Need to Know?" Prepared for the White House Conference on Understanding the Digital Economy, Washington, DC, May 25–26.

David, Paul A., and W. Edward Steinmueller, 2000. "Understanding the Puzzles and Payoffs of the IT Revolution: The 'Productivity Paradox' after Ten Years," in P. A. David and W. Edward Steinmueller, eds., *Productivity and the Information Technology Revolution*, Harwood Academic Publishers.

David, Paul A., and G. Wright, 1999. "General Purpose Technologies and Surges in Productivity: Historical Reflections on the Future of the ICT Revolution," University of Oxford Discussion Paper No. 31, September.

Diewert, W. Edward, and Kevin J. Fox, 1997. "Can Measurement Error Explain the Productivity Paradox?" University of New South Wales, School of Economics Discussion Paper No. 27.

Federal Reserve Bank of Dallas, 1998. "The Right Stuff: America's Move to Mass Customization," *1998 Annual Report*.

Freeman, Christopher, and Carlotta Perez, 1986. "The Diffusion of Technical Innovations and Changes of Techno-economic Paradigm," presented to the Conference on Innovation Diffusion, held in Venice, 17–22 March.

Gibbs, W. Wyat, 1997. "Taking Computers to Task," *Scientific American*, July.

Goldin, Claudia, and Lawrence Katz, 1996. "The Origins of Technology-Skill Complementarity," *National Bureau of Economic Research Working Paper Series*, No. 5657.

Gordon, Robert J., 1996. "Problems in the Measurement and Performance of Service-Sector Productivity in the United States," *National Bureau of Economic Research Working Paper Series*, Number 5519.

Gordon, Robert J., 1997. "Is There a Tradeoff Between Unemployment and Productivity Growth?" in D. Snower and G. De la Dehesa, eds., *Unemployment Policy: Government Options for the Labour Market*, Cambridge: Cambridge University Press, pp. 433–463.

Gordon, Robert J., 1998a. "Monetary Policy in the Age of Information Technology: Computers and the Solow Paradox," prepared for the Conference on Monetary Policy in a World of Knowledge-Based Growth, Quality Change and Uncertain Measurement, Bank of Japan, June 18–19.

Gordon, Robert J., 1998b. "Current Productivity Puzzles from a Long-Term Perspective," upublished manuscript, Northwestern University, September.

Greenan, Nathalie, and Jacques Mairesse, 1996. "Computers and Productivity in France: Some Evidence," *National Bureau of Economic Research Working Paper Series*, No. 15836; also *Monash Department of Econometrics and Business Statistics Working Papers*, No.15/96, September 1997; *National Bureau of Economic Research Working Paper Series*, Fall 1997.

Greenspan, Alan, 1996. "Remarks Before the National Governors' Association," Feb. 5, p. 1.

Griliches, Zvi, 1994. "Productivity, R&D, and the Data Constraint," *American Economic Review* 84: 1–23.

Griliches, Zvi, 1995. "Comments on Measurement Issues in Relating IT Expenditures to Productivity Growth," *Economics of Innovation and New Technology* 3(3–4): 317–321, esp. Table 2 in chapter 10.

Hausman, Jerry A., 1997. "Valuation of New Goods Under Perfect and Imperfect Competition," in Timothy F. Bresnahan and Robert J. Gordon, eds., *The Economics of New Goods*, Chicago: University of Chicago Press for the National Bureau of Economic Research.

Helpman, Elhanan, and Manuel Trajtenberg, 1998. "A Time to Sow and a Time to Reap: Growth Based on General Purpose Technologies," in Elhanan Helpman, ed., *General Purpose Technologies and Economic Growth*, Cambridge, MA: MIT Press.

Jorgenson, Dale W., 1990. "Productivity and Economic Growth," in Ernst R. Berndt and Jack E. Triplett, eds., *Fifty Years of Economic Measurement: The Jubilee of the Conference on Research in Income and Wealth*. Chicago: University of Chicago Press.

Jorgenson, Dale, and Kevin Stiroh, 1995. "Computers and Growth," *Economics of Innovation and New Technology* 3: 295–316.

Lehr, William, and Frank R. Lichtenberg, 1998. "Information Technology and Its Impact on Productivity: Firm-Level Evidence from Government and Private Data Sources, 1977–1993," *Canadian Journal of Economics*.

Lichtenberg, Frank R., 1995. "The Output Contributions of Computer Equipment and Personnel: A Firm-Level Analysis," *Economics of Innovation and New Technology* 3(3–4): 201–217.

Madrick, Jeff, 1997. "The Cost of Living: A New Myth," *The New York Review of Books*, March 6.

Milgrom, Paul R., and John Roberts, 1990. "The Economics of Modern Manufacturing: Technology, Strategy, and Organization," *American Economic Review* 80(3): 511–528.

Milgrom, Paul R., and John Roberts, 1992. *Economics, Organization and Management*, Englewood Cliffs, NJ: Prentice Hall.

Milgrom, Paul R., John Roberts, and Yingyi Qian, 1991. "Complementarities, Momentum, and the Evolution of Modern Manufacturing," *American Economic Review* 81(2): 84–88.

Nakamura, L. I., 1997. "The Measurement of Retail Output and the Retail Revolution," Paper presented at the CSLS Workshop on Service Sector Productivity and the Productivity Paradox, Ottawa, April.

Nelson, Richard R., 1990. "On Technology Capabilities and Their Acquisition," in R. E. Evenson and Gustav Ranis, eds., *Science and Technology: Lessons for Developing Policy*, Boulder, CO: Westview Press, in co-operation with the Economic Growth Center, Yale University.

Norman, Donald A., 1998. *The Invisible Computer: Why Good Products Can Fail, the Personal Computer Is So Complex, and Information Appliances are the Solution*, Cambridge, MA: MIT Press.

Oliner, Stephen D., and Daniel E. Sichel, 1994. "Computers and Output Growth Revisited: How Big is the Puzzle?" *Brookings Papers on Economic Activity* 2: 273–318.

Pine, B. Joseph II, 1993. *Mass Customization: The New Frontier in Business Competition*, Boston: Harvard Business School Press.

Schmalensee, Richard, 1978. "A Model of Advertising and Product Quality," *Journal of Political Economy* 86(3): 485–503.

Schonfield, Erick, 1998. "The Customized, Digitized, Have-It-Your-Way Economy," *Fortune* September: 114–121.

Sichel, Daniel E., 1997. *The Computer Revolution: An Economic Perspective*, Washington DC: The Brookings Institution Press, esp. Table 4.2, Table 5.2.

Solow, Robert M., 1987. "We'd Better Watch Out," *New York Review of Books*, July 12, p. 36.

Stiroh, Kevin J., 1998. "Computers, Productivity and Input Substitution," *Economic Inquiry*, April.

Triplett, Jack E., 1998. "The Solow Productivity Paradox: What Do Computers Do to Productivity?" Prepared for the meetings of the American Economic Association, January, Chicago, Illinois.

Triplett, Jack E., 1999. "Economic Statistics, the New Economy, and the Productivity Slowdown," *Business Economics* 34(2): 13–17.

U.S. Department of Labor, Bureau of Labor Statistics, 1998. *USDL News Release 98-187*, May 6.

Wykoff, Andrew W., 1995. "The Impact of Computer Prices on International Comparisons of Labour Productivity," *Economics of Innovation and New Technology* 3(3–4): 277–294.

Market Structure, Competition, and the Role of Small Business

Understanding Digital Markets: Review and Assessment

Michael D. Smith, Joseph Bailey, and Erik Brynjolfsson

1 Introduction

A basement computer room at Buy.com headquarters in Aliso Viejo, California, holds what some believe to be the heart of the new digital economy. Banks of modems dial out over separate ISP accounts, gathering millions of prices for consumer products: books, CDs, videos, computer hardware and software. Specially programmed computers then sift through these prices, identifying the best prices online and helping Buy.com deliver on its promise of having "the lowest price on earth."

Buy.com's model seems to represent the economic ideal for frictionless markets: low search costs, strong price competition, low margins, low deadweight loss. However, the $1 trillion dollar question[1] for Internet consumer goods markets is: Will strong price competition prevail in electronic markets, or will other market characteristics allow retailers to maintain significant margins on the goods they sell?

To approach this question this paper explores three aspects of business-to-consumer electronic commerce markets. Section 2 discusses several alternative ways to measure efficiency in Internet markets and discusses the empirical evidence relating to these alternatives. Section 3 focuses more specifically on potential sources of price dispersion in Internet markets. Section 4 introduces important developments to watch in electronic commerce markets and discusses how they may affect efficiency and competition in the coming years. The appendix offers an extensive, if necessarily incomplete, bibliography of related research.

2 Characterizing Competition in Electronic Markets

There are a variety of ways to analyze the level of friction in Internet markets. Some studies in this area compare the characteristics of electronic markets to conventional markets, while others analyze behavior within electronic markets. In this section, we identify four dimensions of efficiency in electronic markets: price levels, price elasticity, menu costs, and price dispersion (Table 1).

2.1 Price Levels

In the classic economic models of social welfare, efficiency is maximized when all welfare-enhancing trades are executed. In retail markets where sellers set prices, efficiency occurs when prices are set equal to retailers' marginal costs. This is the efficient outcome because pricing above marginal cost excludes welfare-enhancing trades from consumers who value the product at a level between the price and the marginal cost.

A number of economists have asserted that electronic markets should be more efficient than conventional markets because lower search costs lead to a reduction in information asymmetries. Economic theory predicts that high consumer search costs lead to prices above marginal cost in equilibrium (see, e.g., Hotelling 1929 or Salop 1979). If electronic markets allow consumers to determine retailers' prices and product offerings more easily, their lower search costs should lead to lower prices for both homogeneous and differentiated goods (Bakos 1997).

In theory, more advantageous retailer cost structures should also contribute to lower price levels in electronic marketplaces in several ways. First, low market entry costs should limit the price premiums that existing market participants can sustain by increasing actual or potential competition (Milgrom and Roberts 1982). Second, favorable cost structures should lead to lower equilibrium price levels in a long-run equilibrium by decreasing the underlying costs on which any price premiums are based.

Lee (1997), in one of the first studies of pricing in electronic markets, compared prices in electronic and conventional auction markets for used cars sold from 1986 to 1995. He found that prices

Table 1 Four Dimensions of Internet Market Efficiency

Price Levels: Are the prices charged on the Internet lower?

Price Elasticity: Are consumers more sensitive to small price changes on the Internet?

Menu Costs: Do retailers adjust their prices more finely or more frequently on the Internet?

Price Dispersion: Is there a smaller spread between the highest and lowest cost on the Internet?

in the electronic markets were higher than prices in the conventional markets and that this price difference seemed to increase over time. At first glance, this finding seems to contradict the efficiency hypothesis. But there are two aspects of the study that are important to emphasize: First, this was an auction market, and the characteristics of auction markets differ from those of retail markets. In auction markets efficiency results when a good is sold to the bidder with the highest valuation for that good. Thus, *ceteris paribus*, higher prices may be a signal of greater efficiency in an auction market.Second, Lee was unable to control for the systematic differences between cars sold in the two markets. Specifically, cars sold in the electronic markets were, in general, newer than the cars sold in the conventional markets, and the electronic market cars went through an extra presale inspection process that was not used in the conventional markets.

Bailey (1998a,b) offers a more direct test of the efficiency hypothesis, comparing the prices for books, CDs, and software sold on the Internet and through conventional channels in 1996 and 1997. Like Lee, Bailey found higher prices in the electronic channel for each product category, even though in this study the physical goods were entirely homogeneous and were matched across the channels. Bailey argues that the higher prices he observed could have been caused by market immaturity. This argument is supported, in part, by an analysis of pricing behavior surrounding the entry of Barnes & Noble into the Internet market for books. Bailey notes that during the three months following Barnes & Noble's Internet entry on March 19, 1997, Amazon.com dropped its prices by nearly 10% to match the prices charged by their new competitor.

In a related study, Brynjolfsson and Smith (2000) examined prices for books and CDs sold through Internet and conventional channels in 1998 and 1999.[2] Unlike Bailey, they found that prices are 9–16% lower on the Internet than in conventional outlets— even after accounting for costs related to shipping and handling, delivery, and local sales taxes. The differences in the methodologies used in the two studies (including the retailers, the products, and the time period) prevent direct comparison of results, but one possible explanation for the differences is that Internet markets became more efficient between 1996 and 1999.

2.2 Price Elasticity

Price elasticity measures how sensitive consumer demand is to changes in price.[3] For commodities, price elasticity can be an important signal of market efficiency: in efficient markets, consumers are more sensitive to small changes in prices, at least as long as substitute vendors or products exist. For Internet consumers, higher (absolute values of) price elasticity may result from lower search costs or lower switching costs.

Three studies have looked at aspects of price sensitivity in Internet markets. Goolsbee (2000) used survey data to analyze the sensitivity of consumers to local sales tax rates. He found a high sensitivity to local tax policies: consumers who were subject to high local sales taxes were much more likely to purchase online (and presumably avoid paying the local sales tax). While Goolsbee did not specifically test price elasticity between Internet firms, it does point to a high degree of price sensitivity between the total cost of a good online and the total cost in a conventional outlet.

For differentiated goods, the relationship between price elasticity and efficiency requires more interpretation. There are two reasons why price sensitivity could be lower online than in conventional outlets for differentiated goods. First, lower online search costs could make it easier for consumers to locate products that better meet their needs (Alba et al. 1997). Second, evaluating products online could lead to "missing information" regarding the characteristics of the product (Degeratu, Rangaswamy, and Wu 1998), and missing information could lead consumers to rely more heavily on other signals of quality, such as brand. Either of these factors could soften price competition, but they have opposite outcomes with respect to efficiency.

Two empirical studies have analyzed price sensitivity in electronic markets for differentiated goods. Degeratu, Rangaswamy, and Wu (1998) examined groceries sold through conventional and electronic outlets and found that price sensitivity was lower for online grocery shoppers than for conventional-world shoppers. In a related study, Lynch and Ariely (2000) tested customer price sensitivity by manipulating the shopping characteristics in a simulated electronic market for wine. They found that consumers tend to focus on price when there is little other information available to differentiate products. Providing better product information to customers softens price competition and increases product-customer fit.

2.3 Menu Costs

Menu costs are the costs incurred by retailers in making price changes. In a conventional setting, menu costs consist primarily of the cost of physically relabeling products on shelves (Levy et al. 1997). In an electronic market we hypothesize that menu costs should be lower, since they are comprised primarily of the cost of making a single price change in a central database.

In general, retailers will only make a price change when the benefit of the change exceeds the cost. If menu costs are high, retailers will be less willing to make small price changes and as a result will be less able to adapt to small changes in supply and demand. For this reason menu costs are important in an efficiency context.

Two empirical papers suggest that menu costs are lower online than in conventional outlets. Bailey (1998a) measured the number of price changes undertaken by Internet and conventional retailers. He found that Internet retailers make significantly more changes than conventional retailers and concluded that menu costs are in fact lower on the Internet than in conventional outlets. Brynjolfsson and Smith (2000) compared the propensity of retailers to make small price changes—the types of changes that would be prevented by large menu costs. They found that Internet retailers make price changes that are up to 100 times smaller than the smallest price changes observed in conventional outlets.

2.4 Price Dispersion

The Bertrand model of price competition represents the extreme view of market efficiency. It assumes that products are perfectly homogeneous, consumers are informed of all prices, and there is free market entry, a large number of buyers and sellers, and zero search costs. This setting yields pure price competition: the retailer with the lowest price receives all sales, and as a result all prices are driven to marginal cost. Given the stark assumptions in the Bertrand model, however, it is not surprising that the existence of price dispersion—different prices charged for the same good at the same time—is one of the most replicated findings in economics (see, e.g., Pratt, Wise, and Zeckhauser 1979; Dahlby and West 1986; Sorensen 2000).

Price dispersion is conventionally seen as arising from high search costs (Burdett and Judd 1983; Stahl 1989, 1996) or from consumers who are imperfectly informed of prices (Salop and Stiglitz 1977, 1982; Varian 1980). Since search costs are supposed to be lower in Internet markets (Bakos 1997) and consumers are more readily informed of prices, price dispersion on the Internet should be lower than in comparable conventional markets.

This hypothesis is not supported by existing empirical evidence. Both Bailey (1998a,b) and Brynjolfsson and Smith (2000) found that price dispersion is no lower in Internet markets than in conventional markets. Brynjolfsson and Smith found that prices for identical books and CDs differed by as much as 50% at different retailers; price differences averaged 33% for books and 25% for CDs. The authors attribute their findings to several factors, including market immaturity and heterogeneity in retailer attributes such as trust and awareness.

Clemons, Hann, and Hitt (1998) studied markets for airline tickets sold through online travel agents. They found that prices for airline tickets can differ by as much as 20% across online travel agents, even after controlling for observable product heterogeneity. While this study does not compare the dispersion in online markets to dispersion in conventional markets, the amount of dispersion found is higher than one might expect. The authors attribute the observed price dispersion to retailer segmentation strategies and, in one case, to price discrimination.

2.5 Future Research Directions

To date, empirical studies are mixed on the question of efficiency in Internet markets (Table 2). Both studies of menu costs suggest that such costs are lower in Internet markets, and the most recent test of price levels suggests that prices are lower online for books and CDs. In addition Goolsbee (2000) suggests that consumers are highly sensitive to differences between conventional and Internet prices. At the same time, the three studies of price dispersion all find high degrees of dispersion in Internet markets—a finding inconsistent with a strong efficiency view.

There are a variety of ways to extend the current research to gain a better understanding of the efficiency characteristics of Internet markets.

• Study efficiency in other Internet markets: It is important to confirm the results in the aforementioned studies by measuring the efficiency of other product categories. This will be particularly important for emerging Internet markets for such diverse products and services as pet food, prescription drugs, and financial instruments and for sales outside the United States.

• Analyze changes in efficiency over time: It will be interesting to analyze the behavior of Internet markets over time as markets mature through entry and customer acceptance. This will be important for both relatively mature Internet markets (e.g., books, CDs, hardware, software, and airline tickets) and emerging markets such as prescription drugs. Nascent markets, in particular, may provide an opportunity to observe pricing changes as markets mature over time.

• Examine differences in search behavior for more expensive items: One could also test whether Internet price dispersion varies with product cost. Consumers may be more inclined to search

Table 2 Recent Empirical Research Findings Relating to Internet Efficiency

Study	Data	Finding
Price Levels		
Lee (1997)	Prices for used cars sold in electronic and conventional auction markets, 1986–1995	Prices are higher in electronic auctions and increase over time
Bailey (1998a,b)	Prices for matched set of books, CDs, and software sold through conventional and Internet outlets, 1996–1997	Prices are higher in Internet markets
Brynjolfsson and Smith (2000)	Prices for matched set of books and CDs sold through conventional and Internet outlets, 1998–1999	Prices are lower in Internet markets
Price Elasticity		
Goolsbee (2000)	Survey data for Internet purchases of a variety of goods by 25,000 online users, late 1997	Internet purchases highly sensitive to local tax rates
Degeratu, Rangaswamy, and Wu (1998)	Shopping behavior for groceries sold online (300 Peapod customers) and in conventional outlets (IRI scanner data), 1996–1997.	Price sensitivity lower online
Lynch and Ariely (2000)	Shopping behavior for wine sold in a simulated electronic market	Providing better product information softens price competition and increases fit
Menu Costs		
Bailey (1998a,b)	Prices for matched set of books, CDs, and software sold through conventional and Internet outlets, 1996–1997	Menu costs are lower in Internet markets
Brynjolfsson and Smith (2000)	Prices for matched set of books and CDs sold through conventional and Internet outlets, 1998–1999	Menu costs are lower in Internet markets
Price Dispersion		
Bailey (1998a,b)	Prices for matched set of books, CDs, and software sold through conventional and Internet outlets, 1996–1997	Price dispersion no lower online than in conventional outlets
Clemons, Hann, and Hitt (1998)	Prices quoted by online travel agents for airline tickets, 1997	Substantial price dispersion online (average price differences of up to 20%)
Brynjolfsson and Smith (2000)	Prices for matched set of books and CDs sold through conventional and Internet outlets, 1998–1999	Substantial price dispersion online (average price differences of 25–33%)

aggressively for the best price on expensive items such as cars than they are for low price items such as books and CDs. (Note that Pratt, Wise, and Zeckhauser 1979 found the opposite to be true in conventional markets for a variety of standardized goods.)

• Explore price elasticity in differentiated goods markets: We noted above that electronic markets for differentiated goods may have lower price elasticity than comparable conventional markets for two reasons: "missing information" in the product evaluation, and the ability to find goods that better fit a consumer's preferences. The methodology used by Lynch and Ariely (2000) may provide an interesting way to isolate these two effects and better understand how the observed price elasticity results relate to market efficiency.

• Observe consumer price search behavior: One interesting anomaly in results mentioned previously is that Internet consumers appear to be highly sensitive to prices in conventional outlets (Goolsbee 2000) and yet the price dispersion statistics suggest that consumers may not be as sensitive to price differences between Internet retailers. It would be interesting to explore this issue in more detail to understand how aggressively consumers compare prices in online markets.

3 Sources of Price Dispersion in Electronic Markets

While research to date on price levels, price elasticity, and menu costs are consistent with the hypothesis that the Internet has increased market efficiency, the existence of significant price dispersion in Internet markets and its persistence over time raise interesting questions for the future of competition in electronic markets. In this section we discuss several potential sources of price dispersion in electronic markets. In each case we discuss why the particular factor might be important on the Internet, review the relevant literature, and identify potential areas for future research.

3.1 Product Heterogeneity: The Value of Unmeasured Features

The most obvious source of price dispersion online is product heterogeneity. If the products being compared are different in some way, then it should not be surprising that their prices are different. Even when products are physically identical, there could be other factors that create difference. For instance, they may be available in different locations or time periods—a bottle of wine in a supermarket is not a perfect substitute for the identical vintage in a fine restaurant. It is easy to extend this kind of argument to goods that are accompanied by different levels of customer service, advertising, or even customer awareness. This line of reasoning can be followed a long way, but it usually makes more sense to take George Stigler's advice that "it would be metaphysical, and fruitless, to assert that all dispersion is due to heterogeneity" (Stigler 1961, p. 214). For most purposes, a reasonable approach is to consider product heterogeneity as relating only to the tangible or essential characteristics of the product. These characteristics include differences in the product's physical characteristics or differences in retailer services that must be consumed with the product (e.g., return policies). We discuss other sources of heterogeneity in subsequent sections.

It is possible to control for this type of product heterogeneity using hedonic regressions (see, e.g., Chow 1967; Griliches 1961). Hedonic regression models assume that products can be modeled as (heterogeneous) bundles of (homogeneous) characteristics. In the regression of product prices onto product characteristics, the coefficients on the product characteristics can be interpreted as shadow prices of that characteristic. The shadow prices reveal how much the market values the particular characteristic. For example, the price of a computer can be expressed as a function of its memory, microprocessor, disk storage, and other components (Dulberger 1989; Gordon 1989).

It is important to note, however, that, while product differentiation is an important potential source of price dispersion, it does not seem to explain the dispersion discussed in section 2.4. Clemons, Hann, and Hitt (1998) used hedonic regressions to control for several sources of heterogeneity in airline tickets: arrival and departure times, number of connections, and Saturday night stays. Even after controlling for these sources of price dispersion, they found price dispersion of up to 20%. Similarly, Brynjolfsson and Smith (2000) found little evidence that the most obvious types of heterogeneity could explain the price dispersion they noted. First, they deliberately selected products—books and CDs—that can be perfectly matched across retailers. Books with the same International Standard Book Number (ISBN) are identical down to the commas, regardless of where they are purchased. The authors then used hedonic regressions of book and CD prices onto several retailer service characteristics. They found that the coefficients on the primary service characteristics "either do not vary significantly across retailers or are negatively correlated with price" (p. 22). They suggested that these findings could be due to other unobserved retailer-specific factors such as brand, trust, and awareness. These factors are discussed in more detail below.

3.2 Convenience and Shopping Experience: The Value of Time

Shopping convenience may also provide a source of price dispersion in online markets. Retailers who make it easier to find and evaluate products may be able to charge a price premium to time-sensitive consumers. Sources of convenience may include better search tools, general suggestion tools, extensive product reviews, product samples (e.g., book chapters and CD audio clips), and faster checkout services.

Note that several of the factors mentioned above are purely informational. Product information used to evaluate homogeneous goods is typically separable from the physical product. In and of itself, providing better information on a homogeneous good should not give a retailer strategic advantage. It is possible, however, that product information is a useful strategic tool because of substantial search costs or switching costs in Internet markets. [4] Customers may be drawn to a site because of its outstanding product information and then choose to purchase from that site because of the high search costs to find the good (at a potentially lower price) at another site.

Offering a compelling shopping experience may also affect competition in Internet markets (Novak, Hoffman, and Yung 1998). Several recent papers explore how web design may influence consumer purchase behavior. Mandel and Johnson (1998) showed that background wallpaper can influence the importance of product attributes and consumer choices in online environments. Similarly, Menon and Kahn (1998) found that Internet shopping behavior is influenced by the characteristics of products encountered early in a shopping experience. Specifically, highly novel products lead to less exploration, lower response to promotional incentives, and fewer purchases of other novel products during the rest of the shopping experience.

3.3 Awareness: The Value of Neural Real Estate

It is a truism that the three critical success factors for conventional retailers are location, location, and location. Geography largely determines the set of potential customers that know of a store and make purchases there. Many Internet retailers aggressively purchase premium locations on Internet "portals" and spend hundreds of millions of dollars on advertising through online, print, and traditional broadcast media. This suggests that customer awareness, or "neural real estate," may be just as important in online markets as physical real estate is in conventional markets.

The importance of awareness can be traced to the high search costs associated with locating retailers in Internet markets. These search cost result from the sheer volume of information available. While some retailers such as Amazon.com have used strategic marketing and large advertising budgets to develop high brand awareness, it can be difficult to locate other, more obscure retailers among the millions of Internet sites available online.[5] The heterogeneity in retailer awareness is reflected in a recent Xerox study reporting that just 5% of websites receive nearly 75% of the hits (Adamic and Huberman 1999).

Economists have long recognized the effect of asymmetrically informed consumers on pricing behavior. Salop and Stiglitz (1977) and Varian (1980) have considered markets in which some consumers are aware of all prices in the market while others are aware of the price at only one retailer. Informed customers purchase from the store with the lowest price while uninformed customers purchase if the price they are aware of is lower than their reservation value. The result is that retailers randomize over prices: some retailers always charge a low price while others always charge a high price (Salop and Stiglitz 1977), or retailers occasionally have sales in which they charge a low price on selected items (Varian 1980).

Greenwald and Kephart (1999) applied these models to an Internet setting with analogous results in pricing behavior. They supposed that some consumers have access to price search intermediaries, or shopbots, while others do not. Consumers with access to shopbots purchase at the lowest price, while consumers who do not have access to shopbots purchase if the price they are aware of is lower than their reservation value. This behavior is consistent with that noted by Brynjolfsson and Smith (2000), who observed that retailers with strong customer awareness, such as Amazon.com and CDnow, are able to charge prices that are 7–12% higher than lesser-known retailers such as Books.com and CD Universe.

3.4 Retailer Branding and Trust

It is natural to assume, with Greenwald and Kephart, that shoppers who use shopbots will purchase from the retailer with the lowest price, but conversations with shopbot executives reveal that this is not always the case. These executives observe that some of their visitors regularly buy from branded retailers such as Amazon.com, even when these retailers do not have the lowest price. This suggests that other factors, such as trust, may play an important role in Internet markets.

Trust may take on a heightened importance in electronic markets because of the spatial and temporal separation between buyers and sellers imposed by the medium (Brynjolfsson and Smith 2000). An Internet transaction does not typically involve the simultaneous exchange of money and goods; instead both are typically transmitted from different locations at different times. When selecting a retailer, a consumer may worry that the other party is an expert at attracting traffic and in cashing credit cards but not at actually delivering goods. Consumers may be willing to pay a premium to purchase a product from a retailer they trust. Thus, heterogeneity in retailer trust may lead to price dispersion in online markets.

Recent studies suggest a variety of ways in which retailers may be able to signal trust in an online world:

• Online communities: Having a robust online community housed at a retailer's site may provide a signal of trust. Likewise, reputation systems used in online communities can signal the trustworthiness of other members of the community (Kollock 1999).

• Links from other trusted sites: Trust may be signaled through links from trusted individuals (as in associate programs) or links from respected sites (e.g., Barnes & Noble's link from the online version of the *New York Times Book Review*) (Brynjolfsson and Smith 1999).

• Unbiased product information: Urban, Sultan, and Qualls (1998) used customer feedback data from an online environment called "Truck Town" to demonstrate that unbiased recommendation services can enhance a retailer's trust evaluation among consumers.

• Existing conventional-world brand name: Having a conventional-world brand name can signal trust and soften price competition. Shankar, Rangaswamy, and Pustateri (1998) used survey data to show that prior positive experience with a brand in the physical world can decrease price sensitivity online. Brynjolfsson and Smith (2000) showed that retailers with established conventional-world brand names can charge a price premium of 8–9% over prices at Internet-only retailers.

The role of trust in both Internet and conventional marketing and the cues that help to build trust are explored in more detail by Urban, Sultan, and Qualls (1998).

3.5 Lock-in

Retailers may also be able to charge a price premium by leveraging customers' switching costs. Loyalty programs, long used by airlines, may also prove effective for online shoppers. Varian (this volume) discusses various loyalty programs in existing Internet markets.

There may also be other, more subtle sources of switching costs on the Internet. For example, switching costs may be created through familiarity with a retailer's site. Given the differences in interface design among Internet retailers, a customer who is familiar with an Internet retailer's interface may face a switching cost when shopping at a new retailer whose interface is unfamiliar. Similarly, customization features can introduce switching costs. A customer who has a "one-click" ordering account at a particular retailer may face switching costs when deciding whether to shop somewhere else.

Collaborative filtering tools can be another form of building switching costs. Such tools compare a customer's purchase patterns with those of other like-minded customers to develop personalized recommendations based on a customer's inferred tastes (Shardanand and Maes 1995). Unlike most information used to evaluate homogeneous goods, personalized recommendations are specific to the customer and become more accurate as the customer interacts more with the system. Thus, under the current retailer-owned systems, customers may face a switching cost equal to the decline in the value of the recommendations when switching to another retailer. If the data on a customer's tastes were owned by the customer and were portable from site to site, switching costs would be commensurately lower.[6]

3.6 Price Discrimination

The sources of price dispersion discussed above deal with differences in prices across retailers. Price dispersion may also arise when a single retailer charges different prices based on a consumer's willingness to pay. These price discrimination strategies may take on heightened importance in Internet markets for two reasons. First, while the Internet allows consumers to easily collect retailer information about prices, the same characteristics allow retailers to gather better information about consumer characteristics (Bakos 1998). Second, low menu costs may make it more cost-effective for retailers to change prices online dynamically. The net result is that prices on the Internet need not gravitate to a single value across retailers, time, or customers.[7]

There are a variety of ways for Internet retailers to price-discriminate among consumers. One is to leverage the fact that price-sensitive consumers tend to place a lower value on time than other consumers do. In this situation retailers can create a menu of "prices" and "convenience levels" so that consumers self-select the price corresponding to their willingness to pay (Chiang and Spatt 1982). To obtain a low price a consumer must use an inconvenient or time-consuming process, while a less time-consuming process is associated with a higher price. Below, we identify three ways Internet retailers may be using "convenience" as a price discrimination technique.[8]

First, retailers may be able to establish separate "storefront" interfaces differentiated by their level of convenience. This is the strategy identified by Clemons, Hann, and Hitt (1998) in the Internet online travel agent market. The authors observed that the lowest-priced and the highest-priced online travel agents in their study were both owned by the same parent company. The low-priced agent had a user interface that was very difficult to use while the high-priced agent had a state-of-the-art, user-friendly interface. They concluded that "the difficulty in using [the lower-priced travel agent's] user interface serves as a screen to prevent the time-sensitive travelers from exercising personal arbitrage" (p. 25) and thus facilitates price discrimination.

Price-matching policies—which at first appear to be evidence of strong competition—may provide a second price discrimination technique for Internet retailers.[9] The price-matching system at online retailer Books.com may be an example of such a system. Books.com advertises that it will beat the best price available from the "big 3" Internet book retailers: Amazon.com, Barnes & Noble, and Borders. Figure 1 shows screen shots from such a sequence. At the top, Books.com displays a price of $16.72 for John Grisham's book *The Testament*. Next to this price is a button labeled "Price Compare." If a consumer presses this button, Books.com automatically queries the prices for Amazon.com, Barnes & Noble, and Borders. If Books.com already has the lowest price (which is usually the case), its price remains the same. If it does not have the lowest price, Books.com automatically sets its price to beat the best price offered by its three major competitors. This is shown at bottom, where the new price of $13.65 is displayed. Similar features are appearing in other markets, as exemplified by the electronics retailer NECX.

While this sequence may at first seem to be evidence of strong price competition in Internet channels, three factors suggest that it is more consistent with Books.com using consumer heterogeneity to price-discriminate. First, the price change is not permanent—the lower price is only offered if a consumer asks for it (by pressing the appropriate button). Second, the lower price is only in effect

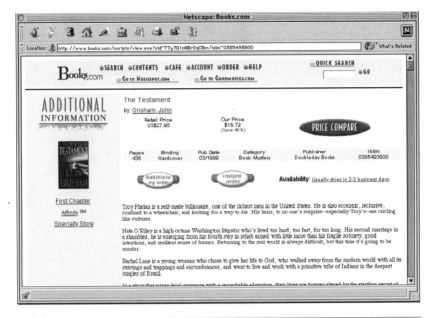

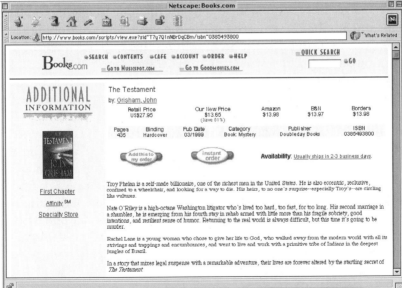

Figure 1 Books.com price before (top) and after (bottom) price comparison.

for the individual transaction: if the consumer comes back later, he or she must again request the lower price. And third, the process is time-consuming (taking up to a minute to complete). A recent sample of 20 books suggests that the expected value to an online consumer from pressing this button is only $0.15. One might suppose that only price-sensitive consumers would be willing to wait up to 1 minute for an expected $0.15 payoff.[10]

Online auctions provide a third example of using convenience to sort consumers by their willingness to pay. Figure 2 displays a screen from an auction conducted by online retailer Shopping.com.[11] Shopping.com auctions several goods that are also available for purchase at Shopping.com's "everyday low price." In Figure 2, Shopping.com is auctioning a Palm V organizer. The winning auction bid is $323, while the regular Shopping.com store price is $333.99—a difference of less than $11. As above, at first glance it appears that Shopping.com is willingly undercutting its own price on this particular good. However, auction shoppers must be willing to wait for the auction to close, accept the uncertainty associated with the auction's outcome, and invest the time necessary to place bids and monitor the progress of the auction.[12] Thus, Shopping.com may also be using a consumer's willingness to participate in the auction as a credible signal of low price sensitivity.

Just as the Internet has provided powerful new tools for consumers in their quest to compare competing retailers and obtain the best possible price, it has also provided a new array of tools for retailers seeking to market to very small groups of customers, in some cases including segments of size less than one,[13] and to adjust those prices dynamically. The end result of this "arms race" may, in some cases, be a reduced reliance on a single one-size-fits-all pricing scheme. As shown by Varian (1985), such price discrimination is often efficiency-enhancing because it can enable consumers with low valuations to get access to the good even if they would have been priced out of the market under a single-price scheme.

3.7 Summary and Areas for Future Research

A better understanding of the sources of price dispersion online may assist consumers, regulators, and marketers in evaluating Internet markets. We have outlined several potential sources of

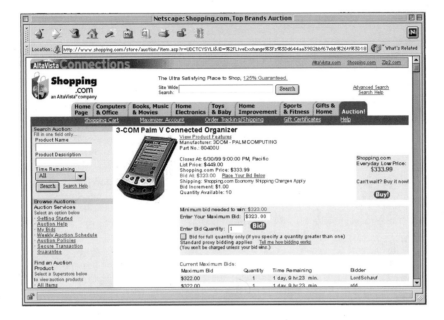

Figure 2 Auction price versus regular Shopping.com price for Palm V Organizer

price dispersion (summarized in Table 3). Future research should focus on verifying and extending this list, measuring the degree of importance of each item, and analyzing changes in these sources of dispersion over time. Here are several potential topics:

• Welfare effects of Internet price discrimination: More research is needed on how flexible pricing systems develop online and how they are used as price discrimination tools. The two examples mentioned above represent early price discrimination models. More sophisticated systems are likely to appear over time. We need to understand the welfare effects of these systems. With respect to welfare analysis, Varian (1985) demonstrates that a necessary condition for third-degree price discrimination to be welfare-enhancing is that it increases market output. A natural question, then, is how these systems affect market participation on the Internet.

• Product information and retailer strategies: We have noted that providing superior product information can be used to signal trust and reliability or to provide shopping convenience. Zettlemeyer

Table 3 Some Research Findings Relating to Sources of Price Dispersion

Study	Summary
Convenience and Shopping Experience	
Mandel and Johnson (1998)	Web page design can affect the importance of product attributes and consumer buying behavior.
Menon and Kahn (1998)	The characteristics of products encountered early in a shopping experience influence subsequent purchases made during the same visit.
Novak, Hoffman, and Yung (1998)	Discuss the flow construct as a way to measure the elements of a "compelling consumer experience online." Present quantitative techniques to measure the flow construct in online environments.
Awareness	
Adamic and Huberman (1999)	Use log files from AOL to show that website popularity is highly concentrated among a few sites online. Propose a model that explains this behavior based on network effects and brand loyalty.
Greenwald and Kephart (1999)	Develop a simulation model similar to Varian (1980) to show that in the presence of asymmetrically informed consumers, retailers will randomize over prices.
Ogus, de la Maza, and Yuret (1999)	Use a simulation model to show that the presence of both network effects and brand loyalty can explain high concentration in Internet markets.
Retailer Branding and Trust	
Kollock (1999)	Discusses the importance of "community" in facilitating the smooth operation of Internet auction markets such as eBay.
Shankar, Venkatesh, and Rangaswamy (1998)	Use survey data for travelers to show that prior positive experience with a brand in the physical world can decrease price sensitivity online.
Urban, Sultan, and Qualls (1998)	Argue that online retailers can build trust among consumers by providing accurate information and unbiased advice. Validate these claims using an online environment for evaluating light trucks for consumer purchase.
Price Discrimination	
Clemons, Hann, and Hitt (1998)	Argue that the site characteristics of two online travel agents owned by the same company may be evidence of the use of a price discrimination strategy by the travel company.
Odlyzko (1996)	Presents many examples of retailers using multiple prices to price-discriminate. Argues that price discrimination may be common on the Internet.

(1996) found that the incentives for providing product information are interdependent with a retailer's conventional strategy and with the reach of the electronic channel. It would be interesting to analyze this theory empirically by tracking differences in the information provided by "pure-play" Internet retailers and retailers who operate conventional outlets or by tracking how these strategies change with the increasing penetration of the Internet.

• The importance of convenience in web page design: Convenience and the customer experience are both important sources of differentiation in online environments, but to some extent they are in opposition to one another. More complex web pages may increase customer download time and detract from the retailer's overall convenience. Delleart and Kahn (1999) found that slower web pages can (but do not necessarily) lead to lower web page evaluations by consumers. It would be interesting to explore the interplay between these two design strategies.

• Importance of trust and awareness in online markets: Ogus, de la Maza, and Yuret (1999) use simulation models to show that the combination of brand loyalty and network effects produce highly concentrated "winner-take-all" Internet markets. Including either of the effects separately, however, does not produce highly concentrated markets. It would be interesting verify their findings through an empirical analysis of Internet markets. It may even be possible to use online experiments to analyze the importance of each factor separately.

• Changes in price dispersion over time: It may also be possible to analyze how the importance of factors such as trust and awareness changes over time. Ward and Lee (1999) argue that as consumers become more experienced with the Internet, they will rely less on brands in their shopping decisions. Likewise, the development of more efficient and well-known price intermediaries may decrease the importance of awareness as a source of price dispersion (Bakos 1998).

4 Developments to Watch

The research on early digital markets not only provides insight into what has occurred but also gives an indication of what the future might hold. There are a number of research issues other than friction and price dispersion that will be worth investigating in electronic markets. These issues tend to focus on broader and more complex areas related to economics, business strategy, and public policy. This section explores four such research issues likely to be among the most important developments to watch in the years ahead.

4.1 Marketing Channels

The first wave of Internet retailers developed a new channel to communicate with their consumers, challenging the established marketing channels of retail stores, catalog sales, and home shopping. This new Internet channel of business-to-consumer interaction was pioneered by pure-play Internet companies such as Amazon.com. The companies with an existing channel watched as the newcomers experimented with this new medium. Once it was known that consumers (and, more particularly, Wall Street) valued Internet retailers, a second wave of Internet retailers emerged that included companies that were expanding from an established marketing channel. These retailers include such industry heavyweights as Barnes & Noble, Macy's, and Compaq.

While the pure-play Internet retailers continued to grow their brand equity and gain market share, Internet retailers with more than one channel began to address problems involving channel conflicts. Channel conflict occurs when a company's Internet channel becomes a competitor for its physical channel. For example, Barnes & Noble has been able to let its physical stores in different geographic locations set their own prices for many titles. With an Internet channel that is available to consumers worldwide, it is not feasible to have prices that vary with geography.[14] Furthermore, companies need to be careful about separating their Internet and traditional channels because they do not want to be taxed for their Internet channel because of their traditional channel retail locations.[15]

It is unlikely that the channel conflicts of today will last forever. As digital markets mature, Internet retailers will either manage their channels simultaneously or will reduce the number of channels. Some retailers, such as Egghead, are already abandoning physical assets and relying solely on their electronic channel. At the same time, some retailers who made a foray into Internet commerce using Marketplace MCI have abandoned their electronic channel. Meanwhile, other retailers are finding ways to use their physical assets to gain a competitive advantage in the electronic channel. Borders.com, for example, allows its Internet customers to return products to the chain's physical outlets. It seems clear that a variety of business models will evolve depending upon market- and firm-level characteristics. Future research can help determine how channel conflict issues will be resolved.

One mechanism to resolve channel conflicts might involve the introduction of auction markets. For example, hotels and airlines might keep their current sales model in place but then sell their excess capacity through an electronic channel via auction. Because the electronic channel then has an associated price uncertainty, it is not selling exactly the same product as the physical channel. Through this differentiation, consumers see the products as less direct substitutes. Increasingly, we may see goods sequentially or even simultaneously available for fixed prices, dynamically up-dated prices, auction prices, and negotiated prices. Another way to use auctions is during the early-stage introduction of a product. Since demand curves are generally unknown for new products, using an electronic auction channel can help firms determine the potential demand for their product and provide consumer feed-back in a timely fashion.

4.2 Intermediation, Disintermediation, and Reintermediation

The shifting roles of intermediaries in electronic markets often lead to changes in the value chain. In a market with friction, intermediation in the value chain can reduce this friction because the intermediaries specialize in certain market roles (Bailey 1998a). In the physical world, for example, distribution of information by an author to all potential readers can be costly. Most authors therefore rely on a publisher who can disseminate their informa-tion at lower cost, thereby reducing market friction, because it specializes in the roles of printing and distribution. With the advent of the Internet, some argue that disintermediation, the removal of intermediaries from the value chain, will occur (Gellman 1996;

Hoffman 1995). In the publishing example, clearly the publisher's printing and distribution roles will no longer be needed once the main medium of dissemination becomes electronic, but this does not mean that intermediaries will be totally removed. Rather, reintermediation will occur, with intermediaries taking on new roles to provide value in new ways. In the publishing example, a new intermediary might provide editorial feedback and peer reviews to the author and help market the information. Two intermediary roles that have been attracting increasing interest include trust and search capabilities.

Trust continues to be an important reason for consumers' emphasis on dealing with known retailers on the Internet, but competition among retailers will become more fluid once consumers can costlessly switch from one retailer to the next. Such competition will be aided by the emergence of trusted third parties (TTPs), intermediaries who will certify the trustworthiness of an Internet retailer. The TTP reintermediation process has already started with companies such as TRUSTe and BBB Online. These two companies will verify the privacy policy of Internet retailers to help protect consumer privacy. Consumers are more likely to trust a retailer if it shows the TRUSTe or BBB Online logo on its web site (*The Industry Standard* 1999). While this is only an initial step in using intermediaries to promote trust, the brand equity that TRUSTe, BBB Online, and other TTPs are building during Internet commerce's growth period will put them in a better position to offer new trust services in the future.

While search costs are likely to decrease in digital markets, consumers may be left with an information overload problem that compels them to use a search intermediary. For example, an Internet search engine can find all documents with the phrase "digital economy," so that this paper, for example, is only one click away. But the engine will also turn up many other web pages related to the "digital economy" that are also one click away. Since the searcher must invest time to filter through all of these matches, and time has value, he or she might find it cheaper to use an intermediary. One such intermediary is the "infomediary," a concept introduced by Hagel and Singer (1999).

When applied to digital markets, infomediaries can help consumers find products that best match their individual preferences.

DealPilot.com, for example, allows consumers to search for the best deals on books, CDs, and videos from more than 100 different Internet retailers. Consumers enter the product(s) they are interested in and are presented with prices and delivery times from the online retailers. Similar systems are available for products as diverse as computer hardware (pricewatch.com), golf clubs (jango .excite.com), and bank certificates of deposit (bankrate.com). For more complex products, second-generation infomediaries such as frictionless.com can rate products based on how well they correspond to the preferences entered by individual customers. By focusing competition on product features and not just price, these tools may soften price competition in online markets (Lynch and Ariely 2000).

4.3 Logistics and Supply Chain Management

Even though the most visible developments in digital markets recently has been in business-to-consumer (B2C) markets, the biggest economic changes are likely to be in the business-to-business (B2B) part of the value chain. B2B electronic commerce has been around longer than B2C commerce, with its origins going back to the introduction of technologies such as electronic data interchange (EDI). Now that the B2C part of the value chain is becoming digital, it is increasingly easy to integrate the whole value chain so that consumers become an important player in all steps of value creation. The most immediate impact of this change will be in logistics and supply chain management.

Traditional logistics issues involve the moving of physical items along the value chain so that a product is available at a retailer when a consumer wants to purchase it. Supply chain management incorporates logistics but examines how information can be used to change how and when products are moved to increase efficiency. By exchanging richer and more timely information, trading partners can also avoid the double marginalization problem of suboptimizing the supply chain (see Milgram and Roberts 1992, p. 550). However, both logistics and supply chain management practices often fall short of incorporating the B2C link.

With the B2C link becoming electronic, consumers are increasingly able to supply information beyond the retailer they transact with and deeper into the value chain. This can affect product offerings. For example, automobile companies such as Ford are starting to use the Internet to share information about product offerings that are still years away from the dealer showroom. By soliciting information from potential consumers, Ford can change the design of a product before it becomes too costly to do so.

4.4 Information Markets

The Internet's ability to deliver a good, as opposed to creating a transaction that requires fulfillment through some other channel, may be the most important development to watch. Information goods have unique properties, including marginal reproduction costs that are close to, if not exactly, zero. For this reason, the pricing strategies for such goods must reflect a new economics. For instance, some of the financial information that is now made available without cost on the web by companies like Etrade was sold through proprietary networks for hundreds of dollars per month just a few years ago. For software, another information good, developers are exploring a new "open source" economic model in which the source code that comprises the good is made freely available for communities of users to explore and help develop.

Information goods may be most affected by the integration of consumers into the value chain. Instead of an information product being created ex ante for consumers to purchase, they can be dynamically rendered based on the wishes of the consumer. Not only will this help Internet retailers price-discriminate, as discussed earlier, it can also dramatically increase the number of product offerings. There is, of course, a potential for mass customization of physical products once the consumer is included in the value chain, but this can be expensive for the producer; for information products, personalization to meet the needs of individual consumers can be done at almost no additional cost.

Digital information goods also raise interesting pricing opportunities. Clearly traditional rules of thumb such as "price equal to marginal cost" or using a standard markup over cost are not very useful in this environment. Instead, value-oriented pricing strategies are more likely to be effective (Varian 1995, 2000). At the same time, the special characteristics of digital goods when combined with the Internet open up new opportunities, including disaggregation of previously aggregated content such as newspaper or journal articles and massive aggregation of content such as that sold by America Online (Bakos and Brynjolfsson 1999, 2000).

A major policy issue relating to the sale of digital goods is that of jurisdiction. When a digital market transaction relies on a physical channel for order fulfillment, jurisdiction can always be resolved by reference to the physical channel. Information goods, however, need not rely on a physical distribution channel. This can be a headache for policymakers trying to prevent fraudulent business activity on the Internet or trying to impose taxes or regulations that would normally be based on jurisdiction.

5 Conclusions

The potential of the emerging digital economy is vast, yet of necessity few business decisions in this area have been able to draw on a significant research foundation. While intuition, trial and error, and venture capital can sometimes substitute for genuine understanding, few areas, if any, could benefit more from well-designed research. In particular, the synergies between rigor and relevance, academia and business, theory and practice, are exceptionally great. The emerging digital economy, with its set of vanishing costs and increasingly universal reach, constitutes a grand experiment that will put many of our theories about what happens at "zero" and "infinity" to the test. At the same time, the managers who best understand the changes taking place will be in the best position to shape those changes. In chaos lies opportunity.

In coming years, electronic markets may dramatically change the way products are bought and sold. Early research suggests that electronic markets are more efficient than conventional markets with respect to price levels, menu costs, and price elasticity. At the same time, several studies find significant price dispersion in Internet markets. This price dispersion may be explained by heterogeneity in retailer-specific factors such as branding and trust, retailer efforts to lock consumers in, and various retailer price discrimination strategies.

At this early stage of the digital revolution in technology and business, many important questions remain to be answered. How will the development of infomediaries and shopbots effect competition on the Internet? Will the importance of brand decrease with the development of third-party rating sites? Will established retailers be able to leverage existing physical assets when competing with pure-play Internet sites? How will the structure of firms adapt to the new digital economy? Questions such as these deserve more attention, and this exploration promises to make the Internet a fertile ground for research and experimentation for years to come.

Appendix: Annotated Bibliography of Selected Electronic Commerce Research Papers

A1 Competition in Electronic Markets

A1.1 Theoretical Analysis of Competition in Electronic Markets

Bakos, J. Yannis, 1997. "Reducing Buyer Search Costs: Implications for Electronic Marketplaces," *Management Science* 43(12).

Uses Salop's circle model to show that if electronic markets have lower search costs than conventional markets, prices in the electronic markets will be lower and more homogeneous.

Bakos, J. Yannis, 1998. "The Emerging Role of Electronic Marketplaces on the Internet," *Communications of the ACM* 41(8): 35–42.

Discusses the effect of the Internet on electronic markets. Hypothesizes that the Internet will (1) increase product offerings, (2) increase customization, (3) increase the ability of consumers to discover prices, and (4) increase the ability of retailers to discover information about consumers and price discriminate.

Odlyzko, Andrew, 1996. "The Bumpy Road of Electronic Commerce," in H. Maurer, editor, *Proceedings of WebNet-96*, World Conference of the Web Society (Association for the Advancement of Computing in Education), pp. 378–389.

Presents many examples of retailers using multiple prices to price discriminate. Argues that the characteristics of electronic markets may give retailers many opportunities to price discriminate.

Ogus, Ayla, Michael de la Maza, and Deniz Yuret, 1999. "The Economics of Internet Companies," Proceedings of *Computing in Economics and Finance 1999*, Meetings of the Society for Computational Economics, June 24–26.

Uses a simulation environment to show that the presence of *both* brand loyalty and network effects leads to highly concentrated Internet markets. The presence of either factor alone leads to significantly less concentrated markets.

Shaffer, Greg, and Florian Zettlemeyer, 1999. "The Internet as a Medium for Marketing Communications: Channel Conflict over the Provision of Information," Working Paper, June.

The authors' model demonstrates that if the Internet allows manufacturers to provide technical/idiosyncratic information directly to customers (without having to use retailers as intermediaries), manufacturers will gain power in the channel. They conclude that the Internet "can potentially harm retailers even if it is not used as a direct sales channel."

Zettlemeyer, Florian, 1996. *The Strategic Use of Consumer Search Cost*, Ph.D. Thesis, Sloan School of Management, Massachusetts Institute of Technology.

Notes that the simple hypothesis that the Internet will lead to lower prices and more information ignores the fact that hybrid firms maximize over conventional and Internet operations. With this factor included in the model, the author finds that the amount of information provided by Internet retailers is tied to the reach of the channel.

A1.2 Empirical Studies of Competition in Electronic Markets

Adamic, Lada A., and Bernardo A. Huberman, 1999. "The Nature of Markets in the World Wide Web," Proceedings of *Computing in Economics and Finance 1999*, Meetings of the Society for Computational Economics, June 24–26.

Uses log files from AOL recording the number of visits to various web sites to show that hits to web sites are highly concentrated among a few sites. The authors suggest that this may be due to brand loyalty and network effects in Internet markets.

Bailey, Joseph P., 1998. *Intermediation and Electronic Markets: Aggregation and Pricing in Internet Commerce*. Ph.D. dissertation, Program in Technology, Management and Policy, Massachusetts Institute of Technology.

Tests Internet market efficiency for books, software, and CDs using three statistics: price levels, price dispersion, and menu costs. Finds higher prices, more dispersion, and lower menu costs for Internet outlets. Uses data from 1996 (exploratory study) and 1997.

Brynjolfsson, Erik, and Michael Smith, 2000. "Frictionless Commerce? A Comparison of Internet and Conventional Retailers," *Management Science* (April).

Extension of Bailey (1998) analyzing Internet market efficiency for books and CDs. Finds lower prices, more dispersion, and lower menu costs for Internet outlets. Uses data from February 1998 through May 1999.

Clemons, Eric K., Il-Horn Hann, and Lorin M. Hitt, 1998. "The Nature of Competition in Electronic Markets: An Empirical Investigation of Online Travel Agent Offerings," Working Paper, Wharton School, University of Pennsylvania, June.

Finds high price dispersion in online markets for airline tickets: prices for tickets offered by online travel agents can vary by as much as 20%. Also finds evidence of the use of separate storefronts with different "ease-of-use" to facilitate price discrimination by sorting customers by their value of time.

Degeratu, Alexandru, Arvind Rangaswamy, and Jianan Wu, 1998. "Consumer Choice Behavior in Online and Regular Stores: The Effects of Brand Name, Price, and Other Search Attributes," Presented at *Marketing Science and the Internet*, INFORM College on Marketing Mini-Conference. Cambridge, MA, March 6–8.

Analyzes prices for online grocery sales and conventional grocery sales. The authors find that price sensitivity can be lower online than in conventional channels. This difference could be due to a lack of product information in the online channel, which would lead to higher brand loyalty (where brand is used by customers as a signal of quality).

Easley, Robert F., and Rafael Tenorio, 1999. "Bidding Strategies in Internet Yankee Auctions," Proceedings of *Computing in Economics and Finance 1999*, Meetings of the Society for Computational Economics, June 24–26.

"Jump bidding" strategies (placing bids that are higher than the amount needed to win the auction) are regularly observed in Internet auctions. Jump bidding can be an equilibrium strategy if consumers face (1) positive costs associated with monitoring auctions and placing bids and (2) uncertainty in the auction's outcome.

Goolsbee, Austan, 2000. "In A World Without Borders: The Impact of Taxes on Internet Commerce," *Quarterly Journal of Economics* (forthcoming).

Uses survey data from online shoppers to impute elasticity with respect to local sales tax rates. Finds that consumers in states with higher local taxes are more likely to purchase online (and thus presumably avoid paying local taxes) than consumers in states with lower local tax rates.

Lee, Ho Geun, 1997. "Do Electronic Marketplaces Lower the Price of Goods?" *Communications of the ACM* 41 (12).

Observes higher prices in Japanese electronic markets for used cars than in conventional used car markets. This could reflect the relative efficiency of the two channels or it could reflect product heterogeneity (cars sold through the electronic channel were newer in general than those sold through the conventional channel).

A2 The Value of Information, Brand, and Trust in Electronic Markets

Kollock, Peter, 1999. "The Production of Trust in Online Markets," in Edward J. Lawler et al., editors, *Advances in Group Processes*, vol. 16 (Greenwich CT: JAI Press).

Discusses the role of community in conveying trust and facilitating the smooth operation of electronic markets. The discussion focuses on communities fostered by eBay and other electronic auctions.

Lynch, John G., Jr., and Dan Ariely, 2000. "Wine Online: Search Cost and Competition on Price, Quality, and Distribution," *Marketing Science* (forthcoming).

Uses laboratory experiments to simulate the sale of wine through electronic channels. These experiments show that providing product information can soften price competition, increase customer loyalty, and increase customer satisfaction.

Shankar, Venkatesh, Arvind Rangaswamy, and Michael Pusateri, 1998. "The Impact of Internet Marketing on Price Sensitivity and Price Competition," Presented at *Marketing Science and the Internet*, INFORM College on Marketing Mini-Conference. Cambridge, MA, March 6–8.

Uses survey data for travelers to show that prior positive experience with a brand in the physical world can decrease price sensitivity in online markets where it may be difficult to evaluate retailer quality.

Urban, Glen L., Fareena Sultan, and William Qualls, 1998. "Trust-based Marketing on the Internet," Working Paper #4035-98, Sloan School of Management, MIT.

Uses a simulated community called "Truck-Town" to analyze the effect of trusted advisers on the operation of electronic markets. Argues that online retailers can build trust among consumers by providing accurate information and unbiased advice. Validates these claims using an online environment for evaluating light trucks for consumer purchase.

Ward, Michael R., and Michael J. Lee, 1999. "Internet Shopping, Consumer Search, and Product Branding," Working Paper, University of Illinois, April.

Observes that recent adopters of the Internet will rely more on brand in their shopping choices, but that this reliance will decrease over time as they gather more experience with the Internet.

A3 The Value of Convenience and Web Content in Electronic Markets

Alba, Joseph, John Lynch, Barton Weitz, Chris Janiszewski, Richard Lutz, Alan Sawyer, and Stacy Wood, 1997. "Interactive Home Shopping: Consumer, Retailer, and Manufacturer Incentives to Participate in Electronic Marketplaces," *Journal of Marketing* 61 (July): 38–53.

Discusses the implications of electronic shopping for consumers and retailers. Technological advancements offer consumers unmatched opportunities to locate and compare product offerings. However, pure price competition may be mitigated by the ability to search for more differentiated products to better fit a customer's needs.

Dellaert, Benedict G. C., and Barbara E. Kahn, 1999. "How Tolerable is Delay? Consumers' Evaluations of Internet Web Sites after Waiting," Working Paper, Center for Economic Research, Tilburg University.

Uses experiments simulating consumer waiting time to show that "waiting can but does not always negatively affect evaluations of Web sites." Argues that the "negative effects of waiting can be neutralized by managing waiting experiences effectively."

Mandel, Naomi, and Eric Johnson, 1998. "Constructing Preferences Online: Can Web Pages Change What You Want?" Working Paper, University of Pennsylvania.

Site design characteristics, such as background wallpaper, can influence customer perceptions of product attributes. Web site design can influence consumer attribute weights and ultimately product choices.

Menon, Satya, and Barbara E. Kahn, 1998. "Cross-Category Effects of Stimulation on the Shopping Experience: An Application to Internet Shopping," Working Paper, Wharton School, University of Pennsylvania, Department of Marketing.

The characteristics of products encountered early in a shopping visit influence shopping behavior during the rest of the trip. Consumers who encounter highly novel products early in their shopping trip will "engage in less arousing activities" during the rest of the shopping event (e.g., less exploration, fewer novel products, less response to promotional incentives, fewer unplanned purchases).

Novak, Thomas P., Donna L. Hoffman, and Yiu-Fai Yung, 1998. "Measuring the Flow Construct in Online Environments: A Structural Modeling Approach," Working Paper, May.

Systematizes the *flow construct* as a way to measure what makes for a "compelling consumer experience" online and then tests this theory using survey data. Shows that this operationalization of the flow construct is a useful way to measure web content.

A4 Bundling and Competition in Information Goods Markets

Bakos, Yannis, and Erik Brynjolfsson, 2000a. "Aggregation and Disaggregation of Information Goods: Implications for Bundling, Site Licenses, and Micropayment Systems," In Brian Kahin and Hal R. Varian, eds., *Internet Publishing and Beyond: The Economics of Digital Information and Intellectual Property* (Cambridge, MA: MIT Press).

Examines where firms will find bundling/aggregation and disaggregation of products optimal. Lower marginal costs of production (e.g., digitized format) favors aggregation. Reductions in transaction and distribution costs (e.g., digital networks) favors disaggregation. Both costs must be taken into account.

Bakos, J. Yannis, and Erik Brynjolfsson, 2000b. "Bundling and Competition on the Internet," *Marketing Science* (April).

Examines the implications of "economies of aggregation" on competition in markets for information goods. Finds that (1) larger bundles are able to outbid smaller bundles for upstream content, (2) bundling makes retailers "tougher" in downstream markets, (3) bundling enhances entry into markets where incumbents aren't bundling, and (4) bundling increases incentives to innovate compared to firms that don't bundle.

A5 Agents, Collaborative Filtering, and Intermediaries

Avery, Christopher, Paul Resnick, and Richard Zeckhauser, 1999. "The Market for Evaluations." *American Economic Review* (forthcoming).

Introduces a mechanism to provide correct incentives for providing evaluations in an electronic market with a collaborative filtering engine. Mechanism solves (1) the underprovision of evaluations as a public good, (2) inefficient ordering of evaluations, and (3) suboptimal quantity of evaluation given a lack of a priori information on quality.

Chavez, Anthony, and Pattie Maes, 1996. "Kasbah: An Agent Marketplace for Buying and Selling Goods," in *Proceedings of the First International Conference on the Practical Application of Intelligent Agents and Multi-Agent Technology*, London, April.

Discusses of the role of agents in creating and mediating electronic markets. Introduces Kasbah as a prototype system for the use of consumer-controlled agents to negotiate deals.

Greenwald, Amy R., and Jeffrey O. Kephart, 1999. "Shopbots and Pricebots," *Proceedings of International Joint Conference on Artificial Intelligence 1999*.

Model similar to that of Varian (1980), where some consumers have access to shopbots (through knowledge of the existence) and some don't. Retailers respond by randomizing over prices: retailers have sales some of the time to capture "informed" consumers and regular prices at other times to capture their share of the "uninformed" consumers.

Sarkar, M., B. Butler, and C. Steinfield (1995), "Intermediaries and Cybermediaries: A Continuing Role for Mediating Players in the Electronic Marketplace," *Journal of Computer-Mediated Communication* 1(3).

Argues that electronic markets will reinforce the position of traditional intermediaries, increase their numbers, and lead to the formation of a new generation of intermediaries called cybermediaries.

Shardanand, Upendra, and Pattie Maes, 1995. "Social Information Filtering: Algorithms for Automating 'Word of Mouth,'" *Proceedings of CHI '95: Mosaic of Creativity*, pp. 210–217.

Discusses the application and design of collaborative filtering algorithms. These algorithms can make personalized recommendations based on observed similarities between the preferences of various users. Introduces *Ringo*, an early collaborative filtering tool, as a case example.

Acknowledgments

We thank Susan Desanti, Howard Frank, and participants at the Conferences on "Understanding the Digital Economy" (Washington, D.C., May 25–56, 1999), "Current Issues in Managing Information Technology" (MIT, June 14–17, 1999), "Reinventing Commerce at Net Speed" (Stanford University, June 21–22, 1999), and "Measuring E-Commerce" (Brookings Institution, September 24, 1999) for valuable comments on this research. The Center for eBusiness @MIT provided generous financial support. Atish Babu and Mohsin Naqvi provided valuable research assistance.

Notes

1. The market capitalization of the 55 stocks that comprise Hambrecht and Quist's "Internet Index" was $1,000,489,700,000 at the time this paper was written.

2. The authors decided not to track software prices because the decline in the number of conventional software retailers from 1997 to 1998 made it difficult to find a representative sample. For example, Egghead Software decided to close their conventional outlets and become a pure-play Internet retailer. Of course, this data problem is itself an interesting bit of evidence on the relative efficiency of the new Internet channel.

3. Price elasticity is defined as the percentage change in quantity sold, q, for a given percentage change in price, p: $(dq/dp).(p/q)$.

4. Brynjolfsson and Smith (1999) note that product information may also serve as a signal of trust and reliability in online markets.

5. To illustrate this, note that the book retailer section in Yahoo lists 6,219 unique sites. Likewise, searching for online bookstores at Altavista returns 5,173,884 possibly relevant web pages.

6. Proposals such as the Platform for Privacy Preference (http://www.w3.org/P3P/) would facilitate such portability.

7. Odlyzko (1996) provides an interesting account of many examples of retailers using multiple prices to price discriminate and argues that this may be quite common on the Internet.

8. Shapiro and Varian (1998) review a variety of other techniques that sellers of information goods use to facilitate price discrimination.

9. See Corts (1996) for a general model of how price matching policies can be used as price discrimination tools.

10. We note that academics also seem prone to push this button independent of price-sensitivity considerations.

11. Similar auctions are conducted by other Internet retailers such as Electronics.net, CompUSA, Nordic Track, Outpost.com, and zones.com.

12. See Easley and Tenorio (1999) for a model of the effect uncertainty and consumer time have on auction bidding behavior.

13. A single individual may choose to have multiple personae: the books recommended when a professor shops to keep up on research may be quite different from those read for entertainment, and the same web store can distinguish and serve both sets of preferences if so informed.

14. It can also be difficult to reliably ascertain the geographic location from which a customer contacts an Internet site, undermining attempts to have web pages customized on this basis.

15. Applicable sales taxes (or "use taxes") must be collected by retailers with physical "nexus" in the taxing jurisdiction. BarnesandNoble.com is considered a separate legal entity from its progenitor, which owns the physical stores.

Bibliography

Adamic, Lada A., and Bernardo A. Huberman, 1999. "The Nature of Markets in the World Wide Web," Proceedings of *Computing in Economics and Finance 1999*, Meetings of the Society for Computational Economics, June 24–26.

Alba, Joseph, John Lynch, Barton Weitz, Chris Janiszewski, Richard Lutz, Alan Sawyer, and Stacy Wood, 1997. "Interactive Home Shopping: Consumer, Retailer, and Manufacturer Incentives to Participate in Electronic Marketplaces," *Journal of Marketing* 61 (July): 38–53.

Bailey, Joseph P., 1998a. *Intermediation and Electronic Markets: Aggregation and Pricing in Internet Commerce.* Ph.D. dissertation, Program in Technology, Management and Policy, Massachusetts Institute of Technology.

Bailey, J. P., 1998b. "Electronic Commerce: Prices and Consumer Issues for Three Products: Books, Compact Discs, and Software," Organisation for Economic Co-Operation and Development, OCDE/GD(98)4.

Bakos, J. Yannis, 1997. "Reducing Buyer Search Costs: Implications for Electronic Marketplaces," *Management Science* 43(12).

Bakos, J. Yannis, 1998. "The Emerging Role of Electronic Marketplaces on the Internet," *Communications of the ACM* 41(8): 35–42.

Bakos, J. Yannis, and Erik Brynjolfsson, 1999. "Bundling Information Goods," *Management Science* 45(11).

Bakos, J. Yannis, and Erik Brynjolfsson, 2000. "Bundling and Competition on the Internet," *Marketing Science* (April).

Brynjolfsson, Erik, and Michael Smith, 2000. "Frictionless Commerce? A Comparison of Internet and Conventional Retailers," *Management Science* (April).

Burdett, Kenneth, and Kenneth Judd, 1983. "Equilibrium Price Dispersion," *Econometrica* (July): 955–969.

Chiang, Raymond, and Chester S. Spatt, 1982. "Imperfect Price Discrimination and Welfare," *Review of Economic Studies* 49(2): 155–181.

Chow, Gregory C., 1967. "Technological Change and the Demand for Computers," *The American Economic Review* (December): 1117–1130.

Clemons, Eric K., Il-Horn Hann, and Lorin M. Hitt, 1998. "The Nature of Competition in Electronic Markets: An Empirical Investigation of Online Travel Agent Offerings," Working Paper, Wharton School, University of Pennsylvania, June.

Corts, Kenneth S., 1996. "On the Competitive Effects of Price-Matching Policies," *International Journal of Industrial Organization* 15: 283–299.

Dahlby, Bev, and Douglas S. West, 1986. "Price Dispersion in an Automobile Insurance Market," *Journal of Political Economy* 94(2): 418–438.

Degeratu, Alexandru, Arvind Rangaswamy, and Jianan Wu, 1998. "Consumer Choice Behavior in Online and Regular Stores: The Effects of Brand Name, Price, and Other Search Attributes," Presented at *Marketing Science and the Internet*, INFORM College on Marketing Mini-Conference. Cambridge, MA, March 6–8.

Dellaert, Benedict G. C., and Barbara E. Kahn, 1999. "How Tolerable is Delay? Consumers' Evaluations of Internet Web Sites after Waiting," Working Paper, Center for Economic Research, Tilburg University.

Dulberger, Ellen R., 1989. "The Application of a Hedonic Model to a Quality-Adjusted Price Index for Computer Processors," in Dale W. Jorgenson and Ralph Landau, editors, *Technology and Capital Formation* (Cambridge, MA: The MIT Press), pp. 37–76.

Easley, Robert F., and Rafael Tenorio, 1999. "Bidding Strategies in Internet Yankee Auctions," Proceedings of *Computing in Economics and Finance 1999*, Meetings of the Society for Computational Economics, June 24–26.

Gellman, Robert, 1996. "Disintermediation and the Internet," *Government Information Quarterly* 13(1): 1–8.

Goolsbee, Austan, 2000. "In A World Without Borders: The Impact of Taxes on Internet Commerce," *Quarterly Journal of Economics* (forthcoming).

Gordon, Robert J., 1989. "The Postwar Evolution of Computer Prices," in Dale W. Jorgenson and Ralph Landau, editors, *Technology and Capital Formation* (Cambridge, MA: The MIT Press), pp. 77–125.

Greenwald, Amy R., and Jeffrey O. Kephart, 1999. "Shopbots and Pricebots," *Proceedings of International Joint Conference on Artificial Intelligence 1999.*

Griliches, Zvi, 1961. "Hedonic Price Indexes for Automobiles: An Econometric Analysis of Quality Change," reprinted in Zvi Griliches, editor, *Price Indexes and Quality Change: Studies in New Methods of Measurement* (Cambridge, MA: Harvard University Press, 1971), pp. 55–87.

Hagel, John, and Marc Singer, 1999. *Net Worth: Shaping Markets When Customers Make the Rules*, Boston, MA: Harvard Business School Press.

Hoffman, Donna L., and Thomas P. Novak, 1996. "Marketing in Hypermedia Computer-Mediated Environments: Conceptual Foundations," *Journal of Marketing* 60(3): 50–68.

Hoffman, Thomas, 1995. "No More Middlemen," *Computerworld* (July 17): 55.

Hotelling, Harold, 1929. "Stability in Competition," *The Economic Journal* (March): 41–57.

The Industry Standard, 1999. "Ecommerce Spotlight: Building Trust Online," February 1, p. 47.

Kollock, Peter, 1999. "The Production of Trust in Online Markets," in Edward J. Lawler et al., eds., *Advances in Group Processes*, vol. 16 (Greenwich CT: JAI Press).

Lee, Ho Geun, 1997. "Do Electronic Marketplaces Lower the Price of Goods?" *Communications of the ACM* 41(12).

Levy, Daniel, Mark Bergen, Shantanu Dutta, and Robert Venable, 1997. "The Magnitude of Menu Costs: Direct Evidence From Large U.S. Supermarket Chains," *The Quarterly Journal of Economics* (August): 791–825.

Lynch, John G., Jr., and Dan Ariely, 2000. "Wine Online: Search Cost and Competition on Price, Quality, and Distribution," *Marketing Science* (forthcoming).

Mandel, Naomi, and Eric Johnson, 1998. "Constructing Preferences Online: Can Web Pages Change What You Want?" Working Paper, University of Pennsylvania.

Menon, Satya, and Barbara E. Kahn, 1998. "Cross-Category Effects of Stimulation on the Shopping Experience: An Application to Internet Shopping," Working Paper, Wharton School, University of Pennsylvania, Department of Marketing.

Milgrom, Paul, and John Roberts, 1982. "Limit Pricing and Entry Under Incomplete Information," *Econometrica* 50: 443–460.

Milgrom, Paul, and John Roberts, 1992. *Economics, Organization, and Management*, Englewood Cliffs, NJ: Prentice-Hall.

Novak, Thomas P., Donna L. Hoffman, and Yiu-Fai Yung, 1998. "Measuring the Flow Construct in Online Environments: A Structural Modeling Approach," Working Paper, May.

Odlyzko, Andrew, 1996. "The Bumpy Road of Electronic Commerce," in H. Maurer, editor, *Proceedings of WebNet-96*, World Conference of the Web Society (Association for the Advancement of Computing in Education), pp. 378–389.

Ogus, Ayla, Michael de la Maza, and Deniz Yuret, 1999. "The Economics of Internet Companies," Proceedings of *Computing in Economics and Finance 1999*, Meetings of the Society for Computational Economics, June 24–26.

Pratt, John W., David A. Wise, and Richard Zeckhauser, 1979. "Price Differences in Almost Competitive Markets," *The Quarterly Journal of Economics* 93(2): 189–211.

Salop, S., 1979. "Monopolistic Competition with Outside Goods," *Bell Journal of Economics* 10: 141–156.

Salop, S., and J. E. Stiglitz, 1977. "Bargains and Ripoffs: A Model of Monopolistically Competitive Price Dispersion," *The Review of Economic Studies* 44 (October): 493–510.

Salop, S., and J. E. Stiglitz, 1982. "The Theory of Sales: A Simple Model of Equilibrium Price Dispersion with Identical Agents," *The American Economic Review* 72(5): 1121–1130.

Shankar, Venkatesh, Arvind Rangaswamy, and Michael Pusateri, 1998. "The Impact of Internet Marketing on Price Sensitivity and Price Competition," Presented at *Marketing Science and the Internet*, INFORM College on Marketing Mini-Conference. Cambridge, MA, March 6–8.

Shapiro, Carl, and Hal R. Varian, 1998. *Information Rules: A Strategic Guide to the Network Economy*, Boston, MA: Harvard Business School Press.

Shardanand, Upendra, and Pattie Maes, 1995. "Social Information Filtering: Algorithms for Automating 'Word of Mouth,'" *Proceedings of CHI '95: Mosaic of Creativity*, pp. 210–217.

Sorensen, Alan T., 2000. "Equilibrium Price Dispersion in Retail Market for Prescription Drugs," *Journal of Political Economy* (August).

Stahl, Dale O., 1989. "Oligopolistic Pricing with Sequential Consumer Search," *The American Economic Review* 79(4): 700–712.

Stahl, Dale O., 1996. "Oligopolistic Pricing with Heterogeneous Consumer Search," *International Journal of Industrial Organization* 14(2): 243–268.

Stigler, George, 1961. "The Economics of Information," *Journal of Political Economy* 69(3): 213–225.

Urban, Glen L., Fareena Sultan, and William Qualls, 1998. "Trust-based Marketing on the Internet," Working Paper #4035-98, Sloan School of Management, MIT.

Varian, Hal R., 1980. "A Model of Sales," *The American Economic Review* 70(4): 651–659.

Varian, Hal R., 1985. "Price Discrimination and Social Welfare," *The American Economic Review* 75(4): 870–875.

Varian, Hal R., 1995. "Pricing Information Goods," Working Paper, pdf version available at http://www.sims.berkeley.edu/~hal/Papers/price-info-goods.pdf.

Varian, Hal R., 2000. "Versioning Information Goods," in Brian Kahin and Hal R. Varian, eds., *Internet Publishing and Beyond: The Economics of Digital Information and Intellectual Property* (Cambridge, MA: MIT Press).

Ward, Michael R., and Michael J. Lee, 1999. "Internet Shopping, Consumer Search, and Product Branding," Working Paper, University of Illinois, April.

Zettlemeyer, Florian, 1996. *The Strategic Use of Consumer Search Cost*, Ph.D. Thesis, Sloan School of Management, Massachusetts Institute of Technology.

Market Structure in the Network Age

Hal R. Varian

E-commerce will undoubtedly change the way business is done. But as I have said elsewhere, "technology changes, economic laws do not." Despite the changes introduced by e-commerce, many of the fundamental principles of competition will still be relevant.

In this chapter I investigate three aspects of competition in e-commerce: marketing, interconnection, and price matching. In each case I will describe the phenomenon, illustrate its relevance for e-commerce, and describe some research issues raised.

Marketing

I will discuss three topics in marketing: versioning, loyalty programs, and promotions.

Versioning

I use the term "information good" to refer to a good that can be distributed in digital form. Examples are text, images, sounds, video, and software. Information goods are characterized by having high fixed costs, or first-copy costs, but very low incremental costs. The challenge in pricing is to find a way to sell to a broad enough audience to cover those high first-copy costs.

One way to accomplish this is to *version* the information good. This means offering a product line of variations on the same underlying good. The product line is designed so as to appeal to different market segments, thereby selling at a high price to those who have a high value for the product, and at a low price to those who value it less.

Versioning is a common strategy for conventional information goods. Books are issued first in hardcover and then in paperback; impatient, high-value users buy the hardcover, while others wait for the paperback. Movies come out in theaters first, then are released six months later in home video.

The flexibility of digital media offers many alternative forms of versioning. Shapiro and Varian (1998) identify the following types:

• *Delay:* Twenty-minute delayed stock quotes are given away, while a real-time feed may be costly.

• *User interface:* The professional version has an elaborate user interface; the popular version has a simple interface.

• *Convenience:* The low-price version is hard to use; the high-price version is simple to use.

• *Image resolution:* Low-resolution images sell for a low price; high-resolution images sell for a high price.

• *Speed of operation:* The low-speed version is cheap; the high-speed version is expensive.

• *Flexibility of use:* A low-end software product may be used only for certain tasks, while the high-end product is more flexible.

• *Capability:* The professional version has more capability and can do more things than the low-end version.

• *Features and functions:* The high-end version has more features and functions.

• *Comprehensiveness:* A high-end database or information service could be more comprehensive than the low-end version.

• *Annoyance:* The low-end product uses "nagware," such as start-up delays or reminders, to induce the consumer to upgrade to a more expensive version.

• *Technical support:* The low-end product has no technical support; the high-end product offers this service.

These are just a few of the dimensions on which one can version information goods. A notable feature of these dimensions is that they often involve first building the high-end product (the immediate, high-resolution, elaborate-user-interface version) and then *degrading* it in some way to produce the low-end version. Often one must go through *extra* processing or programming to create the low-end version of the product.

This, of course, raises public policy questions. Should such deliberate product degradation be allowed? From the viewpoint of economic analysis, the critical issues are the extent of the product degradation and whether the price differentiation increases or decreases the size of the market. The precise statement is this: if price differentiation reduces the size of the market, aggregate welfare necessarily decreases. Conversely, if price differentiation increases the size of the market, aggregate welfare may easily increase. See Varian (1985) for details.

"Aggregate welfare" counts both consumers' surplus and producers' surplus on an equal basis. A single producer does at least as well moving from a flat price to a differentiated price, since it always has the option of not differentiating. Since normally some prices go up and some go down when moving to differentiated pricing, some consumers are made worse off and some better off.[1] On balance, we expect that consumers would be worse off, but there are cases where price discrimination results in a Pareto improvement.[2]

Consider a simple example: a textbook sells in the United States for $50, and a paperback, newsprint version of the same book sells for $5 in India. Does the low-quality version increase overall welfare? To answer this question we have to ask what version *would* have been produced if only one version were allowed. In this case, the likely answer is that only the high-quality, high-price version would have been produced. The ability to produce the low-quality, low-price version increases the availability of the good and increases overall consumer surplus.

An even more dramatic example can be constructed where the cost of production is such that the product could not be produced at all without access to both the U.S. and Indian revenue streams. Here the ability to version, and price discriminate, is critical to the economic viability of the product in question. This case is rather common with information goods because of the high first-copy costs.

One can imagine other cases with the opposite result—cases where versioning ends up reducing the total amount of the product sold. However, these cases do not seem to be very robust, and I believe that, in general, versioning tends to increase overall welfare.

Loyalty Programs

On the Internet, the competition is just a click away. This has the potential to lead to intense price competition for commodity products. ACSES is a search engine for books; it queries roughly 45 sites and reports back price, availability and shipping charges for all books. On a recent query the total price for a particular book varied from $24.07 to $40.94!

Given these dramatically reduced search costs, it is natural for firms to try to build customer loyalty. Obviously the best way to do this is to have low prices, high quality, and good service. But there are other ways: Amazon.com gives out free coffee mugs, t-shirts, upgraded shipping, and other bonuses. They offer customized services based on the shopping history of their customers that would be difficult for competitors to imitate.

Another strategy that I expect to become more widespread is the frequent-purchaser program. Frequent-flyer programs have been around for 25 years and have dramatically changed the pricing and marketing programs of what is essentially a commodity business. Frequent-purchaser programs on the Internet have the same potential.

If all interaction with a customer is via a Web browser, it is trivial to capture that information and offer rewards to customers based on their purchase history. Intermediaries such as Cardpoi/Eå com, SmartFrog.com, Data Marketing Group, and many others allow merchants to monitor and archive consumer purchase information, rewarding them with dollars, points, or prizes.

What should the reward system look like for such loyalty programs? Suppose that Amazon.com and Barnesandnoble.com both use a linear reward system—for each dollar spent, you get one point credit that can be turned in for cash. This system will be attractive to consumers but won't encourage exclusive use, since a point on

BarnesandNoble.com is worth just as much as a point on Amazon.com. What sellers should use is a *nonlinear* rewards scheme—a system that gives customers a big prize after they have hit a certain level. This way, the customer is encouraged to stay with one vendor rather than diversify across vendors. Even better, the sellers could use a sequence of milestones, each more difficult to achieve, that are rewarded by prizes or special services. This strategy is taken right from the airlines, who offer their frequent flyers free flights at certain milestones and first-class upgrades at others.

If such loyalty programs become widespread, as I expect they will, price competition will tend to be reduced, just as it has with the airlines. The competition will occur upfront, in an attempt to encourage new users to sign up with one program or another. All consumers will still benefit from competition, due to the payments and prizes used to reward loyal customers, but heavy purchasers will benefit disproportionately.

Promotions and Shopbots

Kephart and Greenwald (1998) have investigated the "economics of shopbots." In their model, some consumers have access to shopbots that can search out the lowest price for a generic product, while others do not. As they note, their model is similar to that of Varian (1980), in which some consumers read the newspaper for sales, while others shop at random.

It is not surprising that the two models generate similar equilibria: firms randomize their prices—hold "sales"—in order to price discriminate between the searchers and the nonsearchers. Those who invest in using shopbots end up with a lower price, but at the cost of a more elaborate search. In addition, these price-sensitive customers have to give up the benefits conferred by the loyalty programs described above.

The sellers price discriminate between searchers and nonsearchers by randomizing their prices. That way they compete for the searchers, when they happen to have the lowest price, but still manage to charge a relatively high price on average.

Why would anyone *not* use a shopbot? Presumably the answer is the loyalty programs mentioned above: if customers stay with one merchant, they can receive benefits (in the form of lower prices or coffee mugs) that cannot be offered by the low-price merchant.

This suggests that we will see a division between cheap, low-service merchants and high-cost, high-service merchants in cyberspace, just as in the ordinary marketplace. Indeed, it may easily happen that high-service and low-service merchants rely on the same underlying infrastructure. Clemons, Hitt, and Hann (1998) describe a case study of seven online travel agencies and show exactly this outcome: the highest-price and the lowest-price merchants are both owned by the same company!

Research Topics in Marketing

The phenomena of versioning, loyalty programs, and promotions all raise interesting research questions.

• Online merchants will be collecting many megabytes of data about their customers' buying habits. How can these data be analyzed effectively? Many existing techniques rely heavily on parametric forms, but I expect that the massive amounts of data becoming available will readily allow for effective nonparametric analysis. Nevo and Wolfram (1999) have been applying some of these techniques to supermarket scanner data with considerable success.

• It is also worth learning about the people who don't buy. The "clickstream" captures the search process of online users and, to some extent, reflects the underlying cognition surrounding the purchase decision. It would be very helpful to understand this process in more detail.

• Since we expect to see much more price discrimination for information goods, it would be helpful to have better tools for welfare analysis, especially for the case of quality discrimination. Armstrong and Vickers (1999) describe a very promising method of analysis that may help with this issue.

• Loyalty programs push the competition for consumers up front. However, after consumers have chosen a merchant, they tend to be locked-in, allowing the merchant to exploit some monopoly power. In a world of forward-looking, rational consumers, the ex-post monopoly would have small social cost. However, in a world with myopic consumers, the subsequent monopoly may be less benign. A better understanding of the welfare economics of loyalty programs would be helpful.

• A weakness of the standard economic theory of production is that we tend to focus too much on the one-product firm. In the online world there will be dramatic economies of scope. For example, firms can use a single underlying transactions technology that can then be branded in different ways, depending on the market they wish to attract. One would expect that competitive forces would be less strong in such environments, but it would be interesting to work out the details.

Interconnection

Economists say that there is a *network externality* when the value of a good depends on the number of other people who use it. Examples are goods like the telephone network, the fax machine network, the email network, or the Internet itself. Generally, consumers would like to be connected to as large a network as possible. This implies that if there are several different providers of networks, then it is very advantageous to consumers if they interconnect.

In the examples above, telephones, faxes, and email are valuable precisely because they all work according to a common standards and anyone can call, fax or email anyone else who is connected to the network. The Internet is valuable because it is built on a common platform of open standards that allows many different networks to interconnect.

While interconnection is typically in the social interest, it may or may not be in the private interest. There may be cases where a large incumbent finds it attractive to avoid interconnection with new entrants in order to preserve its market power. Shapiro and Varian (1998) discuss several examples.

It is important to understand that if the value of the network increases through interconnection, then there should be a way to divide that increase in value so as to make all participants better off. If the pie gets bigger, everyone can get a larger price. However, the increased size of the pie also means that *threats* not to interconnect become more significant. And, of course, a larger pie is a more tempting target for someone to try to snatch than a smaller one. Let us see how these effects play out in a simple algebraic example. Suppose that the value of a network to a user is proportional to the total number of people on the network, n. For simplicity choose the constant of proportionality to be 1. The value of the entire network is then n^2, in accordance with "Metcalfe's Law."

If two networks of size n_1 and n_2 interconnect, what increase in value accrues to each one? A simple calculation shows that

$$\Delta v_1 = n_1(n_1 + n_2) - n_1^2 = n_1 n_2,$$
$$\Delta v_2 = n_2(n_1 + n_2) - n_2^2 = n_1 n_2. \tag{1}$$

Note the surprising result that each network gets *equal* value from interconnecting. Each person in the large network gets a little bit of extra value from connecting to the small network, but there are a lot of people in the large network. Conversely, each person in the small network gets a lot of extra value from connecting to the large network, but there are only a few people in the small network.

This calculation, simple though it is, gives some insight into why "peering," or settlement-free interconnection, is common among large backbone providers. The gains from interconnection are split more or less equally, even among networks of somewhat different size.

But, in a way, it proves too much, since not all networks are willing to interconnect on a payment-free basis. The answer to this seeming paradox is to look what happens if one network *acquires* the other. Suppose, for example, that network 1 pays network 2 its standalone value and then merges it with its own network. The increase in value is then

$$\Delta v_1 = (n_1 + n_2)^2 - n_1^2 - n_2^2 = 2n_1 n_2.$$

In this case, network 1 captures twice as much value by buying out network 2 rather than interconnecting with it. This is why I said above that the threat of not interconnecting can be valuable, since it can be used to induce another network to merge or be bought out. Essentially the threat of nonconnection increases the larger network's bargaining power.

Of course, the linear-in-value assumption underlying Metcalfe's Law may be wrong, as suggested by Kling (1999). Still, we might expect that the value function is *locally* linear, suggesting that network providers don't have to be perfectly symmetric to gain more or less equally from settlement-free interconnection.

Research Topics in Networks

• The theory of network effects is more evolved than the empirics, and it would be very helpful to have some detailed empirical analyses. This is very hard to do at the "macro" level, due to data limitations, but more feasible at the micro level. See Goolsbee and Klenow (1999) for a nice example of micro analysis of network externalities.

• Interconnection is likely to be a very contentious issues as the Internet evolves, and it is important to try to work out some sensible institutions to facilitate this. Varian (1998), for example, argues that an industry arbitration board might make sense. The problem with such a board would be the temptation to use it as a device for collusion.

• The strategic analysis of interconnection is in its infancy. Much of the analysis based on telecommunications deals with the asymmetric case of local telephony providers interconnecting with long-distance carriers. This is hard enough, but the symmetric case of Internet providers interconnecting is even more difficult. Crémer, Rey, and Tirole (1999) offer a nice start on this set of issues.

Price Competition

I indicated above that the intense price competition would induce online merchants to look for ways to increase customer loyalty. Presumably they will also try to adopt pricing strategies that will reduce the intensity of the competition.

Web-based price comparison agents, sometimes known as "shopbots," have been generally viewed as being beneficial to consumers. This is not totally obvious, however, since shopbots not

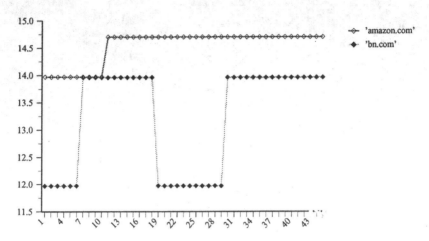

Figure 1 Price matching between Amazon.com and Barnesandnoble.com?

only allow consumers easy access to other firms' prices, they also allow the firms themselves to monitor each other's price movements.

For example, suppose that there are two dominant firms in a given industry, *A* and *B*. *A* adopts the following price strategy: whenever *B* cuts its price, *A* will immediately cut its price by the same amount. Whenever *B* raises its price, *A* will immediately raise its price by the same amount.

What will be the impact of this policy on price competition? The answer depends on how fast "immediately" is. If consumers move more rapidly than the firms, then cutting price may be advantageous to the first price cutter, since the flood of extra consumers makes up for the (small) reduction in price necessary to attract them. But if the firms move faster than consumers, then this may not be the case. Suppose, for example, that firm *B* matches firm *A*'s price change *before* consumers can respond. In this case, there is no flood of consumers from price cutting, and the incentives to cut price are dramatically reduced. If both firms pursue the price-matching strategy, the equilibrium price is the same as if there were a single monopolist. The only check on this upward drift in prices comes from competitive suppliers such as local merchants who may find it difficult to change prices so rapidly.

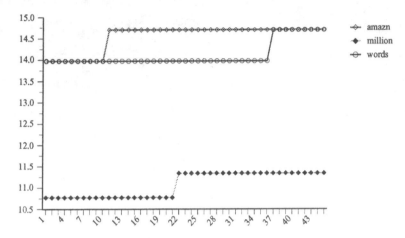

Figure 2 Amazon.com, Wordsworth.com, and BooksAMillion.com.

Does this sort of price matching occur online? Dillard (1999) offers some suggestive evidence. Figure 1 shows the timeline of the price of a bestseller on Amazon.com and Barnesandnoble.com. Amazon.com was selling the book at a higher price initially, and when Barnesandnoble.com raised its price, Amazon.com raised its price even higher. Amazon.com did not respond to Barnesandnoble.com's price cut, and Barnesandnoble.com then returned to its higher price.

Another interesting example is depicted in Figure 2. Here we see Amazon.com leading by raising the price, with Wordsworth and BooksAMillion following shortly after.

Clearly these examples can only be taken as suggestive; it would certainly be worthwhile to look at more cases. One great advantage of the online world is that it is easy to monitor sellers' behavior.

In addition to the theoretical argument, we can also look at experience with pricing on more mature electronic markets. In 1999 NASDAQ paid a $1.01 billion settlement to drop charges of price fixing on their exchange. The charges were prompted by an academic study described in Christie and Schultz (1995). Apparently the traders were able to avoid selling securities at odd-eighth quotes by identifying deviators and refusing to trade with them. This increased the average spread, resulting in higher profits for traders.

Another illustrative example is airline reservation systems such as SABRE. It is common to see competitive carriers engaging in "price signaling" and other techniques to maintain stable, oligopolistic prices. In this industry airlines clearly respond to each other's prices more rapidly than do consumers, and modern information systems apparently help enforce higher prices. (See Nomani [1990] for a popular account of this practice.)

The airline system is different from online merchants in several ways. In particular, there are generally only a couple of major airlines in each city-pair market, whereas there can be dozens of competitors in a market for a commodity product such as books. The price-matching strategy described above may work with two firms, but not with dozens.

Another difference is that entry costs are probably much lower for Internet vendors than for airlines. Although anyone can set up a Web site, however, marketing costs can be prohibitive, especially if one has to compete with entrenched incumbents. Furthermore, marketing costs are entirely sunk costs in the sense that they aren't recoverable if the entrant fails to survive.

Customer loyalty is another issue. A new entrant may spend enough money to get noticed, but will it get patronized? Customers who are building up points through loyalty programs may be loathe to desert their current vendor for a slightly cheaper price.

One scenario is that we will see intense price competition until the small players are weeded out, leaving only a handful of online merchants who can engage in the kinds of price-matching strategies described above. However, the threat of entry and competition from offline vendors may prevent significant abuse of market power. If this scenario is right, online markets may not be as cutthroat as some expect.

Price Matching: Research Questions

• There is an extensive literature on price matching that examines under what conditions it is pro- or anticompetitive; see Corts (1997) for a recent overview of this literature. Current models are not very robust, and more analysis is needed. Shaffer (1999) describes some empirical work, which is very helpful. Empirical work of this sort should be easier to do online than off.

• How can we distinguish "competitive" price matching from "oligopolist" price matching? After all, we *want* firms to cut prices in response to their rivals' cuts. This has been a vexing problem with the airlines, and I don't see much hope of its being resolved easily. It is probably a better idea to focus on ease-of-entry or alternative providers as a means of price discipline.

• Upfront sunk costs are likely to play a large role in online industries. If competition were really so intense as to compete price down to marginal cost, there would be no way to recover those initial upfront investments. Perhaps strategies like loyalty programs and price matching that allow for somewhat lessened competition are healthy. Clearly more research is needed to understand the nature of competition in such environments.

Acknowledgment

Thanks to Carl Shapiro and Marius Schwartz for helpful comments on an earlier version of this paper.

Notes

1. Somewhat surprisingly, there are cases where all prices move in the same direction. See Nahat et al. (1990) for examples.

2. See Hausman and MacKie-Mason (1988) for some theorems about when this can happen in the case of monopolistic price discrimination. In the case of competitive price discrimination, Armstrong and Vickers (1999) show that as long as the markets are competitive enough price discrimination normally results in increase in overall social welfare.

Bibliography

Armstrong, Mark, and John Vickers, 1999. "Competitive Price Discrimination," technical report, Nuffield College, Oxford.

Christie, William, and Paul H. Schultz, 1995. "Are Nasdaq Spreads Determined by Competition or Implicit Collusion?" *Journal of Economic Perspectives* 9(3): 208.

Clemons, Eric K. Lorin M. Hitt, and Il-Horn Hann, 1998. "The nature of competition in electronic markets: A comparison of on-line travel agent offerings," technical report, Wharton School, University of Pennsylvania.

Corts, Kenneth S., 1997. "On the Competitive Effects of Price-Matching Policies," *International Journal of Industrial Organization* 15(3): 299.

Crémer, Jacques, Patric Rey, and Jean Tirole, 1999. "Connectivity in the Commercial Internet," technical report, Institut D'Économie Industrielle, Toulouse.

Dillard, Martin, 1999. "The Economics of Electronic Commerce: A Study of Online and Physical Bookstores," Bachelor's honors thesis, University of California, Berkeley.

Goolsbee, Austan, and Peter J. Klenow, 1999. "Evidence on Learning and Network Externalities in the Diffusion of Home Computers," technical report, University of Chicago, Graduate School of business. http://gsbadg.uchicago.edu/vitae.htm.

Hausman, Jerry A., and Jeffrey K. MacKie-Mason, 1988. "Price Discrimination and Patent Policy," *RAND Journal of Economics* 19(2):265.

Kephart, Jeffrey O., and Amy Greenwald, 1998. "Shopbot Economics," technical report, IBM Institute for Advanced Commerce. http://www.research.ibm.com/infoecon/researchpapers.html.

Kling, Arnold, 1999. "The Last Inch and Metcalfe's Law," technical report, AIMST Essays. http://home.us.net/ arnoldsk/aimst2/aimst212.html.

Nahat, Babu, Krzysztof Ostaszewsky, and P. K. Sahoo, 1990. "Direction of Price Changes in Third-Degree Price Discrimination," *American Economic Review* 80: 1258.

Nevo, Aviv, and Catherine Wolfram, 1999. "Prices and Coupons for Breakfast Cereals," technical report, University of California, Berkeley. http://emlab.Berkeley.EDU/users/nevo/.

Nomani, A., 1990. "Fare Warning: How Airlines Trade Price Plans," *Wall Street Journal*, October 9, page B1.

Shaffer, Greg, 1999. "On the Incidence and Variety of Low-Price Guarantees," technical report, University of Rochester.

Shapiro, Carl, and Hal R. Varian, 1998. *Information Rules: A Strategic Guide the Network Economy*. Boston: Harvard Business School Press. http://www.inforules.com.

Varian, Hal R., 1980. "A Model of Sales," *American Economic Review* 70: 659.

Varian, Hal R., 1985. "Price Discrimination and Social Welfare," *American Economic Review* 75(4): 875.

Varian, Hal R., 1998. "How to Strengthen the Internet backbone," *Wall Street Journal*, June 8, p. A22.

The Evolving Structure of Commercial Internet Markets

Shane Greenstein

1 Introduction

While there has been no shortage of attention paid to the Internet in popular media, few commentators have provided frameworks and data for understanding how commercial processes translate Internet technologies into economic value. This chapter highlights four questions that are central to understanding the structure of virtual activity and changes to that structure: What factors influence how firms organize the "value chain" for delivering electronic commerce? How does the creation of value in this market depend on commercial behavior? Why do vendors approach similar commercial opportunities with similar or different strategies? How does adaptive activity translate technology into a developing market?

I will comment on these four questions and then illustrate them with a familiar story: the rise of the commercial Internet access market, a key element in the value chain of electronic commerce. Because it took only a few years for commercial providers to dominate the market for Internet access in the United States, this is a useful and important way to illustrate the framework. The chapter closes with a survey of open research topics; here I will emphasize the need for measurement methodologies, for more data, and for policy assessment.

Because electronic commerce policy requires analysis of a dynamic evolving market, its framework must be rooted in an understanding of the economics of diffusion, adaptation, and industry evolution. Firms and users select only a few of many possibilities enabled by new technology. Firms package new offerings, launch new services, and tailor the new technology to their particuiar markets. Users survey their options, seek information about possibilities, and, when they are a business, take actions that respond to competitive pressures. Commercial factors play a central role in determining these outcomes. This approach dispels a number of myths about electronic commerce while emphasizing the many avenues open for empirical research.

2 Questions about the Structure of Electronic Commerce

I will focus on electronic commerce after the "commercialization of the Internet," a phrase that is shorthand for three nearly simultaneous events: the removal of restrictions by the NSF over use of the Internet for commercial purposes, the browser wars initiated by the founding of Netscape, and the rapid entry of tens of thousands of firms into commercial ventures using technologies employing the suite of TCP/IP standards. In the first few years after the commercialization of the Internet, the products changed frequently, many firms changed strategies, and the market definition adjusted. The purpose of this section is to identify questions raised by these events.

Value Chain

The commercialization of the Internet gave rise to a value chain for delivering electronic commerce. A "value chain" is comprised of the many activities necessary for the delivery of a final good. What factors influence how firms organize the value chain for delivering electronic commerce? Is this concept useful for understanding this new activity? If not, why not?

The value chain for electronic commerce, if one can be sensibly defined at all, will be quite complicated. It will include at least two dozen distinct categories: client applications, client operating systems, browsers, client hardware, client processors, distributed technologies such as Java and Corba, distribution and mainte-

Table 1   Selected Layers of the Value Chain of Electronic Commerce

Client application	MS Office
Client OS	Windows
Browser	IE, Navigator
Client system	Dell, IBM, Compaq
Client microprocessor	Intel, AMD
Distributed technologies	DCOM, Corba, JAVA-RMI
Distribution and fulfillment	Dell, Compaq, Gateway
Network access	AOL, ISPs, MSN
Internetworking OS	CISCO, Lucent
LAN OS	Novell, Windows NT
Server OS	UNIX, IBM 3090, Windows NT
Server DBMS	Oracle 8, DB2, MS SQL-Server
Server system	HP, SUN, IBM, Windows NT
Groupware	Notes, Many
Custom software	EDS, Perot Systems, Andersen
Enterprise systems	SAP, Baan, Peoplesoft, many
Service and support	IBM (ISSC). Compaq, HP, many
Domain name coordination	Network Solutions, others
Data transport and backbone	Worldcom-MCI, Qwest, Level3, AT&T, many
Internet search and organization	Yahoo!, Excite, Lycos, Netscape, MSN, AOL, @home
Retailing intermediaries	Amazon, E-bay, Yahoo!, MSN, AOL, others

nance of this hardware, network access, internetworking operating systems using TCP/IP and W3C standards, data transport facilities, local area network operating system, server operating system, server database management software, server system hardware, groupware, custom software, enterprise software, enterprise middleware, system software and support, search software, domain name coordination, data transport, retailing intermediaries, and so on. Table 1, modified from Bresnahan (1999), shows some of these.

This value chain is not settled for several reasons. Partly this is because no single firm dominates all phases of the chain or has stamped its unique vision on the organization of transactions. Consequently, it is not obvious that this picture will be the same in ten years. Indeed, nobody in the industry expects it to be close to the same. This is symptomatic of the fluidity of the organization of the value chain.

More to the point, because firms specialize at different layers of the value chain, there is no consensus about how the chain should be organized. This is a situation of "divided technical leadership" (Bresnahan and Greenstein 1999), where many firms possess roughly similar technical capabilities. With only a few notable exceptions, if a firm gets too far from the technical frontier or from satisfying its immediate customer base, it will be replaced relatively quickly by another more sprite and better organized entity from a nearby competitive space.

The vintage of this value chain also affects its stability. It consists of something old and something new, something borrowed and something blue. To be sure, there is new technology here, especially in the wires, cables, hubs, routers, and new switching equipment. Yet it is also a retrofit onto the old telephony communications system, as an incremental change to the established methods for data transport and to the operations of many users' existing client/server systems. It is blue because this design makes the technical perfectionist unhappy: if one were going to build a system from scratch around an Internet protocol, this is not how one would do it. Thus, there is continuing tension between firms that pursue incremental improvements that retrofit to old designs and firms that try to bring dramatic technical advances to users through "green-field" developments.

This value chain is confusing to outsiders because it defies existing classifications of economic activity. It changes too rapidly to be given stable definitions. Moreover, economic activity involves a mix of tangible durable assets and intangible business processes or operation procedures, a combination that tends to defy normal documentation. In addition, mergers occur regularly. As of this writing, there is hardly an end in sight to this type of restructuring.

The final source of confusion arises because the value chain is not "vertical," like the chain found in most manufacturing, for example. A vertical value chain implies that activities must be performed in a hierarchical sequence that is often characterized as linear, leading from upstream to downstream. Instead, the value chain underlying electronic commerce is closer to being a "platform." A platform is a common arrangement of components and activities, usually unified by a set of technical standards and procedural norms, around which users organize their activities (Bresnahan and Greenstein 1999). Platforms have a known interface with respect to particular technologies and are usually "open" in some sense. They are typically associated with substantial externalities, whose value is difficult to capture. Later, I will distinguish between owned technologies as one extreme and nonproprietary specifications as another.

The provision of many activities on the emerging Internet platform positions it somewhere between telecommunications and standard commercial transactions. As in telecommunications services, much activity is geographically based, with great opportunities for location-specific differentiation and packaging as well as geographically situated marketing. As in many intermediary commercial services, many Internet services are bundled to provide not just value to the customer but a kind of channeling of the customer's attention. This presents the supplier with a constellation of opportunities for expanding or marketing the relationship, opening up the boundaries for initiating new supplier services. That is, many Internet services, while layered over telecommunications services, actually compete in the multidimensional, multidirectional market that lies above them. This phenomenon will be illustrated further below.

Creation of Value

Next, consider how this delivery of services creates economic value for society. How does the creation of value in this market depend on commercial behavior?

The first key detail is so familiar that few observers comment on it: data transport services are cheaper at higher volume. This arises because there are economies of scale in aggregation/density. This was true in the voice network and it is still true of data networks, whether it has a PC at the end of it or a mobile intelligent Internet device. It should continue to hold in the future, no matter what structure the TCP/IP network takes (see Aron, Dunmore, and Pampush 1997). In other words, we can expect the high-volume/high-density parts of the emerging Internet platform to contain only a few suppliers in any given location.

The second key detail is somewhat new: the "last mile" of data transport, where the densities are not too large and the volumes are not too high, is becoming a good business in some niches of electronic commerce. Several decades ago it simply was not possible. Now it is, and possibly on a wide scale and for a wide scope of activities, though there is considerable commercial uncertainty over precisely how wide the scope and scale can get. As of this writing, it is already clear that business applications, such as automation of routine business-to-business transactions, can grow considerably. Many are also betting that other activities will shortly display similar economies, even activities such as retailing of goods, delivery of entertainment, organization of virtual games, and development of virtual communities and organizations.

In the commercial world, this new possibility gives rise to hundreds of vexing business decisions. Does it make sense for a small/medium-sized firm to have a large online presence? Does it make sense for someone to get in the business of helping a rural farmer check the financial markets regularly with a Palm Pilot? Does it make sense for a cable company to delivery high-speed data over their cable lines to neighborhoods where only 25 percent of the households have a PC? There is no consensus on how to resolve these issues, even among experts.[1] The key observation is that this uncertainty raises vexing issues for ongoing policy making about electronic commerce, which can no longer be based on old assumptions about the boundaries of commercial behavior.

The standards and processes underlying data interchange form an important technical enabler for this structure, which is why they are a key part of the emerging Internet platform. These are comprised of TCP/IP, W3C, and many other nonproprietary standards, mostly inherited from precommercial days. At many user sites, they are comprised of more proprietary standards, such as AOL's software, Windows, and so on.

Market forces do not provide a natural reason why any particular piece of the dominant standard had to be nonproprietary, nor are there reasons (other than inertia) why it should stay this way. An interesting tension arises because many firms would overlay this system with their own proprietary material if they could. The disputes between TCI/AT&T and AOL in 1999 over interconnection had elements of this tension. So, too, does the dispute between Microsoft and AOL over the use of community chat software. So, too, the dispute between Microsoft and Netscape over the design of browsers and complementary components. The adoption of standards for streaming audio and video have also been influenced by these motives.

That said, today, at least for now, interconnection is easy and does not reside in any firm's unique domain. However, as one can see from table 1, the possibility exists for some firms to acquire dominant positions in one part or another of the value chain. This environment raises alarmist fears in some circles that particular firms may act as a bottleneck on the creation of value. Others see great gains from the privatization of incentives to invest in the emerging platform. This debate will continue for the foreseeable future (for a variety of views, see Eisenach and Lenard 1999), highlighting the need for careful thinking about standards-building processes in the emerging Internet platform.

Though everyone understands that value is being created, it is quite difficult to document even the basic trends. Prices change frequently, and it is not at all clear what economic activity gets priced and what activity does not. The diffusion of new technology has moved rapidly across divides of income, geographic space, and type of application. Just as there is no consensus on how to develop these markets, there is no consensus about the best way to record their progress in creating value.

Same Opportunity, Different Strategy

Why do vendors approach similar commercial opportunities with different strategies? What we see is partly a reflection of the newness of the market and its gold-rush hype. At present it is not hard to start something on the web. Entry costs are low in all but the most technical of frontier activities. It is cheap to put up a web page. It is cheap to open an ISP. In most urban areas, it is not hard to find programming talent. And, for most users of electronic commerce, new applications have been only an incremental change in their lives. Hence, many small firms can give it a whirl and, at least, get a start.

Variety exists for another somewhat less faddish reason. Many vendors are deliberately targeting unique user needs, tailoring their service to the peculiar needs of local markets, to their own special niche, or to bringing their own peculiar background to the fray. Whether this is associated with a different visions of the future, or a different core capability, it results in variety.

Variety thrives because of divided technical leadership. When so many different firms possess similar technical capabilities, only commercial factors distinguish them from each other. This gives commercial firms strong incentives to develop strategies for electronic commerce that strongly differentiate themselves.

As of this writing, two types of strategies tend to characterize electronic commerce entrants. First, a firm may try to combine electronic commerce with nonvirtual activity in some unique way. For example, established media are full of half-breeds like the *Wall Street Journal, The New York Times, Business Week,* and so on, who try to maintain both a virtual and nonvirtual presence and play them off each other. There are also plenty of less-established media doing the same thing, such as *Industry Standard, Wired,* and *Red Herring.*

Half-breeds also exist in retailing, where some firms use their web presence to give users a shopping experience that complements their nonvirtual experience. Dell Computer's establishment of a presence on the web is among the best-known examples. As with most online retailers, there is an important nonvirtual part to their business—in this case, the assembly and delivery of a physical good. But there have been many other firms pursuing different specialties of nonvirtual activity, such as E-Schwab, Microsoft Network, and AT&T Worldnet.

Then there are the pure electronic commerce plays, tailored to visions of unique online needs. The most successful strategies so far have been associated with firms that acquire a role as broker or aggregator of information or web experience. Amazon is among the largest of these firms, as they build a large one-stop shopping experience across books, videos, and other things. E-bay, the auction house, is another, as they try to establish a position as a central virtual location for exchanging unique goods. AOL has pursued a related strategy associated with aggregating entertaining content, simplifying the shopping experience, and establishing virtual communities. There are tens of thousands of other firms trying similar strategies in many fields, from horticultural clubs to healthcare advice.

Characterizing these strategies should continue to provide challenges for policy research. The distinction between electronic commerce and Internet infrastructure will not be very hard and absolute, nor especially useful. Popular conceptions based on electronic retailing by AOL, Amazon, and E-bay are necessarily incomplete. Moreover, much key economic strategy will lie just below the transaction, in the transactions that build the bridges between the virtual world and the nonvirtual, especially as the distinction between electronic commerce and infrastructure becomes more blurry. This will be further illustrated below.

The heart of success strategies may lie in combinations of activities that cannot be replicated easily, combining infrastructure and processes in unique ways. Indeed, there may be no meaningful distinction between the firms that provide Internet access, the organization of the experience by search engines, and the organization of the retail experience. In the future, these firms will be called AOL/Netscape, TCI/@home/Excite, and so on. Similarly, Microsoft has extended its interests into cable modems, WebTV, mobile devices, and satellite (through Teledesic), and they are a large content provider as well. It is not an exaggeration to say that we are headed toward an extraordinary set of arrangements involving confrontations between the strategies pursued by Microsoft, AOL, AT&T, and many others. These confrontations of private interest will situate a number of vexing policy problems.

Adaptation

How does adaptive activity translate technology into a developing market? This last question is perhaps the most important. Adaptive activity is central to growth. Yet it is also most often the activity that goes undocumented.

What is adaptive activity? Firms take an adaptive role when they stand between the many possibilities enabled by new technology and the unique needs of the user. Firms do this when they package new offerings, when they launch new services, and even when they survey a business and tailor the new technology to the user's special needs. These activities may be situated in particular problems, but may generate large spillovers to others in different locations, facing different problems.

Adaptive activity mattered a great deal in the period just after the commercialization of the Internet. Some firms specialized in making electronic commerce easy to use, while others seek to push the technical frontier. Some vendors sought to specialize in a small set of activities, while others sought to offer general solutions. Vendors devised strategies to take advantage of the large gaps in knowledge between themselves and their users.

That said, there seems to be one type of adaptive role that many firms take and one that many firms do not take. The uncommon role is to be a tool builder, a specialist in the emerging platform, defining standards for equipment makers, ISPs, operators of web services, network users, and others. Cisco, Microsoft, Oracle, Sun, IBM, Netscape/AOL and many firms listed in table 1 desire this role.

The more common adaptive role is consulting or, more concretely, translating information about the new technical frontier into information that a user finds valuable. This is not a bad thing, though most commentators underemphasize it. It is the essence of economic development. Consulting services can be either offered as a standalone service or bundled with the sale, installation, and operation of equipment. The key observation is this: in a dynamic environment, every active market participant sells knowledge along with other services, translating technology into value, the key part of economic growth.

Markets for knowledge have generally defied characterization and will likely continue to do so for many reasons. First, the private value of a technology license will diverge from its economic value. Second, the gains from efficient brokering are hard to measure. Third, the value of consulting services varies across location, provider, and time, but bring unmeasured benefits to different locations. Fourth, the transfer of knowledge, especially about the processes necessary to make use of a new technology, is often intangible and invisible to outsiders. This observation will also be illustrated below.

3 The Internet Access Business after Commercialization: An Interpretation

This section will interpret one facet of the value chain of electronic commerce—Internet access—to show in one concrete case how commercial behavior translated the technology behind electronic commerce into actual goods and services. This case will illustrate the fact that this market cannot be understood without using insights and frameworks from the economics of diffusion, adaptation, and industry evolution.

The most recent surveys show that no more than 10 percent of U.S. households get their Internet access from university-sponsored Internet Service Providers (ISPs), with almost all of the remainder using commercial providers (Clemente 1998). As of 1997, ISPs were a $3–5 billion industry (Maloff 1997). What are commercial ISPs in practice? For the most part, they are firms who provide Internet access for a fee. Access can take one of several different forms: dial-up to a local number or 1-800 number at different speeds, or direct access to the user's server using one of several high-speed access technologies.

At the time of the Internet's commercialization, only a few commercial enterprises offered national dial-up networks with Internet access, mostly targeting the major urban areas. At that time it was possible to run a small ISP on a shoestring in either an urban or a rural area. These firms focused primarily on dial-up. Within a few years, however, there were dozens of well-known national networks and scores of less-known national providers offering a wide variety of dial-up and direct access services. There were also many local providers of Internet access that served as the links between end-users and the Internet backbone. Local shoestring operations seemed less common.

Several key factors shaped the structure of this industry in these years: (1) there was an uneven maturity to applications that had commercial value; (2) there was a loosely coordinated diffusion process; (3) a significant set of activities involved intermediary functions; (4) the supply of access approached geographic ubiquity; (5) national, regional, and local ISPs specialized in different markets niches; (6) there were several fleeting business opportunities; (7) adaptive activity is not yet a fleeting business opportunity;

(8) different firms pursued different strategies for offering new services. These are discussed below in turn.

Uneven Maturity in Applications That Had Value to Commercial Users

Internet access technology is not a single invention, diffusing across time and space without changing form. Instead, it is embedded in equipment that uses a suite of communication technologies, protocols, and standards for networking between computers. This technology gains economic value in combination with complementary invention, investment, and equipment.

When electronic commerce based on TCP/IP standards first developed, it was relatively mature in some applications, such as e-mail and file transfers, and weak in others, such as commercial infrastructure and software applications for business use. This was due to the fact that complementary Internet technology markets developed among technically sophisticated users before migrating to a broad commercial user base, a typical pattern for new information technology (Bresnahan and Greenstein 1999). The invention of the World Wide Web in the early 1990s further stretched the possibilities for potential applications, exacerbating the gap between the technical frontier and the potential needs of the less technically sophisticated user.

A Loosely Coordinated Diffusion Process

Unlike the building of every other major communications network in the United States, Internet access was built in an extremely decentralized market environment. Aside from the loosely coordinated use of a few de facto standards, (e.g., the World Wide Web), government mandates after commercialization were fairly minimal. ISPs had little guidance and few restrictions. They had the option to tailor their offerings to local market conditions and to follow entrepreneurial hunches about growing demand.

As a technical matter, there was little barrier to entry into the provision of dial-up access. This was the first obvious adaptation of Internet technologies to commercial use. As a result, commercial factors, and not the distribution of technical knowledge among providers, largely determined the patterns of development of the basic dial-up access market immediately after commercialization.

A Significant Set of Activities Involve Intermediary Functions

The commercial transaction for Internet access between user and vendor could be brief, but most often it was repetitious and ongoing. A singular transaction arose when the vendor performed one activity, setting up Internet access or attaching Internet access to an existing computing network. If the ISP also operated the access for the user, then this ongoing operation provided frequent contact between the user and vendor, and it provided frequent opportunity for the vendor to change the delivery of services in response to changes in technology and changes in user needs.

In many cases, the ISP was better educated about the technology than the user. In effect, the ISP sold its general knowledge to the user in a form that customized it to the user's particular needs and requirements. At its simplest level, the ISP provided a first exposure to a new technological possibility and helped educate the user about its potential. More often the interaction went beyond exposure to electronic commerce and included the installation of equipment, provision of maintenance, and training, as well as application development. These types of knowledge transfers typically involved a great deal of nuance, often escaped attention, and yet were essential to developing electronic commerce as an ongoing and valuable economic activity.

The Supply of Access Approached Geographic Ubiquity

The U.S. telephone system has one pervasive feature: distance-sensitive pricing at the local level. In virtually every part of the country, phone calls over significant distances (more than thirty miles) engender per-minute charges. Hence, Internet access providers had a strong interest in reducing expenses to users by providing local coverage of Internet access for a local population. Unmet local demand represents a gap between what is technically possible and what many users desire. This is a commercial opportunity for an entrepreneurial ISP, a situation where building appropriate facilities could meet local user needs.

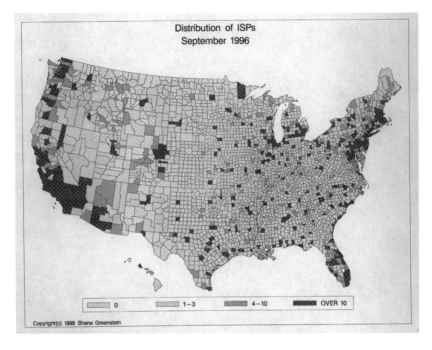

Figure 1a   Distribution of ISPs, September 1996.

Figures 1a and 1b show the density of location of ISPs across the continental United States at the county level for the fall of 1996 and the fall of 1998.[2] Shaded areas are counties with providers; white areas had none. The pictures illustrate the geographic coverage of the industry. ISPs tend to locate in major population centers, but there is also plenty of entry into rural areas. The maps also illustrate the speed of change. Many of the areas that had no coverage in 1996 were covered by a commercial provider in 1998. Many of the areas that had competitive access markets in the early period were extraordinarily competitive by the end of the period. Indeed, Downes and Greenstein (1997) showed that more than 92 percent of the U.S. population had access by a short local phone call to seven or more ISPs. No more than 5 percent did not have such access. Almost certainly the true percentage of the population without access to a competitive dial-up market is even lower than 5 percent.

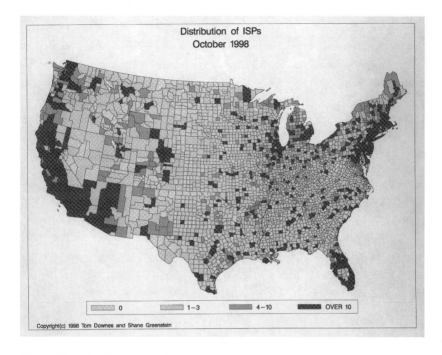

Figure 1b Distribution of ISPs, October 1998.

This near ubiquitous supply of competitive access had two consequences for policy discussions. First, it raised the issue that some low-density areas of the country were getting left behind quickly. Second, in most parts of the country access to the commercial Internet was determined by demand factors—whether the user thought the benefits exceeded the expenses, whether a user could learn how to use the Internet quickly, and so on.

National, Regional, and Local ISPs Specialized in Different Market Niches

An unexpected pattern accompanied this rapid growth in geographic coverage. First, the number of firms maintaining national and regional networks increased over the two years. Table 2 contains the activities of 32 national firms in fall 1996 and 175 in fall 1998. The number of regional firms increased from 186 to over

Table 2 Number of Providers per County, Fall 1996 and Fall 1998

Total number of providers	Counties with this number	Population percentage	Cumulative population percentage	Percent urban counties
Fall 1996				
11	308	59.3	59.3	98.1
10	19	1.0	60.3	68.4
9	17	0.9	61.2	58.8
8	23	1.7	62.9	82.6
7	24	1.5	64.4	91.7
6	41	2.6	66.9	53.7
5	44	2.1	69.0	61.4
4	65	2.5	71.5	44.6
3	107	3.0	74.5	33.6
2	188	3.6	78.1	22.2
1	514	7.9	86.0	18.7
0	1760	13.7	99.7	12.7
Fall 1998				
11	486	69.3	69.3	85.2
10	26	1.1	71.4	50.0
9	28	1.2	71.6	42.9
8	41	1.4	73.0	41.5
7	51	1.5	74.5	43.1
6	40	1.1	75.6	32.5
5	76	1.9	77.5	28.9
4	98	2.0	79.5	20.4
3	224	3.6	83.1	18.3
2	401	5.0	88.1	15.2
1	740	6.5	94.6	13.6
0	928	5.7	100.0	11.6

600.[3] In 1996 most of the national firms were recognizable; they were such firms as IBM, AT&T, Netcom, AOL, and others who had entered the ISP business as a secondary part of their existing services, providing data services to large corporate clients, often with global subdivisions. By 1998 many entrepreneurial firms maintained national networks, and few of these new firms were recognizable to anyone other than long-time followers of this market.

There was also a clear dichotomy between the growth paths of entrepreneurial firms who became national and the regional firms. National firms grow geographically by moving to major cities across the country and then progressively to cities of smaller population. Firms with a regional focus grow into geographically contiguous areas, seemingly irrespective of its urban or rural features.[4]

As it turned out, most of the coverage of rural areas comes from local firms. In 1996 the providers in rural counties with under 50,000 population were overwhelmingly local or regional. Only for populations of 50,000 or above did the average number of national firms exceed one. In fall 1998 the equivalent figure was 30,000, indicating that some national firms had moved into slightly smaller areas. In other words, Internet access in small rural towns is largely done by a local or regional provider. The inference is that it does not pay for many large national providers to provide dial-up service for the home, whereas many small local firms in other lines of business (e.g., local PC retailing) can afford to add Internet access to their existing business. It may also indicate that the local firm may have an easier time customizing the Internet access business to the unique needs of a set of users in a rural setting.

There Were Several Fleeting Business Opportunities

These geographic patterns indicate that the commercialization of the Internet created an economic and business opportunity for providing access. However, this opportunity was fleeting at best. The costs of entry into low-quality dial-up access were low, and commercially oriented firms filled voids in specific places. For any firm with national ambitions, coverage of the top fifty to one hundred cities in the United States was a fleeting advantage and quickly become a necessity for doing business. For any local or regional firm in an urban market, many competitors arose.

It seems unlikely that any firm in the future will get much strategic advantage from the scope of geographic coverage of its dial-up network in the United States. For any firm with a local or regional focus, there will be countless others within every urban area providing similar services. There was much debate among ISPs about the value of providing geographically dispersed service.

Some deliberately chose to focus on a small geographic region and develop a reputation at that local level. Others attempted to create national brand names, focusing their attention on expanding their franchises or geographic reach.

Adaptive Activity Is Not Yet a Nonfleeting Opportunity

A significant set of activities of many providers in the commercial Internet market involve "adaptation." Adaptation services involve one of several activities: Monitoring technical developments, distilling new information into components that are meaningful to unfamiliar users, and matching unique user needs to one of the many possible solutions enabled by advancing technical frontiers.[5] Sometimes adaptation involves heavy use of the technological frontier and sometimes not. In general, it depends on the users, their circumstances, their background, their capital investments, the costs of adjusting to new services, and other factors that influence the match between user needs and technological possibilities.

Adaptation does not happen on its own. In information technology, the agents of change typically come from one of several groups: end-users within an organization, professional staff (such as the MIS group) within an organization, or third-party vendors outside the organization (Bresnahan and Greenstein 1999). If the end-user or their staff does much of the adaptation activity, it becomes an extension of other operations and investments. In contrast, if third parties sell related services to users, adaptation may take several different forms: equipment, consulting about business processes, or both. In this case, third parties—ISPs—took on a central role.

ISPs commercialized their adaptive role by offering new services. Services at ISPs can be grouped into five broad categories: basic access, frontier access, networking, hosting, and web page design (see the appendix of Greenstein 1999 for precise definitions). Table 3 includes lists of activities associated with each category.

Basic access constitutes any service slower than and including a T-1 line. Many of the technologies inherited from the precommercial days were classified as complementary to basic access, not as a new service.

Table 3 Product Lines of ISPs

Category definition	Most common phrases in category	Original Sample
Providing and servicing access though different channels	28.8, 56k, isdn, web TV, wireless, access, T1, T3, DSL, frame relay, e-mail, domain registration, new groups, real audio, ftp, quake server, IRC, chat, video conferencing, cybersitter TM.	3816 (100%)
Networking Service and maintenance	Networking, intranet development, WAN, co-location server, network design, LAN equipment, network support, network service, disaster recovery, backup, database services, novell netware, SQL server	789 (20.6%)
Web Site Hosting	Web hosting, secure hosting, commercial site hosting, virtual ftp server, personal web space, web statistics, BBS access, catalog hosting	792 (20.7%)
Web Page Development and Servicing	Web consulting, active server, web design, java, perl, vrml, front page, secure server, firewalls, web business solutions, cybercash, shopping cart, Internet marketing, online marketing, electronic billing, database integration	1385 (36.3%)
High Speed Access	T3, DSL, xDSL, OC3, OC12, Access rate > 1056k	1059 (27.8%)

Frontier access includes any access faster than a T-1 line, which is becoming the norm for high-speed access for business users. It also includes ISPs that offer direct access for resale to other ISPs or data carriers, and ISPs that offer parts of their own "backbone" for resale to others.[6]

Networking involves activities associated with enabling Internet technology at a user's location. All ISPs do a minimal amount of networking as part of their basic service in establishing connectivity. However, an extensive array of such services, such as regular maintenance, assessment of facilities, and emergency repair, is often essential to keeping and retaining business customers. Note, as well, that some of these experimental services could have been in existence prior to the diffusion of Internet access; it is their offering by an Internet access firm that makes them a source of differentiation from other ISPs.

Hosting is typically geared toward business customers, especially those establishing virtual retailing sites. This requires the ISP to store and maintain information for its access customers on the ISP's servers. Again, all ISPs do a minimal amount of hosting as part of basic service, even for residential customers (e.g., for e-mail). However, some ISPs differentiate themselves by making a large business of providing an extensive array of hosting services, including credit-card processing, site-analysis tools, and so on.

Web Design may be geared toward either the home or business user. Again, many ISPs offer some passive assistance or help pages on web page design and access. However, some offer additional extensive consulting services, design custom sites for users, and provide services associated with design tools and web development programs. Most charge fees for this additional service.

The Rise of Different Strategies for Offering New Services

By 1998 different ISPs had chosen distinct approaches to developing access markets, offering different combination of services and different geographic scopes. Table 3 shows the results of surveys of the business lines of 3816 Internet service providers in the United States who advertised on *thelist* in the summer of 1998 (see the appendix of Greenstein 1999).Virtually every firm in the samples provided some amount of dial-up or direct access and basic functionality, such as e-mail accounts, shell accounts, IP addresses, new links, and FTP and Telnet capabilities, but these 3816 seem to under-represent both very small and quasi-public ISPs (e.g., rural telephone companies).[7]

Of the 3816 ISPs, 2295 (60.1 percent) had at least one line of business other than basic dial-up or direct Internet access. Table 3 shows that 1059 provided high-speed access, 789 networking, 792 web hosting, and 1385 web page design. There is some overlap (shown in figure1): 1869 did at least one of either networking, hosting, or web design; 984 did only one of these three; 105 did all three and frontier access. The analysis sample had similar percentages. For such a cautious method, this reveals quite a lot of different ways to combine nonaccess services with the access business.[8]

These activities contain much more complexity and nuance than table 3 or figure 3 can display. ISPs in urban areas have a greater propensity to offer new services. The largest firms—defined as present in 25 or more area codes—also offer services at slightly higher rates, which is also consistent with the hypothesis that urban areas (where large firms are disproportionately located) tend to receive higher rates of new services. See Greenstein (1999) for further details.

The Research Agenda for Understanding Internet Access

These features of the access business portend an interesting future for this part of the value chain. The locus of adaptations is shifting from developing and maintaining access into related functions. Many ISPs in this business seem to be moving away from their specialization on low-quality access. Access is being provided along with many other complementary services, although the combinations have not yet taken on a set pattern.

Further development of commercial Internet access will accompany and be accompanied by several other activities on the boundaries of these ISPs. This raises questions about changes in the activities of end-users within organizations. As ISPs offer more and more services that integrate with the business processes of their users, they create tighter links with those users. Users will then be left with the option of bringing in-house the creation of new Internet activities or allowing the ISPs to continue advising them on changing their business processes. What will the structure of the ISP industry look like then?

4 The Research Agenda for Electronic Commerce

This section describes the need for original and fundamental empirical research on the changing structure of electronic commerce. While this field raises many challenges for research, the regularity to patterns of behavior helps frame many empirical research issues involving changes in market structure.[9]

Measuring Changes to the Technical Possibilities Frontier and to Pricing

There is a well-known literature in econometrics on hedonic estimation. This has been frequently employed to measure computing industry outcomes. This method provides some insight into the rate of technical improvement in hardware across a class of products. It has also been useful for describing several complementary markets.[10] Since the Internet equipment industry, like the rest of computing, has experienced a dramatic decline in price per unit of features, hedonic curves are a simple way to summarize that change over time. Hedonic techniques also account for changes in prices along the entire product line. This is one tool for focusing attention on improvement in upstream equipment and transmission facilities—along a wide spectrum of sizes, applications, and firms—where almost everything is getting better and cheaper. There has been less attention paid to product turnover—i.e., entry and exit of new designs as a transmission mechanism for the diffusion of new technology—leaving considerable room for further empirical research on product cycles generally.[11] These methods have yet to be applied to the wide class of equipment underlying electronic commerce.

Changes in the Geography of the Provision of Internet Infrastructure

There is wide interest in understanding the Internet's geographic features, which have consequences for the development of a "universally accessible" Internet and for the locus of growth and economic development in any given region.[12] These issues need data collection and new frameworks. The most commonly cited information on the geographic diffusion of the Internet comes from the Matrix Information and Demography Services (MIDS) of Austin, Texas, which has been analyzing the location of "hosts"—i.e., computers connected to the Internet. But it is not clear that there is any relationship between the location of host computers and access to Internet technologies for business and personal use, nor is there any necessary relationship to degrees of economic advance in a region. There is a lot of work that needs to be done in this area, which has attracted increasing attention from geographers.[13]

The Nested Adoption of Electronic Commerce

General-purpose technologies like the ones that drive the Internet do not diffuse immediately without change. Often the critical factor influencing adoption are "co-inventive" activities—inventions that adapt the technology to specific unique users (Bresnahan and Trajtenberg 1997). Co-invention takes time and necessarily occurs in sequence. As the conditions that determine an initial diffusion pattern change, and as users co-invent in reaction to new opportunities, so do the conditions that determine the adoption of Internet technologies change.[14] Hence, a later episode of diffusion can be nested within the factors that determined the first episode. More to the point, any sufficiently complex co-invention activity will result in the nesting of some adoption episodes in others. For example, innovations in personal computing and networking influence the diffusion of online retailing. Innovations in search engines lead many firms to alter their web pages, which induces further changes in interactive access technology, which induces further adoption of software, and so on. There has been very little attention paid to the how the sequence of development of electronic commerce shapes its performance. Is the United States gaining short-term advantages or long-terms disadvantages by being the strong first mover? To what extent are there biases in the resolution of tensions between retrofitting and the green-field development of the value chain of electronic commerce?

Variation in Business Models

Does the availability of new services differ across regions in the United States? Across time? Investment in digital infrastructure induces entry of complementary goods or produces demand-enhancement that differs by company and region. Aside from those identified in the example above, there is room for many more studies of the determinants of differences in the form of commercializing electronic commerce. This topic is difficult partly because the key issues resist data collection, requiring that researchers measure adaptation expenses, how the benefits from new technology get captured by the business, and how these benefits are distributed to the purchasers of the final products. There seem to be opportunities to form links between the broad knowledge of consultants and the specific needs of academics and policy makers.[15]

Variation in User Requirements in the Home

Some statistical research has analyzed the patterns of adoption of IP technologies for nonbusiness use.[16] This is clearly an important determinant of industry structure in electronic commerce, since the diffusion of so many business models and new applications presumes ubiquity or an experienced user base. But adoption and use of the Internet at home depends on historical or previous investments, particularly in such key infrastructure as PCs, cable lines, and local digital phone equipment. PCs, of course, were not oriented toward the diffusion of electronic commerce for many years. Their use was determined by many factors, such as the age, income, and profession of residents of a household, and the conditions of schools, libraries, and retail service facilities in a local region. Does this portend development of non-PC-based models of electronic commerce in the home? Will the have/have-not split in access to electronic commerce be determined by the factors that shape PC adoption?

Variation in User Requirements in Business

Researchers have made interesting progress on understanding the determinants of adoption of new IT in business.[17] These studies could be extended to many of the open questions about the relationship between the diffusion of electronic commerce and its benefits/costs to specific users, especially in different types of business activities. Some buyers may be waiting for adaptation costs to decline, which occurs as the supply of complementary goods increases. In computing, for example, the costs of transition from old technology to new were much higher in complex organizations with idiosyncratic applications. These costs slowed adoption of new technology by some of the very firms that could benefit most from it, inducing a potentially long lag between the invention of new capabilities and their use. These explanations may provide a framework for understanding the development of new services in key industries such as financial services, transportation, and print and publishing.

Markets for Adaptation Services

It would also be interesting to examine the pricing, business models, and success of custom software and related services in a variety of applications to electronic commerce. How effective are they in making adaptations to local conditions and why? Did national firms need to change their sales methods, service, and organizations to try to commercialize this new opportunity? Similarly, there is a need to examine the ability of companies to find and use programmers in their local markets, and of enterprises' ability to deploy managers in the kinds of roles required by new IT. While most data do not directly measure adaptation activity, such activity may leave shadows in features of software, labor practices, management policies, changing job definitions, wages, and output quality. Further studies of the organization of the software industry, training, labor practices, and other adaptation activities would be very useful.[18]

Intermediaries, Local Economic Growth, and Subsidies

The diffusion of an Internet technology is largely shaped by the geographic diversity of local markets and the heterogeneity of firms that commercialize the technology. This dispersion shapes the customization of technology to new users and established businesses. This process is central to the understanding of economic growth, especially because electronic commerce influences information-intensive activities within firms, such as inventory management, sales and distribution, and other coordinative activities.[19] It is also a source of great policy concern in the telecommunications industry, because this relationship shapes the creation and targeting of subsidies associated with new services at schools, libraries and hospitals, as proposed in the 1996 Telecommunications Act.[20] If the absence of new services in low-density areas is due to an absence of local firms with appropriate skills, then policies might either induce commercial firms to expand from high-density areas to low-density areas, or they might encourage investments from stakeholders who are already located in low-density areas. If, on the other hand, the absence of new services in low-density areas is due to an absence of local demand for these services or the absence of local infrastructure, subsidies run the risk of not changing the propensity to experiment in such areas. Indeed, in that case, the subsidy can be very wasteful if it leads to the offering of services that few want.

Restructuring of Intermediary Functions

Many observers feel that TCP/IP-based services will lead to radical restructuring of the formats for, and delivery of, final goods that are information-intensive, such as music or radio, telephony, broadcast television, video gaming, newspapers, magazines, and other print media. Some of this restructuring is symptomatic of the upheaval that is typical of high-technology industries, raising many strategic issues for investors and managers but no substantive issues for policy makers. Some of it raises issues involving the interaction of regulated monopolies with otherwise competitive market environments. There is a need for frameworks and data to understand the key determinants of market structure: the entry and exit of new firms; the value ownership over, and horizontal concentration of, key assets; the persistence of old services and resistance of incumbent firms to new services; and so on. Unlike many of the other topics just raised, this area has already attracted considerable attention from researchers because it overlaps with traditional regulatory concerns about the ownership of key assets in the delivery and transmission of information. Indeed, this literature is too large to summarize here. That said, if the past is any predictor of the future, the demand for empirical research on related topics will exceed the supply for the foreseeable future.

Regulation of Interconnection, Access, and Content

Much regulatory communications policy in the United States presumes and reinforces a distinction in ownership between the firms that provide transport services and the firms that make use of those services in delivering content. This distinction seems vague, at best, in the emerging Internet platform. At worse, it is simply antiquated. This trend raises a question about the wisdom of applying legacy regulatory categories to the behavior of firms, such as ISPs, who cross legacy boundaries. Accordingly, much policy debate has been concerned with redefining the distinction between traditional telephone services and computing services (for a recent summary and critique see Weinberg 1999 or Sidek and Spulber 1998). Should there be a new and possibly sui generis regulatory approach to ISPs, Internet content providers, and providers of new services that combine elements of the old platform with the new, such IP-based telephony? If firms are pursuing business models with only a mild relationship to the regulatory boxes and previous business lines, how should regulators think about these experiments? Is this the key market mechanism for developing complementary Internet services and translating technical advance into economic value? Is it in society's interest to give these experiments sufficient time to generate potential information spillovers, or should the cost of that input be incorporated into the industry's investments and other strategic commitments, thereby minimizing distortions? There is a need for a framework here; and as with the last topic, this area has already attracted considerable attention. Again, it is fair to predict that the demand for research on this topic will exceed the supply for some time.

5 Conclusion

This chapter has offered a set of questions, an illustrative example, and a guide for future empirical research. It has taken just one of many necessary steps toward framing empirical guidelines for analyzing developments in electronic commerce.

It is also worth noting that the nexus of this chapter's questions identifies a particularly vexing and important set of policy issues.

Electronic commerce will undergo considerable change in the next decade as firms respond to better information about demand and the emergence of new technical capabilities. Society benefits from the intermediary activities that firms pursue and from the variety of means different firms adopt to meet user needs. It is precisely that juncture of variety and mediation that keeps observers guessing about the direction of structural change in commercial markets, and that raises the value of empirical research that tries to understand it.

Acknowledgments

I would like to thank the Institute for Government and Public Affairs at the University of Illinois, the Council on Library Resources, and the Consortium for Research on Telecommunication Policy at Northwestern University for financial assistance. Thanks to Oded Bizan, Erik Brynjolfsson, Tim Bresnahan, Greg Crawford, Barbara Dooley, Tom Downes, Brian Kahin, Mike Mazzeo, and Dan Spulber for useful conversations and to many seminar participants. Angelique Augereau, Howard Berkes, and Chris Forman provided outstanding research assistance.

Notes

1. These decisions get attention from policy makers for a good reason: this is where many have/have-not split gets decided. For example, commercial markets have so far determined who has Internet connection to the home and who does not, which regions of the country have easy access and which do not, and so on.

2. This study's data combine a count of the ISP dial-in list from August/September of 1996 and May/June of 1998 in *thedirectory* and a count of the backbone dial-in list for fall 1996 and the summer 1998 issues of *Boardwatch* magazine. For further documentation of these methods, see Greenstein (1997) and Downes and Greenstein (1998). The fall 1996 data cover over 14,000 phone numbers for over 3200 ISPs. The fall 1998 data cover over 65,000 phone numbers for just under 6000 ISPs.

3. In this table a national firm is one that is in more than 25 counties. A regional firm is in more than 3 but less than 25 counties.

4. Some ISPs have told me in interviews that this growth was initially in response to customer requests for local phone numbers for accessing networks (e-mail mostly at first) when these customers traveled outside their primary area. More recently, it ISPs commonly discuss the possibility of developing a large customer base for purposes of "selling the base" to a high bidder in some future industry consolidation.

5. Adaptation has long been a topic of discussion in the economics of technology and economic growth (Bresnahan and Trajtenberg 1995), as well as in the management of technology (Hagerdorn 1998). Studies of this behavior have antecedents in the studies of diffusion and learning by Griliches (1957), Rosenberg (1977), Nelson and Winter (1982), and others. For further development of these views of the ISP market, see Greenstein (1999).

6. Speed is the sole dimension for differentiating between frontier and basic access. This is a practical choice. There are a number of other access technologies now becoming viable, such as wireless access, that are slow and technically difficult. Only a small number of firms in this data set are offering these services, and these are firms offering high-speed access.

7. This site, maintained by Meckler Media, provides an opportunity for both large and small ISPs to advertise their services. ISPs fill out a questionnaire in which the answers are partially formatted, then the answers are displayed in a way that allows users to compare different ISP services. From comparison with other sources, such as Downes and Greenstein (1998), *Boardwatch* magazine, and the National Telephone Cooperative Association directory on Internet Services in rural areas (NTCA 1998), it appears that these 3816 ISPs are not a comprehensive census of every ISP in the country.

8. One of the most difficult phrases to classify was general "consulting." The vast majority of consulting activity is accounted for by the present classification methods as one of these three complementary activities: networking, hosting, and web design.

9. I am grateful to Tim Bresnahan for bringing some of these issues to my attention over the course of many years. These issues partially overlap with our literature review of user-oriented and valuation studies in information technology (Bresnahan and Greenstein 1999).

10. There are many estimates of price changes in computing using hedonic estimates (e.g., Triplett 1989; Dulberger 1989; Gordon 1989; Berndt, Griliches, and Rappaport 1995). Recent research suggests that many of the same trends are found in PC software (Gandal 1994; Brynjolfsson and Kemerer 1996; Groehn 1999). On communications and transmission equipment see Flamm (1989, 1998) and Aron, Dunmore, and Pampush (1997). For some reservations on the use of hedonic estimation, see Bresnahan and Greenstein (1998) or Triplett (1989).

11. See, e.g., Stavins (1995), Greenstein and Wade (1998), and de Figueiredo and Kyle (1999).

12. See, e.g., Moss and Townsend (1996, 1998), Moss and Mitra (1998), Greenstein, Lizardo, and Spiller (1997), and Downes and Greenstein (1998).

13. See http://www4.mids.org/. Also, see http://www.cybergeography.com/atlas/atlas.html for cyber-geography and http://www.telegeography.com/ for international commercial statistics.

14. See Jimeniz and Greenstein (1998), Clemente (1998), Kridel (1997), and Tedlow (1996).

15. There is a long list of commercial firms with active research programs in characterizing business models in electronic commerce at a national or international level, including Juliussen and Juliussen, Forester, the Maloff group, Jupiter Communications, Ziff-Davis, IDG, Boardwatch, Meckler Media, and the Gartner Group.

16. Some recent contributions include Kridel, Rappaport, and Taylor (1997), Goolsbee and Klenow (1999), or Goolsbee (1999). See also Clement (1998) or Maloff (1997).

17. See, e.g., Bresnahan, Brynjolfsson, and Hitt (1999) on the degree of centralization or decentralization within corporation, Hubbard (1998) on the use of computing and global position systems for coordination benefits, and Bresnahan and Greenstein (1997) on the idiosyncratic factors slowing down or speeding up the diffusion of networked IT at mainframe users.

18. For steps in this direction, see, e.g., Mowery (1998), Siwek and Furchtgott-Roth (1998), and Autor (1999).

19. For recent contributions, see, e.g., Roller and Waverman (1997), Moss and Townsend (1998, 1999), Greenstein, Lizardo, and Spiller (1998), Greenstein (1999).

20. This is a growing literature and a topic that is far from settled. For recent contributions, see Werbach (1997), Esbin (1998), Weinberg,(1999), and, for the perspective of rural telephone companies, Garcia and Gorenflo (1998).

References

Aron, Debra, Ken Dunmore, and Frank Pampush (1997). "The Impact of Unbundled Network Elements and the Internet on Telecommunications Access Infrastructure," working paper for the Harvard Information Infrastructure Project, http://ksgwww.harvard.edu/iip/Papers/

Autor, David H. (1998). "Why Do Temporary Help Firms Provide Free General Skills Training?" unpublished dissertation chapter, Harvard University, 1998.

Berndt, Ernst R., Zvi Griliches, and Neal J. Rappaport (1995). "Econometric Estimates of Price Indexes for Personal Computers in the 1990's," *Journal of Econometrics* (July).

Boardwatch (1997). *March/April Directory of Internet Service Providers*, Littleton, CO.

Bresnahan, Timothy (1987). "Measuring the Spillover from Technical Advance: Mainframe Computer in Financial Services," *American Economic Review* (March): 742–755.

Bresnahan, Timothy (1999). "New Modes of Competition: Implications for the Future Structure of the Computer Industry," in Jeffrey A. Eisenach and Thomas M. Lenard, eds., *Competition, Innovation and the Microsoft Monopoly: Antitrust in the Digital Marketplace* (Boston: Kluwer).

Bresnahan, Timothy, Erik Brynjolfsson, and Lorin Hitt (1999). "Information Technology, Organizational Work, and the Demand for Skilled Labor: Firm Level Evidence," working paper, MIT.

Bresnahan, Timothy, and Shane Greenstein (1997). "Technical Progress and Co-Invention in Computing and in the Use of Computers," *Brookings Papers on Economics Activity: Microeconomics,* 1–78.

Bresnahan, Timothy, and Shane Greenstein (1999). "Technological Competition and the Structure of the Computing Industry," *Journal of Industrial Economics* (Winter).

Bresnahan, Timothy, and Shane Greenstein (1998). "The Economic Contribution of Information Technology: Value Indicators in International Perspective." *Organization for Economic and Cooperative Development.* Also available at http://skew2.kellogg.nwu.edu/~greenste/research.html.

Bresnahan, Timothy, Scott Stern, and Manuel Trajtenber (1997). "Market Segmentation and the Source of Rents from Innovation: Personal Computers in the Late 1980s," *Rand Journal of Economics* 28: s17–s44.

Bresnahan, Timothy, and Manuel Trajtenberg (1995). "General Purpose Technologies: Engines of Growth?" *Journal of Econometrics* 65: 83–108.

Brynjolfsson, Erik, and Kemerer (1996). Network Externalities in Microcomputer Software: An Econometric Analysis of the Spreadsheet Market," *Management Science* 42(12): 1627–1647.

Clemente, Peter C. (1998). *The State of the Net: The New Frontier.* New York: McGraw-Hill.

de Figueiredo, John, and Margaret K. Kyle (1999). "Product Entry and Exit in the Desktop Laser Printer Industry," mimeo, MIT Sloan School of Management.

Demsetz, Harold (1988). "The Theory of the Firm Revisited," *Journal of Law, Economics, and Organization* 4: 159–178.

Downes, Tom, and Shane Greenstein (1998). "Do Commercial ISPs Provide Universal Access?" in Sharon Gillett and Ingo Vogelsang, eds., *Competition, Regulation and Convergence: Selected Papers from the 1998 Telecommunications Policy Research Conference* (Mahwah, NJ: Lawrence Erlbaum).

Downes, Tom, and Shane Greenstein (1999). "Universal Access and Local Commercial Internet Markets," mimeo, http://skew2.kellogg.nwu.edu/~greenste/research.html.

Dulberger, Ellen R. (1993). "Sources of Price Decline in Computer Processors: Selected Electronic Components," in Murray F. Foss, Marilyn E. Manser, and Allan H. Young, eds., *Price Measurements and Their Uses* (Chicago: University of Chicago Press).

Dulberger, Ellen R. (1989). "The Application of a Hedonic Model to a Quality Adjusted Price Index for Computer Processor," in Dale Jorgenson and Ralph Landau, eds., *Technology and Capital Formation* (Cambridge MA: MIT Press).

Eisenach, Jeffrey, A., and Thomas M. Lenard (1999). *Competition, Innovation and the Microsoft Monopoly: Antitrust in the Digital Marketplace.* Boston: Kluwer.

Flamm, Kenneth (1990). Chapter in Robert W. Crandall and Kenneth Flamm, eds., *Changing the Rules: Technological Change, International Competition, and Regulation in Communications* (Washington, DC: Brookings Intsitution).

Esbin, Barbara (1998). "Internet over Cable, Defining the Future in Terms of the Past," Working Paper 30, FCC, Office of Planning and Policy, August.

Gandal, Neil (1994). "Hedonic Price Indexes for Spread Sheets and a Test of Network Externalities," *Rand Journal of Economics* 25(1): 160–170.

Garcia, D. Linda, and Neal Gorenflo (1997). "Best Practices for Rural Internet Deployment: The Implications for Universal Service Policy," Prepared for the 1997 Telecommunications Policy Research Conference, Alexandria, VA.

Goolsbee, Austun (1999). "In a World without Borders: The Impact of Taxes on Internet Commerce," mimeo, University of Chicago.

Goolsbee, Austin, and Peter Klenow (1999). "Evidence of Learning and Network Externalities in the Diffusion of Home Computers," mimeo, University of Chicago.

Gordon, Robert J. (1989). "The Postwar Evolution of Computer Prices," in Dale W. Jorgenson and Ralph Landau, eds., *Technology and Capital Formation* (Cambridge, MA: MIT Press).

Greenstein, Shane (1999a). "Building and Developing the Virtual World: The Commercial Internet Access Market," http://skew2.kellogg.nwu.edu/~greenste/research.html

Greenstein, Shane (1999b). "Technological Mediation and Commercial Development in the Early Internet Access Market," http://skew2.kellogg.nwu.edu/~greenste/research.html

Greenstein, Shane, Mercedes Lizardo, and Pablo Spiller (1997). "The Evolution of the Distribution of Advanced Large Scale Information Infrastructure the United States," NBER Working Paper #5929.

Greenstein, Shane, and Jim Wade (1998). "The Product Life Cycle in the Commercial Mainframe Computer Market, 1968–1983," *Rand Journal of Economics* (Winter).

Griliches, Zvi (1957). "Hybrid Corn: An Exploration in the Economics of Technological Change," *Econometrica* 25: 501–522.

Groehn, Andreas (1999). "Network Effects in PC Software: An Empirical Analysis," mimeo, National Bureau of Economic Research, Cambridge, MA.

Hagerdorn, Andrew B. (1998). "Firms as Knowledge Brokers: Lessons in Pursuing Continuous Innovation," *California Management Review* 40(3).

Hubbard, Thomas (1998). "Why Are Process Monitoring Technologies Valuable? The Use of Trip Recorders and Electronic Vehicle Management Systems in the Trucking Industry," mimeo, UCLA.

Jimeniz, Ed, and Shane Greenstein (1998). "The Emerging Internet Retailing Market as a Nested Diffusion Process," *International Journal of Innovation Management* 2(3).

Juliussen, Karen Petska, and Egil Juliussen (1998). *The Internet Industry Almanac*, Austin, TX: The Reference Press.

Kalakota, Ravi, and Andrew Whinston (1996). *Frontiers of Electronic Commerce*, Reading, MA: Addison-Wesley.

Kolstad, Rob (1998). "Becoming an ISP," www.bsdi.com (January).

Kridel, Donald, Paul Rappaport, and Lester Taylor (1997). "The Demand for Access to Online Services and the Internet," mimeo, PNR Associates, Jenkintown, PA.

Leida, Brett (1997). "A Cost Model of Internet Service Providers: Implications for Internet Telephony and Yield Management," mimeo, MIT, Departments of Electrical Engineering and Computer Science and the Technology and Policy Program.

Lerner, Josh (1995). "Pricing and Financial Resources: An Analysis of the Disk Drive Industry, 1980–88," *Review of Economics and Statistics* 77: 585–598

Maloff Group International, Inc. (1997). "1996–1997 Internet Access Providers Marketplace Analysis," Dexter, MO, October.

Meeker, Mary, and Chris Depuy (1996). *The Internet Report*, New York: HarperBusiness.

Moss, Mitchell L., Steve Mitra (1998). " Net Equity: Class Divisions Emerging on the Net," Taub Urban Research Center, New York University, http://urban.nyu.edu/research/net-equity/.

Moss, Mitchell L., and Anthony Townsend (1996). "Leaders and Losers on the Internet," Taub Urban Research Center, New York University, http://urban.nyu.edu/research/l-and-l/.

Moss, Mitchell L., and Anthony Townsend (1998). "Spatial Analysis of the Internet in U.S. Cities and States," Taub Urban Research Center, New York University, http://urban.nyu.edu/research/newcastle/.

Mowery, David (1996). *The International Computer Software Industry: A Comparative Study of Industry Evolution and Structure*, New York: Oxford University Press.

Nelson, R. R. and S. G. Winter (1982). *An Evolutionary Theory of Economic Change*, Cambridge, MA: Harvard University Press.

Northrup, Anthony (1998). *NT Network Plumbing, Routers, Proxies and Web Services*, New York: IDG Books Worldwide.

NTCA (1998). *Membership Directory and Yellow Pages*, Washington DC: National Telephone Cooperative Association.

Roller, H., and L. Waverman (1996). "Endogenous Growth and Telecommunications Infrastructure Investment," mimeo, Organization for Economic Cooperation and Development.

Rosenberg, Nathan (1977). *Perspectives on Technology*, Cambridge, UK: Cambridge University Press.

Rybaczyk, Peter (1998). *Novell's Internet Plumbing Handbook*, San Jose, CA: Novell Press.

Siwek, Stephen E., and Harold W. Furchtgott-Roth (1997). *International Trade in Computer Software*, Westport, CT: Quorum Books.

Spulber, Daniel (1998). *The Market Makers: How Leading Companies Create and Win Markets*, New York: McGraw-Hill.

Stavins, Joanna, 1995, "Model Entry and Exit in a Differentiated-Product Industry: The Personal Computer Market," *Review of Economics and Statistics* 77(4): 571–584.

Tedlow, Richards S., 1996, "Roadkill on the Information Superhighway (logistics of interactive shopping)," *Harvard Business Review* 74 (Nov./Dec.): 164–166.

Trajtenberg, M. (1990). *Economic Analysis of Product Innovation: The Case of CT Scanners*, Cambridge, MA: Harvard University Press.

Triplett, Jack (1989). "Price and Technological Change in a Capital Good: A Survey of Research on Computers," in Dale Jorgenson and Ralph Landau, eds., *Technology and Capital Formation* (Cambridge MA: MIT Press).

Weinberg, Jonathan (1999). "The Internet and Telecommunications Services, Access Charges, Universal Service Mechanisms, and Other Flotsam of the Regulatory System," *Yale Journal of Regulation* (Spring).

Werbach, Kevin (1997). "Digital Tornado: The Internet and Telecommunications Policy," FCC, Office of Planning and Policy Working Paper 29, March.

Small Companies in the Digital Economy

Sulin Ba, Andrew B. Whinston, and Han Zhang

Introduction

Some of the most exciting developments in the digital economy are in the realm of digital products, as reflected in the current burst of activity involving the creation, assembly, procurement, and distribution of digitized content and services. One projection for the future of content provision foresees a world in which rich digital content is distributed to customers as customized bundles of reusable components, based on dynamically updated customer profiles (Parameswaran, Stallaert, and Whinston 1999). This new arena for commercial competition opens the door for the proliferation of small, innovative digital companies.

Small companies have always played an important role in the economy. In fact, many economists argue that a truly competitive economy requires the existence of small companies. Yet the share of total business volume attributable to such companies is declining. In the digital product industry in particular, their share is rapidly shrinking, and we must therefore question the market potential and competitiveness of small companies in this market.

Digital products are often loosely defined to include software, multimedia education and entertainment products such as music and video, and other information-based products that can be digitized and delivered via electronic networks (Choi, Stahl, and Whinston 1997). What binds these products together is the fact that they have been or can be liberated from the physical forms that were once necessary for their delivery, allowing a much greater degree of customization and differentiation.

Naturally, in the digital economy, companies with a large inventory of digital components and the ability to control delivery channels can customize more readily, giving them greater access to consumers. This is the reason for the recent surge of acquisitions and alliances between media and telecommunications giants. Small digital companies usually have a restricted product selection and limited resources to reach consumers. Moreover, electronic commerce involves risks and uncertainties, one of which is the fact that consumers don't have sufficient signals on product quality—what is known as the "asymmetric information problem." Because most small companies do not have a strong brand name to help mitigate the problem, they may have a difficult time attracting customers. This situation will clearly influence competition, and it raises questions about the viability of small firms engaging in such activities. How are small digital companies going to survive in the digital economy? What needs to be done to improve their chances?

In this chapter, we argue that the creation of what we will call *digital intermediaries* could help encourage the growth of small companies in the digital economy. We envision a framework in which digital intermediaries, interacting with both small companies and their potential customers, facilitate product customization and content development. The framework is market-based, unlike a hierarchic structure in which each company does everything on its own. The coordination process is made possible by modern technologies that significantly lower transaction costs (Malone, Yates, and Benjamin 1987). By pooling resources (content from multiple small players) through the market structure, digital intermediaries achieve economies of scale in infrastructure building. They provide quality assurance to consumers, maintain digital components from participating content providers using dynamic catalogues, and ensure content compatibility by enforcing open technology standards.

Products provided to consumers would be customized product bundles generated on the fly from multiple sources according to each customer's preference. Individual content providers would not need to build a relationship directly with consumers.

Another type of intermediary, a trusted third party (TTP), will provide authentication and product or service quality evaluation to both consumers and digital intermediaries. Using reports from TTPs, digital intermediaries will be able to choose the highest-quality content providers, and consumers can get information on which digital intermediaries provide the highest-quality products and services.

The next two sections summarize the opportunities presented to small companies in the digital economy and point out the main challenges facing them. We then outline our framework for helping small companies compete in the new economy, and we conclude by highlighting some public policy issues related to small companies and pointing to future research directions.

The New Opportunities for Small Companies

Only five years after the introduction of the World Wide Web, the digital economy already rivals century-old industries, and it is still growing at an astounding rate (Barua et al. 1999).

On the forefront of the new economy are digital products. Software programs, newspapers, and music CDs no longer need to be packaged and delivered to stores, homes, or news kiosks. They can now be delivered directly to consumers over the Internet. Electronic transactions involving airline tickets and securities already occur in large numbers. Other industries such as consulting services, entertainment, banking and insurance, education, and health care face hurdles but are also beginning to use the Internet to change the way they do business. Over time, the sale and transmission of goods and services electronically is likely to be the largest and most visible driver of the new digital economy (Department of Commerce 1998). These digital products can be assembled, customized, and packaged to meet changing customer demands, and can be delivered instantly when needed.

A large digital product market means vast business opportunities and provides a major arena for small companies to sprout, blossom, and grow. Concentrating on their core digital contents, small companies have an opportunity to play a critical role in the new economy. Moreover, the new information technologies make it easier for small companies to collaborate in the electronic market.

Economists have long recognized the importance of small companies to the economy. The active existence of numerous small business firms, each exercising a reasonable degree of freedom and independence, is considered basic to the maintenance of a competitive market (Beckman 1944; Acs 1999). In addition, small companies are the essential mechanism by which millions enter the economic and social mainstream of the society. In Canada, for example, 57 percent of economic output is generated by an SME (small and medium-sized enterprises) sector consisting of more than 2.2 million firms (OECD Report 1999). In the United States, 47 percent of firms have fewer than ten employees (Acs 1999). In the digital economy, where innovation and change are the rule, it is important to note the crucial role played by new small companies in the experimentation and innovation that lead to technological change and productivity growth.

The New Challenges for Small Companies

The digital economy provides a golden opportunity for small companies, but that does not necessarily mean that they can succeed in the electronic marketplace. In this section, we focus on two sets of issues that will have significant impact on competition in the electronic market: the cost of information infrastructure and information asymmetry.

The Cost Structure of Information Technology

As the digital economy grows, the importance of a widely recognized brand name becomes ever clearer. Consider the case of Amazon.com, which started out as a bookseller but has now expanded its offerings to include a wide variety of products and auctions. The economic explanation for this expansion is that information technology infrastructure has increasing returns to scale. It requires a large initial investment to create an infrastructure that allows efficient processing of information, handling of heavy traffic, and delivery of goods. Once the infrastructure is in place, however, the cost of adding product lines decreases (see figure 1). Given the tremendous investment Amazon.com has made in infrastructure, it is a natural evolution to expand its

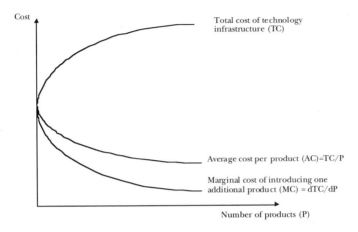

Cost

Total cost of technology
infrastructure (TC)

Average cost per product (AC)=TC/P

Marginal cost of introducing one
additional product (MC) = dTC/dP

Number of products (P)

Figure 1   The cost curves of technology infrastructure and product offering.

product lines to take full advantage of that infrastructure. There is also a prestige that people connect with bigness (Beckman 1944). Many consumers take it for granted that firm size is synonymous with progress, efficiency, and economy. Therefore, the bigger a company gets, the easier it is to win consumer confidence and trust, which makes it easier to lure business away from small companies that do not have an established name in the market.

Asymmetric Information

In a traditional business environment, customers and vendors get to size each other up through direct contact, and the customer can literally get a feel for the quality of the products under discussion. A good reputation stemming from a history of satisfactory transactions will then further enhance the consumer's trust (Johnston 1996; Milgrom, North, and Weingast 1990). The use of trust as a factor in determining interorganizational and interpersonal behavior has been studied extensively (see, e.g., Anderson and Weitz 1989).

In the electronic marketplace, everything is more distant, and two-way trust becomes more difficult to establish. After all, web sites can be counterfeited, identities can be forged, and the nature of transactions can be altered. In order to instill public confidence, companies must find new ways to ensure that consumers trust in their authenticity and in the integrity of their transactions.

The online market certainly offers abundant product choices for consumers. Abundance can lead to confusion, though, when too many choices and too much information make it difficult for consumers to tell which vendors offer quality products. When one agent in a transaction is better informed than the other, we say that information is distributed asymmetrically. For example, a seller may know that a product can vary in quality, but the buyer probably will not (this is the lemon problem). Such situations can lead to market failure (Akerlof 1970).

In the absence of indicators of trustworthiness, online consumers may choose to interact only with firms whose names they recognize. As Kevin O'Connor, the CEO of DoubleClick, has said, "On the Net, consumers have a lot of choices, so brand wins" when consumers don't have enough quality signals (Colvin 1999). A recent study by researchers at Xerox PARC shows that the most popular Web sites command a disproportionate share of Internet traffic—a signature of what economists refer to as a "winner take all" market (Adamic and Huberman 1999). Asymmetric information thus affects market efficiency by skewing competition to favor established brand names.

Will asymmetric information in the electronic marketplace and the cost structure of technology lead to a world of natural monopolies, with Microsoft as *the* software provider and Amazon.com as *the* retailer? Such a situation would lead to market inefficiency and the death of innovation.

Under these circumstances, building an infrastructure to help small companies survive and prosper becomes a top public policy issue. How can we help small digital companies build trust, develop innovative content, and compete with well-established brand names? We next outline a blueprint for a digital product intermediary to illustrate, without going into technical details, what can be done to address this issue.

A New Framework for Small Digital Companies

Adam Smith (1776) used the example of a pin factory to demonstrate the benefits of coordinated specialization and cooperation.

He described how the various stages of pin manufacturing could be most efficiently carried out by workers who specialized in a single task such as pulling wire, straightening it, or cutting it to appropriate lengths. He argued that such specialization, if properly coordinated, would lead to increased output volume. Alchian and Demsetz (1972) took up Smith's argument to assert that resource owners in capitalist society can increase productivity through cooperative specialization and that this results in a demand for economic organizations that facilitate cooperation. These classic economic arguments still hold in the digital economy, although they may no longer be limited to the boundaries of a single firm.

Information technologies and open standards make specialization and cooperation possible within society as a whole. They also reduce transaction costs among collaborators, allowing us to shift resource coordination from a hierarchic approach to a market approach (Malone, Yates, and Benjamin 1987). Like the workers in Smith's pin factory, different digital companies can specialize in different products and collaborate by using the services of digital intermediaries. Conversely, digital intermediaries can customize and integrate digital products from different companies according to consumer demand. This type of collaboration will help small digital companies blossom in the electronic market.

We foresee an electronic marketplace that includes small companies, digital intermediaries, and customers. These small companies may have only a few employees and concentrate on a few specialized products (e.g., accounting software, or educational programs for 3 to 5 year olds). The digital intermediaries will contract with such companies to procure content of different types, with provision for bundling content from different sources for reselling. The content will include both static and dynamic information. Static content may be articles, reports, news items, or books; dynamic content may be sports tickers, stock quotes, and so on. There may also be multimedia content such as digitized music, video clips of news stories, movies, recorded events such as concerts or conferences, live coverage of events, multicast channels of entertainment and news, online radio stations, or distance learning programs. Customers will be able to buy digital products from the digital intermediaries or directly from the originating companies based on the intermediaries' services.

Currently, products are often prebundled by content producers, whether they are in the traditional print business or involved in the electronic delivery of digital content. For example, magazines are bundles of articles. Subscriptions to cable TV are bundles of different types of programs: under the normal basic agreement, a viewer interested only in sports channels is forced to buy a package that includes the home-shopping channel as well. Consumers don't have wide choice about the kinds of bundles they can have. In this type of bundling, product customization is limited because of economies of scale in printing, binding, and shipping. As we move to a world where digital content is delivered electronically, however, printing, binding, and shipping will no longer be necessary, and the opportunities for customization increase.

Small companies have long been good at finding niches in the marketplace. Bigger companies are often resistant to change and less flexible in responding to customer needs. Moreover, in a highly integrated company that markets bundled products using content components that they produce, there may be incentive problems. Current incentive systems, such as stock options, are mostly based on overall firm performance. This creates room for free riders, where individual content providers add only marginally to the value of the product yet derive benefit from the bundle as a whole. In the digital economy, however, small companies will have to develop core competencies and collaborate with each other to construct innovative content tailored to consumers' unique tastes if they are to compete efficiently. Customizing each individual bundle will eliminate the free rider problem because each company must provide its best digital content in order to compete with other content providers.

Figure 2 presents the framework for a digital intermediary specializing in multimedia products for children. In this example, parents can specify what educational programs will be presented to their kids, what music videos their kids can watch, and so on. What they get is a customized program bundle that is well suited to their kids in place of a prefixed bundle determined by a cable provider.

There will be competition among intermediaries both at the level of assembling and customizing bundles and at the level of building content components. (Consider, as an example of how this could

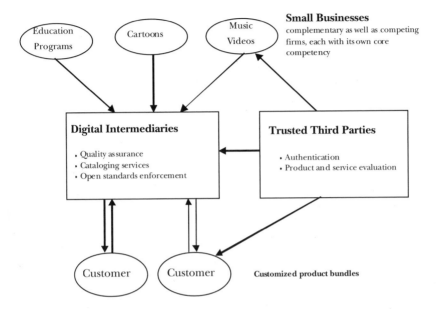

Figure 2 A framework for a digital intermediary.

work, the company Red Hat, which collects a premium for assembling customized versions of Linux, a public-domain operating system whose components are freely available; Red Hat adds value by testing components and using only the ones that are of the highest quality, thus saving users the cost of doing this for themselves.) Since the bundles will be assembled dynamically, firms will easily be able to switch to substitutes and component vendors will need to stay competitive. Thus, an incentive system will be in place that ensures maximum utility for end users.

Trusted Third Parties

Because there are likely to be multiple digital intermediaries providing bundling services, the challenges we outlined above for small companies still need to be addressed. That is, if consumers are to engage in business transactions with a digital intermediary, they must feel confident that the intermediaries are who they claim they are and have a good business reputation. Likewise, digital intermediaries need to feel confident that the content providers are trustworthy players. For convenience, we focus here on the relationship between digital intermediaries and customers; the same issues apply to the relationship between content providers and the digital intermediaries. Trusted Third Parties (TTPs) are a possible solution to problems of authentication and product quality evaluation.

Certification authorities (CAs) have recently emerged to provide authentication services for the digital economy. Major players include VeriSign and GTE CyberTrust. CAs authenticate the identity of each party in a transaction by issuing digital certificates based on technological mechanisms such as the public key cryptography (Schneier 1994) and digital signatures. A certificate is a digitally signed statement by a CA that binds the identity of an individual or organization to a public key. By digitally signing a certificate, a CA vouches for the identity of the public key holder. Digital certificates address some of the major security concerns in online business transactions, namely confidentiality, message integrity, and user authentication. A digital certificate goes a long way toward shoring up consumer confidence.

A digital certificate can be revoked after it is issued. For example, if someone fraudulently gains access to a company's certificate, the CA can revoke the certificate (recording the certificate's serial number in a database that keeps track of all the certificates that have become invalid) as soon as the incident is reported (Ford and Baum 1997). Since certificates must be verified with the issuer before being accepted, the revoked certificate will be easily detected. A stolen certificate therefore quickly loses any value.

One might ask what happens if a business changes its identity after committing a fraud, or if there are significant management changes in a business that could affect its product quality. Strong authentication will help address this issue. TTPs will keep track of the history of certificate holders to make sure they do not change their online identity without securing changes to their certificate stating that this has occurred. In addition, when issuing a certificate to a company, the TTP will tie the management team, key employees, and other critical company information with the certificate and keep track of the company's major business activities. When there are significant management changes in a firm, users will be informed of possible changes in the product or service quality provided by the company. This level of authentication provides extra protection for consumers and endorses businesses that carry the certificate.

Strong authentication services provided by TTPs will be important to digital intermediaries. Carrying a valid digital certificate will help intermediaries overcome initial consumer concern by ensuring that they are who they claim they are. While it vouches for the identity of a certificate holder, however, the current model does not vouch for reputation. Therefore, TTPs need to provide another value-added service: evaluating the product and service quality of digital intermediaries.

For example, BizRate (www.BizRate.com), which calls itself a "trusted infomediary," is a TTP that uses information from consumers to keep track of merchants' reputations. As an independent shopping resource, BizRate evaluates merchants using information provided by actual customers on service attributes such as price, product selection, on-time delivery, and customer support. Only merchants that have undergone a positive evaluation by at least 30 customers are denoted "Customer Certified" (Gold) on BizRate.com. Consumers can check the ratings and review descriptions to find the merchants that best meet their needs. We believe that similar types of TTPs will emerge to establish the reputations of digital intermediaries and digital content providers. The services will be used by consumers to evaluate digital intermediaries and by digital intermediaries to select the best content providers.

Digital Intermediaries

The success of the digital intermediaries depends on the quality of the product bundles they provide to consumers. In addition, intermediaries will need to provide a high degree of product customization, in the form of a wide selection of content providers to meet a wide variety of customer demands.

By offering a digital company's product through their services, intermediaries vouch for the reputation and product quality of that company. This service decreases or even eliminates the need for individual companies to do extensive marketing to build brand equity and reputation, thus saving important resources for product development and innovation.

Small companies can reach a broad set of customers by using intermediaries. Marketing research has shown that renting a reputation—a seller without a brand reputation using reputation spill-over to sell through a reputable seller—is an effective entry strategy (Chu and Chu 1994). In the digital economy, renting a reputation can be used more widely since creators of digital products can be very diverse, and many of them will be small independent players. Investing in reputation building would be a major undertaking, which may not even pay off. Intermediaries, on the other hand, being long-term players, have an incentive to build and maintain a strong reputation.

To provide effective quality assurance to consumers, digital intermediaries need to establish and enforce rules for content creators. By signing up with an intermediary, the content provider guarantees product quality. Deviating would result in being sanctioned by the intermediaries. There are many examples indicating that community standards and extralegal mechanisms work effectively to regulate economic relations (Bernstein 1992; Ellickson 1991). Setting and enforcing quality rules will not only be effective but will be of the utmost importance for ensuring the reputation of the intermediaries.

Interactions between customers and intermediaries will be mediated by directories, catalogue services, and agent-based systems, which are key elements in integrating content and customizing products. Directories, with information on what is available at what location, and what is included in the content, will allow intermediaries to procure and assemble content. Catalogues will allow customers to choose the types of products they wish to purchase. Currently there are several technologies that can be used to build directories and catalogues. For example, the Lightweight Directory Access Protocol (LDAP) (www.umich.edu/~dirsvcs/ldap/) can be used to retrieve and manage a variety of directory information. Resource location standards such as the Resource Description Framework (www.w3.org/RDF/) can be used to describe the content and content relationships available at a particular Web site, and Extensible Markup Language (www.w3.org/XML/) is very flexible in defining new document types.

The catalogues will be dynamically created based on underlying databases available at content providers' sites and will provide an interface that is seamless regardless of the original source or nature of the content. They will provide a vast array of choices that could include a variety of combinations of information components. The agent-based systems will help retrieve information from the catalogues while at the same time assembling profiles of customers. (Incentive systems should be built in to assure customers that such profile information is not abused.) The key to useful agent-based systems and dynamic catalogues is the existence of an adaptive system that can rapidly update the catalogues to reflect individual customer preferences and to make products available on-demand. The agents, in turn, can communicate with each other, ensuring fast dissemination and synchronization of information on demand and supply. Such a seamless flow of information will also lead to efficient content procurement and inventory management.

Public Policy Issues and Future Research

We are still in the earliest moments of an economic revolution. As competition in the electronic market unfolds, a few issues come to mind concerning public policies for small companies and the government's role in helping small companies grow.

First, we need to recognize the tendency for businesses in the online market to grow to achieve economies of scale in the face of expensive infrastructure. Small companies will have to compete through their core competency. Collaborating with other small companies through digital intermediaries may be an effective countermeasure to the huge investment required to set up the technology infrastructure in the digital space. It also compensates for the lack of brand equity and deep pockets.

The second issue is concerned with promoting consumer trust toward small online businesses. Intermediaries are needed to rebalance the playing field and stimulate competition. They should have strong authentication to endorse small companies and quality assurance to protect consumers. This is not only a question of survival for small companies, but also a public policy issue at a larger scale—when there are only a few players in the market, motivation to innovate diminishes. The government needs to recognize the importance of helping small companies build their reputation and establish trust among consumers.

Third, preserving open technology standards should also be a top policy concern. Integrating content, be it software or multimedia objects, from multiple sources requires that content provided by different creators written in different languages for different computing platforms be able to share data and functions. Substitutability of components and bundles will be feasible only if components are interoperable and follow open standards. Conforming to the interoperable standards will generate positive externalities for component vendors as they become candidates for multiple bundles. For the intermediaries, open standards give them a wider range of components to choose from, and make it easier for firms to switch to the bundles they offer. Interfaces between content components should be seamless, and the integration and customization processes should be transparent to customers. Technology compatibility and interoperability are critical, not only to the success of digital intermediaries, but to the wide adoption of electronic commerce in general. Technologies such as Java RMI (Remote Method Invocation) that is not tied to a specific platform or CORBA (Common Object Request Broker Architecture) that is not tied to a specific language or communications protocol are of paramount importance to the future of the digital economy.

The framework we put forward for small digital business raises several research questions, such as the implications of strong authentication, the pricing mechanism for product bundles customized to individual preferences, and the development of technology standards. We believe that these issues are critical to the growth of the digital economy and should be addressed in the near future by the research community as well as by policy makers.

As technology continues to develop, we are likely to see more changes in the economy. How will these changes affect industrial organizational structure? Will the core of the economy shift from large international enterprises to small firms competing and cooperating based on core competencies? Will firms contract in size because coordination costs are significantly lowered by electronic commerce technology? At this stage, the framework we put forth is only a conjecture. Clearly, much empirical research is needed.

References

Acs, Z. J., 1999. "The New American Evolution," in Z. J. Acs, ed., *Are Small Firms Important? Their Role and Impact*, Norwell, MA: Kluwer Academic Publishers.

Adamic, L. A., and B. A. Huberman, 1999. "The Nature of Markets in the World Wide Web," working paper, Xerox Palo Alto Research Center. May. http://www.parc.xerox.com/istl/groups/iea.

Akerlof, G. A., 1970. "The Market for Lemons: Quality Uncertainty and the Market Mechanism," *Quarterly Journal of Economics* 84: 488–500.

Alchian, A. A., and H. Demsetz, 1972. "Production, Information Costs, and Economic Organization," *American Economic Review* 62: 777–795.

Anderson, E., and B. Weitz, 1989. "Determinants of Continuity in Conventional Industrial Channel Dyads," *Marketing Science* 8(4): 310–323.

Barua, A., J. Pinnell, J. Shutter, and A. B. Whinston, 1999. "Measuring the Internet Economy: An Exploratory Study," CREC research report (sponsored by Cisco Systems), June, the Center for Research in Electronic Commerce, University of Texas at Austin. http://crec.bus.utexas.edu.

Beckman, T. N., 1944. "Large versus Small Business after the War," *American Economic Review* 34(1): 94–106.

Bernstein, L., 1992. "Opting Out of the Legal System: Extralegal Contractual Relations in the Diamond Industry," *The Journal of Legal Studies* 21: 115–121.

Choi. S., D. Stahl, and A. B. Whinston, 1997. *Economics of Electronic Commerce*, Reading, MA: Addison-Wesley.

Chu, W., and W. Chu, 1994. "Signaling Quality by Selling through a Reputable Retailer: an Example of Renting the Reputation of another Agent," *Marketing Science* 13(2): 177–189.

Colvin, G., 1999. "How to Be a Great E-CEO," *Fortune*, May 24.

Department of Commerce, 1998. "The Emerging Digital Economy," internal report.

Ellickson, R. C., 1991. *Order without Law*, Cambridge, MA: Harvard University Press.

Ford, W., and M. S. Baum, 1997. *Secure Electronic Commerce: Building the Infrastructure for Digital Signatures & Encryption*, Englewood Cliffs, NJ: Prentice-Hall.

Johnston, J., 1996. "The Statute of Frauds and Business Norms: A Testable Game-theoretic Model," *University of Pennsylvania Law Review* 144(5): 1859–1912.

Malone, T., J. Yates, and R. Benjamin, 1987. "Electronic Markets and Electronic Hierarchies," *Communications of ACM* 30(6): 484–497.

Milgrom, P., D. C. North, and B. R. Weingast, 1990. "The Role of Institutions in the Revival of Trade: The Law Merchant, Private Judges, and the Champagne Fairs," *Economics and Politics* 2(1): 1–23.

OECD Report, 1999. *The Economic and Social Impacts of Electronic Commerce: Preliminary Findings and Research Agenda.*

Parameswaran, M., J. Stallaert, and A.B. Whinston, 1999. "Technological and Organizational Frameworks for Digital Content Provision Industry," working paper, Center for Research in Electronic Commerce, University of Texas at Austin.

Schneier, B., 1994. *Applied Cryptography: Protocols, Algorithms and Source Code in C,* New York: John Wiley.

Smith, A. (1776), *Wealth of Nations* (Oxford University Press edition, 1976).

Small Business, Innovation, and Public Policy in the Information Technology Industry

Josh Lerner

New firms have played a major role in fomenting innovation in information technology. Greenwood and Jovanovic (1999) illustrate these trends dramatically by showing that a group of "IT upstarts"—firms specializing in computer and communications technologies that went public after 1968—now account for over 4% of the total U.S. equity market capitalization. While some of this growth has come at the expense of incumbent information technology firms, the new market value and technological spillovers created by these businesses appear to be substantial.

The role of new firms in the information technology industries has rekindled interest in the relationship between firm characteristics and innovation. Are small businesses more innovative in general? Are high-technology start-ups particularly important? If the answer to either of these questions is yes, how can policymakers encourage such firms?

The relationship between innovation and firm characteristics has been one of the most researched topics in the empirical industrial organization literature. To summarize these discussions and draw implications for policymakers in a few pages is a true challenge! My approach will be to approach the issues selectively. First, I briefly summarize the academic literature on the relationship between firm size and innovation. This work suggests that there is only a very weak relationship connecting firm size, the tendency to undertake R&D, and the effectiveness of research spending. In aggregate, small businesses do not appear to be particularly research-intensive or innovative.

I then turn to one subset of small businesses that does appear to excel at innovation: start-ups backed by venture capital. I highlight some of the contributions of these firms and discuss the reasons for their success. In particular, I highlight the problems posed by the financing of small innovative companies and some of the mechanisms that venture investors employ to guide the innovation process. This will help clarify why venture capital investments are concentrated in information technology industries, and why they appear to spur innovation.

Finally, I consider one specific set of policy issues related to small firms and innovation: recent changes in the intellectual property protection system that appear to favor larger firms. I argue that this is an area that might well reward increased attention by policymakers interested in helping innovative small businesses in information technology and other high-technology industries.

1 Small Business and Innovation

A substantial but largely inconclusive literature examines the relationship between firm size and innovation. These studies have been handicapped by the difficulty of measuring innovative inputs and outputs, as well as the challenges of creating a sample that is free of selection biases and other estimation problems. For a detailed review of this literature, the interested reader can turn to surveys by Baldwin and Scott (1987) and Cohen and Levin (1989).

Much of this work has sought to relate measures of innovative discoveries—R&D expenditures, patents, inventions, or other measures—to firm size. Initial studies focused on the largest manufacturing firms; more recent work has used larger samples and more disaggregated data (e.g., studies employing data on firms' specific lines of business). Despite the improved methodology of recent studies, the results have remained inconclusive: even when a significant relationship between firm size and innovation has been found, it has had little economic significance. For instance, Cohen, Levin, and Mowery (1987) concluded that a doubling of firm size only increased the ratio of R&D to sales by 0.2%.

One of the relatively few empirical regularities emerging from studies of technological innovation is the critical role played by small firms and new entrants in certain industries. The role of entrants—typically *de novo* start-ups—in emerging industries was highlighted, for instance, in the pioneering case study-based research of Jewkes, Sawers, and Stillerman (1958).

Acs and Audretsch (1988) examined this question more systematically. They documented that the contribution of small firms to innovation was a function of industry conditions: the contribution was greatest in immature industries that were relatively unconcentrated. These findings suggested that entrepreneurs and small firms often played a key role in observing where new technologies could be applied to meet customer needs and in introducing products rapidly. These patterns are also predicted in several models of technological competition, many of which were reviewed in Reinganum (1989) as well in the organizational behavior literature (e.g., Henderson 1993).

The 1990s have seen several dramatic illustrations of these patterns. Two potentially revolutionary areas of technological innovation—biotechnology and the Internet—were pioneered by smaller entrants rather than by established drug companies or mainframe computer manufacturers. By and large, these small firms did not invent the key genetic engineering techniques or Internet protocols. The bulk of the enabling technologies were developed with federal funds at academic institutions and research laboratories. It was the small entrants, however, who were the first to seize upon the commercial opportunities of the innovations.

2 Venture Capital and Innovation[1]

One set of small firms appears to have had a disproportionate effect on innovation: those backed by venture capitalists. (Venture capital can be defined as equity or equity-linked investments in young, privately held companies, where the investor is a financial intermediary who is typically actively as a director, advisor, or even manager of the firm.) While venture capitalists fund only a few hundred of the nearly one million firms started in the United States each year, these firms have a disproportionate impact on technological innovation.

This claim is supported by a variety of evidence. One measure, while crude, is provided by the firms that "graduate" to the public marketplace. In the past two decades, about one-third of the companies going public (weighted by value) have been backed by venture investors.

A second way to assess these claims is to examine *which* firms have been funded. Venture capitalists, while contributing a relatively modest share of the total financing, provided critical early capital and guidance to many of the new firms in such emerging industries as biotechnology, computer networking, and the Internet. In some cases, these new firms have used the capital, expertise, and contacts provided by their venture capital investors to establish themselves as market leaders. In other instances, they were acquired by larger corporations, or entered into licensing arrangements with such corporations. In the biotechnology industry, for example, venture capitalists provided only a small fraction of the external financing raised,[2] and only 450 out of 1500 existing firms received venture financing through 1995. These venture-backed firms, however, accounted for over 85% of the patents awarded and drugs approved for marketing. Similarly, venture capitalists have aggressively backed firms in information technology industries, which accounted for 60% of all venture disbursements in 1998.[3] These include many of the most successful firms in the industry, such as Amazon.com, Cisco Systems, Microsoft, Intel, and Yahoo!.

A final way to assess the impact of the venture industry is to consider the impact of venture-backed firms. A mid-1996 survey by the venture organization Kleiner, Perkins, Caufield, and Byers found that the firms that the partnership had financed since its inception in 1971 had created 131,000 jobs, generated $44 billion in annual revenues, and had $84 billion in market capitalization (Peltz 1996). While Kleiner, Perkins is one of the most successful venture capital groups, the results are suggestive of the overall impact of the industry.

Kortum and Lerner (1998) examined the influence of venture capital on patented inventions in the United States across twenty industries over three decades. What they found was that the amount of venture capital activity in an industry significantly increases its rate of patenting. While the ratio of venture capital to R&D has averaged less than 3% in recent years, their estimates suggest that venture capital accounts for about 15% of industrial innovations. (The authors addressed the possibility that their results might be an artifact of the use of patent counts by demonstrating similar patterns when other measures of innovation are used in a sample of 530 venture-backed and non-venture-backed firms. They used several measures to address possible concerns about causality, including exploiting a 1979 policy shift that spurred venture capital fundraising.)

Lending particular relevance to an examination of these firms is the tremendous boom in the U.S. venture capital industry. The pool of venture partnerships has grown tenfold in the last two decades, from under $4 billion in 1978 to about $75 billion at the end of 1999. Venture capital's recent growth has outstripped that of almost every other class of financial product.

It is worth underscoring that the tremendous success of venture-backed firms has not happened by accident. The interactions between venture capitalists and the entrepreneurs they finance are often complex. They can be understood, however, as a response to the challenges posed by the financing of emerging growth companies. Entrepreneurs rarely have the capital to see their ideas to fruition and must rely on outside financiers. Meanwhile, those who control capital—for instance, pension fund trustees and university overseers—are unlikely to have the time or expertise to invest directly in young or restructuring firms. Some entrepreneurs might turn to other financing sources, such as bank loans or the issuance of public stock, to meet their needs. But because of four key factors, some of the most potentially profitable and exciting firms would be unable to access financing if venture capital did not exist.

The first of these factors is uncertainty, which is a measure of the array of potential outcomes for a company or project. The wider the dispersion of potential outcomes, the greater the uncertainty. By their very nature, young companies are associated with significant levels of uncertainty. Will their research program or new product succeed? How will their rivals respond? High uncertainty means that investors and entrepreneurs cannot confidently predict what the company will look like in the future.

Uncertainty affects the willingness of investors to contribute capital, the desire of suppliers to extend credit, and the decisions of a firm's managers. If managers are averse to taking risks, it may be difficult to induce them to make the right decisions. Conversely, if entrepreneurs are overly optimistic, then investors want to curtail various actions. Uncertainty also affects the timing of investment. Should investors contribute all the capital at the beginning, or should they stage their investment through time? Investors need to know how information-gathering activities can address these concerns and when they should be undertaken.

The second factor is asymmetric information (or information disparities). Because of their day-to-day involvement with the firm, entrepreneurs know more about their company's prospects than investors, suppliers, or strategic partners. Various problems develop in settings where asymmetric information is prevalent. For instance, entrepreneurs may take detrimental actions that investors cannot observe—perhaps undertaking a riskier strategy than initially suggested or not working as hard as investors expect. Entrepreneurs might also invest in projects that build up their reputations at the investors' expense.

Asymmetric information can also lead to selection problems. Entrepreneurs may exploit the fact that they know more about the project or their abilities than investors do. Investors may find it difficult to distinguish between competent entrepreneurs and incompetent ones. Without the ability to screen out unacceptable projects and entrepreneurs, investors are unable to make efficient and appropriate decisions.

The third factor affecting a firm's corporate and financial strategy is the nature of its assets. Firms that have tangible assets such as machines, buildings, land, or physical inventory may find financing easier to obtain or may be able to obtain more favorable terms. Absconding with a firm's source of value is more difficult when it relies on physical assets. When the most important assets are intangible, such as trade secrets, raising outside financing from traditional sources may be more challenging.

Market conditions also play a key role in determining the difficulty of financing firms. Both capital and product markets may be subject to substantial variations. The supply of capital from public investors and the price at which this capital is available may vary dramatically. These changes may be a response to regulatory edicts or shifts in investors' perceptions of future profitability. Similarly, the nature of product markets may vary due to shifts in the intensity of competition with rivals or in the nature of the customers. If there is intense competition or a great deal of uncertainty about the size of the potential market, firms may find it very difficult to raise capital from traditional sources.

Venture capitalists have a variety of mechanisms at their disposal to address these changing factors. They will invest in stages, often at increasing valuations. Each refinancing is tied to a re-evaluation of the company and its prospects. In these financings, they will employ complex financing mechanisms, often hybrid securities such as convertible preferred equity or convertible debt. These financial structures can potentially screen out overconfident or underqualified entrepreneurs and reduce the venture capitalists' risks. They will also shift the mixture of investors from whom a firm acquires capital. Each source—private equity investors, corporations, and the public markets—may be appropriate for a firm at different points in its life. Venture capitalists provide not only introductions to these other sources of capital but certification— a "stamp of approval" that addresses the concerns of other investors. Finally, once the investment is made, they monitor and work with the entrepreneurs to ensure that the right operational and strategic decisions are made and implemented.

3 Innovation, Small Business, and Public Policy

If small firms—or even some subset of small firms—are playing an important role in the innovation process, one policy goal should be to address threats to their future development. This is particularly true of threats that have been created by misguided government policies, however good the intentions of their designers. One area that I believe deserves particular attention is patents, the key mechanism for protecting intellectual property.

The U.S. patent system has undergone a profound shift over the past fifteen years. The strength of patent protection has been dramatically bolstered, and both large and small firms are devoting considerably more effort to seeking patent protection and defending their patents in the courts. Many in the patent community— U.S. Patent and Trademark Office (USPTO) officials, the patent bar, and corporate patent staff—have welcomed these changes. But viewed more broadly, the reforms of the patent system and the consequent growth of patent litigation have created a substantial "innovation tax" that afflicts some of America's most important and creative small firms.[4]

Almost all formal disputes involving issued patents are tried in the federal judicial system. The initial litigation must be undertaken in a district court. Prior to 1982, appeals of patent cases were heard in the appellate courts of the various circuits. These differed considerably in their interpretation of patent law. Because few appeals of patent cases were heard by the Supreme Court, substantial differences persisted, leading to widespread "forum shopping" by litigants.

In 1982, the U.S. Congress established a centralized appellate court for patent cases, the Court of Appeals for the Federal Circuit (CAFC). As Robert Merges (1992) observes, "While the CAFC was ostensibly formed strictly to unify patent doctrine, it was no doubt hoped by some (and expected by others) that the new court would make subtle alterations in the doctrinal fabric, with an eye to enhancing the patent system. To judge by results, that is exactly what happened." The CAFC's rulings have been more "propatent" than the previous courts: whereas the circuit courts had affirmed 62% of district court findings of patent infringement in the three decades prior to the creation of the CAFC, the CAFC in its first eight years affirmed 90% of such decisions (Koenig 1980, Harmon 1991).

The strengthening of patent law has not gone unnoticed by corporations. Over the past decade, patents awarded to U.S. corporations have almost doubled. Furthermore, the willingness of firms to litigate patents has increased considerably. The number of patent suits instituted in the federal courts has increased from 795 in 1981 to 1530 in 1997; adversarial proceedings within the USPTO have increased from 246 in 1980 to almost 500 in 1997 (Administrative Office, various years; U.S. Department of Commerce, various years). My analysis of litigation by firms based in Middlesex County, Massachusetts, suggests that six intellectual property-related suits are filed for every one hundred patent awards to corporations (Lerner 1995). These suits lead to significant expenditures by firms. Based on historical costs, I estimate that patent litigation begun in 1991 will lead to total legal expenditures (in 1991 dollars) of over $1 billion, a substantial amount relative to the $3.7 billion spent by U.S. firms on basic research in 1991. Litigation also leads to substantial indirect costs. The discovery process is likely to require the alleged infringer to produce extensive documentation and to allow time-consuming depositions from employees, and may generate unfavorable publicity. An infringer's officers and directors may also be held individually liable.

As firms have realized the value of their patent positions, they have begun reviewing their stockpiles of issued patents. Several companies, including Texas Instruments, Intel, Wang Laboratories, and Digital Equipment, have established groups that approach rivals to demand royalties on old patent awards. In many cases, they have been successful in extracting license agreements or past royalties. For example, Texas Instruments is estimated to have netted $257 million in 1991 from patent licenses and settlements resulting from their general counsel's aggressive enforcement policy (Rosen 1992).

Particularly striking, practitioner accounts suggest, has been the growth of litigation—and threats of litigation—between large and small firms.[5] This trend is disturbing. While litigation is clearly a necessary mechanism to defend property rights, the proliferation of such suits may be leading to transfers of financial resources from some of the youngest and most innovative firms to more established, better capitalized firms. Even if the target firm feels that it does not infringe, it may choose to settle rather than fight. It either may be unable to raise the capital to finance a protracted court battle, or else may believe that the publicity associated with the litigation will depress the valuation of its equity.

These considerations may also lead small firms to reduce or alter their investment in R&D. A 1990 survey of 376 firms found that the time and expense of intellectual property litigation was a major factor in decisions concerning the pursuit of innovation in almost twice as many firms with under 500 employees as in larger businesses (Koen 1990). These claims are also supported by my own study of the patenting behavior of new biotechnology firms that have different litigation costs (Lerner 1995). I found that firms with high litigation costs are less likely to patent in subclasses with many other awards, particularly those of firms with low litigation costs.

These effects have been particularly pernicious in emerging industries. Chronically strained for resources, USPTO officials are unlikely to assign many patent examiners to emerging technologies in advance of a wave of applications. As patent applications begin flowing in, the USPTO frequently finds it difficult to retain the few examiners skilled in the new technologies. Companies are likely to hire away all but the least able examiners. Examiners are valuable not only for their knowledge of the USPTO examination procedure in the new technology, but also for their understanding of what other patent applications are in process but not awarded. (U.S. patent applications are held confidential until the time of award.) As a result, many of the examinations in emerging technologies are performed under severe time pressures by inexperienced examiners. Consequently, awards of patents in several critical new technologies have been delayed and highly inconsistent. These ambiguities have created ample opportunities for firms that litigate their patent awards aggressively. The clearest examples of this problem are the biotechnology and software industries. In these industries, examples abound where inexperienced examiners have granted patents on technologies that were widely diffused but not previously patented (many examples are chronicled in Aharonian 1999).

It might be asked why policymakers have not addressed the deleterious effects of patent policy changes. The difficulties that federal officials have faced in reforming the patent system are perhaps best illustrated by the efforts to simplify one of the most arcane aspects of the system, the "first-to-invent" policy. With the exception of the Philippines, all other nations award patents to firms that are the first to file for patent protection. The United States, however, has clung to the first-to-invent system. In the United States, a patent will be awarded to the party who can demonstrate (through laboratory notebooks and other evidence) that he or she was the initial discoverer of a new invention, even if he or she did not file for patent protection until after others did (within certain limits). A frequently invoked argument for the first-to-invent system is that this provides protection for small inventors, who may take longer to translate a discovery into a completed patent application.

While this argument is initially compelling, the reality is quite different. Disputes over priority of invention are resolved through a proceeding known as an interference before the USPTO's Board of Patent Appeals and Interferences. This is a hearing to determine which inventor made the discovery first.

The interference process has been characterized as "an archaic procedure, replete with traps for the unwary" (Calvert 1980). Interferences consume a considerable amount of resources: adjudication of an average interference is estimated to cost over one hundred thousand dollars (Kingston 1992). Yet in recent years, in only about 55 cases annually has the party that was second-to-file been determined to have been the first-to-invent (Calvert and Sofocleous 1992). Thus, the United States persists in this complex, costly, and idiosyncratic system in order to reverse the priority of 0.03% of the patent applications filed each year.

Yet this system has proved highly resistant to change. Proposals have been offered to shift the United States to a first-to-file system at least since 1967. Recently, USPTO Commissioner Bruce Lehman was forced to withdraw such a proposal. While the protest over his initiative—as in earlier reform attempts—was led by advocates for small inventors, it is difficult not to conclude that the greatest beneficiary from the first-to-invent system is the small subset of the patent bar that specializes in interference law.

It is somewhat puzzling that independent inventors, who are generally unable to afford costly litigation, have been so active in supporting the retention of first-to-invent. A frequently voiced complaint is that small inventors take longer to prepare patent applications, and hence would lose out to better-financed rivals, in a first-to-file world, but this argument appears to be specious for several reasons. First, economically important discoveries are typically the subject of patent filings in a number of countries. Thus, there is already enormous pressure to file quickly. Second, recent reforms of the U.S. system have created a new provisional patent application, which is much simpler to file than a full-fledged application. Finally, as former Commissioner Lehman notes, many of the most vocal independent inventors opposing patent reform are "weekend hobbyists [rather than representatives of] knowl-edge-based industries" (Chartrand 1995).

This case suggests several reasons for the failure of federal reform efforts. First, the issues are complex and sometimes difficult to understand. Simplistic claims frequently cloud discussions. For instance, because firms use patents to protect innovations, it is often argued that a stronger patent system will lead to more innovation. Second, the people with the greatest economic stake in retaining a litigious and complex patent system—the patent bar—have proven to be a powerful lobby. The efforts of the interference bar to retain first-to-invent is a prime example. Finally, the top executives of technology-intensive firms have not mounted an effective campaign around these issues. The reason may be that the companies that are most adversely affected are small, capital-constrained firms that do not have time for major lobbying efforts.

An important policy lesson from this analysis is that we should avoid taking steps in the name of increasing competitiveness that actually interfere with the workings of innovative small businesses. The 1982 reform of the patent litigation process appears to have had exactly this sort of unintended consequence.

Acknowledgments

I thank Paul Gompers and Jenny Lanjouw for helpful discussions. This paper was prepared for the conference "Understanding the Digital Economy: Data, Tools, and Research," and is based in part on Gompers and Lerner (1999) and Lerner (1999).

Notes

1. Unless otherwise cited, the empirical data in this section is from Gompers and Lerner (1999).

2. Expressed in 1995 dollars, venture capitalists provided approximately $7 billion to biotechnology firms between 1978 and 1995. The total financing raised from other sources was about $30 billion (again in 1995 dollars). (See Lerner and Merges 1998.)

3. For a detailed tabulation, see National Venture Capital Association (1999).

4. One might ask why, if these obstacles are important, the share of R&D expenditures being undertaken by small firms has substantially increased in

recent years. The rapid pace of change in many facets of information technology may have created more opportunities for newer organizations. Many observers have noted the difficulties that established organizations have had in responding to rapid technological change: for one example, see Michael Jensen's (1993) discussion of the "major inefficiencies [that exist] in the R&D spending decisions of a substantial number of firms."

5. Several examples are discussed in Chu (1992). Examples may include the dispute between Cetus Corporation and New England Biolabs regarding the taq DNA polymerase and that between Texas Instruments and LSI Logic regarding semiconductor technology.

References

Acs, Zoltan J., and David B. Audretsch, 1988. "Innovation in Large and Small Firms: An Empirical Analysis," *American Economic Review*, 78: 678–690.

Administrative Office of the United States Courts, various years. *Annual Report of the Director*, Washington: U.S. Government Printing Office.

Aharonian, Gregory, 1999. "Internet Patent News Service," http://www.bustpatents.com.

Baldwin, William L., and John T. Scott, 1987. *Market Structure and Technological Change*, Chur, Switzerland: Harwood Academic Publishers.

Calvert, Ian A., 1980. "An Overview of Interference Practice," *Journal of the Patent Office Society*, 62: 290–308.

Calvert, Ian A., and Michael Sofocleous, 1992. "Interference Statistics for Fiscal Years 1989 to 1991," *Journal of the Patent and Trademark Office Society*, 74: 822–826.

Chartrand, Sabra, 1995. "Facing High-Tech Issues, New Patents Chief in Reinventing a Staid Agency," *New York Times*, July 14, p. 17.

Chu, Michael P., 1992. "An Antitrust Solution to the New Wave of Predatory Patent Infringement Litigation," *William and Mary Law Review*, 33: 1341–1368.

Cohen, Wesley M., and Richard C. Levin, 1989. "Empirical Studies of Innovation and Market Structure," in Richard Schmalensee and Robert D. Willig, editors, *Handbook of Industrial Organization*, vol. II (New York: North-Holland).

Cohen, Wesley M., Richard C. Levin, and David C. Mowery, 1987. "Firm Size and R&D Intensity: A Re-Examination," *Journal of Industrial Economics*, 35: 543–563.

Gompers, Paul A., and Josh Lerner, 1999. *The Venture Capital Cycle*, Cambridge: MIT Press.

Greenwood, Jeremy, and Boyan Jovanovic, 1999. "The IT Revolution and the Stock Market," *American Economic Review Papers and Proceedings*, 89: 116–122.

Harmon, Robert L., 1991. *Patents and the Federal Circuit*, Washington: Bureau of National Affairs.

Henderson, Rebecca, 1993. "Underinvestment and Incompetence as Responses to Radical Innovation: Evidence from the Photolithographic Alignment Equipment Industry," *Rand Journal of Economics*, 24: 248–270.

Jensen, Michael C., 1993. "Presidential Address: The Modern Industrial Revolution, Exit, and the Failure of Internal Control Systems," *Journal of Finance*, 48: 831–880.

Jewkes, John, David Sawers, and Richard Stillerman, 1958. *The Sources of Invention*, London: St.Martins Press.

Kingston, William, 1992. "Is the United States Right about 'First-to-Invent'?," *European Intellectual Property Review*, 7: 223–226.

Koen, Mary S., 1990. *Survey of Small Business Use of Intellectual Property Protection: Report of a Survey Conducted by MO-SCI Corporation for the Small Business Administration*, Rolla, Missouri: MO-SCI Corp..

Koenig, Gloria K., 1980. *Patent Invalidity: A Statistical and Substantive Analysis*, New York: Clark Boardman.

Kortum, Samuel, and Josh Lerner, 1998. "Does Venture Capital Spur Innovation?," National Bureau of Economic Research Working Paper No. 6846.

Lerner, Josh, 1995. "Patenting in the Shadow of Competitors," *Journal of Law and Economics*, 38: 563–595.

Lerner, Josh, 1999. "Small Businesses, Innovation, and Public Policy," in Zoltan Acs, editor, *Are Small Firms Important?*, New York: Kluwer Academic Publishing.

Lerner, Josh, and Robert Merges, 1998. "The Control of Strategic Alliances: An Empirical Analysis of Biotechnology Collaborations," *Journal of Industrial Economics* (Special Issue on "Inside the Pin Factory: Empirical Studies Augmented by Manager Interviews."), 46: 125–156.

Merges, Robert P., 1992. *Patent Law and Policy*, Charlottesville, Virginia: Michie Company.

National Venture Capital Association, 1999. *1999 National Venture Capital Association Yearbook*, Arlington, Virginia: NVCA.

Peltz, Michael, 1996. "High Tech's Premier Venture Capitalist," *Institutional Investor*, 30 (June): 89–98.

Reinganum, Jennifer R., 1989. "The Timing of Innovation: Research, Development and Diffusion," in Richard Schmalensee and Robert D. Willig, editors, *Handbook of Industrial Organization*, vol. I (New York: North-Holland).

Rosen, Miriam, 1992. "Texas Instruments' $250 Million-a-Year Profit Center," *American Lawyer*, 14 (March): 56–63.

U.S. Department of Commerce, Patent and Trademark Office, various years. *Annual Report of the Commissioner*, Washington: U.S. Government Printing Office.

Employment, Workforce, and Access

Technological Change, Computerization, and the Wage Structure

Lawrence F. Katz

Wage inequality and educational wage differentials have expanded substantially in the United States over the past two decades. This widening of the wage structure has coincided with the rapid computerization of the workplace. Thus, it is not surprising that many labor market analysts have tried to draw a causal connection between rising earnings inequality and increases in the growth rate of the relative demand for more-skilled workers driven by technological and organizational changes associated with the computer revolution (e.g., Bound and Johnson 1992; Krueger 1993). Such inferences follow a venerable and fruitful tradition extending back to Paul Douglas (1926) and Jan Tinbergen (1975) of viewing the evolution of the wage structure as depending (at least partially) on a race between technological development and educational advance. This hypothesis implies that improvements in access to postsecondary schooling and appropriate skills training may be necessary if the productivity benefits of the new technologies associated with the digital economy are to be more widely shared.

Two key pieces of evidence are often cited as being strongly suggestive of an integral role for skill-biased technological change in the recent rise in U.S. wage inequality.[1] The first is that the relative employment of more-educated workers and nonproduction workers has increased rapidly within detailed industries and within establishments in the United States during the 1980s and 1990s, despite the sharp rise in the relative wages of these groups (Autor, Katz, and Krueger 1998; Lawrence and Slaughter 1993;

Dunne, Haltiwanger, and Troske 1996). This pattern indicates strong within-industry demand shifts favoring the more skilled. Similar patterns of within-industry increases in the proportion of "skilled" workers are apparent in most other advanced nations (Berman, Bound, and Machin 1998; Machin and Van Reenen 1998). Skill-biased technological change (broadly interpreted to be associated with both new production technologies and organizational innovations) is a natural possibility for such unexplained within-sector growth in the demand for skill.[2]

The second piece of evidence from econometric and case-study research is that the relative utilization of more-skilled workers is strongly positively correlated with capital intensity and the introduction of new technologies (Bartel and Lichtenberg 1987; Doms, Dunne, and Troske 1997; Levy and Murnane 1996). These findings imply that physical capital and new technologies are relative complements with more-skilled workers. Such evidence is certainly consistent with the view that the spread of computer technologies has contributed to rapid increases in the demand for skill in recent decades.

Evidence of capital-skill complementarity and rapid skill-biased technological advance is apparent throughout the twentieth century, even in periods of stable or narrowing educational and occupational wage differentials. For example, Goldin and Katz (1998) found that capital-deepening, the diffusion of technologies using purchased electricity, and the introduction of continuous-process and batch-production methods in manufacturing greatly increased the relative demand for white-collar workers and more-educated production workers from 1909 to 1929, but wage differentials by skill actually narrowed during this period. Goldin and Katz (1995, 1999) presented evidence indicating that the rapid increase in the supply of skills arising from the high school movement prevented a rise in wage inequality during the skill-biased technological revolution associated with the electrification of the workplace. Longer-term historical comparisons of changes in technology, the demand for and supply of skills, and wage inequality are prerequisites for a proper assessment of the labor market impacts of computerization and the digital economy.

Although technological advance has clearly contributed substantially to secular increases in the demand for skill over the last century, it is less clear that the large increase in wage inequality of the last two decades necessarily implies acceleration in the pace of demand shifts against less-skilled workers arising from the computer revolution. A slowdown in the rate of growth of the relative supply of more-educated workers from the 1970s to the 1980s may have been an important factor (Katz and Murphy 1992; Murphy and Welch 1992). And much work suggests that changes in pay-setting norms and labor market institutions (e.g., declining union strength and an erosion of the value of the minimum wage in the 1980s) also contributed to the magnitude of recent increases in U.S. wage inequality (DiNardo, Fortin, and Lemieux 1996).

This chapter assesses the burgeoning literature on the role of the spread of computers and computer-based technologies on changes in the demand for skill and in wage inequality over the past two decades.[3] Section I summarizes the nature and magnitude of recent changes in the U.S. wage structure. Section II places these changes into a longer-term historical perspective and examines the evolution of the wage structure and the relative demand and supply for skills from 1940 to 1998. Sharp secular increases in the relative demand for more-educated workers are apparent since 1950 with evidence of some acceleration of such demand shifts with the spread of computers in the 1980s and some slowdown with the evolution of the digital economy in the 1990s. Section III more directly examines the evidence on the spread of computers in the workplace and estimates of the impacts of new computer technologies on the relative demands for different types of workers. Much research has found that increases in the demand for more-educated workers have been concentrated in the most computer-intensive sectors of the economy over the past two decades. But the extent to which this relationship represents a causal effect of computerization on skill demands is difficult to evaluate in a convincing way. Section IV concludes and speculates on new data collection strategies and empirical approaches that might improve our understanding of the labor market consequences of the digital economy.

I Recent Changes in the U.S. Wage Structure

Disparities in the economic fortunes of American families—as measured by income, consumption, and wealth—have increased significantly over the past twenty-five years. Economic inequality in terms of wages, family income, and wealth reached higher levels in the mid-1990s than at any time in (at least) the past sixty years (Goldin and Katz 1999; Wolff 1995, 1998). Labor market changes that have greatly increased overall wage dispersion and shifted wage and employment opportunities in favor of the more educated and more skilled have played an integral role in this process. Many researchers using a variety of data sets—including both household and establishment surveys—have documented these changes and found that wage inequality and skill differentials increased sharply in the United States from the late 1970s to the mid-1990s.[4] While there is much debate about the causes of changes in the wage structure and earnings inequality, there exists substantial agreement on the "facts" that need to be explained.

Recent changes in the U.S. wage structure can be summarized as follows:

• From the 1970s to the mid-1990s wage dispersion increased dramatically for both men and women. The weekly earnings of a full-time, full-year worker in the 90th percentile of the U.S. earnings distribution (someone whose earnings exceeded those of 90 percent of all workers) relative to a worker in the 10th percentile (someone whose earnings exceeded those of just 10 percent of all workers) grew by approximately 45 percent for men and 35 percent for women from 1971 to 1995. Earnings inequality increased even more dramatically if one includes the very top end (top 1 percent) of the distribution. This pattern of rising wage inequality was not offset and actually appears to have been reinforced by changes in working conditions and nonwage compensation (Hamermesh 1999; Pierce 1999). Recent evidence indicates that the U.S. wage structure narrowed slightly from 1996 to 1998 (Bernstein and Mishel 1999).

• Wage differentials by education and occupation increased. The labor market returns to years of formal schooling, workplace training, and computer skills appear to have increased in the 1980s and early 1990s. The earnings of young college graduates increased by 33 percent relative to those of young high school graduates from 1979 to 1995. Wage differentials by age (experience) have expanded for non-college-educated workers. But gender wage differentials have narrowed sharply since 1979.

• Wage dispersion expanded within demographic and skill groups. The wages of individuals of the same age, education, and sex and those working in the same industry and occupation are much more unequal today than twenty-five years ago.

• Increased cross-sectional earnings inequality has not been offset by increased earnings mobility.[5] Permanent and transitory components of earnings variation have risen by similar amounts (Gottschalk and Moffitt 1994). This implies that year-to-year earnings instability has also increased.

• Since these wage structure changes have occurred in a period of sluggish mean real wage growth (deflating wages by official consumer price indices), the real earnings of less-educated and lower-paid workers appear to have declined relative to those of analogous workers two decades ago. The employment rates of less-educated and minority males fell substantially from the early 1970s to the early 1990s (Murphy and Topel 1997). The real wages and employment rates for disadvantaged workers have started to improve over the past few years.

The rise in U.S. wage dispersion has involved both large increases in educational wage differentials and a sharp growth in within-group (or residual) wage inequality. The overall spreading out of the U.S. wage distribution for men and women from 1971 to 1995 is illustrated in figure 1 using data on real weekly wages of full-time, full-year workers from the March Current Population Survey (CPS).[6] The figure shows an almost linear spreading out of the wage distributions for both men and women, substantial gains of women on men throughout the wage distribution, and declines in real earnings for males below the 60th percentile.

The timing of overall rising wage inequality (as measured by the ratio of the wages of the 90th percentile worker to those of the 10th percentile worker) for men and women is illustrated in figure 2. Rising wage inequality (driven initially by increases in within-group

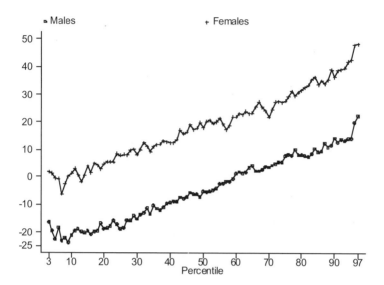

Figure 1 Percentage Change in Real Weekly Wage by Percentile, 1971–1995. Source: Full-time, full-year wage and salary workers from the March Current Population Surveys, 1972–1996. Wages are deflated by the personal consumption expenditures deflator of the national income accounts. See Katz and Autor (1999) for detailed information on the sample selection and data processing procedures.

inequality) began in the 1970s for men. The period from 1980 to 1985, marked by a deep recession and large decline in manufacturing employment, was the period of most rapid growth of wage inequality. The rate of growth of wage inequality appears to have slowed down in the 1990s. Figure 3 combines men and women and presents the evolution of the real hourly wage of 90th, 50th, and 10th percentile workers from 1973 to 1998. The figure highlights the widening of the wage structure in the 1980s as well as some narrowing combined with rapid real wage growth since 1996.

It is sometimes argued that the large increases in wage and family income inequality over the last two decades have had only small consequences for economic welfare because of the large amount of economic mobility in the United States. Although year-to-year earnings mobility is substantial, the evidence from multiple data sources shows no increase in the rate of earnings mobility in the United States over recent decades (Katz and Autor 1999). This

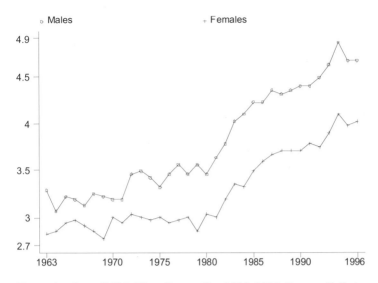

Figure 2 Overall U.S. Wage Inequality, 1963–1996. Source: Full-time, full-year wage and salary workers from the March Current Population Surveys, 1964–1997. The 90-10 wage ratio is the ratio of the weekly earnings of the worker in the 90th percentile of the earnings distribution to the weekly earnings of the worker in the 10th percentile.

means that increases in cross-sectional wage inequality also translate into large increases in permanent (or lifetime) inequality.

A well-known analogy can illuminate the nature of the increase in U.S. wage inequality (Condon and Sawhill 1992; Gottschalk and Danziger 1998). Wage inequality at a point in time is analogous to the situation of a group of people living in an apartment building with units that vary widely in quality. Each individual is assumed to have a one-year lease on a unit, so that the apartment dwellers have unequal accommodations in any given year. Earnings mobility is akin to movement between different apartment units. A substantial fraction of individuals switch apartment units both up and down the quality spectrum each year. But one should not overstate the degree of earnings mobility: those in the top quintile tend to stay in nice apartments, and those in the bottom quintile only rarely make it into the upper units. The rise in wage inequality of the last two decades can be modeled as increased disparities in the quality of the different apartment units: the penthouse has become more

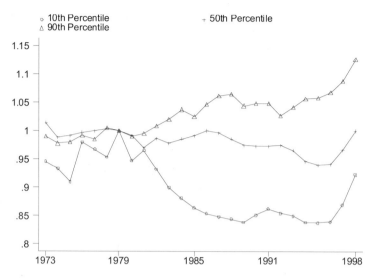

Figure 3 Indexed Real Hourly Wage by Percentile, 1973–1998 (1979=1). Source: Data on hourly wages by decile for all workers are from the May CPS samples for 1973–1978 and from the CPS Merged Outgoing Rotation Group samples for 1979–1998. Jared Bernstein of the Economic Policy Institute provided the underlying data. Nominal wages are deflated by the personal consumption expenditures deflator from the national income accounts. The real wage relative to 1979 is the ratio of the real wage in that year to the real wage in 1979 at the same percentile in the wage distribution.

luxurious, with a better view and upgraded furniture, the middle units are largely unchanged, and the lower units have deteriorated markedly. Since the rate of earnings mobility has not increased and the disparity in apartments has increased, inequality measured over multiple years will increase.[7] A rise in apartment disparities with constant mobility means an increase in the welfare consequences of the rank of the apartment unit to which one gets allocated.

Four primary (and partially complementary) explanations have been offered for the striking increase in wage inequality and returns to skill in the 1980s and early 1990s. The first attributes the primary role to increases in the rate of growth of the relative demand for highly educated and more-skilled workers arising from skill-biased technological changes driven by the diffusion of computer-based technologies (Bound and Johnson 1992; Berman,

Bound, and Machin 1998). The second focuses on the role of globalization pressures (particularly increased trade with less-developed countries and greater foreign outsourcing) in reducing production employment and shrinking the relative demand for the less educated, leading to the loss of wage premia (labor rents) to some blue-collar worker (Borjas and Ramey 1995; Wood 1994; Feenstra and Hanson 1999). The third emphasizes a slowdown in the rate of growth of the relative supply of skills because of the decline in the size of entering labor market cohorts in the 1980s and an increased rate of unskilled immigration (Katz and Murphy 1992; Murphy, Riddell, and Romer 1998; Borjas, Freeman, and Katz 1997). The fourth explanation emphasizes changes in labor market institutions, including the decline in unionization and the value of the minimum wage (DiNardo, Fortin, and Lemieux 1996; Lee 1999).

Sizeable and somewhat accelerated demand shifts favoring more-skilled workers, a reduction in the rate of growth of the relative supply of more-educated workers, and institutional changes all appear to have contributed to the large increase in U.S. wage inequality and educational wage differentials over the past two decades (Katz and Autor 1999). Trade with less-developed countries and outsourcing do not appear to be large enough to be the major culprit (Borjas, Freeman, and Katz 1997; Berman, Bound, and Griliches 1994). Moreover, the slowdown in the growth of wage inequality in the 1990s is not consistent with a major role for trade and outsourcing since these factors have grown much more rapidly in the 1990s than in the 1980s.

II The Relative Supply of and Demand for Skills, 1940–1998

Our understanding of the extent to which the large growth in U.S. wage inequality and educational wage differentials since the 1970s is driven by a technology-based acceleration of relative demand shifts favoring more-skilled workers can be enhanced by examining the evolution of the wage structure and the demand for and supply of skills over a longer time period. Although it is not possible to measure changes in the price and quantity of all skills (many of which are unobservable in available data sets), one can put together reasonably consistent data on the relative quantities and wages of workers by education from 1940 to 1998.

Table 1 displays the evolution of the educational composition of aggregate U.S. labor input (for those aged 18 to 65 years) measured in full-time equivalents (total hours worked) and of the college/high school wage ratio from 1940 to 1998.[8] The educational attainment of the work force increased rapidly over this 58-year period, with a more than fourfold increase in the share of hours worked by those with at least some college. Despite the large increase in the relative supply of the more educated, the college/high school wage differential has grown markedly since 1950, suggesting sharp secular growth in the relative demand for the more educated that started well before the rise in wage inequality of the 1980s.

Figure 4 illustrates the evolution of the college wage premium from 1940 to 1998. A sharp compression of educational wage differentials in the 1940s has been followed by expansions in each subsequent decade except the 1970s. Figure 5 displays the evolution of overall wage inequality (as measured by the 90-10 wage ratio) for men and women separately from 1940 to 1998. These series also indicate a large wage compression in the 1940s followed by widening inequality since 1950, especially in the 1980s. Overall wage inequality and educational wage differentials have tended to move together, with the exception of the 1970s. The college/high school wage gap and overall wage inequality were higher in 1998 than at anytime since 1940. Because the period from 1914 to 1939 was one of substantial declines in educational and occupational wage differentials, however, wage disparities by education and occupation group are still below those in the early part of the century (Goldin and Katz 1999).

Table 2 presents estimates of changes in the college wage premium and in the relative supply of and demand for college equivalents over selected periods from 1940 to 1998.[9] The sharp difference in the behavior of the college relative wage in the 1970s and 1980s can be attributed both to slower relative supply growth and faster relative demand growth in the 1980s. A comparison of the period of large increase in the college wage premium from 1980 to 1998 with the period of little change from 1960 to 1980

Table 1 U.S. Educational Composition of Employment and the College/High School Wage Premium, 1940–1998 (Full-Time Equivalent Employment Shares by Education Level, in percent)

	High School Dropouts	High School Graduates	Some College	College Graduates	College/HS Wage Ratio
1940 Census	67.9	19.2	6.5	6.4	1.65
1950 Census	58.6	24.4	9.2	7.8	1.38
1960 Census	49.5	27.7	12.2	10.6	1.49
1970 Census	35.9	34.7	15.6	13.8	1.59
1980 Census	20.7	36.1	22.8	20.4	1.48
1980 CPS	19.1	38.0	22.0	20.9	1.43
1990 CPS	12.7	36.2	25.1	26.1	1.66
1990 Census	11.4	33.0	30.2	25.4	1.73
Feb. 90 CPS	11.5	36.8	25.2	26.5	1.70
1998 CPS	9.4	33.3	28.3	29.1	1.75

Sources: Data for 1940 to 1990 are from Autor, Katz, and Krueger (1998, Table I). Data for 1998 are from the 1998 Merged Outgoing Rotation Groups of the CPS using the same methodology.

Notes: Full-time equivalent (FTE) employment shares are calculated for samples that include all individuals aged 18–65 in paid employment during the survey reference week for each Census and CPS sample. FTE shares are defined as the share of total weekly hours supplied by each education group. The tabulations are based on the 1940 to 1990 Census Integrated Public Use Micro samples; the 1980, 1990, and 1998 CPS Merged Outgoing Rotation Group samples; and the February 1990 CPS. The 1990 Census, February 1990 CPS, and 1998 CPS samples use the new Census education variable. The Data Appendix to Autor, Katz, and Krueger (1998) discusses how the old and new education coding schemes are made comparable.

The college/high school wage ratio for each year is the (exponentiated) weighted average of the estimated college (exactly 16 years of schooling or bachelor's degree) and postcollege (17+ years of schooling or a postbaccalaureate degree) log wage premium relative to high school workers (those with exactly 12 years of schooling or a high school diploma) for that year, where the weights are the employment shares of college and postcollege workers in 1980. The details of the specifications and estimation approach are given in Autor, Katz, and Krueger (1998).

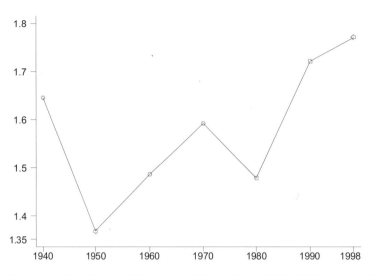

Figure 4   The College/High School Wage Ratio, 1940–1998. Source: Table 1.

suggests a deceleration in relative supply growth is more important than an acceleration in relative demand growth in explaining the recent expansion of educational wage differentials. A marked increase in the rate of growth of relative demand is apparent in the 1980s, followed by a substantial decrease in the 1990s.

Table 2 implies strong secular relative demand growth for college workers since 1950. It is thus necessary to reconcile the large increases in the college wage premium in the face of large relative skill supply increases. The 1970s were an exceptional decade of rapid relative supply growth, with the labor market entry of the baby-boom generation and increased college enrollments associated with the Vietnam War. The 1980s were the decade of most rapid relative demand growth, possibly suggesting an impact of the spread of personal computers and microprocessor-based technologies. The slowdown in demand growth in the 1990s indicates that the period of the explosion of Internet commerce and communication has not been one of particularly rapid shifts in demand for college-educated workers.

Table 2 also indicates that the average rate of growth of relative demand for college workers was more rapid during the past twenty-eight years (1970–1998) than during the previous thirty years

Technological Change and the Wage Structure

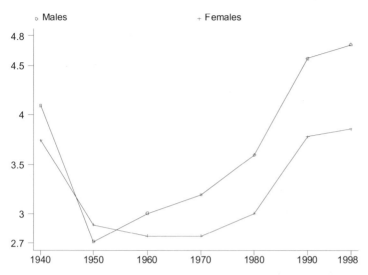

Figure 5 Overall U.S. Wage Inequality, 1940–1998. Source: Estimates are for the weekly wages of full-time, full-year workers not employed in agriculture and earning at least half of the federal minimum wage. The estimates for 1940–1990 are from Katz and Autor (1999, Table 8), and the estimated changes from 1990 to 1998 are from Bernstein and Mishel (1999). The 90-10 wage ratio is the ratio of the earnings of the worker in the 90th percentile of the earnings distribution to the earnings of the worker in the 10th percentile.

(1940–1970). This pattern is suggestive of an increased rate of skill-biased technological progress starting in the early 1970s, as has been hypothesized by Greenwood and Yorukoglu (1997). But the evidence for a discrete trend break in overall demand growth is not very strong. And this conclusion depends on including the 1940s, a decade of strong institutional intervention in the labor market, in the earlier period.

How can we explain the strong trend growth in the relative demand for skills over the past fifty years and the decadal fluctuations in the growth rate? A common approach is to conceptualize relative demand shifts as coming from two types of changes: those that occur within industries (shifts that change the relative factor intensities within industries at fixed relative wages) and those that occur between industries (shifts that change the allocation of total labor between industries at fixed relative wages). Sources of within-industry shifts include pure skill-biased technological change,

Table 2 Growth of College/High School Relative Wage, Supply, and Demand, Selected Periods, 1940–1998 (Annualized Percent Changes)

	Relative Wage	Relative Supply	Relative Demand
1940–50	−1.86	2.35	−0.25
1950–60	0.83	2.91	4.08
1960–70	0.69	2.55	3.52
1970–80	−0.74	4.99	3.95
1980–90	1.51	2.53	4.65
1990–98	0.36	2.25	2.76
1940–70	−0.11	2.61	2.45
1970–98	0.38	3.33	3.86
1940–60	−0.51	2.63	1.92
1960–80	−0.02	3.77	3.74
1980–98	1.00	2.41	3.81

Source: Autor, Katz, and Krueger (1998, Table II), updated to 1998.

Notes: The relative wage measure is the log of the college/high school wage ratio from Table 1. The relative supply and demand measures are for college equivalents (college graduates plus half of those with some college) and high school equivalents (those with 12 or fewer years of schooling and half of those with some college). The implied relative demand changes assume an aggregate elasticity of substitution between college equivalents and high school equivalents of 1.4. The relative supply measure adjusts for changes in the age-sex composition of the pools of college and high school equivalents; see Autor, Katz, and Krueger (1998) for details.

changes in the relative prices (or supplies) of nonlabor inputs (e.g., computer services or new capital equipment), and changes in outsourcing activity. Between-industry shifts in relative labor demand can be generated by sectoral differences in productivity growth and by shifts in product demand across industries arising either from domestic sources or from shifts in net international trade that change the domestic share of output in an industry at fixed wages. Shifts in employment between industries will have a larger effect on relative skill demands as the differences in skill intensities across industries increase.

This conceptualization has led to the use of decompositions of aggregate changes in the utilization of more-skilled labor into between-industry and within-industry components as a guide to the importance of product demand shifts as opposed to skill-biased technological change (or outsourcing) as sources of relative demand changes (Berman, Bound, and Griliches 1994; Katz and Murphy 1992). This research shows that throughout the twentieth century the industrial and occupational distribution of employment has shifted in favor of more-educated workers (Autor, Katz, and Krueger 1998; Goldin and Katz 1995; Juhn 1999). But measured between-industry shifts appear to explain no more than 20–40 percent of the secular growth in the relative demand for more-skilled workers. Substantial within-industry demand shifts must also have been a major factor. The pervasiveness of occupational and educational upgrading (even in industries outside of manufacturing with little foreign outsourcing) is quite suggestive of significant skill-biased technological change.

Autor, Katz, and Krueger (1998), using three-digit Census industries, find that the rate of within-industry relative demand growth for college workers increased from the 1960s to the 1970s and remained at a higher level in the 1980s through 1996. The large jump in within-industry skill upgrading occurred in service industries in the 1970s and in manufacturing industries in the 1980s. This timing pattern appears consistent with an earlier impact of computerization (through organizational applications of computers) on many service industries in the 1960s and 1970s and the somewhat later large-scale impact of microprocessor technologies on manufacturing production processes. These findings motivate a more detailed and direct look at the evidence on the impact on labor demand of skill-biased technological change and the spread of computers.

III Technological Change, Computerization, and the Demand for Skills

The deteriorating labor market outcomes of less-educated workers in most OECD economies from the 1970s to the mid-1990s, despite their increasing relative scarcity, strongly implies a strong decline in the relative demand for less-skilled workers. Skill-biased technological change and increased exposure to international competition from less-developed countries have been offered as the leading explanations for this demand shift.

Much indirect evidence suggests a dominant role for skill-biased technological change (associated with changes in production techniques, organizational changes, and reductions in the relative prices of computer services and new capital equipment) in the declining relative demand for the less skilled. First, the magnitude of employment shifts to skill-intensive industries as measured by between-industry demand shift indices is too small to be consistent with explanations giving a leading role to product demand shifts (such as those relating it to increasing trade with developing countries). Moreover, estimates of between-industry demand shifts show little evidence of acceleration in recent decades. Second, despite increases in the relative wages of more-skilled workers, the composition of U.S. employment continues to shift rapidly toward more-educated workers and higher-skill occupations within industries and even within establishments (Autor, Katz, and Krueger 1998; Dunne, Haltiwanger, and Troske 1996). Third, within-industry skill upgrading, despite rising or stable skill premia, is found in almost all industries in many other developed economies in the 1980s. The cross-industry pattern of the rate of skill upgrading in manufacturing industries appears to be quite similar among advanced nations (Berman, Bound, and Machin 1998). These findings suggest an important role for *pervasive* skill-biased technological change concentrated in similar industries in all OECD countries as a major source of changes in relative skill demands.

There also exist strong positive correlations between industry-level indicators of technological change (computer investments, the growth of employee computer use, research and development expenditures, utilization of scientists and engineers, and changes in capital intensity measures) and the within-industry growth in the relative employment and labor cost share of more-skilled workers (Autor, Katz, and Krueger 1998; Berman, Bound, and Griliches 1994; Machin and Van Reenen 1998; Wolff 1996). The causal interpretation of contemporaneous correlations of technology indicators such as R&D intensity and computer use with skill upgrading is unclear because R&D activities directly use highly educated workers and because other sources of changes in the use of skilled workers could drive variation across industries in purchases of computers. But Autor, Katz, and Krueger (1998), Machin and Van Reenen (1998), and Wolff (1996) find that lagged computer investments and R&D expenditures predict subsequent increases in the pace of skill upgrading. This pattern is consistent with a recent survey of U.S. human resource managers indicating that large investments in information technology lead to changes in organizational practices that decentralize decision-making, increase worker autonomy, and increase the need for highly educated workers (Bresnahan, Brynjolfsson, and Hitt 1999).

Plant-level studies of U.S. manufacturing by Bernard and Jensen (1997) and Doms, Dunne, and Troske (1997) find strong positive relationships between within-plant skill upgrading and both R&D intensity and computer investments, although Doms, Dunne, and Troske (1997) find little relationship between a plant-level indicator of the number of new factory automation technologies being used and subsequent within-plant skill upgrading. Case studies by the Bureau of Labor Statistics show that large labor-saving production innovations were adopted in the 1970s and 1980s in the electrical machinery, machinery, and printing and publishing sectors—industries that are among the leaders in the rate of skill upgrading in most developed countries (Berman, Bound, and Machin 1998; Mark 1987).

The diffusion of computers and related technologies represents a possibly significant measurable source of recent changes in the relative demand for skills. The share of U.S. workers using computers on the job, an extremely crude measure of the diffusion of computer-based technologies, increased from 25 percent in 1984 to 51 percent in 1997 (Friedberg 1999).[10] Although most workers use computers largely for common applications (word processing, spreadsheets, and databases), Friedberg (1999) finds that approximately 47 percent of those with workplace computers used them for electronic mail or other communication tasks in 1997. Table 3 shows that the growth in workplace computer use has not been uniform across demographic or skill groups. Women, college-educated workers, whites, and white-collar workers are more likely to use computers and to have experienced wage growth since 1979 than men, non-college-educated workers, blacks, and blue-collar workers, respectively.

Krueger (1993) and Autor, Katz, and Krueger (1997) document a wage premium associated with computer use (conditional on a

Table 3 Percent of Workers in Various Categories Who Directly Use a Computer at Work, 1984–1997

	1984	1989	1993	1997
All workers	24.4	37.3	46.6	50.6
Education				
< High School	4.9	7.7	9.5	11.7
High School	18.5	28.5	34.1	36.4
Some College	31.2	44.8	53.1	56.2
College +	41.2	58.6	70.2	75.9
Race and Sex				
White, male	21.6	32.9	42.3	46.3
White, female	30.5	44.9	54.8	58.9
Black, male	12.6	21.7	29.7	32.3
Black, female	22.6	33.8	43.3	47.8
Occupation				
Professional, Technical	38.1	54.4	65.7	73.1
Managers, Administrators	42.5	61.8	73.7	78.7
Sales	23.9	35.5	49.8	55.8
Clerical	47.4	66.8	77.4	78.6
Craft	10.1	15.2	23.5	25.3
Operatives	5.8	9.6	15.7	18.6
Laborers	3.2	6.6	11.7	12.8
Service	6.0	9.8	15.1	16.8

Source: Friedberg (1999, Tables 2 and 4).

Notes: Tabulations of computer use at work from the October 1984, 1989, 1993, and 1997 CPS samples for individuals aged 18–64 at work or with a job in the survey reference week. A computer is defined as a PC or desktop terminal with a keyboard and monitor.

large set of controls for observed worker characteristics) that increased from 18 percent in 1984 to 20 percent in 1993. The extent to which this computer wage premium represents a measure of the true returns to computer skills (the treatment effect of computer use) or reflects omitted characteristics of workers and their employers is a subject of much controversy (see, for example, DiNardo and Pischke 1997). But the causal interpretation of such regressions does not directly address the issue of whether the spread of computer technologies has changed organizational practices and altered relative skill demands.

Computer technology may affect relative labor demand in several ways.[11] Computer business systems often involve the routinization of white-collar tasks. Simpler, repetitive tasks have proved more amenable to computerization than complex, idiosyncratic tasks. Microprocessor-based technologies have similarly facilitated the automation of many production processes in recent years. The direct substitution of computers for human judgment and labor is likely to prove more important in clerical and production jobs than in managerial and professional jobs. Computer-based technologies may also increase the returns to creative use of greater available information to tailor products and services more closely to customers-specific needs and to develop new products. Computers, the Internet, and electronic commerce also raise the returns to the use of marketing and problem-solving skills to improve the match between customers' idiosyncratic preferences and existing products and services. Bresnahan (1999) posits such an organizational complementarity between computers and workers who possess both greater cognitive skills and greater "people" or "soft" skills.

The direct substitution and organizational complementarity channels both predict that an increase in the relative demand for highly educated workers and occupations stressing "soft" skills should be associated with computerization. These predictions are consistent with the findings of Autor, Katz, and Krueger (1998) that increased computer intensity is associated with increased employment shares of managers, professionals, and other highly educated workers, and with decreased employment shares of clerical workers, production workers, and less-educated workers. Bresnahan, Brynjolfsson, and Hitt (1999) also find in firm-level data that greater use of information technology is associated with the employment of more-educated workers, greater investments in training, broader job responsibilities for line workers, and more decentralized decision-making.

Several conceptual issues concerning how technological change affects the labor market merit further consideration in our attempt to sort out the long-run implications of computerization and the rise of the digital economy. One possibility is that skilled workers are more flexible and facilitate the adoption of new technologies, so that all technological changes increase the relative demand for more-skilled labor over some transitional period (Bartel and Lichtenberg 1987; Greenwood and Yorukoglu 1997). As technologies diffuse and become mature and more routinized, the comparative advantage of the highly skilled declines. In this case the demand for skilled labor depends on the rate of innovation. Periods of large increases in the skill premium correspond to technological revolutions.[12]

Under this interpretation, the apparent slowdown in growth of the relative demand for skill in the 1990s could reflect such a maturing of the computer revolution. The naive measure of employee computer use in table 3 does show a slowdown in the rate of diffusion from the 1984–1993 period to the 1993–1997 period. This interpretation also implies that the expansion of the Internet and electronic commerce may have much smaller labor market impact than the spread of large-scale computing operations in the 1970s and of personal computers in the 1980s and early 1990s. Of course, we may only be observing the tip of the iceberg, and there may be major organizational changes associated with electronic communications that could lead to large transitory impacts on the relative demand for skills. Furthermore, the improvements in the relative and real labor market position of less-skilled workers over the past few years may largely reflect transitory factors associated with extremely strong macroeconomic conditions (Katz and Krueger 1999).

An alternative (but potentially complementary) hypothesis is that distinctive technological innovations may have different skill biases. While the technological changes associated with electrification and computerization may have been skill-biased, other innovations need not be. Mechanization in the nineteenth century is associated with the movement from artisanal production (intensive in skilled craft workers) to factory production (intensive in unskilled labor); it appears to have been largely deskilling, even though more flexible workers were probably needed to assist in the introduction of factory methods (Goldin and Katz 1998). Under this scenario it is the inherent skill-biased nature of twentieth-century innovations rather than an accelerating rate of innovation that is the source of secular within-industry growth in the relative demand for skill.[13]

IV Conclusions and Research Directions

Strong secular growth in the relative demand for more-educated and more-skilled workers has been apparent throughout the twentieth century in the United States. Skill-biased technological changes ranging from electrification to computerization have been major factors in this steady growth in the relative demand for skill. The overall rate of relative demand growth for college-educated workers appears to have been particularly rapid in the 1980s and then to have slowed in the 1990s. The pace of within-industry skill upgrading increased from the 1960s to the 1970s throughout the economy, further increased in manufacturing in the 1980s, and has remained high in the 1990s. Indicators of employee computer usage, computer capital intensity, and the rate of investment in information technologies are higher in industries with more rapid rates of skill upgrading in each of the last several decades. Thus skill-biased technological and organizational changes that accompanied the computer revolution appear to have contributed to faster growth in relative skill demand within industries starting in the 1970s.

Although the strong observed conditional correlations of computer measures and the growth in the relative utilization of highly educated workers may not simply reflect causal relationships, it is clear that whatever is driving the rapid rate of relative demand growth for more-skilled workers over the past few decades is concentrated in the most computer-intensive sectors of the U.S. economy. But these patterns leave substantial room for fluctuations in the rate of growth of the supply of college equivalents, globalization forces, and changes in labor market institutions to also have contributed to recent movements in U.S. wage inequality and educational wage differentials.

Our understanding of how computer-based technologies are affecting the labor market has been hampered by the lack of large representative data sets that provide good measures of workplace technology, worker technology use, firm organizational practices, and worker characteristics. Research on representative national data sets has been forced to use crude measures of employee computer usage from the occasional supplements to the CPS or has had to link CPS data on worker characteristics to noisy measures of industry-level information technology investments and capital stocks. Matched employer-employee data sets with detailed information on technologies, worker attributes, and personnel practices would greatly enhance our ability to sort out how new technologies are affecting skill demands and the organization of work. The linked data sets for manufacturing workers and plants from the 1990 Census of Population, the Longitudinal Research Database, and the 1988 and 1993 Survey of Manufacturing Technologies used by Doms, Dunne, and Troske (1997) provide a fine example of data collection efforts moving in this direction. But we need such data sets also for nonmanufacturing industries.

The other major methodological issue involves moving from correlations between technology indicators and skill upgrading to learning more about causal relations from an examination of "exogenous" changes in firms' access to or costs of purchasing new technologies. Studies of the effects on skill demands of the differential effects of tax changes on firms' investment incentives might be a useful start. Case studies of how sharp changes in firm technologies and computer use affect organizational practices and relative skill demands also are proving fruitful (e.g., Levy and Murnane 1996; Ichniowski, Shaw, and Prennushi 1997; Bresnahan, Brynjolfsson, and Hitt 1999).

Several issues concerning how the digital economy is affecting the labor market merit further study. A first research issue concerns how the growth of the Internet is affecting the geographic distribution of production and employment opportunities among large cities, smaller cities, suburban areas, and rural areas (Gaspar and Glaeser 1998; Kolko 1999). A second topic involves the sources of employee training in a rapidly changing digital economy. Autor (1999) has documented an increasing role of temporary help firms in providing limited computer skills training.

A final issue for further scrutiny is how the Internet job search and computer-oriented labor market intermediaries (the rapidly growing temporary help industry) are affecting labor market matching and the ability of the economy to operate with a low unemployment rate. There has been a striking decline in short-term unemployment in the United States in the 1990s, with a lower proportion of the labor force flowing through unemployment by 1997 than at any time in the past forty years (Katz and Krueger 1999). Suggestive evidence indicates improvements in labor market matching and greater labor market competition stemming from the growth of labor market intermediaries may be playing a role in reducing labor market bottlenecks and potentially lowering the natural rate of unemployment. Increased software compatibility across work sites that allows new employees to integrate quickly into many computer-oriented jobs may be having a similar effect.

Notes

1. Skill-biased technological change refers to any introduction of a new technology, change in production methods, or change in the organization of work that increases the demand for more-skilled labor (e.g., college graduates) relative to less-skilled labor (e.g., workers who are not college graduates) at fixed relative wages.

2. Foreign outsourcing of less-skilled jobs is another possible explanation for this pattern (Feenstra and Hanson 1999). But large within-industry shifts toward more skilled workers are pervasive even in sectors with little or no observed foreign outsourcing activity.

3. See Autor, Katz, and Krueger (1998) and Bresnahan (1999) for more detailed and technical treatments of these issues.

4. See Katz and Autor (1999) and Levy and Murnane (1992) for reviews of the literature on U.S. wage structure changes and for more detailed references; see Gottschalk and Smeeding (1997) for comparisons of wage structure changes among OECD countries.

5. Earnings mobility measures how individuals move in the earnings distribution between two points in time. The greater the extent of earnings mobility, the greater the likelihood an individual will move among various parts of the distribution over time.

6. Nominal wages are converted into constant dollars using the chain-weighted personal consumption expenditures deflator of the national income accounts. Many experts believe this deflator may fail to adequately capture consumer gains from new goods and quality improvement and thereby overstate the rate of increase of the cost of living (Boskin *et al.* 1998). Such adjustments would increase the estimates of real wage growth for all workers (by possibly 0.5 to 1 percent a year) but would not change conclusions about the growth of wage inequality or educational wage differentials.

7. Mobility can offset increases in cross-sectional inequality only if the rate of mobility also increases.

8. The increases in the educational attainment of the U.S. work force since 1940 may overstate increases in the relative supply of more-skilled workers to the extent that the "unobserved" quality of more-educated workers declines with some re-labeling of less-skilled workers into higher education categories. Juhn, Kim, and Vella (1996) examine this issue using Census data from 1940 to 1990 and find that conclusions concerning changes in relative supply and implied relative demand shifts are not much affected by adjustments for such re-labeling.

9. The basic approach, following Katz and Murphy (1992) and Autor, Katz, and Krueger (1998), is to examine the relative wage of two "pure" skill groups (college graduates and high school graduates) and to relate this relative wage to changes in the relative quantities and demands for equivalents of these pure skill classes. College equivalents are given by college graduates plus half of those with some college; high school equivalents are half of those with some college plus workers with twelve or fewer years of schooling. Demand shifts for college equivalents are calculated under the assumption that the aggregate elasticity of substitution between college and high school equivalents is 1.4, approximately in the middle of the range of recent estimates (Katz and Autor 1999).

10. The rapid spread of computers in the work place appears to have occurred at a similar pace in other OECD countries (Card, Kramarz, and Lemieux 1996).

11. See Bresnahan (1999) for a descriptive theory of and illuminating historical evidence on how computerization influences labor demand and organizational practices.

12. See Galor and Moav (2000) for an insightful model of the rate of technological innovation, changes in educational attainment, and the evolution of wage inequality.

13. See Acemoglu (1998) for an insightful model of how increases in the proportion of more-educated workers (as have occurred throughout the twentieth century) can induce the development of skill-complementary technologies.

References

Acemoglu, Daron, 1998. "Why Do New Technologies Complement Skills? Directed Technical Change and Wage Inequality." *Quarterly Journal of Economics* 113 (November): 1055–1089.

Autor, David H., 1999. "Why Do Temporary Help Firms Provide Free General Skills Training?" Unpublished paper, Harvard University, April.

Autor, David H., Lawrence F. Katz, and Alan B. Krueger, 1997. "Computing Inequality: Have Computers Changed the Labor Market?" NBER Working Paper No. 5956, March.

Autor, David H., Lawrence F. Katz, and Alan B. Krueger, 1998. "Computing Inequality: Have Computers Changed the Labor Market?" *Quarterly Journal of Economics* 113 (November): 1169–1213.

Bartel, Ann and Frank Lichtenberg, 1987. "The Comparative Advantage of Educated Workers in Implementing New Technologies." *Review of Economics and Statistics* 69 (February): 1–11.

Berman, Eli, John Bound, and Zvi Griliches, 1994. "Changes in the Demand for Skilled Labor within U.S. Manufacturing Industries: Evidence from the Annual Survey of Manufactures." *Quarterly Journal of Economics* 109 (May): 367–397.

Berman, Eli, John Bound, and Stephen Machin. 1998. "Implications of Skill-Biased Technological Change: International Evidence." *Quarterly Journal of Economics* 113 (November): 1245–1279.

Bernard, Andrew, and J. Bradford Jensen, 1997. "Exporters, Skill Upgrading, and the Wage Gap." *Journal of International Economics* 42: 3–31.

Bernstein, Jared, and Lawrence Mishel, 1999. "Wages Gain Ground." EPI Issue Brief #129, Economic Policy Institute, Washington, DC, February.

Borjas, George J., Richard B. Freeman, and Lawrence F. Katz, 1997. "How Much Do Immigration and Trade Affect Labor Market Outcomes?" *Brookings Papers on Economic Activity*, no. 1, 1–90.

Borjas, George J., and Valerie Ramey, 1995. "Foreign Competition, Market Power and Wage Inequality." *Quarterly Journal of Economics* 110 (November): 1075–1110.

Boskin, Michael J., Ellen R. Dulberger, Robert J. Gordon, Zvi Griliches, and Dale W. Jorgenson, 1998. "Consumer Prices, the Consumer Price Index, and the Cost of Living." *Journal of Economic Perspectives* 12 (Winter): 3–26.

Bound, John, and George Johnson, 1992. "Changes in the Structure of Wages in the 1980s: An Evaluation of Alternative Explanations." *American Economic Review* 82 (June): 371–392.

Bresnahan, Timothy F., 1999. "Computerisation and Wage Dispersion: An Analytical Reinterpretation." *Economic Journal* 109 (June): 390–415.

Bresnahan, Timothy F., Erik Brynjolfsson, and Lorin M. Hitt, 1999. "Information Technology, Workplace Organization and the Demand for Skilled Labor: Firm-level Evidence." NBER Working Paper No. 7136.

Card, David, Francis Kramarz, and Thomas Lemieux, 1996. "Changes in the Relative Structure of Wages and Employment: A Comparison of the United States, Canada, and France." NBER Working Paper No. 5487.

Condon, Mark, and Isabelle Sawhill, 1992. "Income Mobility and Permanent Income Inequality." Unpublished paper, Urban Institute, Washington DC.

DiNardo, John, Nicole Fortin, and Thomas Lemieux, 1996. "Labor Market Institutions and the Distribution of Wages, 1973–1992: A Semi-Parametric Approach." *Econometrica* 64: 1001–1044.

DiNardo, John, and Jörn-Steffen Pischke, 1997. "The Returns to Computer Use Revisited: Have Pencils Changed the Wage Structure Too?" *Quarterly Journal of Economics* 112 (February): 291–303.

Doms, Mark, Timothy Dunne, and Kenneth R. Troske, 1997. "Workers, Wages, and Technology." *Quarterly Journal of Economics* 112 (February): 253–290.

Douglas, Paul, 1926. "What is Happening to the 'White-Collar-Job' Market?" *System: The Magazine of Business* (December).

Dunne, Timothy, John Haltiwanger, and Kenneth R. Troske, 1996. "Technology and Jobs: Secular Changes and Cyclical Dynamics." NBER Working Paper No. 5656.

Feenstra, Robert C., and Gordon H. Hanson, 1999. "The Impact of Outsourcing and High-Technology Capital on Wages: Estimates for the United States, 1979–90." *Quarterly Journal of Economics* 114 (August): 907–940.

Friedberg, Leora, 1999. "The Impact of Technological Change on Older Workers: Evidence from Data on Computers." Unpublished paper, University of California at San Diego, April.

Galor, Oded, and Omer Moav, 2000. "Ability-Biased Technological Transition, Wage Inequality and Economic Growth." *Quarterly Journal of Economics* 115 (May), forthcoming.

Gaspar, Jess, and Edward Glaeser, 1998. "Information Technology and the Future of Cities." *Journal of Urban Economics* 43: 133–156.

Goldin, Claudia, and Lawrence F. Katz, 1995. "The Decline of Non-Competing Groups: Changes in the Premium to Education, 1890 to 1940." NBER Working Paper No. 5202.

Goldin, Claudia, and Lawrence F. Katz, 1998. "The Origins of Technology-Skill Complementarity." *Quarterly Journal of Economics* 113 (August): 693–732.

Goldin, Claudia, and Lawrence F. Katz, 1999. "The Returns to Skill in the United States across the Twentieth Century." NBER Working Paper No. 7126.

Gottschalk, Peter, and Sheldon Danziger, 1998. "Family Income Mobility: How Much is There, and Has it Changed?" In J. Auerbach and R. Belous, eds., *The Inequality Paradox: Growth of Income Disparity* (Washington, DC: National Policy Association), 92–111.

Gottschalk, Peter, and Robert Moffitt, 1994. "The Growth of Earnings Instability in the U.S. Labor Market." *Brookings Papers on Economic Activity*, No. 2, 217–272.

Gottschalk, Peter, and Timothy M. Smeeding, 1997. "Cross-National Comparisons of Earnings and Income Inequality." *Journal of Economic Literature* 35 (June): 633–687.

Greenwood, Jeremy, and Mehmet Yorukoglu, 1997. "1974." *Carnegie Rochester Series on Public Policy* 46: 49–95.

Hamermesh, Daniel, 1999. "Changing Inequality in Markets for Workplace Amenities." *Quarterly Journal of Economics* 114 (November): 1085–1123.

Ichniowski, Casey, Kathryn Shaw, and Giovanna Prennushi, 1997. "The Effect of Human Resource Practices on Productivity: A Study of Steel Finishing Lines." *American Economic Review* 87 (June): 291–313.

Juhn, Chinhui, 1999. "Wage Inequality and Demand for Skill: Evidence from Five Decades." *Industrial and Labor Relations Review* 52 (April): 424–443.

Juhn, Chinhui, Dae Il Kim, and Francis Vella, 1996. "Education and Cohort Quality." Unpublished paper, University of Houston.

Katz, Lawrence F., and David H. Autor, 1999. "Changes in the Wage Structure and Earnings Inequality." In O. Ashenfelter and D. Card, eds., *Handbook of Labor Economics*, vol. 3A (Amsterdam: North-Holland).

Katz, Lawrence F., and Alan B. Krueger, 1999. "The High-Pressure U.S. Labor Market of the 1990s." *Brookings Papers on Economic Activity*, no. 1, 1–87.

Katz, Lawrence F., and Kevin M. Murphy, 1992. "Changes in Relative Wages, 1963–87: Supply and Demand Factors." *Quarterly Journal of Economics* 107 (February): 35–78.

Kolko, Jed, 1999. "The Death of Cities? The Death of Distance? Evidence from the Geography of Commercial Internet Usage." Unpublished paper, Harvard University, March.

Krueger, Alan B., 1993. "How Computers Changed the Wage Structure: Evidence from Micro Data." *Quarterly Journal of Economics* 108 (February): 33–60.

Krussell, Per, Lee E. Ohanian, José-Víctor Ríos-Rull, and Giovanni L. Violante, 1997. "Capital-Skill Complementarity: A Macroeconomic Analysis." Federal Reserve Bank of Minneapolis, Staff Report 239.

Lawrence, Robert Z,. and Matthew J. Slaughter, 1993. "International Trade and American Wages in the 1980s: Giant Sucking Sound or Small Hiccup?" *Brookings Papers on Economic Activity*, no. 2, 161–226.

Lee, David S., 1999. "Wage Inequality in the U.S. during the 1980s: Rising Dispersion or Falling Minimum Wage?" *Quarterly Journal of Economics* 114 (August): 977–1023.

Levy, Frank, and Richard Murnane, 1992. "U.S. Earnings Levels and Earnings Inequality: A Review of Recent Trends and Proposed Explanations." *Journal of Economic Literature* 30: 1333–1381.

Levy, Frank, and Richard Murnane, 1996. "With What Skills Are Computers a Complement?" *American Economic Review* 86 (May): 258–262.

Machin, Stephen, and John Van Reenen, 1998. "Technology and Changes in Skill Structure: Evidence from Seven OECD Countries." *Quarterly Journal of Economics* 113 (November): 1215–1244.

Mark, Jerome, 1987. "Technological Change and Employment: Some Results from BLS Research." *Monthly Labor Review* 110: 26–29.

Murphy, Kevin M., W. Craig Riddell, and Paul M. Romer, 1998. "Wages, Skills and Technology in the United States and Canada." In E. Helpman, ed., *General Purpose Technologies* (Cambridge, MA: MIT Press).

Murphy, Kevin M., and Robert H. Topel, 1997. "Unemployment and Nonemployment." *American Economic Review* 87 (May): 295–300.

Murphy, Kevin M., and Finis Welch, 1992. "The Structure of Wages." *Quarterly Journal of Economics* 107 (February): 285–326.

Pierce, Brooks, 1999. "Compensation Inequality." Unpublished paper, U.S. Bureau of Labor Statistics.

Tinbergen, Jan, 1975. *Income Differences: Recent Research.* Amsterdam: North-Holland.

Wolff, Edward, 1995. *Top Heavy: A Study of the Increasing Inequality of Wealth in America.* New York: Twentieth Century Fund Press.

Wolff, Edward, 1996. "The Growth of Information Workers in the U.S. Economy, 1950–1990: The Role of Technological Change." Unpublished paper, New York University.

Wolff, Edward, 1998. "Recent Trends in the Size Distribution of Household Wealth." *Journal of Economic Perspectives* 12 (Summer): 131–150.

Wood, Adrian, 1994. *North-South Trade, Employment and Inequality.* Oxford: Clarendon Press.

The Growing Digital Divide: Implications for an Open Research Agenda

Donna L. Hoffman and Thomas P. Novak

Introduction

That portion of the Internet known as the World Wide Web has been riding an exponential growth curve since 1994 (Network Wizards 1999; Rutkowski 1998), coinciding with the introduction of NCSA's graphically based "browsing" software interface Mosaic (Hoffman, Novak, and Chatterjee 1995).

Currently, over 43 million hosts are connected to the Internet worldwide (Network Wizards 1999). In terms of individual users, somewhere between 40 and 80 million adults (eStats 1999) in the United States alone have access to around 800 million unique pages of content (Lawrence and Giles 1999), globally distributed on what is arguably one of the most important communication innovations in history.

Enthusiasm for the anticipated social dividends of this "revolution in democratic communication" (Hoffman 1996) that will "harness the powerful forces of science and technology"(Clinton 1997a) for all members of our society appears boundless. The Internet is expected to do no less than transform society. Nowhere has this confidence been expressed more clearly than in President Clinton's aggressive objective to wire every classroom and library in the country by the year 2000 (NetDay 1998), followed by every home by the year 2007, so that "every 12-year-old can log onto the Internet" (Clinton 1997b).

Yet even as the Internet races ambitiously toward critical mass, some social scientists have begun to examine carefully the policy implications of *current* demographic patterns of Internet access and usage (Hoffman and Novak 1998; Hoffman, Kalsbeek, and Novak 1996; Hoffman, Novak, and Venkatesh 1997; Katz and Aspden 1997; Wilhelm 1998). For while Clinton's "Call to Action for American Education" (Clinton 1997a) may guarantee universal access for our nation's next generation, we must ask whether the 200 million Americans presently over the age of 16 are equally likely to have access to the Internet. The findings thus far are both obvious and surprising, with important implications for social science research and public policy.

Looming large is the concern that the Internet may not scale *economically* (Keller 1996), leading to what Lloyd Morrisett, former president of the Markle Foundation, has called a "digital divide" between information "haves" and "have-nots." That is, although the decentralized nature of the Internet means that it can easily expand in terms of the number of people who can access it, an individual's access may be constrained by his or her particular economic situation.

For example, although almost 70 percent of the schools in this country have at least one computer connected to the Internet, less than 15 percent of classrooms have Internet access (Harmon 1997). Not surprisingly, access is not distributed randomly; it is correlated strongly with income and education (Coley, Cradler, and Engel 1997). A recent study of Internet use among college freshman (Sax et al. 1998) found that nearly 83 percent of all new college students report using the Internet for school work, and almost two-thirds use email to communicate. Yet, closer examination suggests a disturbing disparity in access. While 90.2 percent of private college freshman use the Internet for research, only 77.6 percent of students entering public black colleges report doing so. Similarly, although 80.1 percent of private college freshman use email regularly, only 41.4 percent of students attending black public colleges do so.

Furthermore, although numerous studies (CyberAtlas 1999; Maraganore and Morrisette 1998) suggest that the gender gap in Internet use appears to be closing over time and that Internet users are increasingly coming from the ranks of those with lower education and income (Pew Research Center 1998), the perception persists that the gap for race is not decreasing (Abrams 1997).

In examining the evidence supporting the notion of a digital divide, we will highlight studies focusing on key differences in PC ownership, Internet access, and Web usage between whites and African Americans in the United States.

Evidence for a Digital Divide

Katz and Aspden (1997) found that Internet users were generally wealthier and more highly educated. Sparrow and Vedantham (1995: 19) summarize the broader information technology situation as follows:

> Information technologies include basic telephone service, personal computing, and computer networking. Although these technologies are becoming everyday conveniences for many Americans, some communities are being left out. Disparities exist in levels of access between rich and poor and between suburban and inner-city residents.

Hoffman and Novak (1998) examined racial differences in Internet access and use in 1997 and found that, overall, whites were significantly more likely than African Americans to have a computer in their household and were also more likely to have PC access at work. Whites were significantly more likely to have ever used the Web at home, whereas African Americans were more likely to have ever used the Web at school. As one might expect, increasing levels of income corresponded to an increased likelihood of owning a home computer, regardless of race. But while income explained race differences in computer ownership and Web use, whites were still more likely to own a home computer than were African Americans and to have used the Web recently, even controlling for differences in education.

Hoffman and Novak's most striking findings, however, were for students. They found no differences between white and African American students when the students had a home computer. However, among students without a computer in the home, white students were much more likely than African American students to have used the Web, and also more likely to have used the Web at locations other than home, work, or school-for example, at libraries, friends' houses, or community access points. They concluded that "access translates into usage" and that whites are more likely than African Americans to use the Web because they are more likely to have access.

Babb (1998) investigated home computer ownership and Internet use among low-income individuals and minorities. She found that African Americans and Hispanics were less likely to own computers, even after adjusting for income and education, and termed this finding, consistent across seven different data sets under examination, "the single most important finding" of her study.

The Digital Divide Is Increasing over Time

In 1998, the Commerce Department's National Telecommunications and Information Administration (McConnaughey and Lader 1998) analyzed data on computer penetration rates from the October 1997 Current Population Survey (CPS) as part of an ongoing examination of the digital divide. This analysis represented an update from their 1995 study of similar data from the November 1994 CPS. The authors concluded that the gap between the technology "haves" and "have-nots" had *increased* between 1994 and 1997, with African Americans and Hispanics actually farther behind whites in terms of home computer ownership and Internet access and with an even wider gap between individuals at upper and lower income levels.

The NTIA examined the digital divide again a year later (Department of Commerce 1999), using Census data from December 1998. Although they found that more Americans than ever before were connected to the Internet, the data clearly showed a persistent digital divide between the "information-rich" and the "information-poor." Upper-income households were much more likely to have Internet access and PCs at home. Furthermore, whites were more likely than African Americans or Hispanics to have Internet access. Additionally, rural Americans were less likely to have Internet access than Americans in urban locations. The report also revealed that, compared to 1994, gaps in home Internet access had widened between whites and African Americans.

Hoffman, Novak, and Schlosser (1999) systematically investigated differences over time in home computer ownership, Internet access, and usage between whites and African Americans in the United States. Their comparative analysis was based on primary data from three population-projectable, nationally representative surveys of Internet use among Americans (Nielsen Media Research 1997a;b; 1998), including the first survey on Internet use to collect data on race and ethnicity (Hoffman, Kalsbeek, and Novak 1996; Nielsen Media Research 1997a).

In terms of Internet access, use, and PC ownership across three time points (January 1997, September 1997, and June 1998), Hoffman, Novak, and Schlosser found that the digital divide continues. Web users in general were wealthier, while those without Internet access in general were poorer. Similarly, Web users were better educated, while those without access were most likely to have a high school education or less. These effects were more pronounced for African Americans than for whites and persisted over time. Furthermore, differences in Internet access, having ever used the Web, and home computer ownership between whites and African Americans actually increased over time.

Among recent Web users, who by definition have access somewhere, Hoffman, Novak, and Schlosser found that the gaps in usage had largely disappeared. Over time, African Americans were nearly as likely to be long-term users as their white counterparts, and they used the Web just as recently and frequently.

Among other results, they reported that men were still more likely to have ever used the Internet than women, but that, consistent with other surveys, the gender gap was closing rapidly. However, white men and women were more likely to have access, to use, and to own PCs than their African American counterparts. Furthermore, although the percentage of white men and women owning a PC has increased, it has not increased for African American men and women.

Students were more likely to have access, to have ever used, and to own computers than nonstudents, and that rate was increasing. However, white students were more likely to have access and to have ever used the Web than African American students, and also more likely to own home computers. For those without a home PC, the gaps appear to be increasing between white and African American students.

Not surprisingly, increasing levels of education lead to higher levels of access, use, home PC ownership, and PC access at work. But Hoffman, Novak, and Schlosser found that these levels were higher for whites than for African Americans and persisted even after adjusting for education. Also not surprisingly, higher income corresponded to higher levels of access, use, home PC ownership, and PC access at work. At incomes below $40,000, whites were more likely than African Americans to have Internet access, to own, or to use a PC, whereas the gaps greatly diminished at incomes above $40,000.

In the next section, we use this research on the digital divide to formulate a series of discussion and policy points relevant to the development of an open research agenda concerning the socioeconomic impact of the Internet and electronic commerce in the United States and globally.

Developing a Research Agenda

Computers in the Home

The gap between whites and African Americans in computer ownership has been cited as the key explanation for corresponding gaps in Web usage. A Yankelovich Monitor study (*Interactive Daily* 1997) "suggests that what bars entry to cyberspace among African Americans is owning a home PC, not lack of interest in the Internet." In addition, a Forrester Research study (Walsh 1999) cites "technology optimism" as an important predictor of technology adoption. More rigorous research is required to understand the relevance of such factors in predicting the increasing gaps in access and usage noted above.

While previous research has shown that inequalities in Internet access in schools persist (Educational Testing Service 1997; Sax et al. 1998), the research reviewed above suggests that inequalities in Internet access at home may be even more problematic. The role of access to the Internet at home needs to be much more clearly understood (Abrams 1997).

Gaps in general Web access and use between African-Americans and whites appear to be driven by whether or not there is a computer present in the home. Access to a personal computer, whether at home, work, school, or somewhere else, is important because it is currently the dominant mechanism by which individuals can access the Internet. We believe that access translates into usage. Overall, individuals who own a home computer are much more likely than others to use the Web. This suggests that programs that encourage home computer ownership (see, for example, Roberts 1997) and the adoption of inexpensive devices that enable Internet access over the television should be aggressively pursued.

Internet Adoption

A number of reasons have been provided in the popular press for the gap between whites and African Americans in computer ownership. Price and value are often cited as explanations. For example, Malcolm CasSelle, cofounder of NetNoir, asserted that "African Americans just don't perceive the value of the Internet. Many blacks would pay $500 for a TV, and you could get a computer, though maybe not a top-of-the-line one, for not much more than that" (Holmes 1997). Similarly, Larry Irving, Assistant Secretary of Commerce, noted that WebTV is in the under-$500 price range and "laptop and PC prices are coming down. As that continues to happen, the Internet will become more prevalent in the African American community" (Holmes 1997).

Morrisette (1999) projected that by the year 2003, over half of all households in the United States will have access to the Internet, but that PC penetration could stall at 60 percent of households. Research is needed on what motivates individual-level adoption of home computers and related technologies, as well as Internet adoption, both within and outside the home. Additionally, research is needed on the long-term impact of home computer ownership on Internet access and use. The stalling of PC penetration is a critical issue, but one that may prove illusory in the long run as prices drop and Internet appliances emerge. This issue illustrates one of the main problems involved in the design of research in a rapidly moving market.

The main ways that people are originally introduced to the Internet are, in order, being taught by friends or family, learning at work, or teaching themselves (Katz and Aspden 1997). Recent Internet users are less likely to learn at work than to be taught by friends/family or themselves. This reinforces the importance of the presence of a computer at home, or the opportunity to access the Web from locations other than the home, in stimulating Web use.

Insight into the importance of reducing this gap in Web use between whites and African Americans is provided by Anderson and Melchior's (1995) discussion of *information redlining*, which they define as the relegation of minorities into situations where satisfying their information needs is weighed against their economic and social worth. From the point of view of those affected, this is both an access issue and a form of discrimination.

The new technologies of information are not simply tools of private communication in the way that a telephone is, or tools of entertainment in the way that a television is. They provide direct access to information sources that are essential in making social choices and keeping track of developments not only in the world at large, but also within one's immediate neighborhood. Unless all neighborhoods are properly served, there is no way out of information redlining for most disadvantaged groups.

There are also interesting differences in media use between whites and African Americans that also deserve further probing. For example, although the overall rate of home PC ownership among African Americans is flat or even decreasing, the rates of cable and satellite dish penetration are increasing dramatically. At a minimum, these results suggest that African Americans may have better immediate prospects for Internet access through cable modems and satellite technology. It follows directly that marketing Internet access via these technologies to African Americans should be investigated.

Web Use outside the Home

In addition to gaps in home computer ownership, the implications of differential Internet access at locations outside the home, including school, the workplace, and other locations needs to be clearly understood. Research suggests that additional access points stimulate usage. Further research is needed on the impact of multiple access points on Web use, particularly for individuals who have no access at home.

Public-private initiatives such as Bell Atlantic's efforts in Union City and Bill Gates's announcement of a $200 million gift to provide library access to the Internet are steps in the right direction (Abrams 1997). It has also been asserted that "community networks and public access terminals offer great potential for African-American communities" (Sheppard 1997). Furthermore, the creation of E-rate funds (Schools and Libraries Corporation 1998) provides a significant opportunity for researchers to explore the factors important in stimulating Web usage among those least likely to have access.

School Web Use

The role of Web access in the schools, compared to other locations, needs to be clearly understood. Students enjoy the highest levels of Internet access and Web use, especially when there are computers in their households. However, white students are still more likely than African-American students to have access to and to use the Internet, and these gaps persist over time. Indeed, our findings closely parallel statistics comparing student Internet use at private universities and black public colleges (Sax et al. 1998). As a report by the Educational Testing Service (1997) found:

• There are major differences among schools in access to different kinds of educational technology.

• Students attending poor and high-minority schools have less access to most types of technology than students attending other schools.

• It will cost about $15 billion-approximately $300 per student-to make all our schools "technology-rich." This is five times what we currently spend on technology, but only 5 percent of total education spending.

Anderson and Melchior (1995) cited lack of education as an important barrier to technology access and adoption. Access to technology does not make much sense unless people are educated in using the technologies. Our data do not speak to the quality of the hardware/network connections, or the quality of information technology education that is provided by school. As noted by the

ETS report, creation of educational opportunities requires financial commitment that cannot be generated by the minority groups from their own resources.

Comparisons of All Racial/Ethnic Groups

We also need to do comparisons that involve such minorities as Hispanics, Asian Americans, and Native Americans. For a comprehensive understanding of technology adoption and its impact on the digital economy, we need to know the differences in Internet access and use among *all* racial and ethnic groups in the United States. Future studies need to oversample members of minority groups so that there will be sufficient numbers of all such groups to perform poststratification adjustments to create weights that yield population-projectable results for each minority group.

Differences in Search Behavior

We need to understand why African Americans and whites differ in their Web search behavior. Such differences could have important implications for the ultimate success of commercial efforts online. White Web users are more likely to report searching for product- or service-related information than African Americans. One possibility is that despite the existence of sites such as NetNoir (www.netnoir.com/) and Black Entertainment Television (www.msbet.com/), African Americans may not perceive general-purpose sites as an effective way to locate compelling Web content (*New Media Week* 1997). This suggests that there is a need for search engines and portals targeted to the specific interests of racial/ethnic groups.

Shopping Behavior

There appear to be no differences between African Americans and whites in the incidence of Web shopping. Is this because race doesn't matter for the "lead users" who are most likely to shop online, or is it because commercial Web content better targets racial and ethnic groups than does noncommercial Web content? Previous research (Novak, Hoffman, and Yung 1999) suggests that more skill is required to shop online than to search. More generally, consumer behavior in the commercial Web environment is complex and only weakly understood. Further research is needed on the differences in consumer behavior on the Web and the implications of such differences for commercialization.

Multicultural Content

Studies on the extent of multicultural content on the Web are needed. Another possibility for the gap between African Americans and whites in Web search behavior is that there is insufficient content of interest to African Americans. *Interactive Marketing News* (1997) claimed that "while there are about 10 million sites on the Web, there are fewer than 500 sites targeted" to African Americans. However, others have commented on the multicultural diversity of the Web. Skriloff (1997) reported, "there are thousands of Web sites with content to appeal to Hispanics, African Americans, Asian-Americans, and other ethnic groups. . . . A Web search for Latino sites, reported in the February/March 1997 issue of *Latina* Magazine, turned up 36,000. Many of these sites are ready-for-prime time with high-quality content, graphics, and strategic purpose."

Community Building

Are there different cultural identities for different parts of cyberspace? Schement (1997) notes that by the year 2020, major U.S. cities such as Los Angeles, Chicago, and New York will have increasingly divergent ethnic profiles and will take on distinctive cultural identities. An important question is whether there are divergent ethnic profiles for different areas of cyberspace. While the research conducted to date does not directly address this issue, our review above provided some preliminary evidence of divergent ethnic profiles for various Web usage situations. For example, African Americans appear to be more likely to use the Web at school and at other locations, and in some cases are more likely to use the Web at work. How much of this is driven by the lack of a PC in the home and how much by other factors we have yet to hypothesize and investigate?

In addition to facilitating community building at the global level, the Web also facilitates neighborhood-level community building. Clearly, the Internet can be used as a vehicle for empowering communities (Anderson and Melchior 1995; Blumenstyk 1997; Schwartz 1996). Thus, we should expect to find neighborhood Web sites emerging as an important aspect of cyberspace, and that these Web sites will parallel the ethnic profiles of the corresponding physical communities.

Income and Education

Income matters, but only above a certain level. Household income explains race differences in Internet access, use, home computer ownership, and PC access at work. In terms of overall access and use, higher household income positively affects access to a computer. But at lower incomes, gaps in access and use between whites and African Americans exist and have been increasing. Research is necessary to determine the most effective means to ensure access for lower-income Americans and especially for African Americans.

The situation is different with education. As with income, increasing levels of education positively influences access, Web use, PC ownership, and PC access at work. However, whites are still more likely than African Americans to have access to and to use the Internet, and to own a home computer, and these gaps persist even after controlling for educational differences.

The policy implications of this finding need to be carefully considered: To ensure the participation of all Americans in the information revolution, it is critical that we improve the educational opportunities for African Americans. How this might best be achieved is an open research question.

Interestingly, Cooper and Kimmelman (1999) argue that the Telecommunications Act of 1996 has had the unintended and unfortunate consequence of increasing the division between the telecommunications "haves" and "have-nots." As evidence, they point to (1) increased concentration and less competition in the telecommunications and cable industries, (2) significant increases or flat prices, instead of declines, in cable, long-distance, and local phone rates, and (3) a growing disparity between those market segments who are heavy users of telecommunications networks, including the Internet, and those whose use is more modest.

Concluding Remarks

The consequences of the digital divide for American society could well be severe (Beaupre and Brand-Williams 1997). Just as Liebling (1960) observed for the freedom of the press, the Internet may allow equal economic opportunity and democratic communication, but it will do so only for those with access. Moreover, the U.S. economy as a whole could be at risk if a significant segment of our society lacks the technological skills needed to keep American firms competitive.

This goal of this chapter has been to stimulate discussion among scholars and policymakers in how differences in Internet access and use among different segments of our society affects their ability to participate in the emerging digital economy and to reap the rewards of that participation. We have reviewed recent research investigating the relationship of race to Internet access and usage over time and have developed a set of issues supported by that research that can serve as a framework for future work.

Acknowledgments

The authors gratefully acknowledge a research grant from the John and Mary R. Markle Foundation in support of this research and thank Nielsen Media Research for generously providing access to the original data.

References

Abrams, Alan (1997). "Diversity and the Internet," *Journal of Commerce*, June 26.

Anderson, Teresa E., and Alan Melchior (1995). "Assessing Telecommunications Technology as a Tool for Urban Community Building," *Journal of Urban Technology* 3(1): 29–44.

Babb, Stephanie F. (1998). "The Internet as a Tool for Creating Economic Opportunity for Individuals and Families," Unpublished Doctoral Dissertation, University of California, Los Angeles.

Beaupre, Becky, and Oralandar Brand-Williams (1997). "Sociologists Predict Chasm between Black Middle-Class, Poor Will Grow," *The Detroit News*, February 8.

Blumenstyk, Goldie (1997). "An Experiment in 'Virtual Community' Takes Shape in Blacksburg, Va.," *The Chronicle of Higher Education* 43(19): A24–A26.

Clinton, William J. (1997a). "State of the Union Address," February 4. [http://www.whitehouse.gov/WH/SOU97/]

Clinton, William J. (1997b). "Remarks by the President at Education Announcement/Roundtable," Office of the Press Secretary, April 2. [http://www.iitf.nist.gov/documents/press/040297.htm]

Coley, Richard J., John Cradler, and Penelope K. Engel (1997). "Computers and Classrooms: The Status of Technology in U.S. Schools," ETS Policy Information Report. ETS Policy Information Center. Princeton, NJ. [http://www.ets.org/research/pic/compclass.html]

Cooper, Mark, and Gene Kimmelman (1999). "The Digital Divide Confronts the Telecommunications Act of 1996: Economic Reality Versus Public Policy," The First Triennial Review, February, Consumers Union. [http://www.consunion.org/other/telecom4-0299.htm]

CyberAtlas (1999). "As Internet Matures, So Do Its Users," April 26. [http://www.cyberatlas.com/big_picture/demographics/inteco.html]

Department of Commerce (1999). "Falling Through the Net: Defining the Digital Divide," National Telecommunications and Information Administration. [http://www.ntia.doc.gov/]

Educational Testing Service (1997). *Computers and Classrooms: The Status of Technology in U.S. Schools,* Policy Information Center. [http://www.ets.org/research/pic/compclass.html]

eStats (1999). "Net Market Size and Growth: U.S. Net Users Today," May 10. [http://www.emarketer.com/estats/nmsg_ust.html]

Harmon, Amy (1997). "Net Day Volunteers Back to Wire Schools for Internet," *New York Times,* October 25.

Hoffman, Donna L. (1996). "Affidavit: ACLU v. Reno." [http://www2000.ogsm.vanderbilt.edu/affidavit.html]

Hoffman, D. L., W. D. Kalsbeek, and T. P. Novak (1996). "Internet and Web Use in the United States: Baselines for Commercial Development," Special Section on "Internet in the Home," *Communications of the ACM* 39 (December): 36–46. [www2000.ogsm.vanderbilt.edu/papers/internet.demos.July9.1996.html]

Hoffman, D. L., and T. P. Novak (1998). "Bridging the Racial Divide on the Internet," *Science* 280 (April 17): 390–391.

Hoffman, D. L., T. P. Novak, and P. Chatterjee (1995). "Commercial Scenarios for the Web: Opportunities and Challenges," *Journal of Computer-Mediated Communication,* Special Issue on Electronic Commerce, 1(3). [http://jcmc.huji.ac.il/vol1/issue3/hoffman.html]

Hoffman, D. L., T. P. Novak, and A. E. Schlosser (1999). "The Evolution of the Digital Divide: How Gaps in Internet Access May Impact Electronic Commerce," Working Paper, Project 2000. [http://ecommerce.vanderbilt.edu/]

Hoffman, D. L., T. P. Novak, and A. Venkatesh (1997). "Diversity on the Internet: The Relationship of Race to Access and Usage," paper presented at the Aspen Institute's Forum on Diversity and the Media , Queenstown, Maryland, November 5–7, 1997. [http://www2000.ogsm.vanderbilt.edu/papers/aspen/diversity.on.the.internet.oct24.1997.html]

Holmes, Tamara E. (1997). "Seeing a Future with More Blacks Exploring the Internet," *USA Today*, February 20.

Interactive Daily (1997). "More African-Americans Plan To Go Online," February 18.

Katz, James, and Philip Aspden (1997). "Motivations for and Barriers to Internet Usage: Results of a National Public Opinion Survey," paper presented at the 24th Annual Telecommunications Policy Research Conference, Solomons, Maryland, October 6, 1996.

Keller, James (1996). "Public Access Issues: An Introduction," in Brian Kahin and James Keller, eds., *Public Access to the Internet* (Cambridge, MA: The MIT Press).

Lawrence, Steve, and C. Lee Giles, (1999). "Accessibility of Information on the Web, " *Nature* 400 (July 8): 107–109.

Liebling, A. J. (1960). *The New Yorker* 36 (May 14): 105.

Maraganore, Nicki, and Shelley Morrisette (1998). "The On-Line Gender Gap Is Closing," *Data Insights, Forrester Research Reports* 1(18). December 2.

McConnaughey, James W., and Wendy Lader (1998). "Falling through the Net II: New Data on the Digital Divide," U.S. Department of Commerce, National Telecommunications and Information Administration, July 28. [http://www.ntia.doc.gov/ntiahome/net2/falling.html]

Morrisette, Shelley (1999). "Consumer's Digital Decade," *Forrester Report* (January). Forrester Research, Inc. [http://www.forrester.com/]

NetDay (1998). [http://www.netday96.com/]

Network Wizards (1999). "Internet Domain Survey," July. [http://www.nw.com/zone/WWW/report.html]

New Media Week (1997). "BET, Microsoft Sees Potential in African-American Audience," March 3.

Nielsen Media Research (1997a). "The Spring '97 CommerceNet/Nielsen Media Internet Demographic Survey, Full Report." Interviews conducted in December 1996/January 1997. Volumes I and II.

Nielsen Media Research (1997b). "The Fall '97 CommerceNet/Nielsen Media Internet Demographic Survey, Full Report." Interviews conducted in August/September 1997. Volumes I and II.

Nielsen Media Research (1998). "The Spring '98 CommerceNet/Nielsen Media Internet Demographic Survey, Full Report." Interviews conducted in May/June 1998. Volumes I and II.

Novak, T. P., D. L. Hoffman, and Y. F. Yung (1999). "Modeling the Flow Construct in Online Environments: A Structural Modeling Approach," manuscript under review, *Marketing Science*.

Pew Research Center (1998). "Online Newcomers More Middle-Brow, Less Work-Oriented: The Internet News Audience Goes Ordinary," The Pew Research Center for the People and the Press. [http://www.people-press.og/tech98sum.htm]

Roberts, Regina M. (1997). "Program Lowers Costs of Going Online; Families Can Get Break on Equipment," *The Atlanta Journal and Constitution*, June 19.

Rutkowski, Anthony M. (1998). "Internet Trends," Washington, DC: Center for Next Generation Internet. [http://www.ngi.org/trends.htm]

Sax, L. J., A. W. Astin, W. S. Korn, and K. M. Mahoney (1998). "The American Freshman: National Norms for Fall 1998," Higher Education Research Institute, UCLA Graduate School of Education & Information Studies. [http://www.acenet.edu/news/press_release/1999/01January/freshman_survey.html]

Schement, Jorge Reina (1997). "Thorough Americans: Minorities and the New Media," paper presented at the Aspen Institute Forum, October 1996.

Schools and Libraries Corporation (1998). "First Wave of E-Rate Funding Commitment Letters Sent," November 23 news release.

Schwartz, Ed (1996). *NetActivism: How Citizens Use the Internet*, Sebastopol, CA: O'Reilly & Associates.

Sheppard, Nathanial (1997). "Free-Nets Reach out to Communities' Needs," *The Ethnic NewsWatch*, April 30.

Skriloff, Lisa (1997). "Out of the Box: A Diverse Netizenry," *Brandweek*, February 17.

Walsh, Ekaterna O. (1999). "The Digital Melting Pot," *The Forrester Brief*, March 3, Forrester Research, Inc.

Wilhelm, Anthony (1998). "Closing the Digital Divide: Enhancing Hispanic Participation in the Information Age," Claremont, CA: The Tomas Rivera Policy Institute, April.

Extending Access to the Digital Economy to Rural and Developing Regions

Heather E. Hudson

1 Introduction

The convergence of telecommunications, information technologies, and electronic media has made possible new forms of economic interaction that have been characterized as the "digital economy." This chapter examines ways of conceptualizing access to this emerging digital economy and identifies research questions that need to be addressed to formulate policies and strategies to extend access, both to rural and disadvantaged populations in industrialized countries and to people in the developing world.

2 Information Gaps

2.1 Gaps within Industrialized Countries

In industrialized countries, there is growing concern that a "digital divide" separates those with access to information technologies and the skills and resources to use them from the rest of the society. In the United States in 1997, 93.8 percent of households had telephone service, 36.6 percent had personal computers, and 26.3 percent had modems. The number of households with access to e-mail increased nearly 400 percent between 1994 and 1997.[1] Despite an overall trend of growth in access, there is a widening gap between high- and low-income households, and between Whites and Blacks, Hispanics, and native American populations, in computer ownership and online access.

In rural areas, distance no longer accounts for difference in household access to a telephone; income levels are now a better predictor. But there is a gap in connectivity to the Internet between rural and urban areas. At every income level, households in rural areas are significantly less likely—sometimes half as likely—to have home Internet access than households in urban or central city areas;[2] and those who are connected typically pay more than their urban counterparts for Internet access.

2.2 Gaps in Developing Countries

Access to information and communications technologies (ICTs) remains much more limited in the developing world. In its Statement on Universal Access to Basic Communication and Information Services, the United Nations noted:

The information and technology gap and related inequities between industrialized and developing nations are widening: a new type of poverty—information poverty—looms. Most developing countries, especially the Least Developed Countries (LDCs), are not sharing in the communications revolution, since they lack:

• affordable access to core information resources, cutting-edge technology, and sophisticated telecommunications systems and infrastructure;

• the capacity to build, operate, manage, and service the technologies involved;

• policies that promote equitable public participation in the information society as both producers and consumers of information and knowledge; and

• a workforce trained to develop, maintain, and provide the value-added products and services required by the information economy.[3]

Table 1 shows the gap in Internet access between the industrialized and developing worlds. More than 85 percent of the world's Internet users are in developed countries, which account for only about 22 percent of the world's population.[4] Of course, Internet access requires both communications links and information technologies, particularly personal computers or networked computer terminals. While there is much less access to telecommunications overall in developing countries than in industrialized countries,

Table 1   Internet Access by Region, June 1999

	People connected (millions)	Percentage of global connections	Percentage of global population
Canada and U.S.	97.0	56.6	5.1
Europe	40.1	23.4	13.7
Asia/Pacific	27.0	15.8	56.2
Latin America	5.3	3.1	8.4
Africa	1.1	0.6	12.9
Middle East	0.9	0.5	3.6

Source: Henry et al. (1999).

Table 2   Access Indicators

Country Classification	Telephone lines/100	PCs/100	Internet hosts/10,000	Internet users/10,000
High Income	56.1	30.4	450.4	1396.5
Upper Middle	16.5	4.1	18.2	141.7
Lower Middle	8.2	1.3	1.6	24.7
Low Income	1.4	0.3	0.1	3.9

Source: International Telecommunication Union (1999b).

the gap in access to computers is much greater than the gap in access to telephone lines or telephones. High-income countries had 22 times as many telephone lines per 100 population as low-income countries, but 96 times as many computers. As prices for computers continue to decline, however, access may become more related to perceived value than to price (table 2).

Typically, a high percentage of people in developing countries live in rural areas (as much as 80 percent of the population in the least-developed countries), where access to communication networks is much more limited than in urban areas (table 3). It should be noted that table 3 overestimates rural access because "rest of country" includes everything except the largest city. Also, facilities are not likely to be evenly distributed throughout the country, so that in poorer nations there may be many rural settlements without any communications infrastructure at all.

Table 3 Access to Telecommunications

Country	Teledensity (Tel Lines/100)		
Classification	National	Urban	Rest of country
High Income	56.1	60.2	47.8
Upper Middle	16.5	24.3	13.8
Lower Middle	8.2	23.3	6.6
Low Income	1.4	5.7	1.4

Source: International Telecommunication Union (1999b).

3 The Importance of Access

What is the significance of these digital divides? The theoretical underpinning of research on the impact of ICTs in general is that information is critical to the social and economic activities that comprise the development process. The ability to manipulate information is obviously central to activities that have come to be known as the "information sector," including education and research, media and publishing, information equipment and software, and information-intensive services such as financial services, consulting, and trade. But information manipulation is also critical for management, logistics, marketing, and other functions in economic activities ranging from manufacturing to agriculture and resource extraction. Information is also important to the delivery of health care and public services. If information is critical to development, then ICTs, as the means of accessing, processing, and sharing information, are links in the chain of the development process itself.

In general, the ability to access and share information can contribute to the development process by improving:

• *efficiency*, or the ratio of output to cost;

• *effectiveness*, or the quality of products and services; and

• *equity*, or the distribution of development benefits throughout the society.

Much of the research to date on the socioeconomic effects of new communications technologies has examined the role of information networking through telecommunications. The extended impact of the combination of networks and information technologies is just beginning to be understood. The United States and the OECD are in the early stages of collecting data on the growth of electronic commerce and analyzing its impact. The U.S. Department of Commerce states that the output of IT industries contributed more than one-third of the growth of real output in the overall U.S. economy between 1995 and 1998 (Henry et al. 1999).

While we are in the early stages of understanding the emerging digital economy, it seems clear that more than access will be necessary to foster participation. The critical factors will likely include a workforce with sufficient general education and specialized training and an institutional environment that fosters innovation and productivity.

4 Access Parameters

4.1 Access vs. Service

The terms "universal access" and "universal service" are sometimes used interchangeably and typically refer to telecommunications networks. Here we must also consider access to the technologies connected to these networks that make possible the information processing necessary to participate in the digital economy. Typical end users require personal computers with sufficient speed and capacity to process data from the World Wide Web (or networked terminals with central access to sufficient capacity) and connections to value-added services such as Internet service providers (ISPs). Access is thus a broader concept than service and involves the following components and issues:

- *Infrastructure:* reach of networks and services (e.g., to rural areas or to low-income populations in inner cities); available bandwidth (e.g., broadband capacity for high-speed Internet access);
- *Range of Services* (e.g., basic voice service—plain old telephone service, or "POTS"—or value-added services such as ISPs);
- *Affordability:* pricing of installation, monthly service fees, usage fees by time or volume, and so on;

- *Reliability:* quality of service, as indicated by frequency and extent of outages, breakdowns, circuit blockage, circuits degraded by noise or echoes, and so on.

Another important aspect of access is specifying the users of telecommunications services. We might consider several categories:

- *The public:* broken down by geographic or demographic characteristics such as urban/periurban/rural/remote or age, gender, ethnicity, etc.;

- *Commercial enterprises:* large and small businesses and entrepreneurs; critical sectors such as agriculture, transportation, manufacturing, or tourism;

- *Public services:* government and public service sectors such as health care and education; nonprofit and nongovernmental organizations (NGOs).

4.2 Universal Access: A Moving Target

Universal access is a dynamic concept with a set of moving targets. The unit of analysis for accessibility could be the household, the municipality, or even institutions such as schools and health centers. Moreover, we must periodically reconsider our definition of basic service to take into consideration changes in technology and user needs. Thus, we should state goals not in terms of a specific technology or service provider (such as wireline or wireless service provided by a telephone company) but in terms of functions and capabilities, such as the ability to transmit voice and data. Because information access is so important for socioeconomic development, the units of analysis for access should include not only the individual but the community as a whole and institutions such as schools, clinics, libraries, and community centers.

The economic and demographic diversity common to inner cities, rural areas, and developing countries will require a variety of goals for information infrastructure policies. Rapid technological change also dictates that the definitions of basic and "advanced" or "enhanced" services will change over time. We might, for example, propose a multitiered definition of access, identifying requirements within households, within communities, and for education and social service providers, as follows:

Level One: community access (through kiosks, libraries, post offices, community centers, telecenters, etc.).

Level Two: institutional access (schools, hospitals, clinics, etc)

Level Three: household access.

Universality has been defined differently in various countries. In North America and Europe, the goal has been to provide basic telephone service to every household, with the assumption that businesses and organizations would all have access to at least this grade of service. The Maitland Commission of the International Telecommunication Union (ITU) called for a telephone within an hour's walk throughout the developing world. Some developing countries set targets of public telephones within a radius of a few kilometers in rural areas.[5] Others, including China, India, Mexico, Nepal, and Thailand, aim for at least one telephone per village or settlement.

It is interesting to note that for Internet access, the United States is applying the community and institutional access models more commonly found in developing countries. The U.S. Telecommunications Act of 1996 specifies that "advanced services" should be provided at a discount to schools, libraries, and rural health centers. "Advanced services" are currently interpreted as Internet access. In the future, it is likely that "advanced services" will be redefined, perhaps to include access to new generations of services available through the Internet or its successors. It should also be noted that industrialized countries such as the United States and Canada have extended the concept of basic service beyond quality adequate for voice to include single-party service and circuits capable of supporting the capacity of current modems, with the assumption that people will want to communicate electronically from their homes.[6] These criteria are also likely to be revised over time to keep pace with the demands of the digital economy.

5 Understanding the Demand for Information Services

As noted above, income may be the best underlying predictor of access to the tools of the digital economy. Because higher-income populations tend to be better educated, they have not only the

Table 4   Teledensity vs. TV Density

	Telephone lines/100	TV sets/100	Ratio of TV sets to telephone lines
High-Income Countries	56.1	64.8	1.2
Upper Middle-Income Countries	16.5	28.2	1.7
Lower Middle-Income Countries	8.2	24.5	2.3
Low-Income Countries	1.4	6.6	4.7

Source: International Telecommunication Union (1999b).

money but the skills to use new technologies and services, and they are more likely than poorer people to use these tools in their work. Also, higher-income populations tend to live in urban and suburban areas where communication networks are more available in developing countries and more affordable almost everywhere.

Yet income may not fully explain the pattern of demand for information technologies and services, nor can lack of access to telephone lines necessarily be attributed to lack of demand or purchasing power. For example, in industrialized countries, both TV sets and telephone lines are almost universally available. In middle-income countries, however, there are twice as many TV sets as telephone lines, while in low-income countries, there are more than five times as many TV sets as telephone lines (table 4). It appears that where television is available, a significant percentage of families will find the money to buy TV sets. Thus, even in the poorest countries, there may be much more disposable income available than per capita GDP data would indicate, and there may be significant demand for other information services. (The exponential growth of cellphone subscribers in Uganda is another example of unanticipated demand for information services in a low-income country.) Another conclusion that can be drawn from this analysis is that changing the policy environment to create incentives to serve previously ignored populations may significantly increase access among these groups.

Indicators other than population and household income may be better predictors of demand for communication services. One study estimates that rural users in developing countries are able collectively to pay 1–1.5 percent of their gross *community* income for telecommunications services.[7] The ITU uses an estimate of 5 percent of *household* income as an affordability threshold. To generate revenues to cover capital and operating costs of the network, the average household income required would be $2060; for a more efficiently run network, it would be $1340.[8] Using the higher estimate, 20 percent of households in low-income countries could afford a telephone; in lower middle-income countries the range could be from 40 percent to 80 percent, while in upper middle-income countries such as Eastern Europe, more than 80 percent of households could afford telephone service.[9] It should be possible to use similar approaches to forecast affordability of access to the Internet in developing regions.

Other approaches may also be used to gauge demand for information services. For example, the presence of video shops indicates sufficient disposable income to afford TV sets, videocassette players, and cassette rentals. Telephone service resellers (such as in Indonesia, Senegal, and Bangladesh), local cable television operators (common in India), and small satellite dishes on rural homesteads and urban flats (common in Eastern Europe and many Asian countries) also signal demand and ability to pay for information services. The existence of video rental outlets, phone shops, and storefront copy centers is also evidence of entrepreneurs who could possibly operate other information service businesses.

Collectively, expenditures on rural and regional telecommunications in developing countries are between 1 and 2 percent of national GDP. Revenue forecasts are often based on the traffic generated from the rural area, but they should also include urban-to-rural traffic. For example, foreigners working in the Arabian Gulf states call family members in rural communities of Egypt, Yemen, India, and Pakistan. In South Africa, mine workers call their families in rural townships as well as in neighboring countries. As more rural communities have e-mail and Internet access, we should expect urban-to-rural traffic to increase since urban businesses can place orders from rural suppliers, individuals and travel agencies can make reservations for rural tourist facilities, and urban relatives can more easily contact rural family members. Of course, rural-to-urban traffic to send messages and access websites is also likely to increase.

6 Technological Trends

From the service providers' perspective, there have traditionally been few incentives to provide access to low-income customers, who are presumed to have limited demand for new services, and to rural and remote regions, where the cost of extending or upgrading facilities and services is assumed to be higher than expected revenues. However, technological innovations, many of which were initially designed for other applications, are now creating opportunities to reduce costs and/or increase revenues in these populations.

The tremendous capacity of fiberoptic backbone networks and the increased capacity available to end users through enhancements of the wireline local loop such as ISDN (Integrated Services Digital Network) and DSL (Digital Subscriber Line) as well as coaxial cable and hybrid fiber coax (HFC) make it possible to provide increased bandwidth for accessing the Web to households and small businesses. Moreover, the capacity of these technologies to carry voice and video as well as data can provide a wider range of services at potentially lower cost to customers than separately delivered services. Of course, these technologies are being targeted initially at larger businesses or more affluent residential customers, but the widespread availability of wireline in telephone networks, coaxial cable television networks, and fiberoptic backbones should make increased bandwidth affordable for residents of inner cities, small businesses, and nonprofit organizations. In rural areas, both terrestrial wireless and satellites offer greater capacity without the cost of building out fiber and cable networks. More information on these technologies can be found in the appendix to this chapter.

These technological trends have significant implications, particularly for rural and developing regions:

• *Distance is no longer a barrier* to accessing information. Technologies are available that can provide interactive voice, data, and multimedia services virtually anywhere.

• *Costs of providing services are declining.* Satellite transmission costs are independent of distance; transmission costs using other technologies have also declined dramatically. Thus communications services can be priced not according to distance, which penalizes rural and remote users, but per unit of information (message, bit) or unit of time.

- *The potential for competition is increasing.* Lower costs make rural/remote areas more attractive. New competitors can offer multiple technological solutions, including wireless, satellite, copper, cable, etc.

In addition, it is no longer technically or economically necessary to set rural benchmarks lower than urban benchmarks for access—either to basic telecommunications or to the Internet. The U.S. Telecommunications Act of 1996 requires that rural services and prices be *reasonably comparable* to those in urban areas. This standard rejects the assumption that "something is better than nothing" in rural areas because minimal service was all that is either technically feasible or economically justifiable. As noted above, advances in technologies such as terrestrial wireless and satellite systems now allow for higher quality at lower cost in rural areas. These changes in policy and technology will be particularly critical in enabling rural residents to participate in the digital economy.

While the industrialized countries must upgrade outdated wireline networks and analog exchanges in rural areas, developing countries can leapfrog old technologies and install fully digital wireless networks. At the same time, developing country regulators can adopt rural comparability standards to avoid penalizing rural services and businesses in access to information services. In the Philippines, as an example, after extensive discussion, government and industry representatives agreed on rural benchmarks that include digital switching, single-party service, and line quality sufficient for facsimile and data communications.[10]

7 Policies and Strategies for Increasing Access

7.1 Innovative Private-Sector Strategies

A variety of innovative strategies have been adopted to provide community access to telecommunications and, more recently, to the Internet. Some countries, such as Chile and Mexico, have mandated that operators install payphones in rural communities; South Africa has also required its wireless operators to install fixed rural payphones. Franchised payphones have been introduced in Indonesia, India, Bangladesh, and other countries in order to involve entrepreneurs where the operator is still government-owned. Indonesia's franchised call offices known as Wartels (Warung Telekomunikasi), operated by small entrepreneurs, generate more than $9,000 per line, about 10 times more than Telkom's average revenue per line.[11] Franchised telephone booths operate in several francophone African countries; in Senegal, phone shops, known locally as telecenters, average four times the revenue of those operated by the national carrier.[12] In Bangladesh, Grameen Phone has rented cellphones to rural women who provide portable payphone service to their communities. These examples demonstrate how simple resale can create incentives to meet pent-up demand even if network competition has not yet been introduced.

Innovative operators are also using information technology to extend access to previously unserved customers. Prepaid phone cards, widely available in Europe and Japan, have been introduced in developing countries to eliminate the need for coin phones (which require coin collection and may be subject to pilferage and vandalism). Cellular operators have now extended this concept to offer prepaid cellular service using rechargeable smart cards, so that telephone service is now available to customers without credit histories or even bank accounts. In South Africa, the cellular carrier Vodacom has introduced prepaid calling cards; Vodacom sold more than 300,000 prepaid starter packs and one million recharge vouchers for cellular use in 1997.[13] In Uganda, within one year of licensing a second cellular operator, its prepayment strategy coupled with aggressive marketing and attractive pricing resulted in there being more cellular customers than fixed lines in the country. For most of the new subscribers, a cellphone is their first and only telephone.[14]

Innovative approaches are also helping to extend access to the Internet. Virtually every major city in the developing world now has cybercafes or privately operated telecenters equipped with personal computers linked to the Internet. The African Communications Group plans wireless kiosks for Internet access, with web pages enabling artisans, farmers, and other small entrepreneurs to set up shop in the global marketplace.[15] Initiatives to support public

Internet access through community telecenters are being supported by several development agencies, including the ITU, Unesco, United Nations Development Program (UNDP), Canada's International Development Research Centre (IDRC), and the U.S. Agency for International Development (USAID). South Africa is also supporting the installation of telecenters equipped with phone lines, facsimile, and computers with Internet access through a Universal Service Fund; South Africa also plans to provide Internet access to government information and electronic commerce services through post offices. Many other countries are extending public access to the Internet through telecenters, libraries, post offices, and kiosks.

Access to telephones through booths, kiosks, and telecenters can be coupled with electronic messaging to provide "virtual telephone service." TeleBahia in northeastern Brazil offers a virtual service for small businesses without individual telephones. These customers rent a voice mail box for a monthly fee and check their messages from a payphone, providing a means for clients to contact them. African Communications Group is setting up wireless public payphones and providing voice mail accounts and pagers that announce incoming messages. The recipient calls back or leaves a voice mail message using a phone card; the service is priced for people making $200 per month.[16] (Similar systems are used for migrant farm workers in California to enable them to stay in touch with their families, and in homeless shelters to enable job seekers to be contacted by employers.)

Telecenters and other public facilities can provide access to e-mail, which is much faster than the postal service and cheaper than facsimile transmission. For example, a message of 2,000 words takes ten minutes to read over a telephone, two minutes to send by fax, and about four seconds to transmit via 28.8 kbps modem.[17] Such services can be valuable even for illiterates. For example, a Member of Parliament from Uganda stated that his father sent many telegrams during his lifetime but could neither read nor write. Local scribes wrote down his messages. Similarly, "information brokers" ranging from librarians to cybercafe staff can help people with limited education to send and access electronic information.

7.2 Service Obligations

Many countries include a universal service obligation (USO) as a condition of the license. The cost of USOs may vary depending on geography and population density. British Telecom's USO costs just 1 percent of its total revenue base.[18] Latin American countries with USOs include Argentina, Chile, Mexico, Peru, and Venezuela. In Mexico, the privatized monopoly operator, TelMex, must provide service to all communities with at least 500 population by the year 2000. In the Philippines, local exchange obligations are bundled with cellular and international gateway licenses; licensees are required to install up to 300,000 access lines in previously unserved areas within three years.[19]

Some countries use a "carrier of last resort" model that imposes an obligation to provide service if no other carrier has done so. Typically, the dominant carrier bears this obligation and is entitled to a subsidy to provide the service. This approach can be problematic, however, if it provides no incentive for the carrier of last resort to use the most appropriate and inexpensive technology and to operate efficiently. It can also serve as a justification for the dominant carrier to be protected from competition because it has additional costs and obligations not required of new competitors.

7.3 Subsidies

A variety of schemes can be used to subsidize operators that serve regions where revenues would probably not cover costs. Subsidies may be paired with USOs to compensate the carrier with the obligation to serve.

• *Internal Cross-Subsidies:* The traditional means of ensuring provision of service to unprofitable areas or customers has been through cross-subsidies, such as from international or interexchange to local services. Technological changes and the liberalization of the telecommunications sector now make it impracticable to rely on internal cross-subsidies. For example, customers may bypass high-priced services by using callback, VSATs, or Internet telephony.

• *Targeted Subsidies:* In a competitive environment, cross-subsidies cannot be maintained. Carriers that have relied on revenues from one service to subsidize another now face competitors that can underprice them on individual services. Also, new entrants cannot survive if their competitors are subsidized. Therefore, if subsidies are required, they must be made explicit and targeted at specific classes of customers or locations. For example, carriers may be subsidized to serve locations that are isolated and/or have very low population density. This approach is used in the United States and has recently been mandated in Canada. Subsidies may also target economically disadvantaged areas or groups that could not afford typical prices for installation and usage, or whose demand for service is significantly lower than average. Some operators may offer interest-free loans or extended payment periods to assist new subscribers to connect to the network. In the United States, the Lifeline program subsidizes basic monthly services charges for low-income subscribers. The subsidy funds come from a combination of carrier contributions and surcharges on subscriber bills. Some 4.4 million households receive Lifeline assistance. Also in the United States, the Linkup program subsidizes network connections for low-income households.

• *Route Averaging:* Australia, Canada, the United Kingdom, and the United States require that rates be averaged so that all customers pay uniform distance charges, regardless of location. Thus, for example, the rate per minute between Sydney and Melbourne would be the same as the rate over an equal distance in the Australian Outback, where costs are much higher. Such policies can bridge the digital divide by reducing rural access costs.

7.4 Rural Telecommunications Funds

Funds for subsidies may be generated from sources such as contributions required from all carriers (e.g., a percentage of revenues or tax on revenues), a surcharge on customer bills, or government funds (from general tax revenues or other government sources).

Some countries with many carriers rely on settlement and repayment pooling schemes among operators to transfer payments to carriers with high operating costs. For example, the U.S. Universal Service Fund is mandated by the Federal Communications Commission (FCC) but administered by the carriers through the National Exchange Carriers Association (NECA); it transfers funds to subsidize access lines to carriers whose costs are above 115 percent of the national average.[20]

In Poland, more than 7,885 localities were connected between 1992 and 1996 with funding of US $20 million from the state budget.[21] In 1994, Peru established a rural telecommunications investment fund, FITEL (Fondo de Inversion de Telecomunicaciones), which is financed by a 1 percent tax on revenues of all telecommunications providers, ranging from the country's newly privatized monopoly operator, Telefonica/ENTEL, to cable TV operators. Since it was established, it has generated an average of US$450,000 per month and is growing by US$12 million annually.[22] Private-sector operators may apply to FITEL for financing.[23]

7.5 Bidding for Subsidies

Rather than designating a single carrier of last resort, some countries are introducing bidding schemes for rural subsidies. In Chile, a development fund was established in 1994 to increase access for the approximately 10 percent of the population in communities without telephone access. The regulator estimated the required subsidies, distinguishing between commercially viable and commercially unviable projects, and put them out to competitive tender. There were 62 bids for 42 of the 46 projects. Surprisingly, 16 projects were awarded to bids of zero subsidy; as a result of preparing for the bidding process, operators were able to document demand and willingness to pay in many communities. Once completed, these projects will provide service to about 460,000 people, about one-third of the Chilean population without access.[24] Peru is introducing a similar program.

7.6 Licensing Rural Operators

Some countries grant monopoly franchises to rural operators. For example, Bangladesh has licensed two rural monopoly operators, which are allowed to prioritize the most financially attractive customers and charge an substantial up-front subscriber connection fee. The Bangladesh Rural Telecommunications Authority

(BRTA) is profitable, even though it must provide at least one public call office (PCO) in each village that requests one.[25]

Other countries are opening up rural areas to competition as part of national liberalization policies. Argentina allows rural operators to compete with the two privatized monopolies, Telecom and Telefonica. Some 135 rural cooperatives have been formed to provide telecommunications services in communities with fewer than 300 people.[26] Finland's association of telephone companies has created several jointly owned entities that provide a range of rural, local, and long-distance services in their concession areas, in competition with the national operator.[27] In Alaska, a second carrier, GCI, competes with AT&T Alascom to provide long-distance services in rural and remote areas. This competition has benefited Alaskan schools by making it easier for them to gain access to the Internet. GCI has assisted school districts in applying for E-rate subsidies for Internet access, apparently viewing this initiative as a win-win opportunity for both schools and the telephone company.

Although in most countries a single carrier provides both local and long-distance services, it is also possible to delineate territories that can be served by local entities. In the United States, the model of rural cooperatives fostered by the Rural Utilities Service (formerly Rural Electrification Administration) has been used to bring telephone service to areas ignored by the large carriers. As noted above, wireless technologies could change the economics of providing rural services, making rural franchises much more attractive to investors. As a result of availability of funds from the RUS for upgrading networks, rural cooperatives in the United States typically offer higher-quality networks and better Internet access than are provided by large telephone companies serving rural areas.

Third parties may also be permitted to lease capacity in bulk and resell it in units of bandwidth and/or time appropriate for business customers and other major users. This approach may be suitable where excess network capacity exists (e.g., between major cities or on domestic or regional satellites). Resale is one of the simplest ways to introduce some competition and lower rates for users, but it is not legal in many developing countries, even where some excess capacity exists in backbone networks.

8 Topics for Research

8.1 Tracking Information Gaps

It will be important to develop methods to track disparities in access to the technical components of the digital economy, such as connectivity (via telecommunications infrastructure) and information processing and storage (at present, this primarily means personal computers). Data such as those available through NTIA's Digital Divide studies will provide a valuable resource for monitoring such trends.[28] Other countries should develop similar sets of indicators, based on their own demographics and definitions of disadvantaged groups. At the international level, it would be useful to create a common set of indicators that could be tracked through census data. (South Africa, for example, included questions on telephone access for the first time in its 1996 census.) Such data would then provide a means for monitoring access on a global basis, while enabling each country to track progress toward its own goals.

There is also a need for research to determine which underlying factors best explain variations in access. In the United States, the possible factors that tend to be emphasized are race, ethnicity, and location, though there are clearly other factors (such as income and education) that also influence access. Cross-country analyses could be helpful in isolating the full range of factors that form barriers to access. A first step would be more detailed statistical analyses on census data such as those reported in NTIA's "Falling through the Net" studies.[29]

Other industrialized countries show trends in access broadly similar to those in the United States. Typically, access is greater among groups with higher incomes and more education, and somewhat greater in urban than in rural areas. However, the percentage of the population with Internet access at home or at work in the United States, Canada, the Nordic countries, and Australia is more than double the percentage in the United Kingdom, and more than triple the percentage in Germany, Japan, and France.[30] It would be interesting to learn what enabling or inhibiting factors are contributing to these disparities.

Beyond access, research will be needed to understand what factors influence use of ICTs once they are accessible, either through individual ownership and connectivity or through public sites such as schools and libraries. Among youth, are there specific factors, such as exposure at an early age, that are preconditions for later use? Among adults, are there information-seeking behaviors or social norms that influence use? For example, in some cultures, women may be discouraged from using technology; also, older or less educated people may feel more comfortable using an "information broker" such as a librarian, social worker, or extension agent to find information they need or to contact others electronically.[31]

Data from various sources such as the census, government reports, and statistics compiled by regulators, consulting firms, Internet-tracking web sites, and others can be useful in measuring change in access and seeking explanations for trends in the utilization of information technologies. Sharing data sets through web sites would enable researchers around the world to undertake comparative studies.[32]

8.2 Beyond Correlation

Since the 1960s, researchers have documented a close correlation between access to infrastructure (typically measured by teledensity) and economic growth (typically measured by per capita GDP). Of course, correlations do not imply causality, so that in general, the question has remained unanswered as to whether general economic growth has led (or, in research terms, "caused") growth in infrastructure investment, or vice versa. A landmark study by Hardy (1980) showed causality working in both directions—that is, investment increased as economies grew, but telecommunications investment itself made a small yet significant contribution to economic growth. As the cost of investing in infrastructure (e.g., the cost per line) has dropped, this finding has become more significant, as it suggests that early investment in infrastructure can contribute to economic growth.

Studies of outliers and anomalies could also improve our understanding of correlational trends. For example, why are the Scandinavian countries (Finland, Sweden, Norway, Denmark) in the top ten countries in Internet hosts per 1,000 population, and what impact is this high level of access likely to have on their economies? Does the fact that Israel, Ireland, and Taiwan have more Internet hosts per 1,000 population than France and Japan indicate future trends in economic growth, or is it a short-term artifact of national policies? Are middle-income countries such as Egypt and Jordan that have better Internet access than other economically similar countries likely to reap greater economic benefits than countries with below-average access such as Tunisia and Algeria? Among the "Asian Tigers," does the greater Internet access of Singapore, Hong Kong, and Taiwan give them an advantage over South Korea, Malaysia, and Thailand?[33]

It will be important to continue these lines of research on the transition to a digital economy, including not only on infrastructure but also on indicators such as density of personal computers and Internet hosts, and on economic indicators of both per capita GDP and of information-related work and the creation of new enterprises. Findings from such studies will be helpful in ascertaining whether policies such as incentives to upgrade or extend infrastructure and to foster innovative applications of information technologies can contribute to economic growth.

8.3 Usage of Information Technologies

In addition to analyzing trends and effects of national access to the global digital economy, it will be important to understand what factors influence actual usage of available facilities. Since computer use requires literacy and more skill than using a telephone, we could expect that education rather than income would be a better predictor of demand for information services in developing countries. U.S. data appear to indicate that education is critical to adoption; people with more education are not only more likely to use networked computers at work but to have access to the Internet at home. Are there other factors, such as households with children who have used computers at school, that are likely to encourage access? And are there strategies, such as community access or training, that could increase utilization? To what extent is the existence of "information brokers" such as librarians, telecenter trainers, or extension agents important in encouraging access?

Anecdotal evidence from projects such as Seniornet in the United States and telecenters in developing countries indicates that information brokers can be very important as facilitators, especially in introducing Internet usage to such populations as senior citizens and women. For example, at telecenters in Mali, Uganda, and Mozambique, 30–45 percent of the users are women, despite the fact that women typically have less education and exposure to technology than men in these societies.[34]

8.4 Institutional and Community Access

The Telecommunications Act of 1996 mandated policies designed to foster access to "advanced services" for schools, libraries, and rural health-care facilities. At present, access to the Internet is considered an "advanced service," with subsidy programs implemented to increase access. An evaluation of the so-called E-rate Program should include demographic data on users, purposes, and frequency of use, and data on the impact of access on education and health-care delivery. A primary research question is to what extent the subsidy programs have increased Internet access to these three target institutions. A second question is what factors explain disparities in participation in these programs? Are some states or organizations more effective in encouraging participation than others? Is the role of the telecommunications carriers significant? The third and most important set of research questions can be summarized as: What difference does it make? Does improved access to the Internet improve education or rural health care? Does library access to the Internet increase Internet usage by people in the community without other access, and if so, with what effect?

The subsidies mandated by the Telecommunications Act and community access policies in several other countries are based on the assumption that publicly accessible Internet facilities will increase the number of Internet users and will provide access to otherwise disadvantaged groups. Research is needed to determine success factors for various models of community access such as libraries, publicly supported telecenters, and privately owned kiosks or cybercafes. Again, demographic information on users, applications, and volume of usage should be collected, for example, from a sample of libraries participating in the E-rate Program and from case studies of public access models in other countries.

Research is also needed on the sustainability of various community access models. For example, beyond individual access, what entrepreneurial and technical skills are most important in establishing and operating businesses that provide access to information technologies and services or are intensive users of such services? Where such skills are lacking or in short supply, how can they be developed? What approaches are most successful in sustaining noncommercial forms of access such as school networks, libraries, and nonprofit telecenters?

8.5 Rural Access

Although, as we have noted, technological innovations have reduced the cost of providing reliable telecommunications facilities and increased bandwidth in rural areas, policies in many countries are still based on the assumption that prices for access will necessarily be higher and services more limited in those areas. Little-publicized sections of the Telecommunications Act of 1996 state that rural prices and services should be "reasonably comparable" to urban prices and services. To understand factors contributing to rural access to the digital economy, it would be useful to examine how the comparability in services and prices stipulated in the Act has been operationalized as a standard. For example, are there still significant disparities between urban and rural prices and service standards in the United States?[35] Has there been any change in such disparities since the passage of the Act? Has any other country adopted a specific rural comparability benchmark or goal, and if so, with what effect?

This set of research questions could be expanded to include other issues related to the availability and affordability of facilities and services. For example, to what extent is poor or nonexistent telecommunications infrastructure inhibiting the growth of Internet use in the developing world? Once reliable networks are in place, will disparities in Internet access decrease dramatically, or are there other factors such as pricing that will influence usage? Are there lessons from the analysis of anomalies proposed above that could be useful in developing policies to foster Internet access?

8.6 Impact of New Technologies

In addition to the studies on the economic impact of telecommunications access noted above, there is an extensive body of literature on the impact of new technologies beginning with the diffusion of radio and television.[36] These studies show that among individuals, there is a continuum in the adoption of new technologies from innovators through early adopters to laggards, and that various institutional factors can be important in the adoption of such technologies. In the 1970s, evaluations of experimental satellite projects showed that information technologies could improve some elements of education, training, and health care delivery but that other factors, such as perceived benefits by decision makers and sustainability, were critical to the creation of an institutional commitment to the technologies and services past the pilot phase.[37] This literature should be reviewed to ascertain whether it provides insights and methodologies that can be applied to the study of the diffusion of the digital economy and its associated innovations.

9 Conclusion

Innovative technologies, strategies, and policies are needed to increase access to the facilities and services of the emerging digital economy. Effective applications of these facilities may require training, mentoring, and in certain cases facilitation through intermediaries. In this chapter we have concentrated on the many research questions that remain to be answered, ranging from how access should be defined and measured, to what factors influence diffusion of these new technologies and services, to how electronic access to information services can benefit rural and disadvantaged populations.

Appendix: Technologies and Services for Extending Access

Technological innovations that can help to achieve universal access to telecommunications in rural and developing countries include wireline, terrestrial wireless, satellite technologies, and digital services.

Wireline

• *Digital Subscriber Line (DSL):* This technology could be appropriate for urban settings where copper wire is already installed, since its range is limited. It should be noted, however, that copper wire is prone to theft in some countries: Telkom South Africa reported more than 4,000 incidents of cable theft in 1996, at an estimated cost of R 230 million (about US$ 50 million).[38]

• *Hybrid Fiber/Coax (HFC):* A combination of optical fiber and coaxial cable can provide broadband services such as TV and high-speed Internet access as well as telephony; this combination is cheaper than installing fiber all the way to the customer premises. Unlike most cable systems, HFC allows two-way communication. The fiber runs from a central switch to a neighborhood node; coax links the node to the end user such as the subscriber's home or business. Developing countries with HFC projects include Chile, China, India, South Korea, and Malaysia.[39]

Terrestrial Wireless

• *Wireless Local Loop (WLL):* Wireless local loop systems can be used to extend local telephone services to rural customers without laying cable or stringing copper wire. WLL costs have declined, making it competitive with copper; wireless allows faster rollout to customers than extending wire or cable, so that revenue can be generated more quickly; it also has a lower ratio of fixed to incremental costs than copper, making it easy to add more customers and serve transient populations. Wireless is also less vulnerable than copper wire or cable to accidental damage or vandalism. Examples of countries with WLL projects include: Bolivia, Czech Republic, Hungary, Indonesia, and Sri Lanka.[40]

• *Cellular:* Cellular technology, originally designed for mobile services (such as communication from vehicles), is now being introduced for personal communications using small portable handsets. In developing countries without sufficient wireline infrastructure, wireless personal technology can be provided as a primary service. In China, there are more than 10 million wireless customers; other developing countries where wireless is used as a primary service include Colombia, Lebanon, Malaysia, the Philippines, Sri Lanka, South Africa, Venezuela, and Thailand.[41]

- *Wireless Payphones:* Cellular installations can be used to provide fixed public payphones. For example, new cellular operators in South Africa were required to install 30,000 wireless payphones within five years as a condition of the license. By March 1997, almost 15,000 wireless payphones had been installed.[42] Alternatively, a cellular subscriber may resell access. Entrepreneurs in Bangladesh offer payphone service using cell phones leased from Grameen Phone, which they carry by bicycle to various neighborhoods.

- *Multi-Access Radio:* Time division multiple access (TDMA) radio systems are a means of providing wireless rural telephony. They typically have 30–60 trunks and can accommodate 500–1,000 subscribers. Their range can be extended using multiple repeaters.[43]

- *Cordless:* Short-range cordless extensions can provide the link from wireless outstations to subscriber premises. The DECT (Digital European Cordless Telephone) technology standard will also allow the base station to act as a wireless PBX and further reduce cost.[44] For example, DECT has been used in South Africa for the link to rural subscribers.[45]

Satellite Technologies

- *Very Small Aperture Terminals (VSATs):* Small satellite earth stations operating with geosynchronous (GEO) satellites can be used for interactive voice and data, for data broadcasting, and for broadcasting. For example, banks in remote areas of Brazil are linked via VSATs; the National Stock Exchange in India links brokers with rooftop VSATs; China's Xinhua News Agency uses VSATs for broadcasting news feeds to subscribers. VSATs for television reception (known as TVROs, for television receive only) deliver broadcast signals to viewers in many developing regions of Asia and Latin America.

- *Demand Assignment Multiple Access (DAMA):* In geostationary satellite systems, instead of assigning dedicated circuits to each location, DAMA allows the terminal to access the satellite only on demand and eliminates double hops between rural locations served by the same system. The system is very cost effective because satellite transponder expense is reduced to a fraction of that associated with a fixed-assigned system for the same amount of traffic. Moreover, digital DAMA systems provide higher bandwidth capabilities at much lower cost than analog. Both AT&T Alascom and GCI are introducing DAMA for their rural satellite networks in Alaska.

- *Global Mobile Personal Communications Systems (GMPCS):* Using low earth-orbiting (LEO) satellites, these systems (e.g., Iridium, Globalstar, ICO) will be able to provide voice and low-speed (typically 2400–9600 kbps) data virtually anywhere, using handheld transceivers. The downside is that the price per minute for these services may be much higher than national terrestrial services, and the first generation of LEOs has very limited bandwidth.

- *Internet via Satellite:* Internet gateways can be accessed via geostationary satellites. For example, MagicNet in Mongolia and some African ISPs access the Internet in the United States via PanAmSat, and residents of the Canadian Arctic use the Anik satellite system, while Alaskan villagers use U.S. domestic satellites. These systems are not optimized for Internet use, however, and may therefore be quite expensive. Several improvements in using GEOs are becoming available:

  - *DirecPC:* This system, designed by Hughes, uses a VSAT as a downlink from the ISP, but provides upstream connectivity over existing telephone lines. Some rural schools in the United States are using DirecPC for Internet access.

  - *Interactive Access via VSAT:* Several companies are developing protocols for fully interactive Internet access via satellite.[46]

  - *High-Bandwidth LEOs:* Future LEO systems are being planned to provide bandwidth on demand. Constellations of LEO satellites such as Teledesic, Cyberstar, or Skybridge may provide another means of Internet access via satellite.[47]

  - *Data Broadcasting:* Satellites designed for digital audio broadcasting (such as Worldspace) can also be used to broadcast web pages to small receivers. Users would not have fully interactive service, but could receive regular downloads of specified pages addressed to their receivers.

Digital Services

• *Compressed Voice:* Compression algorithms can be used to "compress" digital voice signals, so that eight or more conversations can be carried on a single 64 kbps voice channel, thus reducing transmission costs.

• *Compressed Video:* Compressed digital video can be used to transmit motion video over as few as 2 telephone lines (128 kbps), offering the possibility of low-cost videoconferencing for distance education and training.

• *Internet Telephony (Voice over IP):* Some carriers are beginning to offer dial-up access to Internet telephony. The advantage of using Internet protocols for voice as well as data is much lower transmission cost than over circuit-switched telephony networks. IP telephony may eventually operate on separate data networks.

Notes

1. McConnaughey and Lader (1998). Native Americans are not disaggregated in this study because of small sample size; however, based on census and other data, they appear to fall below national rates, particularly in rural areas, including Indian reservations.

2. Ibid. See also Fact Sheet: Rural Areas Magnify "Digital Divide" (www.ntia.doc.gov/ntiahome/digitaldivide/factsheets/rural.htm).

3. United Nations Administrative Committee on Coordination (1997).

4. It should be noted that Japan and Australia are included in the Asia/Pacific in this chart; the estimate in the text includes them with industrialized countries of Europe and North America.

5. See International Telecommunication Union (1998), p. 9.

6. See the CRTC Decision (www.crtc.gc.ca).

7. Kayani and Dymond (1997), p. xviii

8. International Telecommunication Union (1998), p.35.

9. Ibid., p. 37. It should be noted that this calculation appears to assume even distribution of income throughout the society at higher income levels, which is not necessarily true.

10. Meeting at Department of Transport and Communications attended by the author, Manila, January 1998.

11. International Telecommunication Union (1998), p. 77.

12. Ibid., pp. 77–78.

13. Ibid., p. 44.

14. Personal interview, Uganda Communications Commission, Kampala, November 1999.

15. Petzinger (1998).

16. Ibid. The Africa Communications Group is to be known as Adesemi Communications International.

17. M. Hegener, quoted in International Telecommunication Union (1998), p. 80.

18. Office of Telecommunications, *A Framework for Effective Competition*. (London: OFTEL, 1994), quoted in Kayani and Dymond (1997), p. 53.

19. Hudson (1997b).

20. See www.neca.org, and information on the Universal Service Fund on the FCC's website, www.fcc.gov.

21. International Telecommunication Union (1998), p. 78.

22. Ibid., p. 79.

23. Kayani and Dymond (1997), pp. 63–64.

24. International Telecommunication Union (1998), p. 79.

25. Kayani and Dymond (1997), p. 18.

26. Ibid.

27. Ibid., p. 19.

28. See www.ntia.doc.gov/ntiahome/digitaldivide.

29. Unfortunately, while the above study analyzes census data to show access by race, location, and education as well as income, it does not include statistical analysis that would indicate whether income is the underlying variable accounting for much of the disparity across these other variables.

30. International Telecommunication Union (1999), p. 22.

31. For example, peasant farmers in Ecuador found out how to eliminate a pest that was destroying their potato crop through the assistance of a field worker who posted their question on several Internet news groups (personal communication, October 1999).

32. See, for example, data on rural telecommunications services available at www.rupri.org and reported in Hobbs and Blodgett (1999).

33. International Telecommunication Union (1999), pp. 22, 38.

34. Author's field research and unpublished reports, 1999.

35. The data set available through www.rupri.org would be a good starting point.

36. See, for example, Schramm, Lyle, and Parker (1961) and Rogers (1995)

37. Hudson (2000).

38. International Telecommunication Union (1998), p. 60.

39. Kayani and Dymond (1997).

40. International Telecommunication Union (1998), p. 53.

41. Ibid., p. 49.

42. Ibid., p. 50.

43. Kayani and Dymond (1997), p. 27.

44. Ibid., p. 48.

45. A disadvantage of all of these wireless technologies is limited bandwidth. While they can be used for email, they do not provide sufficient capacity for accessing the World Wide Web at present. However, a new protocol known as WAP (wireless application protocol) being developed to enable cell phone users to access the web may also make it possible to access text on the web using very limited bandwidth.

46. See www.alohanet.com; also *The Red Herring*, September 29, 1998 (www.redherring.com/mag/issue59/limit/html).

47. Hudson (1998b).

References

Cronin, Francis J., Elisabeth K. Colleran, Paul L. Herbert, and Steven Lewitzky, 1993a. "Telecommunications and Growth: The Contribution of Telecommunications Infrastructure Investment to Aggregate and Sectoral Productivity," *Telecommunications Policy* 17(9): 677–690.

Cronin, Francis J., Edwin B. Parker, Elisabeth K. Colleran, and Mark A. Gold, 1993b. "Telecommunications Infrastructure and Economic Development," *Telecommunications Policy* 17(6): 415–430.

Hardy, Andrew P., 1980. "The Role of the Telephone in Economic Development," *Telecommunications Policy* 4(4): 278–286.

Henry, David et al., 1999. *The Emerging Digital Economy II*. Washington, DC: U.S. Department of Commerce.

Hobbs, Vicki M., and John Blodgett, 1999. "The Rural Differential: An Analysis of Population Demographics in Areas Served by Rural Telephone Companies," paper presented at the Telecommunications Policy Research Conference, September. See also www.rupri.org.

Hudson, Heather E., 1984. *When Telephones Reach the Village: The Role of Telecommunications in Rural Development*. Norwood, NJ: Ablex.

Hudson, Heather E., 1990. *Communication Satellites: Their Development and Impact*. New York: Free Press.

Hudson, Heather E., 1995. *Economic and Social Benefits of Rural Telecommunications: A Report to the World Bank.*

Hudson, Heather E., 1997a. *Global Connections: International Telecommunications Infrastructure and Policy.* New York: John Wiley.

Hudson, Heather E., 1997b. "Converging Technologies and Changing Realities: Toward Universal Access to Telecommunications in the Developing World," in *Telecom Reform: Principles, Policies, and Regulatory Practices* (Lyngby, Denmark: Technical University of Denmark).

Hudson, Heather E., 1998a. "African Information Infrastructure: The Development Connection," in *Proceedings of Africa Telecom 98* (Geneva: International Telecommunication Union).

Hudson, Heather E., 1998b. "The Significance of Telecommunications for Canadian Rural Development," Testimony on Behalf of the Public Interest Advocacy Centre et al., Canadian Radio Television and Telecommunications Commission Hearing on Telecom Public Notice CRTC 97-42, Service to High-cost Serving Areas, April.

Hudson, Heather E., 2000. "Beyond Infrastructure: A Critical Assessment of GII Initiatives," in Sharon Eisner Gillett and Ingo Vogelsang, ed., *Competition, Regulation, and Convergence: Current Trends in Telecommunications Policy Research* (Mahwah, NJ: Lawrence Erlbaum).

International Telecommunication Union, 1998. *World Telecommunication Development Report 1998.* Geneva: ITU.

International Telecommunication Union, 1999a. *Challenges to the Network: Internet for Development.* Geneva: ITU.

International Telecommunication Union, 1999b. *World Telecommunication Development Report 1999.* Geneva: ITU.

Jordan, Miriam, 1999. "It Takes a Cell Phone: Nokia Phone Transforms A Village in Bangladesh," *Wall Street Journal*, June 25.

Kayani, Rogati, and Andrew Dymond, 1997. *Options for Rural Telecommunications Development.* Washington, DC: World Bank.

Margherio, Lynn, et al., 1998. *The Emerging Digital Economy.* Washington, DC: U.S. Department of Commerce.

Mayo, John K., Gary R. Heald, and Steven J. Klees, 1992. "Commercial Satellite Telecommunications and National Development: Lessons from Peru," *Telecommunications Policy* 16(1): 67–79.

McConnaughey, James W., and Wendy Lader, 1998. *Falling Through The Net II: New Data on The Digital Divide.* Washington, DC: National Telecommunications And Information Administration.

National Research Council, Board on Science and Technology for International Development, 1990. *Science and Technology Information Services and Systems in Africa.* Washington, DC: National Academy Press.

O Siochru, Sean, 1996. *Telecommunications and Universal Service: International Experience in the Context of South African Telecommunications Reform.* Ottawa: International Development Research Centre.

Parker, Edwin B., and Heather E. Hudson, 1995. *Electronic Byways: State Policies for Rural Development through Telecommunications,* 2nd edition. Washington, DC: Aspen Institute.

Petzinger, Jr., Thomas, 1998. "Monique Maddy uses Wireless Payphones to Battle Poverty," *Wall Street Journal,* September 25, B1.

Rogers, Everett, 1995. *Diffusion of Innovations,* 4th edition. New York: Free Press.

Saunders, Robert, Jeremy Warford, and Bjorn Wellenius, 1994. *Telecommunications and Economic Development,* 2nd edition. Baltimore: Johns Hopkins University Press.

Schramm, Wilbur, Jack Lyle, and Edwin B. Parker, 1961. *Television in the Lives of Our Children.* Stanford, CA: Stanford University Press.

Telecommunications Act of 1996. U.S. Congress. Public Law 104-104, February 8.

United Nations Administrative Committee on Coordination (ACC), 1997. "Statement on Universal Access to Basic Communication and Information Services," April. Quoted in International Telecommunication Union (1998), p. 10.

World Information Technology and Services Alliance, 1998. *Digital Planet: The Global Information Economy.* Washington, DC: WITSA.

Websites

Aloha Networks: www.alohanet.com

Alaska Public Utilities Commission: www.state.ak.us/local/akpages/COMMERCE/apuc.htm

Canadian Radio Television and Telecommunications Commission (CRTC): www.crtc.gc.ca.

Department of Commerce: www.ecommerce.gov/ece/.

Federal Communications Commission: www.fcc.gov.

General Communications Inc. (GCI): www.gci.com.

National Computer Board of Singapore: www.ncb.gov.sg.

National Exchange Carriers Association: www.neca.org.

National Telecommunications and Information Administration: www.ntia.doc.gov.

The Red Herring: www.redherring.com.

Vitacom, Inc.: www.vitacom.com.

Organizational Change

IT and Organizational Change in Digital Economies: A Sociotechnical Approach

Rob Kling and Roberta Lamb

1 The Digital Economy and Organizational Change

Many people are enthusiastic about the prospects of a digital economy (sector) energizing the larger U.S. economy. Much of the speculation and reporting so far has emphasized new business models, which is always a fun topic. Such reports usually assume, however, that business firms and public agencies can easily adapt themselves to take advantage of new models once they have decided that they are appropriate. But the fact is that, regardless of the specific models that are devised and selected, they must still be enacted by *organizations* in order to realize their expected economic and social value, and we know that organizations are imperfect implementers of business strategies—even strategies that appeal to experienced managers.

For example, between 1993 and 1995, Business Process Re-engineering (BPR) was enthusiastically advanced by the popular business press and was tried by a substantial number of major business firms, despite high costs and a failure rate of 75 percent (Bashein, Markus, and Riley 1994). Many professional managers who became wary of BPR have now turned to Knowledge Management as "the next big thing," despite considerable confusion about what this term means in practice and about how organizations must change to take advantage of its insights. The lack of success of such efforts to change organizations should make us cautious about forecasting how easy it will be for organizations to implement new business strategies that depend in critical ways on complex forms of information technology (IT).

Thirty years of systematic, empirically grounded research on IT and organizational change suggests that many organizations have trouble changing their practices and structures to take advantage of IT. Of course, computerized information systems are widely used in industrialized countries to support an immense variety of organizational activities. But researchers have found that it requires complex organizational work to implement information systems. In addition, there are sometimes major differences between the ways that systems were originally envisioned and how they are used in practice. The body of research that examines topics like these is called Organizational Informatics (OI). OI research has led us to a deeper understanding of IT and organizational change, and the highlights of this understanding form the substance of this chapter.

Before we discuss key ideas from OI, it will help to characterize what we mean by the digital economy, so that we can better understand the enabling role that IT is to play. The term "digital economy" was popularized by pundit and consultant Don Tapscott in his 1996 book *The Digital Economy*. Tapscott provides many engaging examples of the roles IT plays in business operations, and he is specially enthusiastic about the role of the Internet in fostering electronic commerce. But he doesn't provide a significant analytical conception of a digital economy. In fact, he often uses the term "digital economy" interchangeably with "new economy" (which is a different construct—one that emphasizes high growth, low inflation, and low unemployment).

A recent U.S. Commerce Department report, *The Emerging Digital Economy*, is much more analytical. It characterizes a "digital economy" based on industries and forms of IT-enabled business activity that are likely to be significant sources of economic growth in the next decade. These include the IT industry itself, electronic commerce among businesses, the digital delivery of goods and services, and the IT-supported retail sale of tangible goods. Tapscott includes in his definition a wide variety of IT-enabled activities, such as Boeing's "paperless design" of the Model 777 wide-body jet airplane using mainframe-based CAD systems. In contrast, *The Emerging Digital*

Economy emphasizes systems and services that utilize the Internet rather than proprietary commercial networks.

Our approach builds on both of these points of view, focusing on important forms of IT-enabled business activity. These developments were initiated (in the United States) in the 1950s, long before the Internet was conceived. They were widely expanded during the 1960s, 1970s, and 1980s, before the Internet was reconceived as a commercial service. We have much to learn from these computerization projects about the character of organizational change in response to new technologies. There will continue to be important proprietary networks for the foreseeable future, such as those that clear checks between banks and communicate credit card transactions between merchants and banks. While the Internet is likely to become the major enabler of growth in electronic commerce, we should not conceptualize a digital economy in ways that make the Internet central by definition.

The "digital economy" is conceptualized differently than the better understood and more carefully studied "information economy" (Porat 1977; Cooper 1981; Katz 1984; Robinson 1986; Jussawalla and Lamberton 1988; Kling 1990; Schement 1990; Engelbrecht 1997). In brief, the digital economy includes goods or services whose development, production, sale, or provision is critically dependent upon digital technologies. In contrast, the information economy includes all informational goods and services, including publishing, entertainment, research, legal and insurance services, and teaching in all of its forms. These are overlapping but different conceptions. The digital economy can include some forms of production that are excluded from the information economy, such as computer-controlled manufacturing, while the information economy includes many services that are only partly included in today's digital economy, such as all K-12 education, all legal services, all forms of entertainment, and so on.

We identify four subsectors of a Digital Economy:

• *Highly digital goods and services:* These are goods that are delivered digitally and services of which substantial portions are delivered digitally. Examples include interbank fund transfers, on-line information services (e.g., Lexis/Nexis, DIALOG), electronic journals, and some software sales. This subsector may soon include a significant portion of music sales. It can also include distance education that is enacted primarily on-line, although many distance education courses are not wholly conducted on-line: students may be required to attend a face-to-face orientation meeting and to purchase books and other materials through specialty stores. By acknowledging that many of these services are highly digital rather than purely digital, we can better understand the organizational activities that are required to support them.

- *Mixed digital goods and services:* These include the retail sale of tangible goods such as music, books, and flowers via the Internet, as well as services such as travel reservations. While a significant fraction of some of these products, such as pop music, may be sold in purely digital form within the next decade, there is a durable market for tangible goods. For example, around Valentine's Day, many people want "real flowers," not digital simulacra. In addition, people who make airline reservations to fly to a resort hotel usually want a "real flight" and a "real hotel room." In practical terms, the retail sale of tangible goods usually rests on the availability of inventory, distribution points, and high-quality delivery services (e.g., Federal Express) as well as advertising and on-line sales and secure banking to support the front end of the transaction. The production and distribution system for tangible goods can be the same one that is used for mail catalog or telephone sales; the Internet serves as another sales channel.

- *IT-intensive services or goods production:* These are services that depend critically on IT for their provision. Examples include most accounting services in the United States, data-intensive market research, and complex engineering design. They also include the manufacture of tangible goods in whose production IT is critical (such as precision machining that uses computerized numerical control or chemical process plants that are controlled by computer). This set of activities was the major focus of computerization between the 1950s and the early 1990s.

- *The segments of the IT industry that support these three segments of the digital economy:* The goods and services of the IT industry that most directly support the foregoing three segments of the digital economy include a large fraction of the computer networking subindustry, PC manufacturing, and some IT consulting firms. (Some analysts characterize the IT industries in more expansive terms and add communications equipment—including broadcast—and communications services—including all telephone as well as all radio, television, and cable broadcasting; see (Margherio et al. 1998, Appendix I.) The industrial classification codes don't always align well with the boundaries of a digital economy (e.g., some computer networking is classified within telephone communications), but we see no substantive rationale for gerrymandering all of the telephone industry and the broadcast industry into the Digital Economy.

Taken together, these four segments represent a significant level of economic activity that will grow in the next decades. Most of the systematic analytical, empirically grounded research on IT and organizations has been focused on the third sector: IT-intensive services or goods production. We believe, however, that many of the key concepts and theories that have come from this research provide a useful basis for understanding important aspects of the first and second subsectors and also help inform a research agenda.

2 Information Systems as Sociotechnical Networks

It is easy for business analysts and IT specialists to become enthusiastic and even evangelical about the prospects of a digital economy as a source of business innovation and economic growth (Tapscott 1996). This professional enthusiasm has led, unfortunately, to a literature that emphasizes streamlined "success stories" and dresses up legitimate kinds of "old technology" examples in new language to signify new practices.

A close reading of *The Emerging Digital Economy* (Margherio et al. 1998.), is instructive. Most of the projects are described in terms of a series of tasks and give us little clue about how organizations changed to accommodate new practices. Improvements in organizational subsystems are treated as organization-wide gains. For example, a description of how General Electric's Lighting Division developed an on-line procurement system focuses on efficiencies in the procurement department (faster orders, 30 percent cost reduction, and 60 percent staff reduction). But there is no account of the costs of developing the new procurement system, deploying and maintaining numerous new workstations in the Lighting

Division, training those who request materials ("the internal customers") to specify orders correctly on-line or to use the on-line
forms efficiently with digital drawing attachments, and so on.
There may still be important net savings after these costs are
factored in, but the cost reductions would not be so dramatic. The
magnitude and characteristics of the co-requisite organizational
changes would also be clearer.

Most seriously, this expanded view suggests that IT should not be
conceptualized simply as a "tool" that can be readily applied for
specific purposes. GE Lighting's on-line procurement system is a
complex technological system in which the orchestration of digitized product drawings and purchase orders has to be synchro-
nized. Its operation contains important social elements governing
authorizations to initiate an electronic purchase order, control
over product drawings that are subject to engineering or manufacturing changes, and so on. In short, organizational researchers
have found that systems like this are better conceptualized as
"sociotechnical networks" than as tools. In practice, the boundaries
between what is social and what is technological blurs because some
of the system design encodes assumptions about the social organization of the firm in which it is embedded.

A different kind of example comes from the experience of
Charles Schwab and Co. in developing an on-line trading operation (e.Schwab) in 1995–1996 (Schonfield 1998). Like many firms,
Schwab initially set up a small new division to develop the software,
systems, and policies for e.Schwab. To compete with other Internet
brokerages, Schwab dropped its commissions to a flat fee that was
about one-third of its previous average commission. Schwab's
regular phone representatives and branch officers were not allowed to help e.Schwab customers. Those customers were allowed
one free phone call a month; all other questions had to be e-mailed
to e.Schwab. While over a million people rapidly flocked to e.Schwab,
many of these customers found the different policies and practices
to be frustrating. In 1997, Schwab's upper managers began integrating e.Schwab and "regular Schwab." This integration required
new, more coherent policies as well as training all of Schwab's
representatives to understand e-trades. It also required the physical
integration of e.Schwab's staff with their "jeans and sneakers"

culture into the offices of regular Schwab staff with their "jacket and tie" culture. One side result of all this was a more flexible dress code in Schwab's headquarters.

e.Schwab has been discussed in some business articles as a tool or a technological system. But the policies and procedures for any trading system—including pricing, trade confirmations and reversals, and advice—are integral to its operation. These are social practices without which there is no e.Schwab. Consequently, the standard "tool view" is insufficient for understanding the design of e.Schwab, its operations, and consequently the character of the organizational change required to develop this line of business.

These brief examples illustrate an approach to understanding IT as a sociotechnical network. Table 1 characterizes some of the key differences between the standard (tool) models of IT and organizational change and the sociotechnical models. The sociotechnical approach has been developed by analytical, empirically anchored researchers who have studied IT and social change in a diverse array of public and private sector organizations over the last 25 years (see Kling and Scacchi 1982; Kling 1992, 1999; Kling and Star 1998; Kling et al. 2000). The research is robust insofar as it rests on studies of diverse kinds of IT—from accounting systems through engineering design to knowledge bases—and varied organizations.

Unfortunately, the standard model still underpins many of the stories about electronic commerce that appear in the professional and popular business and technological magazines. The major predictive error that results from relying upon this model is that one overestimates the ease of "going digital" by substantially underestimating the complexity and time of the required organizational changes.

3 Illustrations from Organizational Informatics Research

A socially rich view of highly digital and mixed digital products and services—one that follows a sociotechnical model rather than the standard model—can help policymakers and practitioners anticipate some of the key organizational shifts that accompany introductions of new technologies. That view is supported by the large

Table 1 Conceptions of IT in Organizations in Accounts of the Digital Economy

Standard (Tool) Models	Sociotechnical Models
IT is a tool.	IT is a sociotechnical network.
Business model is sufficient.	Ecological view is needed.
One-shot implementation.	Implementation is an ongoing social process.
Technological effects are direct and immediate.	Technological effects are indirect and involve different time scales.
Incentives to change are unproblematic.	Incentives may require restructuring and may be in conflict with other organizational actions (section 3.1).
Politics are bad or irrelevant.	Politics are central and even enabling (section 3.2).
IT infrastructures are fully supportive. Systems have become user-friendly, people have become "computer-literate," and these changes are accelerating with the "net-generation."	Articulation work is often needed to make IT work, and sociotechnical support is critical for effective IT use (section 3.3).
Social relationships are easily reformed to take advantage of new conveniences, efficiencies, and business value.	Relationships are complex, negotiated, multivalent; the nature of the relationship with the customer makes a difference in what can become digital—including trust (section 3.4).
Social effects of IT are big but isolated and benign.	Potentially enormous social repercussions from IT—not just quality of working life but overall quality of life (section 3.5).
Contexts are simple (described by a few key terms or demographics).	Contexts are complex (matrices of businesses, services, people, technology, history, location, etc.).
Knowledge and expertise are easily made explicit.	Knowledge and expertise are inherently tacit/implicit.

and growing body of carefully designed empirical studies under the rubric of organizational informatics (OI) (Kling 1996; Kling and Star 1998). We will summarize here a few OI studies that exemplify some important contrasts between socially rich and socially thin accounts about IT and incentives, politics, support, interorganizational relationships, and social repercussions (as outlined in table 1). These studies illustrate the ways in which a sociotechnical perspective can guide researchers toward important insights about technology and organizational change.

3.1 Organizational and Social Incentives Shape IT Configurations and Use

OI researchers have found repeatedly that *incentives matter* in shaping the adoption and discretionary use of new technologies. People need good reasons to change their organizational practices, and they need the time and the training to make those changes. In many cases, work incentives require restructuring in ways that conflict with other organizational actions. Too often, however, the sponsors of new technologies hold the standard-model view that incentives are unproblematic. They believe that information workers will "naturally" see the advantages of using a new technology, like Lotus Notes, and adopt it immediately.

Lotus Notes at Alpha Consulting
Alpha Consulting is a pseudonym for an international consulting firm with tens of thousands of employees worldwide, and about 10,000 of them in the United States. In 1989, the vice president of information systems bought 10,000 copies of Lotus Notes, software that can act as an e-mail system, a discussion system, an electronic publishing system, and/or a set of digital libraries. At that time, Notes was superficially similar to an Internet-like system with bulletin boards and posting mechanisms, discussion groups and electronic mail. The VP believed that the firm's line consultants, who worked on similar projects in offices all over North America (although none were located in his corporate office), could use some kind of computerized communication and information system to store and share what they knew. He also believed that Lotus

Notes 1.0 was such a powerful new technology that it would sell itself. No consulting applications of Lotus Notes existed yet, but the VP did not see this as a problem. To the contrary, he thought that examples might hinder new uses—the main thing to do was to roll it out rapidly to the consulting staff and let them use it to find creative ways to share information.

Alpha Consulting's IT staff used Notes fairly aggressively for sharing information about their own projects. And the tax consultants in Washington, D.C., used Notes as they monitored the behavior of the Internal Revenue Service and the U.S. Congress and disseminated tax advisories to Alpha Consulting offices around the country about changes in tax legislation that might affect their clients (Mehler 1992). The line consultants, however, who were supposed to become the program's primary users, seemed uninterested in learning the program, gave up quickly if they encountered early problems, and as a group did not spend much time with it. The senior line consultants, who were partners in the firm, tended to be modest users. The more numerous junior line consultants, called associates, were low users.

This outcome might puzzle technology enthusiasts, like the Alpha Consulting VP, who hold to the standard model. If we do a sociotechnical analysis, in contrast, we see easily that reimbursement incentives go a long way toward explaining these results (Kling 1999.) The partners, who had substantial job security, could afford to experiment with Notes. Many of the IT staff were technophiles who were also willing to explore an interesting new application. The tax consultants, who were located in Washington, D.C., had a significant incentive to show that they were visible and valuable in the firm. Notes gave them the ability, in effect, to publish their advice electronically and make it quickly available to consultants around the firm. They hoped it would enhance their visibility and thus show that the Washington office was not just overhead, but an important and contributing part of the firm.

It was not clear to the line consultants, however, what their incentives were for using Notes. Alpha Consulting—like many large consulting firms in North America—reviews its consultants every two years for "up or out" promotions. At major firms, about half of the associates are fired at each review, while the few consultants who are promoted up through the ranks to the status of partners can expect annual incomes over $300,000. Alpha Consulting's associates were valued for their billable hours and were effectively required to bill almost all of their time. "Billable hours" means having an account that they can charge their time to. Consultants who wanted to use Notes had to have an account to charge their time against, and the initial learning time was on the order of 20–30 hours. In 1991, the consultants were billed at about $150 an hour, and so they had to find a client who would be willing to pay $3,000 to $4,500 for them to learn a system whose value wasn't yet clear to them. There were no exemplary demonstrations showing them how other successful line consultants used Notes. Consequently, relatively few associates saw value in the program.

Lotus Notes at Ernst & Young
An organization with a different explicit incentive system might use Notes very differently. Ernst & Young (E&Y), another major consulting firm, created an organization whose charter was to organize E&Y's consultants' know-how in specific high profile areas. By 1997, E&Y had developed 22 cross-office networks of consultants with expertise about certain industries, organizational reforms, and technologies that were a focus of E&Y's business (Davenport 1997; Gierkink and Ruggles, n.d.). Each network was assigned one line consultant, on a short-term half-time basis, to codify in Notes databases the group's insights from specific consulting projects, to prompt line consultants to add their own insights, and to edit and prune a project's discussion and document databases. Some developed topical "Power Packs" in Notes—structured and filtered sets of on-line materials, including sales presentations and proposal templates. Davenport (1997) observed that these "knowledge networkers" became network domain experts whose consulting services were in demand throughout the firm, and that Notes served as their information support system.

The case of E&Y illustrates the importance of conceptualizing the design of computer and networked systems as a set of interrelated decisions about technology and the organization of work. Unfortunately, thinking and talking about computerization as the development of sociotechnical configurations rather than as the installation and use of a new technology is not commonplace. It is common for managers and technologists to discuss some social repercussions of new technologies, such as the sponsorship of projects, training people to use new systems, and controls over access to information. However, these discussions usually treat all or most social behavior as separable from the technologies, whereas the E&Y case suggests that a more integrated sociotechnical view is critical. We include this example not to show that E&Y executives were "smarter" than Price-Waterhouse executives, but to demonstrate the value of research guided by a sociotechnical approach. Because some E&Y managers were cognizant of the Price-Waterhouse failures through the publication of OI studies, E&Y was able to avoid making the same mistakes.

Different incentive systems for different groups is one way to view a key concept that helps to integrate seemingly disparate cases— one that may helpfully guide implementations of highly digital and mixed digital products and services such as web-based publishing. Authors and publishers, for example, are conflicted about putting their intellectual property on the web. They may gain a wider reading audience, but at the same time they risk losing revenues by providing works in a form that is easily copied and distributed. Varied and conflicting consequences in different settings is a common finding in OI research. Our job as researchers is not simply to document the various consequences of computerization, but also to theorize them (see Lamb 1996; Robey 1997).

3.2 IT Implementations Have Important Political Dimensions

OI researchers have also found that organizational politics can have significant effects on the outcomes of new technology implementations. A sociotechnical view of the backroom manipulations of key players assumes that these can be enabling and even central to the success or failure of the implementation of complex systems such as financial accounting systems and material resource planning (MRP) systems. Many standard-model discussions, particularly those that report on successful implementations, simply ignore behind-the-scene activities, implying that they are irrelevant (see, e.g., the account of an implementation of an inventory control system by IBM's Personal Systems Group in Margherio et al. 1998). Other accounts, particularly those that report on failed IT implementations, dismiss the political wrangling as unusual or aberrant. The following OI research examples show that organizational change, technology implementation, and political activities can be associated in complex ways. Key organizational actors can both promote and thwart the changes needed to encourage widespread use of a new technology. They can also vie for power by backing competing technologies. The two cases show that it can be folly to ignore organizational histories when trying to evaluate what has made a new technology implementation successful—more so if one seeks to emulate that success.

PRINTCO

PRINTCO is the pseudonym for a medium-sized manufacturing firm (about 800 employees) that designed, manufactured, and marketed several lines of medium-speed dot matrix line printers for the minicomputer and small business computer marketplace in the 1970s and 1980s (Kling and Iacono 1986). A case study from the 1980s may seem anachronistic when we are discussing current IT developments, but it will help to illustrate some organizational dynamics of upgrading IT that are as pertinent today as then.

In 1977, as PRINTCO was growing by diversifying the variety of printers it produced, it found that the new products greatly complicated the logistics of managing inventory. The material control managers began looking for more sophisticated MRP software to help resolve manufacturing problems such as capacity planning, tracking multiple simultaneous revisions of products, and accounting for planned orders. An informal committee found an MRP package that satisfied their preferences, but it ran on a Data General (DG) minicomputer, a DG S350 Eclipse, rather than on their IBM System 34. The new MRP package was also written in BASIC—a new language for PRINTCO's manufacturing division, all of whose administrative information systems were written in RPG-II.

The conversion began in 1980, but 18 months later it was still not complete. Unexpected problems plagued the project, such as lack of on-site vendor support from DG and difficulties in hiring programmers with the necessary skills, in addition to the complexities of making large-scale modifications to poorly documented system code. The senior vice president of manufacturing saw an impending crisis and formed a data processing steering committee to help guide the Data Processing (DP) manager. Some months later, the steering committee hired a new DP manager with stronger managerial skills but weaker technical skills. They also ended the conversion project, deciding instead to upgrade the existing IBM System 34 and enhance the MRP system. Unfortunately, the new DP manager decided to support the purchase of a more sophisticated computer (an IBM System 38). When the steering committee saw little progress on the enhancements of their MRP system after 10 months, they replaced the new DP manager with the manager of engineering services, who was promoted to the role of operations director. Almost immediately, they opted to buy an IBM 4331, found new MRP software to satisfy their preferences, and started a new conversion project.

Because of problems in DP, no one paid much attention to the proliferation of microcomputing at PRINTCO. At first, a few departments obtained DEC LSI-11 microcomputers from test equipment cast off by other departments. They upgraded them into usable computing equipment with the help of their own skilled staff. Soon 6–10 LSI-11s were scattered around the firm. One staff member in the test equipment area became the informal expert in operating, programming, and using the microcomputers.

PRINTCO's management was not simply replacing one MRP system with another. They were also attempting to replace the existing social organization of computing in their firm with an altered configuration. Management generated a lot of action that substantially strengthened the infrastructure for computing support at PRINTCO, but their fiscally conservative approach stopped short of doing what was needed to complete the conversion. The existing RPG-II programmers, for example, attended several BASIC programming classes at local colleges, but the simple class exercises did not teach them to program complex MRP applications with DG's proprietary BASIC, and their learning curve was steep. PRINTCO's managers assumed that their information systems staff had all the skills necessary for most computing tasks or could easily acquire them. They did not realize that the skills and work routines of the department were very specialized and limited. Later, key managers tried to hire people who could program in both BASIC and RPG-II to expedite the conversion, but they could not locate and hire new programmers with programming skills in both languages at the offered rate. And they were not willing to create a DP milieu that would attract programmers with appropriate developmental skills to effectively convert their software. PRINTCO's managers were acting in ways they knew (standard operating orientations), such as minor reorganizations and changing managers. These kinds of changes did not really shake up their organization, and they were not effective either.

While PRINTCO management was focused on the MRP system crisis, other staff in the organization, especially test-engineers, had to develop their own microcomputing environments. Many of these staff had the skills to develop an adequate infrastructure of support for their own work groups, but because they were effectively cut out of discussions about the conversion project, the firm never took advantage of their expertise. These staff viewed their micros as tools that helped them develop small-scale systems independently of the ineffective DP shop. Their micro revolution lasted a year before control over computing equipment and programming was recentralized under DP. During the conversion project, however, two parallel computing environments were developing independent of each other. Each required investments of time and money from the organization. Each was left to run its own course with little direction and modest resources.

Golden Triangle
Pfeffer's (1981) account of the design of a financial information system at Golden Triangle further illustrates the ways in which IT implementations are often entwined with power struggles within an organization. Golden Triangle Corporation is a major chemical manufacturing concern that operates internationally, with sales in excess of $3 billion. It is organized into a staff group that includes accounting and four fairly autonomous operating groups. Within each operating group, divisions are headed by general managers. Divisional accountants report directly to these general managers,

with only an indirect relationship to corporate accounting, which is supposed to provide "broad policy guidelines" (Markus 1980: 7–8).

In 1971, Golden Triangle had seven different computerized systems and numerous manual systems in use in the divisions. It was hoped that the introduction of the financial information system would standardize these systems by collecting and summarizing financial data from input covering transactions involving expenses, revenues, assets, and liabilities and storing all transactions in a single, centralized data base. The system would output monthly balance sheets as well as profit-and-loss statements by division and for the whole company. Prior to the development of the new system, "divisional accountants had collected and stored transaction data however they saw fit, but had reported summary data to corporate accountants in a standardized format" (Markus 1980: 7). Clearly, the introduction of a standardized system would profoundly change the relationship between corporate and divisional controllers, as well as between the division and headquarters operating managers.

Over the years Golden Triangle had grown by the acquisition of newer, more rapidly growing divisions that would attempt to operate independently and resist control from corporate headquarters and the original chemical division. To complicate matters further, corporate accounting was headed by someone who was a long-standing enemy of the controller of the original chemical division. Much more than managerial control and effective resource deployment was at stake. A single, centralized database would enhance corporate accounting's power over the various division controllers. Divisions would be unable to resist or delay in the furnishing of information, and any alleged misreporting of figures would also be stopped by the centralized system. Of course, the divisions saw the new system as a loss of autonomy and control over their operations information.

In many respects, the design of the financial information system was a political choice. Corporate accounting used an outside vendor to implement it, to avoid having to rely on internal operating support. The divisions fought cooperation with the new system, attacking its design, technical adequacy, and feasibility. This process dragged on for years, costing numerous hours of effort and meetings. Divisional accountants even attempted to sabotage the system. During the conflict, the head of accounting for the chemical division was reorganized out of his job, which alleviated tensions and drastically altered the political rationale that had originally driven system design.

As we consider the potentially radical organizational restructurings that highly digital and mixed digital products and services will require, like those that are currently under way at Schwab, the lessons learned from these cases could provide critical guidance. In some ways, technology can be held hostage by the political milieu, as at PRINTCO. In other organizations, such as Golden Triangle, key actors may enlist the technology as a political tool. Even successful IT implementations cannot always be easily understood or emulated without an adequate description of the attendant political arrangements.

3.3 Sociotechnical Support Is Critical for Effective IT Use

Discussions about supporting IT infrastructures are often constrained by the physical architectures of systems and networks. In practice, a "supporting infrastructure" involves a much wider range of "systems" and "networks" that includes organizational practices, key support staff, and access to technical and social skill sets. These extensions are often referred to as "the hidden costs of computing" because most IT systems are built around a set of assumptions and defaults that makes deviation difficult and expensive. Processing errors is very costly, even though some systems may require users to do this routinely in order to achieve desired results (Gasser 1986). Suchman (1997) terms this ongoing additional support required to make information technologies function for the organization "articulation work." As organizations seek to collaborate with other organizations, infrastructural demands escalate. Most accounts, however, portray IT infrastructures as fully supportive—they rarely refer to the articulation work needed to make IT implementations usable and dependable. The brief description of a Collaborative Planning Forecasting Replenishment system in Margherio et al. (1998) gives few clues that would help us understand the challenges member firms faced as they each implemented the system within their own organizations. But another account of a collaborative effort among geneticists at 50 organizations shows clearly that supporting infrastructure and articulation work are key components of networked collaboration.

Worm Community System

The Worm Community System (WCS) was a large-scale, custom-software, collaborative system designed to serve a geographically dispersed community of geneticists. Ultimately, WCS was used by 250 geneticists at 50 commercial and university laboratories. It was based on Internet communication technologies, and it allowed geneticists to publish and share documents and data, to create links among the content, and to analyze, navigate, and select among its contents. WCS also included access to relevant external databases, such as Medline and Biosis, as well as newsletters and meeting information. Although the system had a well-designed interface that users found easy to manipulate, many still found the system difficult to access and use routinely. This failure was due not to any inadequacies from an end-user point of view—the system met the demands of the geneticists—but to the fact that demands on university computer support staff were often greater than their system skills and availability.

The social infrastructure of networked computer systems like WCS—which includes not only hardware and software, but also knowledgeable, skilled support staff to maintain system availability and to respond to user problems or questions—is not usually homogeneous, and therefore equally robust, across all collaborating sites. In short, lack of attention to local infrastructure can undermine the workability of larger-scale projects. WCS is no longer used. Much of its functionality has been added to newer web-based systems developed for the genome projects. These preserve some of the best features of WCS, like the link-following capability, nice graphical displays, and easy-to-use interface, and they are better integrated to the desktop tools, operating systems, and networking skill sets that are commonly supported for web browsing.

In some cases, the need to provide an adequate infrastructure in support of collaborative knowledge work can trigger a local organizational transformation and large-scale infrastructural change as support practices, tools, computers, and networks are upgraded to meet system operational requirements and as new staff are hired or existing staff are retrained to acquire the needed system skills. There is a small body of OI research that amplifies these ideas. Web models of computing (which are not related to the WWW) treat the infrastructure required to support a computerized system as an integral part of it (Kling and Scacchi 1982; Kling 1992.) Star and Ruhleder (1996) have also shown that subtle individual and organizational learning processes underlie the development of local computing infrastructure—including the ability of professionals with different specialties to communicate about computerization issues. We expect these concepts to become even more relevant as organizations find new technologies to support their interorganizational networks.

3.4 Interorganizational Computer Networks Are Also Social Networks

Many network characterizations seem to suggest that the most important relationships can all be wired directly, and that they can be easily established and reformed. The Automotive Network Exchange (ANX), for example, a high-maintenance, tightly managed, virtual private network for automotive design, has been characterized as a network of routinized interactions among a stable set of participants (Margherio et al. 1998). In sharp contrast, OI studies show that interorganizational relationships are complex, dynamic, negotiated, and interdependent. As the following study shows, a sociotechnical approach can expose the complexities of using on-line technologies in support of interorganizational relationships and can help to explain why some firms find on-line technologies essential while others use them very little, or not at all.

Interorganizational Relationships and Information Services (IRIS)
In a recent study of on-line information resources, we examined the differences in on-line information use among 26 California firms in three industries: biotechnology, law, and real estate (Lamb 1997). We found that there are as many differences among firms

within an industry as there are between firms in different industries. Five factors seem to affect differences in the use of on-line information:

1. Interaction with regulatory agencies, as illustrated by biotechnology firms who submit documentation about product and product effects to regulatory agencies for review and approval, and by law firms whose clients are governed by such agencies.

2. Demonstration of competence and superior service to clients, as illustrated by the packaging of information from on-line and other information sources in the real estate industry, and by the profiling of competitors and markets in all three industries.

3. Opportunities to obtain information from other organizations through load-shifting, whether through outsourcing, partnering, or purchasing information services.

4. Existence of industry-wide information infrastructures to provide critical information, such as law libraries and real estate multiple listing services.

5. Client expectations for timely, cost-effective information exchanges, such as corporate clients' demands for immediate, specialized legal advice outside "normal" business hours.

These factors describe a set of influences that come from the interorganizational relationships of the firm. Some, such as profiling, have a technical orientation, and some, such as documentation, have an institutional orientation. The first two factors lead to increased use of on-line information resources. Firms that interact directly with regulators and those that see a need to demonstrate competence use more on-line information than firms that don't. The third factor leads to decreased use. When firms have an opportunity to shift data-gathering responsibilities to another firm, they will do less of it themselves. The fourth factor may also lead to decreased use if the infrastructure provides an alternative to going on-line, such as publicly supported law libraries. But it will lead to increased use if the infrastructure is on-line, such as the multiple listing services of the real estate industry. The fifth factor may, similarly, lead to either decreased or increased on-line activity, depending on the types of resources (including support staff) that

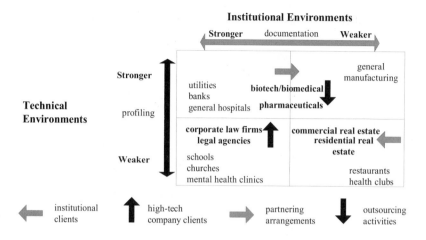

Figure 1 Informational environments with interorganizational influences.

are available to busy firm members in the evenings or on weekends; but time pressures generally lead to increased use of on-line information resources.

All organizations face varying degrees of technical and institutional demands from their environments. Scott (1987) has categorized industries as being more strongly or weakly influenced by these demands (see figure 1). The IRIS study shows that, in addition to such general influences, firms in each quadrant may have more or less incentive to gather data and use information resources depending on the clients they serve or wish to attract. Thus client relationships have a very strong impact on data-gathering practices and the use of information resources (in figure 1, see the arrows placed next to the "corporate law firms" and "commercial real estate" labels). Firms that work closely with institutions, such as federal regulators, report gathering more data overall than firms that do not interact with regulators as intensively; and when firms partner with one another, they may shift the responsibilities for gathering data across organizational boundaries (in figure 1, see the arrows placed next to the "biotech/biomedical" label).

The IRIS study shows that careful and effective designs for interorganizational networks must take into account the nature of interorganizational relationships. It also suggests that it is not "just a matter of time" before all organizations adopt on-line technologies. Some firms have less need and fewer incentives to use on-line technologies by the very nature of their industry, their clientele, and their interorganizational relationships. Although small firms are commonly portrayed as being more enabled to reach customers via the Internet, much still depends on their main business. There will be many more opportunities in e-commerce for providers of highly digital goods and services than for vendors of physical products and personal relationships.

3.5 Profitable Electronic Retailing May Weaken Community Life

The power of on-line technologies to strengthen or reshape relationships is not restricted to organizations. Internetworking has the potential to reshape relationships within our local communities and to affect the way we live, work, and shop. The authors of *The Emerging Digital Economy* (Margherio et al. 1998) report that companies are beginning to use the Internet to enhance and manage customer service and customer relations by operating around the clock and around the world. Going beyond standard-model assumptions of workforce flexibility, they also discuss the skills that workers and consumers will need as well as expected consumer behaviors in the Cybermall to come. Sociotechnical analyses, however, go even further toward examining the social repercussions of sweeping reforms like Internet shopping.

Irvine, California
Some technology developers and enthusiasts believe that Cyberspace will radically reshape our physical space. The visions of utopian planners have, in fact, frequently shaped our landscapes and lifestyles (Kling and Lamb 1998). The city of Irvine, California, is a case in point. Irvine is a postsuburban version of the "city of efficient consumption" (Goodman and Goodman 1960). It is characterized by a fundamentally decentralized spatial arrangement "in which a variety of commercial, recreational, shopping, arts, residential, and religious activities are conducted in different places and are linked primarily by private automobile transportation—[making it] complex, seemingly incoherent and disorient-

ing, and yet dynamic and lively" (Kling, Olin, and Poster 1995: viii).
Broad boulevards allow shoppers speedy access to local shopping
centers, and Irvine residents can conveniently reach 12-lane free-
ways for their workday commutes.

Irvine is a city of efficient consumption because its developers
and planners consciously control how citizens can exercise their
economic power as consumers. Although Irviners often have more
discretionary income than citizens of neighboring cities, their
discretion is locally limited to a relatively small number of choices
among restaurants, movie theaters, sporting facilities and retail
outlets. The number, location, and type of consumer services have
been planned by the community developers to maximize financial
returns on their investment. The Irvine Company, as the original
developer of the area, still owns most retail commercial property.
It rents to retail shops that agree to pay a monthly rental fee plus a
percentage of their gross monthly revenues. This arrangement
favorably predisposes The Irvine Company toward high-revenue-
producing renters or low-risk renters whose gross revenues can be
reasonably estimated beforehand. Not surprisingly, national and
regional chain stores, which already have wide name recognition,
rent most of the available shopping mall space.

When Irvine residents interact with nonresidents who work in
Irvine retail outlets, there is little chance that the interaction will
blossom into an ongoing relationship. The types of efficient, high-
volume transactions favored by national and regional chain stores
allow for only a brief encounter between a customer and a service
provider. And since these types of service provider jobs are not well
paid, there is usually high personnel turnover, further lessening
the probability of an ongoing relationship. As Gutek (1995) has
observed, the prevalence of services marked by minimal and
impersonal interactions is not unique to new cities. It is a growing
phenomenon in many service industries, including retail sales,
social services, education, and medical care. Social scientists worry
that this phenomenon contributes to the deterioration of a sense
of community. These interactions seem disconnected from real
life. What's the difference between this type of an encounter and
a fully automated electronic encounter, complete with computer-
controlled voice synthesis? For the most part, though, Irvine resi-

dents seem comfortable with the encounter-based service format. It is often convenient, but it is not their only option. If they want more personalized service, they can afford to go elsewhere and pay more for it.

Wal-Mart vs. the Web
Some California commercial realtors speculate that the Cybermall is about to do to Wal-Mart and The Irvine Company what Wal-Mart was accused of doing to small downtown retailers in the 1980s and 1990s. According to London (1995), as the expansion of Internet retailing brings more choice, lower prices, and better service to consumers, it will result in a downsizing of all physical-space retailers. He is not suggesting that traditional retail shopping centers will be eliminated, but that in order to remain profitable, shopping center owners will have to rethink how retailers pay rent. If local stores become mere showcases for products and services, like some Gateway computer stores, with the actual purchase being made on-line, the shopping center owner will not be able to depend on retail receipts for revenue.

But Internet retailing doesn't threaten only small shopping centers and retailers. The "big box" discounters, such as Wal-Mart, Circuit City, Costco, and CompUSA, will also be challenged. Their centers usually have a warehouse-type interior, and their selling approach has changed the nature of retail consumer relationships—inadvertently making it more comfortable for consumers to shop on-line. "The emphasis is on large selection, discounting, and convenience. They have de-emphasized customer service and presentation. The concept has taken the nation by storm and appears to represent a permanent change in the nature of shopping" (London 1995).

Faced with declining market share for the past two decades, traditional "downtown" retailers and those in regional community centers have been forced to establish alternative marketing or rehabilitation plans. London has participated in at least one physical rehabilitation of a small shopping center. The project, which may indicate the shape of malls to come, involved an inspired thematic concept. The center's pedestrian-only streets became an extension of those of the community. The developers simulated a dynamic downtown retail center—a pseudo-community that they hope will redefine why people go shopping, where they go, and how they spend their time. As our shopping habits become more rationalized, and more often on-line, we may also be inadvertently encouraging the developers who have planned our postsuburban landscapes to begin planning more and more of our "quality" life experiences.

4 Conclusions

The foregoing analysis of prior research amply demonstrates the ways in which sociotechnical IT studies can foster a deeper understanding of organizational change in increasingly digitally enabled environments. Table 1 and section 3 of this chapter identify a few key areas where sociotechnical perspectives diverge from mainstream conceptualizations of IT in organizations, and where further research may amplify our abilities to benefit economically and socially from new information technologies. From these areas, a few key empirically researchable questions emerge:

1. What are the organizational and social processes, the technological opportunities and constraints, and the dynamics of key combinations that influence how organizations "go digital"? How do these shape the development of new services, business viability, and so on? (As an example, how do these processes work in a bookselling environments like those of amazon.com, Barnes & Noble, Borders, and independent bookstores?)

2. What organizational and social processes influence how whole industries "go digital"? How can we understand differences between industries, such as travel versus steel manufacturing?

3. Which kinds of customers and services seem to be advantaged by digitally supported goods and services, and which kinds of customers and services are cut back or cut out?

Questions such as these should be studied with some significant historical perspective and ecological awareness. For example, firms like amazon.com could not have functioned on the Internet alone: they rely on a financial infrastructure (credit cards) and a distribution infrastructure (rapid national shipments of small parcels).

Some of this infrastructure has been developing over a 100-year period, since the advent of mail order!

This research agenda is preliminary and far from exhaustive. But we believe that it provides a starting point for discussions that will lead to a robust research program that examines the social, technical, and organizational aspects of the emerging digital economy. Sociotechnical perspectives can continue to guide researchers of e-commerce and new technology configurations, as they have guided IT researchers in the studies we highlighted. Moreover, like Ernst & Young, organizations can continue to learn important lessons from both the successful and the failed implementations that these studies analyze. A research program that fosters this approach and supports the longitudinal research that such studies often require will ensure that insightful analyses are available for thoughtful managers of IT systems in the emerging digital economy.

Acknowledgments

Blaise Cronin and Suzanne Iacono were invaluable discussants when we were preparing this manuscript. Brian Kahin provided helpful comments on an intermediate draft. The development of the digital economy model owes much to Ph.D. students in seminar L764 at Indiana University, especially Chris Ferguson, Joanna Fortuna, and PyungHo Kim.

References

Bashein, B. J., M. Lynne Markus, and Patricia Riley, 1994. "Business Process Reengineering: Preconditions for Success and How to Prevent Failures," *Information Systems Management* (Spring).

Bishop, Ann, and Susan Leigh Star, 1996. "Social Informatics for Digital Libraries," *Annual Review of Information Science and Technology (ARIST)* 31: 301–403

Clement, Andrew, 1994. "Computing at Work: Empowering Action by 'Low-level Users,'" *Communications of the ACM* 37(1): 52–65.

Cooper, Michael D., 1983. "The Structure of the Information Economy," *Information Processing and Management* 19: 9–26.

Davenport, Thomas, 1997. "Knowledge Management Case Study: Knowledge Management at Ernst & Young," http://www.bus.utexas.edu/kman/E&Y.htm.

Engelbrecht, Hans-Jurgen, 1997. "A Comparison and Critical Assessment of Porat and Rubin's Information Economy and Wallis and North's Transaction Sector," *Information Economics and Policy* 9(4): 271–290.

Fishman, Robert, 1987. *Bourgeois Utopias: The Rise and Fall of Suburbia*, New York: Basic Books.

Forsythe, Diana, 1992. "Blaming the User in Medical Informatics," *Knowledge and Society: The Anthropology of Science and Technology* 9: 95–111.

Forsythe, Diana, 1994. "Engineering Knowledge: The Construction of Knowledge in Artificial Intelligence," *Social Studies of Science* 24: 105–113.

Fuller, Steve, 1995. "Cyberplatonism: An Inadequate Constitution for the Republic of Science," *The Information Society* 11(4): 293–303.

Gasser, Les, 1986. "The Integration of Computing and Routine Work," *ACM Transactions on Office Information Systems* 4(3): 205–225.

George, Joey, Suzanne Iacono, and Rob Kling, 1995. "Learning in Context: Extensively Computerized Work Groups as Communities-of-Practice," *Accounting, Management and Information Technology* 5(3/4): 185–202.

Gierkink, Tia, and Rudy Ruggles, n.d. "Leveraging Knowledge for Business Value: Creating Living Knowledge Representations through the Power of Communities," http://www.businessinnovation.ey.com/mko/html/levera.html.

Goodman, Percival, 1960. *Communitas: Means of Livelihood and Ways of Life*, New York: Vintage Books.

Grudin, Jonathan, 1989. "Why Groupware Applications Fail: Problems in Design and Evaluation," *Office: Technology and People* 4(3): 245–264.

Gutek, Barbara, 1995. *The Dynamics of Service: Reflections on the Changing Nature of Customer/Provider Interactions*, San Francisco: Jossey-Bass.

Harris, Douglas H., ed., 1994. *Organizational Linkages: Understanding the Productivity Paradox*, Washington, DC : National Academy Press.

Jewett, Tom, and Rob Kling, 1991. "The Dynamics of Computerization Social Science Research Team: A Case Study of Infrastructure, Strategies, and Skills," *Social Science Computer Review* 9(2): 246–275.

Jussawalla M., and D. M. Lamberton, eds., 1988. *The Cost of Thinking: Information Economies of Ten Pacific Countries*, Norwood, NJ: Ablex Publishing.

Katz, Raul L., 1986. "Measurement and Cross-National Comparisons of the Information Work Force," *The Information Society* 4(4): 231–277.

Kling, Rob, 1990. "More Information, Better Jobs?: Occupational Stratification and Labor Market Segmentation in the United States' Information Labor Force," *The Information Society* 7(2): 77–107.

Kling, Rob, 1992. "Behind the Terminal: The Critical Role of Computing Infrastructure in Effective Information Systems Development and Use," in William Cotterman and James Senn, eds., *Challenges and Strategies for Research in Systems Development* (New York, Wiley), pp. 153–201. Also available at http://www-slis.lib.indiana.edu/kling/pubs/webinfra.html.

Kling, Rob, ed., 1996. *Computerization and Controversy*, 2nd ed., San Diego, CA: Academic Press.

Kling, Rob, 1999. "What Is Social Informatics and Why Does It Matter?" *D-Lib Magazine* 5(1), http://www.dlib.org:80/dlib/january99/kling/01kling.html.

Kling, Rob, Holly Crawford, Howard Rosenbaum, Steve Sawyer, and Suzanne Weisband, 2000. *Information Technologies in Human Contexts: Learning from Organizational and Social Informatics.* Bloomington, IN: Center for Social Informatics, Indiana University. Also available at http:/www.slis.indiana.edu/CSI.

Kling, Rob, and Suzanne Iacono, 1984. "The Control of Information Systems Development after Implementation," *Communications of the ACM* 27(12).

Kling, Rob, and Suzanne Iacono, 1986. "PrintCo Case," in Henry C. Lucas, Jr., *A Casebook for Management Information Systems,* 3rd ed. (New York: McGraw-Hill).

Kling, Rob, and Suzanne Iacono, 1989. "The Institutional Character of Computerized Information Systems," *Office: Technology & People* 5(1): 7–28.

Kling, Rob, and Tom Jewett, 1994. "The Social Design of Worklife with Computers and Networks: An Open Natural Systems Perspective," in Rob Kling and Tom Jewett, eds., *Advances in Computers,* vol. 39 (New York: Academic Press).

Kling, Rob, and Roberta Lamb, 1998. "Bits of Cities: Utopian Visions and Social Power in Place-Based and Electronic Communities," in Emmanuel Eveno, ed., *Urban Powers and Utopias of the World* (Toulouse: Presses Universitaires du Mirail).

Kling, Rob, Spencer Olin, and Mark Poster, 1995. "Beyond the Edge: The Dynamism of Postsuburban Regions," in Rob Kling, Spencer Olin, and Mark Poster, eds., *Post-suburban California: The Transformation of Orange County since World War II* (Berkeley, CA: University of California Press).

Kling, Rob, and Walt Scacchi, 1982. "The Web of Computing: Computing Technology as Social Organization," in *Advances in Computers,* vol. 21 (New York: Academic Press).

Kling, Rob, and Susan Leigh Star, 1998. "Human-Centered Systems in the Perspective of Organizational and Social Informatics," *Computers and Society* 28(1): 22–29. Also available at http://www-slis.lib.indiana.edu/kling/pubs/CAS98A-O.htm.

Lamb, Roberta, 1996. "Informational Imperatives and Socially Mediated Relationships," *The Information Society* 12(1): 17–37. Also available at http://info.cwru.edu/rlamb/infoim19.html.

Lamb, Roberta, 1997. *Interorganizational Relationships and Information Services: How Technical and Institutional Environments Influence Data Gathering Practices,* unpublished Ph.D. dissertation, University of California, Irvine.

London, Gary, 1995. "Are Shopping Centers A Vestigial Remain of Times Past?" The London Group Realty Advisers, October 5, available as http://www.londongroup.com/retail.html.

Lucas, Henry C., Jr., 1986. *A Casebook for Management Information Systems,* 3rd ed., New York: McGraw-Hill.

Margherio, Lynn, Dave Henry, Sandra Cooke, and Sabrina Montes, 1998. "The Emerging Digital Economy," Washington, DC: U.S. Department of Commerce.

Also available at http://www.ecommerce.gov/emerging.htm.

Markus, M. Lynne, 1979). *Understanding Information System Use in Organizations: A Theoretical Approach*, unpublished Ph.D. dissertation, Case Western Reserve University.

Markus, M. Lynne, 1980. "Organizational Design and Information Systems," unpublished manuscript, Sloan School of Management, MIT.

Markus, M. Lynne, 1981. "Systems in Organizations: Bugs and Features," in Jeffrey Pfeffer, *Power in Organizations*, (Marshfield, MA: Pitman Publishing).

Markus, M. Lynne, 1994. "Finding a Happy Medium: The Effects of Electronic Communication on Social Life at Work," *ACM Transactions on Information Systems*.

Mehler, Mark, 1992. "Notes Fanatic," *Corporate Computing* 1(2): 160–164.

Orlikowski, Wanda J., 1993. "Learning from Notes: Organizational Issues in Groupware Implementation," *The Information Society* 93(3): 237–250. Reprinted in Kling (1996).

Orlikowski, Wanda J., 1996. "Evolving with Notes: Organizational Change around Groupware Technology," in Claudio Ciborra, ed., *Teams, Markets and Systems : Business Innovation and Information Technology* (Cambridge: Cambridge University Press).

Orr, Julian, 1996. *Talking about Machines: An Ethnography of a Modern Job*, Ithaca, NY: Cornell University Press.

Parker, Edwin, 1981. "Information Services and Economic Growth," *The Information Society* 1(1): 71–78.

Pfeffer, Jeffrey, 1981. "Golden Triangle," in Jeffrey Pfeffer, *Power in Organizations* (Marshfield, MA: Pitman Publishing), pp. 275–277.

Porat, Marc Uri, 1977. *The Information Economy: Definition and Measurement*, U.S. Office of Technology Special Publication 77-12(1), Washington, DC: Department of Commerce, Office of Telecommunications.

Robey, Dan, 1997. "The Paradox of Transformation: Using Contradictory Logic to Manage the Organizational Consequences of Information Technology," in Christopher Sauer and Phillip Yetton, eds., *Steps to the Future: Fresh Thinking on the Dynamics of Organizational Transformation* (San Francisco: Jossey-Bass).

Robinson, S., 1986. "Analyzing the Information Economy: Tools and Techniques," *Information Processing and Management* 22: 183–202.

Schement, Jorge R., 1990. "Porat, Bell, and the Information Society Reconsidered: The Growth of Information Work in the Early Twentieth Century," *Information Processing and Management* 26(4): 449–465.

Schonfeld, Eric, 1998. "Schwab Puts It All Online: Schwab Bet the Farm on Low-cost Web Trading and in the Process Invented a New Kind of Brokerage," *Fortune* 138(11). Also available at http://cgi.pathfinder.com/fortune/technology/1998/12/07/sch.html.

Scott, W. Richard, 1987. *Organizations: Rational, Natural, and Open Systems,* 2nd ed., Englewood Cliffs, NJ: Prentice-Hall.

Star, Susan Leigh, and Karen Ruhleder, 1996. "Steps towards an Ecology of Infrastructure: Design and Access for Large-scale Collaborative Systems," *Information Systems Research* 7: 111–138.

Suchman, Lucy, 1996. "Supporting Articulation Work," in Rob Kling, ed., *Computerization and Controversy,* 2nd ed. (San Diego, CA: Academic Press).

Tapscott, Don, 1996. *The Digital Economy: Promise and Peril in the Age of Networked Intelligence,* New York: McGraw-Hill.

Tyre, M. J., and W. J. Orlikowski, 1994. "Windows of Opportunity: Temporal Patterns of Technological Adaptation in Organizations," *Organization Science* 5(1): 98–118.

Wagner, Ina, 1993. "A Web of Fuzzy Problems: Confronting the Ethical Issues," *Communications of the ACM* 36(4): 94–101.

Wellman, Barry, Janet Salaff, Dimitrina Dimitrova, Laura Garton, Milena Gulia, and Caroline Haythornthwaite, 1996. "Computer Networks as Social Networks: Virtual Community, Computer Supported Cooperative Work and Telework," *Annual Review of Sociology* 22: 213–238.

Wellman, Barry, and Gulia Milena, 1999. "Net Surfers Don't Ride Alone: Virtual Communities as Communities," in Marc Smith and Peter Kollock, eds., *Communities in Cyberspace* (London: Routledge).

White, Joseph B., Don Clark, and Silvia Ascarelli, 1997. "This German Software Is Complex, Expensive, and Widely Popular," *Wall Street Journal,* March 14: A1, A8.

Wigand Rolf, Arnold Picot, and Ralf Reichwald, 1997. *Information, Organization and Management: Expanding Markets and Corporate Boundaries,* Chichester: John Wiley.

Xenakis, John J., 1996. "Taming SAP," *CFO: The Magazine for Senior Financial Executives* 12(3): 23–30.

Organizational Change and the Digital Economy: A Computational Organization Science Perspective

Kathleen M. Carley

As we move into the twenty-first century, technological advances are transforming simple objects such as microwaves, VCRs, computers, locks, and lighting systems into intelligent objects by giving them the ability to perceive their environment, process information, make decisions, act, and communicate. The integration of computers into an increasing number of devices is making commerce electronic, actors artificial, spaces intelligent,[1] and the social and economic world digital.

Intelligent spaces will be characterized by the ubiquitous provision and distribution of information in networks of agents (Kurzweil 1988). These networks will include human as well as artificial agents such as organizations, webbots, and robots. The agents will act and interact in an environment characterized by vast quantities of distributed but potentially integratable information, where the interface between the analog and digital worlds is seamless.

Intelligent spaces will have four main characteristics:

• Ubiquitous access: Agents (human or artificial) will have technology to access or provide information wherever and whenever it is useful, thus both acting and remotely enabling other agents to act.

• Large scale: Vast quantities of information will be automatically collected, stored, and processed by vast numbers of agents.

• Distributed cognition and intelligence: Information, access to information, and information processing and communication capabilities (i.e., intelligence) will be distributed across agents, time, space, physical devices, and communications media (Hutchins 1991, 1995).

• Invisible computing: The interface between the digital world and the analog world will become seamless as computers are miniaturized, made reliable and robust, and are embedded into all physical devices.

As spaces become intelligent and information becomes digitized, a new sociopolitical and economic system will emerge. We will call this system the digital economy.

As spaces become intelligent, there will be unprecedented increases in the size and complexity of the interaction and knowledge networks in which human and other agents are embedded. Technology is increasing the amount of information humans have access to, when and where they have access to information, and how they can process information. Whether or not t†°se changes will foster social equality and improve individual and organizational performance is a matter of debate (Ebo 1998; Kiesler 1996). Whatever happens, people will still be people, and we will still need organizations to overcome our limitations (March and Simon 1958; Pew and Mavavor 1998; Prietula and Watson, forthcoming). Coordination, communication, and the diffusion of new technologies will still center around knowing who knows who and who knows what (Wellman 1998; Wellman et al. 1996; Rice and Aydin 1991; Aydin and Rice 1992; Contractor and Eisenberg 1990).

If we are to turn the potential of intelligent spaces into a reality in which individual and organizational performance is improved, we must overcome the digital, physical, and cognitive barriers that prevent people and organizations from working with others effectively. People need to be able to locate others who have needed information or resources, interact with those others, acquire the information, and understand the impact of these interactions. Increasing professional specialization combined with the speed at which ideas can be developed in a digital economy create an unprecedented need for quickly and efficiently locating and working with others.

Today, communication takes place in a limited environment. There are digital barriers to locating information, physical barriers to interaction, and cognitive barriers to understanding the impact of interactions. Overcoming these barriers will benefit both science and industry. Simply making spaces intelligent, making computers invisible, digitizing all data, putting everything and everyone on the web, and carrying out all transactions electronically will not allow us to overcome these barriers. Technology alone cannot create a truly digital economy (Kiesler 1996).

In theory, providing the physical world with the instrumental means to be more intelligent enables individuals, groups, and organizations to do more in less time and to connect to a widening circle of others. Research in telework, however, has shown that such technological changes can have mixed results: they lead to higher levels of productivity, improved working-time arrangements, and new employment opportunities for some (through greater decentralization and increased worker autonomy and mobility), but they generate increased isolation, marginalization, exploitation, and stress for others (DiMartino and Wirth 1990). It is difficult to measure the overall impact of computers and the internet on productivity, performance, and effectiveness, but it does appear that productivity and connectivity are closely linked. Increasing connectivity has often had the direct effect of increasing costs and delaying productivity gains (Dutton 1996; Anonymous 1988).

The movement to intelligent spaces will likely increase the complexity of underlying interaction and knowledge networks that comprise what we shall call the individual's "infosphere" (Figure 1). We expect the complexity of the infosphere to increase faster than our ability to manage and monitor this space.

The term infosphere was coined by the military to refer to the collection of remote instruments, appliances, computational resources, agents (human and artificial), and information accessible from an individual's working environment, such as the cockpit of a plane, the bridge of a ship, or the office. All agents are surrounded by such information spheres. For humans, the infosphere is largely determined by the type of technology that is immediately accessible. Thus, your infosphere is generally larger in your office than it is in your car, when you are walking down a hallway, or when you are sitting on a mountain top.

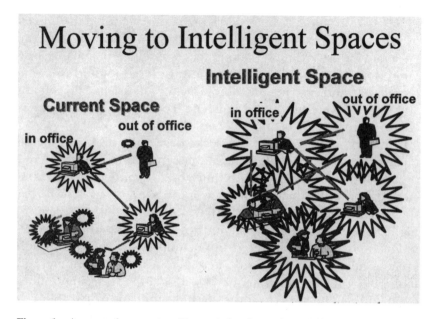

Figure 1 As spaces become intelligent, infospheres (stars indicating the amount of information a person has access to in that physical location) grow and changes occur in the interaction networks (bold lines indicating who interacts frequently with whom).

As the physical spaces humans inhabit become more intelligent, each individual's infosphere will expand and become less likely to change in size as the individual moves from one physical location to another. In intelligent spaces, when people move, their infosphere moves with them. As infospheres expand, the networks in which people are embedded and those to which they have access become potentially unbounded. Examples of these networks are the social network (who interacts with whom), the knowledge network (who knows what), and the information network (what information is related to what other information).

Technological change may lead to nonlinear rates of network change and to altered network structures (Kaufer and Carley 1993). However, technological change will not obviate the need for networks or the fundamental sociocognitive processes surrounding them (Wellman et al. 1996). Thus, the impact of technological change on organizations can be characterized in terms of alterations on and variations from existing forms and in terms of community creation and maintenance (Butler 1999).

Computational Organization Science

Two adages underlie much of current research on organizations: (1) *it is who you know not what you know that matters,* and (2) *knowledge is power.* Both adages imply that there are multiple adaptive intelligent agents whose actions and relations determine their decisions and performance and those of the organizations in which they work. There is a hidden conflict between these two adages, however, with the first focusing on the social network and the second focusing on the knowledge network.

Research on organizations that has sought to keep these networks separate has had limited success in addressing the impact of IT, e-commerce, or the web on organizations and society as we move to a digital economy. To achieve such understanding, we must recognize that that social and knowledge networks are linked in an ecology of networks and that a change in any one evokes a cascade of changes in the others. A high-level view of this ecology in shown in Table 1.

Research across a large number of fields (from anthropology to computer science) has contributed to our understanding of the processes at work in each cell in Table 1. Nevertheless, our understanding of how the entire ecology of networks interacts and affects social and economic outcomes is incomplete, particularly as it relates to knowledge. Further, most of the measures that have been developed have been tested only on small networks (less than 5000 nodes, often less than 100 nodes). We need further research to understand which of these measures scale, and continue to provide information, when the network has many more nodes and ties.

The complexity of interactions implied by this ecology of networks, particularly when it is populated by humans and artificial agents (such as webbots) who have the ability to learn, adapt, and evolve as a group, is difficult to comprehend, let alone reason about. A new approach that has tremendous potential for improving our ability to understand, reason, and manage the digital economy is computational analysis. In particular, computational

Table 1 The Ecology of Networks in Which Individuals and Organizations Reside

	People	Knowledge	Organizations
People	**Social Network**	**Knowledge Network**	**Work Network**
Tie	*Who knows who*	*Who knows what*	*Who works where*
Phenomenon	Social Structure	Culture	Organizational demography
Learning	Structural learning	Individual learning	Turnover-based learning
Knowledge		**Information Network**	**Competency Network**
Tie		*What informs what*	*What is where*
Phenomenon		Intellectual formation	Core comptencies
Learning		Discovery	R&D and Strategic Learning
Organizations			**Interorganizational Network**
Tie			*Organizational linkages*
Phenomenon			Industry-level structure
Learning			Mimicry, transference, best practice adoption

organization science offers a perspective on organizations and groups that has emerged in the past decade in response to the need to understand, predict, and manage organizational change caused by changing technology (Carley and Gasser 1999).

Computational organization science views organizations as complex, computational, adaptive systems composed of complex, computational, adaptive agents. Human organizations can be viewed as computational because many of their activities transform information from one form to another and because organizational activity is information-driven. This new perspective places individuals and organizations in an ecology of networks. We then use knowledge about the distribution of agents and knowledge across these networks to predict organizational behavior (Cyert and March 1963). Affecting the ways in which people and organizations navigate within and operate on these networks should allow us to improve overall performance.

From the perspective of computational organization science, organizations are synthetic agents. Within organizations, cognition, knowledge, and learning reside in the minds of the participant agents and in the connections among agents. Consequently, both individuals and organizations as agents are constrained and enabled by their positions in the ecology of networks (Granovetter 1985).

The computational approach works synergistically with other approaches to extend and evaluate theoretical arguments in complex, dynamic domains such as the ones that characterize the digital economy. The computational approach is strongest when the underlying models are empirically grounded and embed, are driven by, or are validated against other forms of data such as anthropological case studies, laboratory experiments, survey results, and large-scale data that can be automatically collected over the web. Multidisciplinary teams are thus needed to support the effort of modeling and theory building, as are data archives, model archives, and canonical task sets.

Every type of scientific research has critical limitations that affect the extent to which one can generalize from its findings. For example, analyses based on surveys are limited by the ways in which questions are asked, whether questions are always asked in the same order, and the samples surveyed. Human experiments are limited by experimental design, the subject pool, and the nature of the manipulation and controls applied. Computational analysis is limited by the assumptions made in constructing models and the ways in which the basic processes are modeled. For each method, researchers have developed procedures for overcoming the limitations. For example, specialized sampling procedures can increase the generalizability of the results of survey analysis. Similarly, in computational analysis, using Monte Carlo techniques to average out assumptions about parameter values (Balci 1994), using empirical data to calibrate the model (Carley 1999), and docking two or more models with different core processes (Axtell et al. 1996) are among the techniques that can increase the generalizability of findings.

Computational organization scientists focus on two distinct but complementary types of organizations (Carley and Gasser 1999).

The first type is the human organization that continually acquires, manipulates, and produces information (and other goods) through the interlocked activities of people and automated information technologies. The second is the artificial organization comprised of multiple distributed agents that exhibits properties such as collective action and collective task assignment. Computational analysis is used to improve our understanding of the fundamental principles of organizing heterogeneous agents and the nature of organizations as computational entities operating in the ecology of networks. Here I will consider three general findings repeatedly demonstrated by research in this area for multiple models and under a wide range of assumptions: emergent behavior, path dependence, and inevitability of change.

• *Emergent Behavior.* Although organizational performance is dependent on the intelligence of the agents within the organization, it is not determined exclusively by an aggregation of individual agent activity. Organizations in particular, and multiagent systems in general, often show an intelligence and a set of capabilities that are distinct from the intelligence and capabilities of the composite agents (Epstein and Axtell 1997; Padgett 1997; Zeggelink, Stokman, and van de Bunt 1996; Kauffman 1993; Macy 1991; Axelrod and Dion 1988). This means that we cannot predict the behavior of groups, organizations, and markets by looking at the average behavior, or even the range of behaviors, of the ensemble members. Rather, the networks affecting and affected by these agents constrain and enable what actions are taken when and by whom, and the efficiency of those actions. These networks and the agents' learning procedures dictate what changes can occur, are likely to occur, and will have what effect (Carley and Newell 1996).

In order to predict the behavior of groups, organizations, or markets we need to understand interactions and changes in the underlying networks and the ways in which member learning alters these networks. Computer modeling, because it can take into account the complexities of network dynamics, facilitates accurate prediction and helps us to move from saying simply that interesting complex behaviors will emerge to saying what behaviors will emerge. Research is needed on the behaviors that emerge under different conditions and on the scenarios that are likely or infeasible given the constraints of human cognition, socioeconomic policies, and the way in which the extant networks change, constrain, and enable individual behavior.

• *Path Dependence.* Individual and organizational performance is dependent on the history behind the current situation (Richardson 1996). What individuals can learn is a function of what they currently know and who they know. Thus, individuals with different backgrounds learn different things when faced with the same new information. Organizational performance is determined by structure, culture, and the experience of the organization's members. In particular, organizational performance is affected by the group work experience of members, which can affect both team mental models (Kim 1993) and transactive memory of who knows what (Wegner 1995).

For this reason two organizations that start identically but differ in when they adopt new technology are likely to have dramatically different performance profiles. Organizations that adopt the best practices of other organizations may not reap the rewards seen by the originator of the best practice. Research is needed to convert this notion of path dependence into a tool for determining whether, and under what conditions, a person or organization can achieve a targeted goal. We need to be able to predict, a priori, what path to follow and how to recover from a wrong path.

• *Inevitability of Change.* Individuals learn continuously (Newell 1990). Whether they actively seek information, simply absorb information presented to them, or generate new information, they are learning. As individuals learn, the knowledge networks change and sometimes the information network changes. Since organizations are composed of individuals, changes in the knowledge network lead to changes in the competency network. Learning also alters whom individuals interact with and thus affects the social network (Carley 1991).

Changes in the social or knowledge network can lead to or be motivated by changes in the job network. At the organizational level such changes might be characterized as evolution or organizational adaptation (Moss 1990). Changes in the social network, the competency network, or the job network can result in changes in the organizational network. Change, for the most part, is inevitable and must therefore be an expected part of organizational planning. Under such conditions, managerial strategy becomes decision making about how to structure and position the firm so as to manage and profit from changes in underlying networks. Organizational design becomes a dynamic process (Cohen 1986). Thus, research is needed on how to manage change and create an environment that controls the rate and type of change in these networks.

Before discussing specific results relating to the digital economy it is worth noting that the ecology of networks in Table 1 provides a distinctive way of classifying organizations. Previous classification schemes have been based on strategy (Romanelli 1989), product service (Fligstein 1985), or some combination of technology, coordination, and control (Aldrich and Mueller 1982). Such schemes provide little guidance for exploring how IT will be adopted by or will affect organizations, how change should be managed, and how organizations change. Computational and empirical research based on a network approach has been able to make useful predictions about the impact of IT and changes in performance that might result from reengineering (see, e.g., Levitt 1994).

Intelligent Spaces and the Ecology of Networks in a Digital Economy

Researchers in computational organization science employ computer models to predict, explain, and manage organizations. The accuracy of the predictions depends in part on the level of detail in the models. More detailed models lead to more accurate predictions.

To move beyond the general findings described in the last section, which are robust yet vague in providing specific guidance with respect to the digital economy, we need to look at predictions made by specific models. One core area where computational models have been useful is the study of information diffusion and belief formation.

To illustrate these results we will focus on the CONSTRUCT model (Carley 1990; 1991, 1995, 1999). CONSTRUCT is one of the few validated computational models concerned with information diffusion that takes IT into account. It is a multiagent model of social and organizational change in which there are many heterogeneous agents all of which can be intelligent, adaptive, and capable of learning, making decisions, and communicating. CONSTRUCT allows us to examine the impact of different types of IT on information diffusion, belief formation, and group performance. The exact processes embodied in the agent depend on whether the agent is human or some form of IT such as books or webbots. Using CONSTRUCT, the researcher can predict change in the social network from change in the knowledge network, and vice versa, for a group.

The first issue the model needs to address is how to represent, measure, and model IT. Research in this area has demonstrated that IT is both an agent and an agent enhancer. Most research on the social or organizational impacts of technology assumes that the reason IT does or does not effect change is because it changes the information-processing capabilities of humans. For example, email changes communication patterns because it enables asynchronous, high-speed communication and is archivable. Yet IT is also an agent; that is, it has the ability to create and communicate information, make decisions, and take action. As spaces become intelligent, this aspect of IT is likely to become more important. Treating IT as an agent has helped us understand the effects of previous technology (Kaufer and Carley 1993) and has led to important new findings about the potential impact of IT. This approach could allow us to model more accurately the behavior of organizations in which humans, webbots, robots, avatars, and so forth work together to perform various tasks (Kaplan 1999).

Viewing IT as an enhancer has led many researchers to predict that IT will speed things up and make interaction and knowledge networks bigger. Computer-based studies using CONSTRUCT suggest that the movement to intelligent spaces will have other important effects on groups and may alter the underlying social and political order. First, to the extent that discovery is facilitated by increased information sharing, the increase in the rate of information diffusion, which is a function of the amount of information there is to diffuse, may be less than expected. Second, IT does not affect all individuals in the same way, nor will it necessarily decrease the socioeconomic distance between disparate groups. Rather, since individuals who know more have more ability to learn new information, and since individuals who know more people have more sources of new information, IT could increase the socioeconomic distance between intellectual haves and have-nots (Carley 1995; Allstyne and Brynjolfsson 1995). Third, IT will alter not only the rate of information diffusion but also the relative rates of diffusion.

Consider the case of a scientist who has made a discovery. Who will learn of the discovery first: other scientists or the general public? In a predigital economy, where spaces were not intelligent and access was not ubiquitous, historical studies have shown that the answer was usually other scientists.

Simulation studies using CONSTRUCT predict that as spaces become intelligent discoveries will diffuse much faster to both scientists and the general public (Figure 2). Every new communication technology, from the printing press to email to the web, has increased the diffusion rate of new ideas. More importantly, the computational models suggest that the order in which people get information is likely to change as the world becomes digitized. Our scientist's discovery, for example, will most likely diffuse to the general public before it gets to other scientists.

This will change the role of knowledge-intensive professionals. Many professions, including medicine, law, science, and engineering, have developed norms, procedures, educational programs, and information checking and balance schemes based on the assumption that new information would become known first to insiders in the profession (Abbott 1988). How these procedures will change with the presence of digital experts and ubiquitous information is an open question. For example, how will doctor-patient-nurse relationships change when patients learn about new drugs and procedures prior to doctors?

As we develop a better understanding of how to model IT, we will be able to use computational analysis to address these issues and to explore whether specific policies and security procedures will ensure that the right information reaches the right people in the right order to achieve desired outcomes. Research is needed in the

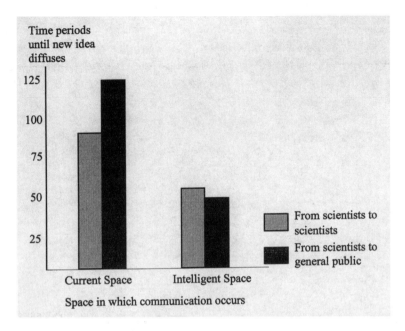

Figure 2 Communication in intelligent spaces will alter the relative rate at which information diffuses to different groups.

creation of computational tools for evaluating the potential short- and long-term impact of policies and procedures on access to information, on changes in information flow, and on the consequent effects on individual, group, and organizational behavior and performance. Part of this research agenda should include improved procedures, tools, and techniques for designing, building, evaluating, and teaching with computational models.

These results and others suggest that organizations and society will need to erect barriers around people and knowledge to help control information flow, maintain information superiority, and promote organizational performance. The point for research is, where and how should these barriers be erected?

Erecting barriers is not the only approach to altering the rate of information diffusion. Another approach is to encourage or discourage information-seeking behavior. For example, some web proponents argue that all organization members should be both taught and encouraged to surf the web so that they can gather information that will enhance the way they do their job. Simulation

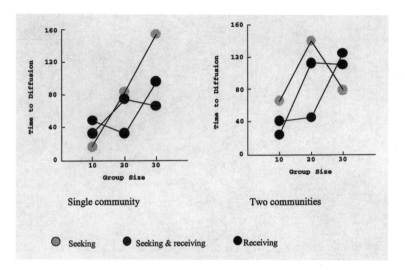

Figure 3 In intelligent spaces, group size, knowledge distribution, and procedures for learning new information still affect who learns what when.

studies using CONSTRUCT to explore the relative rates of information diffusion in intelligent spaces when individuals surf, actively seek, and passively receive information reveal that active information seeking does not guarantee faster diffusion (Figure 3).

The rate at which information diffuses depends on whether individuals are actively seeking out someone to give them the new information or are receiving it because someone they happen to interact with happens to give it to them. Actively seeking information can actually slow down the rate of information diffusion, and this effect, even in an intelligent space, may be more pronounced the larger the group. Thus, if the organization's goal is to slow diffusion, they might place people in larger groups, or they might encourage active searching rather than generic surfing (Figure 3, left).

This assumes that information is distributed more or less randomly through the community or organization. If there are knowledge cliques, such as occur when a community is divided into subcommunities or an organization is divided into divisions, then a different picture emerges (Figure 3, right). The partitioning of knowledge across subgroups slows down the rate of diffusion, even when there are no active barriers to the flow of information. This effect is strongest when individuals are passive information receivers, and it is stronger the larger the number of people who are connected.

Let's put these results in the context of the web. If people and organizations put up sites more or less randomly and there is no underlying division of knowledge or people across sites, then as more sites are erected and more people actively try to find information on the web, it may take longer for new ideas to diffuse. But if groups establish distribution lists, so that people are sometimes sent information and must sometimes seek it out, then as more sites are erected and more people start using the web, the effect of size will be mitigated. And if clusters form or are constructed of people and knowledge (e.g., by similar sites linking to each other, or by sites of the same type putting up similar information), then as long as people spend at least part of the time seeking information, simply having more sites and more people on the web may not determine the rate at which new ideas diffuse. While we now know that clustering networks can facilitate communication and comprehension, we do not know what the optimal size, location, or composition of those clusters should be.

A popular image of IT associated with a digital economy has been that it eradicates social boundaries, eliminates the role of social networks, and diminishes the importance of who knows who and who knows what in determining individual and organizational performance. The view that is emerging from computational analysis of social and organizational systems is almost the opposite (Alstyne and Brynjolfsson 1995). A growing body of research is demonstrating that the impact of making spaces intelligent is very context dependent and that knowing the distribution of connections among people, information, and organizations is necessary for understanding the impact of different types of IT.

A growing body of research, sometimes under the rubric of small-world phenomena, is demonstrating that e-commerce, the web, and IT, far from reducing the role of networks in a digital economy, actually require network structuring (i.e., the placement of non-random connections) in the social, knowledge, organizational, and other networks if the digital economy is to be effective and efficient. Web managers for companies are often aware of this and take care in exactly how they place links in the web-based organizational network (Gant 1998). We have suggested such structuring can actually reduce search time for new information. In practical terms, putting up web pages pointing to sets of group-relevant web pages should actually enable new information to diffuse faster. However, how many or which groups you should point to is not known.

Adaptive Organizations

While rapid information diffusion is valuable to organizations, performance depends not only on getting new information but on making the right decisions over sustained period of time. That is, organizations need to adopt strategies of change, do R&D, engage in alliances, and so forth to ensure high performance now and in the future as the environment changes. Much of the research in this area suggests that organizations need to develop competencies, that they need to learn how to learn, and that they need to trade off between exploiting known competencies and exploring new options (Levinthal and March 1981). Despite the growing body of work on organizational learning, the picture that is emerging with respect to intelligent spaces and the digital economy is woefully incomplete.

One interesting question is, what is happening in the high-technology industry itself? Many studies point to increased outsourcing and the development of new forms of organization (Pinchot 1994; Worhington 1997). One such form is the "networked organization," which is alternatively defined as a virtual organization formed through longstanding linkages among a set of organizations and as an organization in which work is coordinated on an as-needed basis with emergent teams rather than through a strict hierarchy (Nadler 1992; Nohira and Eccles 1992).

Chowdhury (1998) and Casciaro (1999) have gathered data for the past decade from newspapers and trade journals on joint ventures, partnerships, mergers, teaming, and other forms of alliance involving over 200 corporations in the telecommunications, electronic, and media industries (which are arguably at the heart of technology development, service development, and usage for the digital economy). These studies show, first, that over the past decade the interorganizational network has become increasingly structured and dense; that is, many new organizational linkages have been forming. Second, because most organizations work in multiple industries, standard industry-level SIC codes are not particularly useful means for classification. Third, and most intriguing, the best predictor of where organizational linkages will form is "my enemies' friends are my friends too" (Chowdhury 1998). That is, two competing organizations often linked to the same third organization. These links are not sales agreements, so it is not the case that the competitors are buying a common commodity. What is passing through the links is expertise and knowledge. Thus one possible explanation is the shared need to know about third-party information that is uniquely held by only one company (the friend of one's competitor). Another possible explanation is that when two companies link to the same third party, they can indirectly learn about the types of things their competitor is learning about and so stay abreast of recent developments. Fourth, over time, organizations develop a portfolio of ties in which the different sectors are represented only once (Casciaro 1999). Further research is needed to show exactly why these linkages are forming and how long they last.

A second set of questions center around the issues of how organizations adapt and how a digital economy will affect this adaptation. Work in computational organization science speaks to these questions (Levinthal and March 1981; Lant 1994; March 1996). As in the last section, more detailed predictions and explanations require utilization of more detailed models. To illustrate the findings in this area we use the ORGAHEAD framework (Carley and Svoboda 1996; Carley and Lee 1998; Carley 1998).

ORGAHEAD is multiagent model of organizational behavior and adaptation. ORGAHEAD makes it possible to examine how changes in IT and the nature of the task environment affect adaptation and performance in organizations engaged in classification and situation awareness tasks. At the operational level within ORGAHEAD individual agents learn how to get the job done through experience and communication with others. Basically, information and decisions flow up the chain of command and performance evaluations and change orders flow down. Experiential learning is modeled using standard human learning models. At the strategic level, the CEO or change agent can attempt to predict the future (albeit faultily) and to move ahead by engaging in different strategies for change (upsizing, downsizing, redesigning, retasking). The flow of strategic decisions, with the organization becoming increasingly risk averse, is captured as a simulated annealing process. Within this environment, different aspects of the digital economy, such as its impact on the amount and quality of information and the rate at which decisions must be made, can be tested in isolation or collectively.

It is often asserted that IT and the web have given rise to a constantly changing environment to which organizations must continuously adapt. One question is, how and how fast must organizations change to maintain high performance? Studies using ORGAHEAD suggest that the adaptive organizations that exhibit high sustained performance actually change less than other organizations in a rapidly changing environment. Moreover, adaptive organizations tend to be larger and to have more connections in the social or knowledge network (depending on the task environment) than their maladaptive counterparts. Whether and under what conditions who-knows-who connections can be traded for who-knows-what connections is a topic for further study.

Hierarchies tend to be more robust than flatter, more teamlike structures and are thus better able to withstand information and communication errors and personnel turnover. This appears to be particularly true for complex tasks involving large amounts of information. It is often asserted, conversely, that in a rapidly changing environment flatter structures are better because they can adapt more rapidly. Computer modeling, however, suggests that speed is not the only important factor in effecting and sustaining high performance in rapidly changing environments. Learning also matters. In a fast-moving digital economy there is less time to do error checking, and with more people and more information there are more chances of information and communication errors. Since telework and rapidly changing technology encourage turnover and job shifts, organizations will need to adapt by finding ways to do error checking and retain expertise. One response is to be hierarchical, not necessarily in management but in a checks-and-balances approach; another response is to expend effort on retraining, just-in-time training, training tools embedded in technology, and lifelong learning.

Computational research also suggests that adaptive organizations tend to change in different ways than do maladaptive organizations. For example, studies using ORGAHEAD (Carley and Lee 1998) suggest that adaptive organizations change the network of connections—retasking, changing the knowledge network by changing who is doing what, and redesign, changing the social network by changing who reports to whom. In contrast, maladaptive organizations spend most of their time changing the "nodes" in the network through alternate bouts of hiring and firing. Future work should examine how these changes interact with technology transfer and the migration of personnel between organizations.

Finally, adaptive organizations tend to start by getting the right people (hiring plus judicious firing) and then spend their time responding to the environment by altering connections. In contrast, maladaptive organizations tend to engage in frequent cycles of upsizing and downsizing. These results suggest that as we move to intelligent spaces, organizations must make it easy for their personnel to move between tasks, groups, departments, and divisions if they want to achieve sustained high performance. Internal organizational boundaries should be treated as permeable and internal transfers as natural. Research is needed to suggest what tasks this approach is valuable for and whether redesign and retasking are valuable in a multiorganization system where personnel can move between companies as well as between divisions within a single company.

Future Directions

Organizations are heterogeneous, complex, dynamic nonlinear adaptive and evolving systems. Organizational action results from interactions among adaptive subsystems (both human and artificial), emergent structuration in response to nonlinear processes, and detailed interactions among hundreds of factors. As such, they are poor candidates for analytical models. Because of the natural complexity of the object of study, existing models and theories of the organization are often vague, intuitive, and underspecified. Scientific progress will be more readily achievable if the theories become more explicit and better defined. Computational organization science helps to achieve this.

This chapter has explored the value of computational theorizing for understanding organizational change as we move to a digital economy. Computational models can be used to address organizational change in other ways as well. For example, such models can be used to demonstrate lower bounds on or the tractability of organizational information-processing phenomena—for example, the minimal information necessary to reach distributed agreement or awareness or the tractability of an organizational decision or negotiation processes (Rosenschein and Zlotkinx 1994). Experimental and empirically based computational models can also provide computationally plausible accounts of organizational activity (Jin and Levitt 1996; Decker 1996). Such models have the potential to be useful as both didactic devices and managerial decision aids (Baligh, Burton, and Obel 1990; Burton and Obel 1998).

Additional work is needed in developing computational frameworks in which models of organizations, markets, and societies can be rapidly developed and tested. The issues here go far beyond developing a multiagent language. The usefulness of such frameworks will be enhanced by linking them directly to online databases.

Using the common representational scheme implicit in Table 1 enables cross-model comparison as well as direct comparisons of model predictions, human laboratory data, and survey data. This common representational scheme is also leading to the development of powerful and comprehensive measures of organizations that go well beyond the social network measures (Krackhardt 1994; Wasserman and Faust 1994) employed currently to understand the structuring of personnel networks and their impact on organizational performance.

In the near future it will be possible to collect data in exactly the format needed by computational models, and the models can already generate data in a form that is directly comparable to that generated by the human organization and used by managers, human resources personnel, and intelligent agents to manage, monitor, and analyze the organization. This commonality will allow researchers to validate the computational models. Equally important from a digital economy perspective, the models can themselves serve as artificial agents or artificial organizations doing some of the work that might in a nonintelligent space be done by humans or human organizations. Moreover, the computational models can be used as virtual laboratories drawing on web-accessible data in which practitioners and researchers can conduct what-if analysis on the impact of new IT.

An extremely important future direction is to develop an understanding of, and tools for, the management of change. Little is known about what people need to manage interaction and knowledge in intelligent spaces. Will providing people with tools for integrating and visualizing knowledge (both theirs and others) actually improve the way in which they work? Will being able to analyze, visualize, and manage interaction and knowledge networks enable people, groups, and organizations to be more effective and more productive, to reduce uncertainty, and to improve performance? It is reasonable to expect that as we enter the age of intelligent spaces true productivity gains will require better tools to manage and monitor infospheres and networks.

Today, in many organizations, the automation of basic processes is insufficient to eliminate inefficiencies and guarantee sustained performance. Similarly, success in integrating distributed work activities will rest on how well the users of a network can coordinate their activities (Rogers 1992). Network management involves being able to search for relevant people and knowledge, dynamically generate and evaluate the capability of groups of people and knowledge that are networked together to achieve some goal, and assess the vulnerability of the system to various types of dysfunction (such as loss of personnel or knowledge).

We have some understanding of the social and psychological factors involved here, but we have few tools that can aid managers in thinking through these issues, or help us track the networks in and among companies, or automatically gather the relevant measures. Nor do we have an infrastructure for collecting and correlating all of the existing data about human behavior that are needed to serve as an empirical foundation for such models.

Issues such as these are particularly relevant in the area of security. It is often assumed that issues of security are by and large technological. Encryption, firewalls, and distributed computing and storage are all seen as technological schemes to limit the free and easy access of information by anybody at any time. Security, however, is also a social and organizational issue. Consider the concept of inevitable disclosure. The idea here is that if enough people working for one company are hired by a second company, then whether or not they as individuals know trade secrets and whether or not there is any intent on the part of individuals or the second company to gain knowledge peculiar to the first company, trade secrets and core competencies will inevitably be disclosed. This is an area filled with research needs and policy implications.

Acknowledgments

Much of the work reported here was supported by the National Science Foundation, under grants NSF CSS9711548, NSF IRI9633 662, and NSF GRT9354995. In addition support was provided by the Institute for Complex Engineered Systems and the Center for Computational Analysis of Social and Organizational Systems, http://www.ices.cmu.edu/casos, at Carnegie Mellon University.

Note

1. I am using an information-processing view of intelligence. Thus I consider any agent that can perceive its environment, acquire information, process information, make decisions, learn, and communicate to be intelligent. The degree of intelligence would vary with the number, extensiveness, and quality of these capabilities.

References

Abbott, Andrew D., 1988. *The System of Professions: An Essay on the Division of Expert Labor*. Chicago: University of Chicago Press.

Aldrich, H. E. and S. Mueller, 1982. "The Evolution of Organizational Forms: Technology, Coordination, and Control." In B. M. Staw and L. L. Cummings, eds., *Research in Organizational Behavior*, vol. 4 (Greenwich, CT: JAI Press), 33–87.

Alstyne, M. v., and E. Brynjolfsson, 1995. "Communication Networks and the Rise of an Information Elite—Does Communication Help the Rich Get Richer?" Paper presented at the International Conference on Information Systems, Amsterdam.

Anonymous, 1988. "Communications: A Direct Connection to Productivity." *Computerworld* 22 (Jan 6, 1A):17–22.

Axtell, R., R. Axelrod, J. M. Epstein, and M. D. Cohen, 1996. "Aligning Simulation Models: A Case Study and Results." *Computational and Mathematical Organization Theory* 1(2): 123–142.

Aydin, C., and R. E. Rice, 1992. "Bringing Social Worlds Together: Computers as Catalysts for New Interactions in Health Care Organizations." *Journal of Health and Social Behavior* 33(2): 168–185.

Axelrod, Robert M., and Doug Dion, 1988. "The Further Evolution of Cooperation." *Science* 242 (Dec. 9): 1385–1390.

Balci, O., 1994. "Validation, Verification, and Testing Techniques Throughout the Life Cycle of a Simulation Study." *Annals of Operations Research* 53: 121–173.

Baligh, Helmy H., Richard M. Burton, and Borge Obel, 1990. "Devising Expert Systems in Organization Theory: The Organizational Consultant." In Michael Masuch, ed., *Organization, Management, and Expert Systems* (Berlin: De Gruyter), 35–57.

Burton, Richard M., and Borge Obel, 1998. *Strategic Organizational Design: Developing Theory for Application.* Dordrecht: Kluwer Academic Publishers.

Butler, Brian, 1999. "Communication Cost, Attitude Change, and Membership Maintenance: A Model of Technology and Social Structure Development." CASOS working paper, Carnegie Mellon University.

Carley, Kathleen, 1990. "Group Stability: A Socio-Cognitive Approach." In E. Lawler, B. Markovsky, C. Ridgeway, and H. Walker, eds., *Advances in Group Processes: Theory and Research,* vol. 7 (Greenwich, CT: JAI Press), 1–44.

Carley, Kathleen, 1991. "A Theory of Group Stability." *American Sociological Review* 56(3): 331–354.

Carley, Kathleen, 1995. "Communication Technologies and Their Effect on Cultural Homogeneity, Consensus, and the Diffusion of New Ideas." *Sociological Perspectives* 38(4): 547–571.

Carley, Kathleen M., 1998. "Organizational Adaptation." *Annals of Operations Research* 75: 25–47.

Carley, Kathleen M., 1999. "On the Evolution of Social and Organizational Networks." In Steven B. Andrews and David Knoke, eds., special issue of *Research in the Sociology of Organizations* on "Networks In and Around Organizations." (Greenwich, CT: JAI Press), 3–30.

Carley, Kathleen M., 1999. "Validating Computational Models." CASOS Working Paper, Carnegie Mellon University.

Carley, Kathleen M., and Les Gasser, 1999. "Computational Organization Theory." In Gerhard Weiss, ed., *Distributed Artificial Intelligence* (Cambridge, MA: MIT Press).

Carley, Kathleen M., and Ju-Sung Lee, 1998. "Dynamic Organizations: Organizational Adaptation in a Changing Environment." In Joel Baum, ed., *Advances in Strategic Management*, vol. 15 (Stamford, CT: JAI Press), 269–297.

Carley, Kathleen M., and David M. Svoboda, 1996. "Modeling Organizational Adaptation as a Simulated Annealing Process." *Sociological Methods and Research* 25(1): 138–168.

Casciaro, Tiziana, 1999. "The Formation of Strategic Alliance Networks." Unpublished Ph.D. dissertation, Social and Decision Sciences Department, Carnegie Mellon University.

Chowdhury, Sumit, 1998. "Struggle for Power and Influence: A Network Study of Mergers, Acquisitions, Strategic Alliances and Competition in the Communication, Information and Entertainment Industries." Unpublished Ph.D. dissertation, Heinz School of Public Policy and Management, Carnegie Mellon University.

Cohen, M. D., 1986. "Artificial Intelligence and the Dynamic Performance of Organizational Designs." In J. G. March and R. Weissinger-Baylon, eds., *Ambiguity and Command: Organizational Perspectives on Military Decision Making* (Marshfield, MA: Pitman).

Contractor, N., and E. Eisenberg, 1990. "Communication Networks and New Media in Organizations." In J. Fulk and C. Steinfield, eds., *Organizations and Communication Technology* (Newbury Park: Sage Publications).

Cyert, Richard Michael, and James G. March, 1963. *A Behavioral Theory of the Firm.* Englewood Cliffs, NJ: Prentice-Hall.

Decker, Keith, 1996. "TAEMS: A Framework for Environment Centered Analysis and Design of Coordination Mechanisms." In G.M.P. O'Hare and N. R. Jennings, eds., *Foundations of Distributed Artificial Intelligence* (New York: John Wiley).

Di Martino, V., and L. Wirth, 1990. "Telework: A New Way of Working and Living." *International Labour Review* 129(5): 529–554.

Dutton, William H., ed., 1996. *Information and Communication Technologies: Visions and Realities.* Oxford: Oxford University Press.

Ebo, Bosah, 1998. *Cyberghetto or Cybertopia?: Race, Class, and Gender on the Internet.* Westport, CT: Praeger.

Epstein, Josh, and Rob Axtell, 1997. *Growing Artificial Societies.* Cambridge, MA: MIT Press.

Fligstein, Neil, 1985. "The Spread of the Multi-divisional Form among Large Firms, 1919–1979." *American Sociological Review* 50: 377–391.

Gant, Diana, 1998. "The Web of Affiliation: Theoretical Motives for the Strategic Establishment of Inter-organizational Relationships." Unpublished Ph.D. dissertation, Social and Decision Sciences Department, Carnegie Mellon University.

Granovetter, Mark, 1985. "Economic Action and Social Structure: The Problem of Embeddedness." *American Journal of Sociology* 91: 481–510

Hutchins, Edwin. 1991. "The Social Organization of Distributed Cognition." In L. B. Resnick, J. M. Levine, and S. D. Teasley, eds., *Perspectives on Socially Shared Cognition* (Washington DC: American Psychological Association).

Hutchins, Edwin, 1995. *Cognition in the Wild.* Cambridge, MA: MIT Press.

Jin, Yan, and Raymond Levitt, 1996. "The Virtual Design Team: A Computational Model of Project Organizations." *Computational and Mathematical Organization Theory* 2(3): 171–196.

Kaplan, David, 1999. "The STAR System: A Unified Multi-Agent Simulation Model of Structure, Task, Agent, and Resource." Unpublished Ph.D. dissertation, Heinz School of Public Policy and Management, Carnegie Mellon University.

Kaufer, David S., and Kathleen M. Carley, 1993. *Communication at a Distance: The Effect of Print on Socio-Cultural Organization and Change.* Hillsdale, NJ: Erlbaum.

Kauffman, S. A., 1993. *The Origins of Order: Self-Organization and Selection in Evolution.* New York Oxford University Press.

Kiesler, Sara, ed., 1996. *Culture of the Internet.* Hillsdale, NJ: Erlbaum.

Kim, D. H., 1993. "The Link Between Individual Learning and Organizational Learning." *Sloan Management Review* (Fall): 37–50.

Krackhardt, David, 1994. "Graph Theoretical Dimensions of Informal Organizations." In K. M. Carley and M. J. Prietula, eds., *Computational Organization Theory.* Hillsdale, NJ: Erlbaum.

Kurzweil, Raymond, 1988. *The Age of Intelligent Machines.* Cambridge, MA: MIT Press.

Lant, Theresa L., 1994. "Computer Simulations of Organizations as Experimental Learning Systems: Implications for Organization Theory." In K. M. Carley and M. J. Prietula, eds., *Computational Organization Theory* (Hillsdale, NJ: Erlbaum), 195–216.

Levinthal, Daniel A., and James G. March, 1981. "A Model of Adaptive Organizational Search." *Journal of Economic Behavior and Organization* 2: 307–333.

Levitt, Raymond E., Geoff P. Cohen, John C. Kunz, Chris I. Nass, Torre Christiansen, and Yan Jin, 1994. "A Theoretical Evaluation of Measures of Organizational Design: Interrelationship and Performance Predictability." In K. M. Carley and M. J. Prietula, eds., *Computational Organization Theory* (Hillsdale, NJ: Erlbaum), 1–18.

March, James G., 1996. "Exploration and Exploitation in Organizational Learning." In M. D. Cohen and L. S. Sproull, eds., *Organizational Learning* (Thousand Oaks, CA: Sage).

March, J. G., and H. Simon, 1958. *Organizations.* New York: John Wiley.

Macy, Michael W., 1991. "Learning to Cooperate: Stochastic and Tacit Collusion in Social Exchange." *American Journal of Sociology* 97(3): 808–843.

Moss, Scott, 1990. "Equilibrium, Evolution and Learning." *Journal of Economic Behavior and Organization* 3(1): 97–115.

Nadler, David A., Marc S. Gerstein, and Robert B. Shaw, 1992. *Organizational Architecture: Designs for Changing Organizations.* San Francisco: Jossey-Bass.

Newell. A., 1990. *Unified Theories of Cognition.* Cambridge, MA: Harvard University Press.

Nohria, Nitin, and Robert G. Eccles, eds., 1992. *Networks and Organizations: Structure, Form, and Action.* Boston, MA: Harvard Business School Press.

Padgett, John F., 1997. "The Emergence of Simple Ecologies of Skill." In W. B. Arthur, S. N. Durlauf, and D. A. Lane, eds., *The Economy as an Evolving Complex System II* (Reading, MA: Addison-Wesley), 199–222.

Pew, Richard W., and Anne S. Mavavor, eds., 1998. *Modeling Human and Organizational Behavior: Application to Military Simulations* (Final Report, National Research Council). Washington, DC: National Academy Press.

Pinchot, Gifford, and Elizabeth Pinchot, 1994. *The End of Bureaucracy and the Rise of the Intelligent Organization.* San Francisco, CA: Berrett-Koehler Publishers.

Prietula, M., and H. Watson, forthcoming. "A Behavioral Theory of the Firm: Organizational and Economic Perspectives." *Organizational Science.*

Rice, R. E., and C. Aydin, 1991. "Attitudes towards New Organizational Technology: Network Proximity as a Mechanism for Social Information Processing." *Administrative Science Quarterly* 36: 219–244.

Richardson, G. P., 1996, *Modeling for Management I: Simulation in Support of Systems Thinking.* Brookfield, VT: Dartmouth Publishing Co.

Rogers, Y., 1992, "Ghosts in the Network: Distributed Troubleshooting in a Shared Working Environment." Cognitive science research paper no. CSRP 253, University of Sussex, School of Cognitive and Computing Sciences.

Romanelli, E., 1989. "Environments and Strategies of Organizational Start-up: Effects on Early Survival." *Administrative Science Quarterly* 34: 369–387.

Rosenschein, S., and G. Zlotkin, 1994. *Rules of Encounter: Designing Conventions for Automated Negotiation among Computers.* Cambridge, MA: MIT Press.

Wasserman, Stanley, and Katie Faust, 1994. *Social Network Analysis: Methods and Applications.* Cambridge: Cambridge University Press.

Wegner, D. M., 1995. "A Computer Network Model of Human Transactive Memory." *Social Cognition* 13(3): 319–339.

Wellman, Barry, 1998. *Networks in the Global Village.* Boulder CO: Westview Press.

Wellman, Barry, Janet Salaff, Dimitrina Dimitrova, Laura Garton, Milena Gulia, and Caroline Haythornthwaite, 1996. "Computer Networks as Social Networks: Virtual Community, Computer Supported Cooperative Work and Telework." *Annual Review of Sociology* 22: 213–238.

Worthington, John, 1997. *Reinventing the Workplace*. London: Architectural Press.

Zeggelink, Evelien P. H., Franz N. Stokman, and G. G. van de Bunt, 1996. "The Emergence of Ggroups in the Evolution of Friendship Networks." *Journal of Mathematical Sociology* 21: 29–55.

The Truth Is Not Out There: An Enacted View of the "Digital Economy"

Wanda J. Orlikowski and C. Suzanne Iacono

Our title—with apologies to all *X-Files* fans—is intended to signal the key message of our chapter, which is that in many discussions of the digital economy in both the popular press and academic circles, there is a tendency—rhetorically and theoretically—to objectify "the digital economy," to treat it as if it were an external, independent, objective, and inevitable phenomenon, literally something "out there." We believe that such ways of conceptualizing the digital economy are inappropriate and misleading. In contrast, we want to suggest that the digital economy is nothing more or less than a social production—a product of our own making. As such, it is most certainly not "out there," but emerges in complex and nonlinear ways from our ongoing efforts, energies, and enterprises, both individual and collective. The digital economy is a phenomenon that we are, literally, enacting—that is, bringing into existence through our actions—everyday and over time. These actions are taken by us both individually and institutionally, as governments, communities, vendors, public and private organizations, workers, managers, consumers, citizens, hackers, pundits, lobbyists, and policy makers. We thus have the opportunity, the challenge, and, perhaps more importantly, the responsibility to shape this phenomenon in ways that reflect what it is we want—for ourselves, our organizations, our communities, and our economies.

In this chapter we consider the phenomenon now called "the digital economy" from a microsocial and organizational change perspective. Rather than focusing on market forces or technological infrastructure (the basic components of a digital economy conceptualized as "out there"), we start with the assumption that organizational practices play a key role in creating and sustaining this phenomenon. As organizations invest in new technologies, use them to internetwork with other organizations, and implement new cross-boundary work practices and processes, they literally enact the digital economy. Considering the critical role of organizations in carrying out these activities, we were surprised to find that there has been little systematic research on the relationship of internetworking to organizational change processes. We argue that such a research agenda is critical if we are to begin shaping and directing the digital economy to reflect our aspirations and values.

In the next section of this chapter, we discuss some of the lessons learned from prior research into technological change in organizations and discuss their relevance for understanding the digital economy. We then examine what we currently know about the role of organizations in the digital economy, and we conclude by considering some research questions raised by taking an enacted view of organizations in the digital economy.

Thinking about the Digital Economy

At some time in the past 40 years, most organizations in the industrialized world have computerized significant aspects of their work processes. Under a variety of mantles such as manufacturing resource planning, office automation, computer-supported cooperative work, supply-chain management, and virtual integration, organizations continue to invest in information technology. Each wave of technology brings with it a new set of technological artifacts whose design and use are informed by the organizational problems of their era, the current expectations about their value and function, and the processes through which they are appropriated into organizations. Each wave is usually associated with rhetoric about the potential impacts, both positive and negative, of the new technologies (Iacono and Kling 1999; Wiener 1954; Yates 1999).

Much of the rhetoric following the advent of the digital economy has highlighted its apparently transformative nature. For example,

Cairncross (1997, p. 119) writes that "The changes sweeping through electronic communications will transform the world's economies, politics, and societies," and even lead to "world peace." Shaw (1999, pp. 15–16) similarly predicts that the digital economy will lead to "plug-and-play inter-operability and modularity, customer-centric, friction-free, global supply-chains. Cairncross (1997), Dyson et al. (1996), and Toffler (1980) all predict that geographic distance will be "obliterated" by the availability of electronic communications to connect globally distributed institutions and people.

Such broad predictions are useful in encouraging new ways of thinking about these new phenomena, and they may mobilize some organizations, individuals, and even governments into action. They become problematic, though, when they are taken literally, because they mislead on two counts. First, they mislead on a factual level in the sense that generalized, "transformative" predictions are rarely accurate. Consider the following "death of distance" prediction made in 1847 by a U.S. congressman trying to convince his colleagues to fund the development of the telegraph (Davis 1997, p. 10, emphasis added):

The influence of this invention on the political, social and commercial relations of the people of this widely extended country will of itself amount to a revolution unsurpassed in world range by any discovery that has been made in the arts and sciences. Space will be, to all practical purposes of information, *annihilated* between the states of the Union and also between the individual citizens thereof.

The history of such predictions should have taught us that we cannot predict, with any accuracy, the social, economic, and technological changes and consequences likely to accompany unprecedented shifts in ways of working and living. We should not expect that today's pundits and technology advocates will be more prescient than their predecessors.

Second, sweeping predictions mislead on a theoretical level. That is, the promise of friction-free supply chains, obliteration of distance, and world peace creates the impression that the digital economy is an external and independent set of (largely) technological forces, from which individuals, organizations, and economies will necessarily reap significant benefits. Such conceptualizations do not take into account the difficult and often precarious process of realizing predicted changes. Decades of research on technological change in organizations have taught us that implementing change is a profoundly complex and uncertain endeavor (Attewell and Rule 1984; Carley 2000; Kling and Lamb 2000; Markus and Robey 1988; Orlikowski 1996). Not only is success not guaranteed, but significant unintended consequences are likely to occur.

The predictions embedded in the contemporary discourse about the digital economy reflect two particular and long-standing approaches to the relationship between technology and organizations: (1) technological determinism and (2) strategic choice (Markus and Robey 1988). Research on earlier technologies has shown that these approaches are not effective ways of understanding how organizational change processes are related to new technologies (Kling and Scacchi 1982). We do not expect them to be particularly effective here either. We shall therefore propose an alternative approach, which we call an *enacted* view. We briefly discuss each theoretical approach below.

Technological Determinism

This approach posits technology to be an external, largely independent phenomenon that determines or forces change in the social system (Marx and Smith 1994). Given this assumption, determinists focus on measuring and modeling the changes caused by technology, so that future changes in social systems can be predicted (Attewell and Rule 1984). Historically, predictions made about technological impacts have varied over time as well as by kind of technology being examined. From the late 1950s through the early 1970s, it was predicted that the use of mainframe computers in large hierarchical organizations would increase centralization and managerial authority, eliminate middle management, lead to massive work automation and job loss, and increase worker deskilling (Blauner 1964; Leavitt and Whisler 1958; Zimbalist 1979). In the 1980s and early 1990s, it was predicted that extensive internal computer networking and the rise of personal computing would increase decentralization, improve information sharing, and expand collaboration (Applegate et al. 1988; Giuliano 1982; Huber 1990). In the mid to late 1990s, with the exponential growth in the use of the Internet and the World Wide Web, predictions have been made about technological causes of transformations in markets—toward "friction-free" electronic commerce (Bakos 1998; Martin 1996; Shaw 1999)—and in organizations—toward "virtual," networked forms of work and governance (Davidow and Malone 1992; Mowshowitz 1997; Turoff 1997). Empirical work on new technologies and organizational change over the past three decades has not supported such a simple, deterministic model. Instead, researchers have found, for example, that the same technology implemented in different organizations can result in different practices and outcomes (Barley 1986), that the implementation of a new technology does not necessarily mean that it will be used or that use will occasion the benefits or intentions of the designers (Orlikowski 1992), and that different social groups can conceptualize the same technology in different and often contradictory ways (Iacono and Kling, 1999).

Strategic Choice

The second common approach to technology posits it to be a malleable resource that can be put to a variety of uses (with a range of effects) depending on managerial or organizational strategies, ideologies, and political dynamics (Child 1972; Daft and Lengel 1986; Noble 1985; Thomas 1994; Zuboff 1988). This approach suggests that we should focus on identifying the motivations, objectives, and interests of relevant players as a way of predicting particular changes and outcomes. Commentators working from a rationalist position portray managers as making choices about which technologies they will purchase through strategic alignment of the technology's characteristics with their organizational environments, and then deciding who in the organization should use them for specific "value-adding" processes or tasks. The assumption is that the choice of the product (e.g., a new flexible or collaborative tool) determines the outcomes (e.g., more flexible or collaborative work practices). Commentators working from a labor process perspective see managers deploying technology with the intent of controlling and deskilling workers, thus decreasing corporate reliance on human labor and skills.

In both cases, commentators share the strategic choice presumption that managers rather than users are the key actors in shaping technology to particular organizational or economic ends. In fact, however, once a new technology is deployed, developers and managers often have little control over how specific workgroups and teams will use it. Instead, users shape the technology to their own needs—for example, by developing "workarounds" (Gasser 1986), by only using the most basic features (Bullen and Bennett 1991), or by improvising with the technology to generate new uses (Mackay 1988; Orlikowski 1996).

Enacted Approach

An alternative approach to understanding the relationship between technology and organizations is to see this relationship as an ongoing sociotechnical production. It is through our actions, both individual and collective, and either deliberate or not, that outcomes associated with technological change emerge. Technology in this view is neither an independent, external force completely outside of our influence, nor a fully malleable resource that can be thoroughly controlled and bent to our will. Rather, the organizational changes associated with the use of technologies are shaped by human actions and choices, while at the same time having consequences that we cannot fully anticipate or plan. This approach we term an *enacted* view.

An enacted view represents a historical and proactive stance with respect to the world. Its strong focus on human agency (Giddens 1984) leads to the core assumption that the economic, institutional, infrastructural, technological, political, and social arrangements that shape our lives don't exist "out there" as part of nature, nor are they imposed on us by the will of the gods or a brilliant leader. Rather, they are equally shaped by our actions, individual and collective, intended and unintended.

This view suggests that the digital economy is neither an exogenous nor a completely controllable phenomenon, but an ongoing social product, shaped and produced by humans and organizations, and having both intended and unintended consequences. It is our individual and institutional actions in developing, constructing, funding, using, regulating, managing, supporting, amplifying, and modifying the phenomenon we refer to as the "digital economy" that enacts it over time.

Implications of Using Technologies in Organizations

Given the fundamental role of technologies in the digital economy, it may be instructive to review some of the lessons learned in three decades of studying technologies in organizations. While the findings have often been tied to specific contexts, particular time periods, and certain types of technologies, they have also yielded deeper and more general insights about the nature of technologies, their use by people in organizations, and resulting outcomes. These insights, which we have grouped into three clusters here, should aid our understanding of the digital economy.

1. Technology Is Social, Dynamic, and Multiple

Technologies—whether hardware, software, networks, or techniques—are human artifacts, produced through a social process of design, development, and maintenance. As such, their form, function, and operation reflect the interests, assumptions, values, objectives, resources, materials, and skills of their makers. Thus, technologies are not neutral, objective, or independent; they are social because they are constructed by people.

Technologies are also dynamic. Even after a technological artifact appears to have solidified, with the discourse around its functions and features apparently having reached "closure" (Bijker 1997; Pinch and Bijker 1984), the stability of the actual artifact is still only provisional. It is provisional because new materials might be invented, different features might be developed, existing functions may fail and be corrected, new standards could be set, and users can adapt the artifact for new and different uses (Mackay 1988; von Hippel 1988). Technologies are thus never fully stabilized or "completed," even though we may choose to treat them as "black boxes" for a period of time. By temporarily bracketing the dynamic nature of technological artifacts, we assign a "stabilized-for-now" status (Schryer 1993) to our technological products. Such bracketing is an analytic and practical convenience only, because technological artifacts continue to evolve, are tinkered with (by users, designers, and regulators), modified, improved, rebuilt, etc. Typically, such change is not predetermined or predictable, but implemented by people influenced by competitive, technological, political, cultural, and environmental forces (e.g., feature wars with competitors, privacy or decency concerns, technological innovations, security legislation, climatic conditions, earthquakes, poor maintenance).

All technologies are thus social and dynamic, produced by people over the lifetime of their use. This applies, in particular, to contemporary internetworking technologies. For example, the World Wide Web (WWW) was first proposed in 1989 by Tim Berners-Lee of CERN as a hypertext, networked system for sharing information within the high-energy physics research community. No one, least of all its inventor (Berners-Lee 1996), envisioned the changes associated with this technology. Planned and designed as a particular artifact for a particular community, the WWW was taken up by other individuals and communities, used in different ways, and adapted, enhanced, and expanded to accommodate those differences in use and community. Today, the WWW continues to be adapted, enhanced, and expanded by individuals and organizations around the world.

Technology is also multiple. It does not consist of a single thing but is typically a multiplicity of tools and a variety of different configurations of often fragile and fragmentary components. In addition, the interconnections among these components are only partial and provisional, and they need bridging, integration, and articulation in order to work together. We have a tendency to talk of technology, systems, and networks as if they were wholes—monolithic, uniform, and unified. For example, we talk about "the Internet" or "the Digital Economy" as if these were single, seamless, and stable—the same at every time and every place, always operating, flawlessly connecting everyone, anytime, anywhere. While such simplifications make it easy to talk about new technologies, they also mislead because they obscure the many ways in which technologies are not fully formed, coherent, integrated, and dependable, and the many ways in which they may and do break down, wear down, and shut down.

In our talk and visions we tend to focus on the apparent solidity and sensibility of the technological artifacts to which we have assigned rhetorically powerful and provocative labels. But in focusing on coherent labels, we can lose sight of the multiplicity of components that need to work together to produce the artifacts we can name (e.g., hardware devices, software applications, middleware, telecommunications, interfaces, training services, access protocols, business models, and workflow processes). These components are far from unitary, unified, or uniform. They are often characterized by brittle interconnections and complex interdependencies. And we should have no illusions that such multiplicity and connectivity will disappear. On the contrary, it is likely to increase as people keep developing, experimenting, and inventing new technologies, evolving components and uses, yielding ever more interfaces, interdependencies, and applications.

The fragility of our multiple, interdependent technologies often becomes salient when a new component needs to be integrated into an existing system, when someone wants to use it for novel purposes, or when there is a breakdown or public protest. For example, many corporations have explicit e-commerce strategies for collecting consumer information and monitoring online activity, in what Culnan and Milberg (1999) describe as the second exchange. When the public finds out about these invasions into their privacy, they often take action (Markoff 1999). Consider the case of Lotus *Marketplace*. When people learned that Lotus Development Company and Equifax Inc., the national credit reporting company, were in a joint venture to market Lotus *Marketplace*, a database that would have contained the names, addresses, and buying habits of 80 million U.S. households, more than 30,000 messages of protest flooded into Lotus Development Company, many of them sent by email (Brody 1992). These actions, which have been called the first "electronic sit-ins," forced Lotus and Equifax to abandon the product.

2. Technology Must Be Used to Have Effect, and Such Use Is Varied, Embedded, and Emergent

To be useful, technology must be used, and when we fail to pay attention to what people actually *do* with a technology, we often end up focusing on the wrong thing, such as the artifact itself, its features, or the discourse around it. But technology is not valuable, meaningful, or consequential until people engage with it in practice. Neglecting the centrality of use leads to simplistic assumptions such as: if people are given technology, they will use it; they will use it as the creators intended; and such use will produce expected outcomes. Such assumptions reflect a "build it and they will come" approach to technology. Research, however, indicates that such fields of dreams exist only in the movies!

Because of simplistic assumptions about technology and its use, many organizations have concentrated resources, attention, and effort on getting the right technologies to the right place at the right time, effectively ignoring "right use." In learning theory, Argyris and Schön (1978) were thinking of this general tendency when they distinguished between "espoused theories" (what we say about how we act) and "theories-in-use" (what our actions reveal about how we act). They note that people are usually unaware of this distinction, and that an important part of learning is recognizing and dealing with it. Similarly, people typically do not differentiate between what we may call "espoused technologies" and "technologies-in-use." *Espoused technologies* refer to our expectations about the generalized use of hardware and software components and the broad discourses associated with their functions and features. *Technologies-in-use* refer to the situated ways in which we actually use specific technological features in particular ways depending on our skills, tasks, attention, and purposes, and varying by time of day, situation at hand, and pressures of the moment.

For example, one study examined the use of the Lotus *Notes* in a multinational consulting firm that had adopted the technology to facilitate knowledge sharing among consultants across the firm (Orlikowski 1992). The managers implementing *Notes* concentrated their energies and resources on installing *Notes* within the firm's infrastructure and on every consultant's desktop. They believed that their deployment of the technology was successful, as measured by the number of user accounts established, the number of servers installed, and the number of databases created. Focusing on the espoused technologies, these managers did not attend much to the technologies-in-use, that is, to what consultants were actually doing with *Notes* in their everyday consulting practice. Such attention would have revealed that consultants were not using the technology to share knowledge, choosing instead either to not use

Notes or to use it only to transfer files or send memos. This consulting firm, like most professional services firms, had a competitive "up or out" career path and individualistic work norms; hence, sharing knowledge through *Notes* with anonymous others across the global firm was countercultural and, not surprisingly, did not happen.

Because technologies-in-use are, by definition, distinct from espoused technologies, we cannot use the features and functions of the latter to predict the former. Consider the HomeNet project, a multiyear research study at Carnegie Mellon University examining the Internet usage of about 100 families in Pittsburgh during their first few years online (Kraut et al. 1998, p. 21). The surprising finding so far is that "Using the Internet at home causes small but reliable declines in social and psychological well-being." Many find this result disquieting, at odds with both popular beliefs and personal experiences. Users of the WELL, for example, a virtual community on the Internet, report quite different experiences. As chronicled by Rheingold (1993), members of the WELL offer each other social ties, friendship, and emotional support. Similarly, Galegher et al. (1998) report intense emotional and practical support offered by online networks of electronic support groups.

How can we explain these differences in experiences with the same technology? One possible explanation lies in the difference between espoused technologies and technologies-in-use. Stories of the WELL and electronic support groups are descriptions of technologies-in-use. The HomeNet project's measures of "Internet use"—number of hours connected to the Internet—reflect espoused technology. They don't tell us what people were actually doing with the Internet and how they were using it—whether they were surfing the web, shopping for books, interacting with friends, participating in an electronic support group, etc. The meaning of the HomeNet results may be less paradoxical if represented in terms of technologies-in-use. Thus, the decline in social and psychological well-being found by the HomeNet researchers may be associated with the specific technologies-in-use (not yet described in the research) generated by 169 people in Pittsburgh, rather than the result of some general and universal "use of the Internet." Other technologies-in-use generated by using the Internet—as suggested by the experiences of WELL users and members of online support networks—may result in different social and psychological outcomes. Clearly, we need to look not just at the use of technology in general, but at specific uses by particular people in particular times and places. Use of technology is varied, embedded in various contexts, and consequently has a variety of outcomes.

The distinction between espoused technologies and technologies-in-use may also help us make sense of and address the debate that has formed around the existence and meaning of the so-called productivity paradox—the idea that the increased investment in information technology is not yet producing increased productivity. While the force behind this debate has generally been defused due to recent empirical work linking organizational IT investments to increases in organizational revenues (Smith, Bailey, and Brynjolfsson 2000), and the explanation that productivity gains are linked to IT "regime transitions" rather than simple technology substitution (David 2000), we argue that—for organizations—it would be more appropriate and more meaningful to look for returns on the *use* of information technology rather than only for returns on *investments* in information *technology*. Information *technology* per se cannot increase or decrease the productivity of workers' performance, only their *use* of the technology can. This differentiation may sound like semantic hair-splitting, but how people talk has profound implications for how they think and act in the world. By emphasizing technology in their talk, people tend to emphasize *espoused technologies* in their allocation of resources, attention, and measures. And such an emphasis, as our examples of *Notes* and HomeNet showed, typically leads to a neglect of *technologies-in-use*. By not understanding (and supporting) what actually happens at the moment of use, commentators miss the crucial point that it is how people *use* technology in their day-to-day activities—not the mere presence of the technology on the desktop or factory floor—that determines actual effects and work productivity.

Use of technology is also emergent. It typically departs from the expectations of its original inventors, designers, and promoters. Indeed, our own experiences with technology reveal that we do not passively or mindlessly follow the dictates of the machine or its designers' specifications. Rather, we constantly make choices about whether, how, when, where, and for what purposes to use technology. When the order entry system slows to a crawl at peak times, we bypass it. If we can't figure out how to program the VCR, we only use it to play prerecorded videos. When we want to use a spreadsheet tool, we learn the basic functions we need and ignore the advanced features. As the Internet keeps evolving, we keep adjusting how we use it as we figure out what is possible (and what others are doing). We are purposive, knowledgeable, adaptive, and inventive agents who engage with technology to accomplish various and changing ends. Where the technology does not help us achieve those ends, we abandon it, or work around it, or change it, or improvise new ends.

People engage artfully with the technologies they encounter in their lives, using them in a multiplicity of ways not imagined at their design and construction (cf. Gasser 1986). For example, in a study of a customer support department's use of *Notes* (Orlikowski and Hofman 1997; Orlikowski 1996), we found that the staff's initial use of the technology to support call tracking evolved over time as they learned more features and experimented with different types of use. Over a period of about two years, the use of the technology had changed dramatically from the initial, simple model of documenting a problem to a more complex model of collaborative problem-solving. Similarly, uses of the WWW have evolved considerably beyond the ones imagined by its inventor (Berners-Lee 1996). From the initial vision of project home pages for high-energy physicists to intranets, extranets, and e-commerce for everyone, we have seen an explosion of emergent and diverse uses. It should be clear, then, that any understanding of technology and what it might mean for organizations or economies must begin with an understanding of how and why people engage with it initially and over time.

3. Use of Technology Has Unintended Consequences

All action in the world, including the development and use of technology, has unintended consequences. Because each of us participates in multiple social systems, our every action can have multiple implications. For example, when we use money to buy a product, in addition to participating in a purchasing transaction, we are reinforcing the prevailing market economy and the legitimacy of money to mediate such transactions. Similarly, an unintended consequence of the increased use of the WWW by people around the world is the extension and reinforcement of English (the *lingua franca* of the Internet) as the language of the global economy. Consider, too, how the increased use of technology throughout the economy has had the unintended consequence of increasing vulnerability to technical breakdown and error, manifest recently in the heightened state of anxiety and activity around the Y2K problem and various computer viruses. One such virus—the "Love Bug"—launched on May 3, 2000, attacked an estimated 45 million home, office, and government computers around the world, causing an estimated two billion dollars in damage. One final example of unintended consequences of the global economy is the creation of a new and growing class of workers that Iyer (1998) calls the "business homeless." These are people who jet-lag their way through the world's airports, spending more time on airplanes than most flight attendants, and becoming in the process "glazed nomads" with "decentered souls."

That technology in use always has outcomes not intended or envisioned by its designers and implementers is a central finding of the research conducted over the past few decades on social issues of computing. This finding has been stable across time periods, type of information technology, and social context (Barley 1988; Button 1993; Gasser 1986; Kling and Scacchi 1982; Kraut et al. 1988; Iacono and Kling, 1999; Orlikowski 1992, 1996; Sproull and Kiesler 1991; Thomas 1994). As a result, our studies of and practices within the digital economy should take into consideration not only the possibility but the likelihood that there will be many and various unintended consequences of living and working in the digital economy.

Organizations and the Digital Economy

While little research to date has generated deep understanding of the relationship between organizations and the digital economy, three aspects of this relationship may serve as starting points for developing such an understanding: extent of organizational engagement in the digital economy, rationale for engagement, and nature of engagement.

Extent of Organizational Engagement in the Digital Economy

In the early 1990s, NSF transferred most Internet operations to commercial providers. By 1995, restrictions on commercial use of the Internet were lifted and organizations were increasingly investing in internetworking technologies to interact and connect with other organizations and their customers (National Research Council 1999). Internetworking refers to the use of special-purpose computers or hosts to connect a variety of separate networks for transmitting data, files, and messages in text, audio, video, or graphic formats over distances. For example, organizations exchange email with people outside the organization. They develop web sites to provide online information for external consumption. They build intranets and extranets, and they are shifting some of their operational systems onto the Internet, where many expect the bulk of their future business activities to be conducted. This "net presence" strategy adopted by many organizations constitutes one common aspect of the digital economy.

Today, the Internet is the largest internetwork. As a result of the increasing use of the Internet by organizations, Internet traffic, defined as data flow on the U.S. Internet backbone, has roughly doubled in size each year for the past decade (Guice 1998). Internet traffic and counts of hosts and users are routinely tracked by various monitoring services. In 1981, there were 621 connected hosts. According to recent estimates, over 43 million hosts are now connected (Network Wizards 1999), and 254 million connected hosts are projected by the year 2000 (Matrix Information and Directory Services 1997). One recent survey of the number of people connected to the Internet estimates that there are 163 million users worldwide, with 90 million in North America (NUA Ltd. 1999). A number of surveys have focused on the demographics of Internet users (Hoffman et al. 1996), their attitudes and uses (Chung 1998), and changes in well-being (Kraut et al. 1996, 1998).

Given all this attention to contouring the size, shape, and scope of the Internet in terms of individuals and computers, it is surprising that little attention has been paid to organizations and their connections to the Internet. The only estimates we have are based on figures from DomainStats.com (a database run by NetNames, the company that registers domain names). They report that there are almost 16 million registered domain names worldwide (a doubling of the numbers in less than one year). Almost 9.5 million of them are registered to commercial organizations (.com domains). Almost one million are registered to nonprofit organizations (.org domains). Almost 6,000 are registered to educational institutions (.edu domains), and over 700 are registered to the U.S. government (.gov domains). While these figures may be seen as rough surrogates of organizational presence on the net, they are also misleading. For example, international domains are registered at the top level by their country of origin (e.g., .ca for Canada, .fr for France), not by their type. Additionally, it is not clear whether domain name registration satisfies legal or even common assumptions about what constitutes an organization. Several organizations might share the same domain name (e.g., if they are subsidiaries), or one organization might have many domain names (e.g., for different divisions). And many domain names are simply registered to individuals who plan to use them or sell them at a later date.

This lack of attention to mapping the presence, power, and performance of internetworked organizations is particularly surprising given that the predominant domain on the Internet is that of commercial organizations and the expectation is that business-to-business transactions will account for the majority of activity in the digital economy. In 1998, $43 billion were spent on e-commerce business-to-business transactions, five times that spent on business-to-consumer transactions. Forrester Research projects that e-commerce business-to-business transactions will grow to $1.3 trillion by 2002, while in that same time period e-consumer business will grow to $95 billion (Tedeschi 1999). Clearly, much research and monitoring of organizational engagement in the digital economy will be necessary to assess its extent, effectiveness, and consequences.

Rationale for Organizational Engagement in the Digital Economy

There are two common answers to the question of why organizations are engaging with the digital economy. The most frequent one is that the Internet has opened up a new marketplace for buying and selling. Rao et al. (1998) argue that there has been a "stampede of businesses to the Net" as a result of a number of trends: the commercial advent of the WWW in 1994; the availability of user-friendly browsers on many desktops; the tremendous growth in the number of Internet users; and the low marginal costs associated with offering products or services to customers via the Internet. Others point out that by lowering the search costs for alternative products, electronic markets will benefit consumers through greater price competition and lower prices (Elofson and Robinson 1998). Additionally, use of the Internet is seen to open up new markets by moving organizations closer to their customers (Palmer and Griffith 1998). From this perspective, the rationale underlying organizational engagement in the digital economy is based on the resource needs of organizations, expectations of reduced costs and access to new markets, and the availability of cost-effective internetworking technologies.

A variant of this answer focuses less on immediate economic gains and more on issues of long-term organizational survival. Here, engagement in the digital economy is seen to be an essential aspect of a flexible and learning organization. Organizations can no longer learn all they need to know internally (Powell 1996). New ways of gaining information are essential. For example, marketing information can be gained from electronic communities and online focus groups (Kannan et al. 1998). Commercial firms develop partnerships and maintain continuing communication with external parties such as research centers, laboratories, and even former competitors. Because they provide a means of gaining access to new knowledge and a way of exploiting those capabilities for innovation and experimentation, these linkages are seen to be necessary for the long-term economic viability of organizations.

A second type of rationale focuses on epochal social transformations and argues that the United States is shifting from a society where industrial activity and modernist systems dominate to one in which information and postmodern systems will prevail (Bell 1979; Lyotard 1984). Toffler (1980) coined the term "the Third Wave economy" to refer to an economy based on information, reflecting what he sees as the central event of the past century—the death of matter. He and his colleagues posit the inevitability of a Third Wave economy, arguing that Internet connections are nothing less than the first step in the creation of a new civilization.

These two rationales evince the two approaches to technology-based organizational change we discussed above. The first answer, characterized by "strategic choice" assumptions, is grounded in both conventional economic analysis of information flows along value chains (Porter and Millar 1985) and the resource-dependence view of organizations (e.g., Pfeffer 1987). Engaging in internetworking is a strategic choice to enhance organizational performance. The second answer reflects the approach of technological determinism and is based on an assumed causal relationship between the technological infrastructure of an era (e.g., farm implements, factories, and computers) and the organizations, societies, and economies that result. The belief is that inter-networking is imperative given the certain coming of the digital economy.

While these two approaches offer some insight into internetworking processes, they ignore the difficulties of implementing technological change in organizations and the challenges of dealing with unintended consequences. For example, a story in the *Washington Post* (March 6, 1999) describes the dilemma faced by the U.S. government as it tries to keep open channels of communication with its constituencies while also limiting the amount of email received by its employees. In 1999, the Forest Service was swamped by thousands of emails from environmentalists and forest industries. Concerned that the agency's system might crash, Forest Service Chief Michael P. Dombeck announced a policy change, declaring that all email from constituents to Forest Service employees must go through him. We suspect that this story of email overloading the Forest Service workers is not an isolated incident. However, neither strategic choice nor technological determinism is particularly helpful in informing organizations how to respond effectively to the increasing demands of external constituents.

Internetworking has become part of doing business. However, many organizations are struggling with issues of how permeable their boundaries should be, how they will structure interactions with the outside world, how tightly or loosely coupled they should be with various stakeholders, and how exactly to integrate transactions and interactions into their own work practices. Moving beyond these struggles will require extensive experimentation and ongoing research.

Nature of Organizational Engagement in the Digital Economy

The artifacts of internetworking and the ways in which they have been used by organizations have changed over the years. During the earliest period, computer science departments in a few universities across the country and a small number of R&D organizations such as Rand Corporation and Bolt, Beranek & Newman helped to develop the Arpanet. Over time the development of other nets such as NSFnet and Bitnet allowed use to expand to include specific scientific communities. At that point, internetworking was understood as a way for distributed scientists to share distributed resources such as rare scientific instrumentation and large-scale databases or to achieve relatively unrestricted exchange of data and information. By the late 1980s, the use of email to communicate with distant scientific colleagues became popular. Being on the Internet primarily meant access to email for long-distance communication and collaboration. In the early 1990s, such usage spread more generally to public agencies, colleges, and universities. Other Internet services became popular, as did the notion of sharing information across organizations and with the general public.

Today, what it means for an organization "to be on the net" continues to evolve. Starting in 1995, private organizations and political groups in the United States have created WWW sites to advertise and market their products to a larger audience. Increasingly, organizations in countries around the globe are developing their own web sites, and some form of Internet presence has become an obligatory part of doing business in the late 1990s.

At this stage of development and use of the Internet, we can identify at least four modes in which organizations internetwork: (1) communicating via email; (2) generating a web presence; (3) establishing buyer-supplier transaction networks; and (4) creating real-time virtual integration. While some organizations might have one or two capabilities, such as web sites and email, others might employ all of them or be developing new ones. Much research remains to be done on the possible consequences of each of these ways of organizational engagement with the digital economy in terms of such factors as privacy, overload, surveillance, connection, dependence, fragmentation, and isolation. We briefly describe each mode below.

1. *Communicating via Email:* Since 1992, the number of corporate email addresses worldwide has gone from 1 million to 167 million. In 1998, email surpassed the telephone as the most frequently used communication medium in the office. Three billion email messages are sent each day by 100 million users (Yehling 1999). Early studies of email use focused on related changes within a single organization (Sproull and Kiesler 1991) or research community (Hesse et al. 1993; Orlikowski and Yates 1994). We now need to investigate changes in organizational processes and work practices resulting from email use, particularly across heterogeneous, global organizations or virtual communities, and with external constituents.

2. *Generating a Web Presence:* Presumably, most organizations with registered domain names plan to or already have web sites. Investigations into the qualitative aspects of such web sites has just begun. One research project analyzed the "openness" of governmental web sites, where openness was measured by degree of interactivity and transparency (Demchak et al. 1999). Culnan (1999), in a study for the Federal Trade Commission, investigated the extent to which customers interacting with web sites are informed of their privacy rights. The London School of Economics recently conducted a comprehensive survey of corporate web sites, ranking them according to quality and business value (see *The Financial Times,* May 17, 1999). We expect more research on the nature, use, and implications of web sites, particularly as organizations are pressured to produce high-quality sites while also providing significant consumer protection.

3. *Establishing Buyer-Supplier Transaction Networks:* Electronic marketplaces and buyer-supplier networks have received considerable research attention (Bakos 1998). Most of this research focuses on market dynamics, economics, or quantitative shifts in the makeup of industries, for example, rather than on organizational change processes or outcomes. In effect, organizations and their members are transparent players in these depictions of electronic markets. Research is clearly needed to examine the organizational role and consequences of constituting such electronic markets.

4. *Creating Real-Time Virtual Integration:* A more experimental and less common form of internetworking is real-time direct accessibility across organizational boundaries. Research suggests that such

internetworking is particularly challenging for organizations. For example, a recent investigation of telemedicine applications in three Boston hospitals looked at a videoconferencing system used by nurses to conduct presurgery assessment of patients living at a distance (Tanriverdi and Iacono, 1999). The researchers found that while the technology was easy to install, it was difficult getting people to collaborate and coordinate their activities on a regular basis. This confirms the well-established research finding that simply having technology in place is no guarantee of effective use. In this case, having technology available for interconnecting across hospitals did not ensure that interorganizational processes were integrated. Also necessary were new strategies, protocols, roles, and management techniques for working together across organizational and functional boundaries.

Despite the predominance of commercial, for-profit organizations on the Internet and their predicted role as major players in the digital economy, we do not have good understandings of who these organizations are, the change processes they are undergoing, the kinds of uses they make of the Internet, and what the consequences of these changes are for their members. We also do not know which organizations are not connecting and why, and what types of challenges organizations face when attempting to participate in the Internet. What it means for organizations to "be on the Internet" will also evolve as new technologies, business models, regulations, laws, and organizational processes emerge. Further research on various modes of internetworking is necessary if we want to be able to guide the evolution and emergence of the digital economy.

Suggestions for Future Research

We have argued that it is organizations (and the people in them) that create the digital economy as they develop and implement internetworking technologies and new organizational and interorganizational practices. We have also argued that these processes are not well explained by technological determinism or strategic choice. Consequently, we propose that an enacted perspective on the digital economy may be particularly useful. Taking such an enacted view seriously leads to a number of implications for our understanding of organizations in the digital economy. First of all, it eschews any notion that either technology or the economy is an unstoppable, independent, or deterministic force, outside the control of social institutions and individuals. It also eschews any notion that we can control, predict, or precisely model what the digital economy will be and what its organizational effects might be. The enacted view therefore suggests that in assessing the future of organizations in the digital economy we should start with three assumptions: (1) time-, context-, and technology-specific generalizations will be most useful; (2) as knowledgeable human agents, we can choose how and why we use internetworking technologies, thus significantly influencing the shape and consequences of the digital economy; and (3) we need to answer the question, what sort of digital economy do we collectively want to create?

We propose that research into the relationship between the digital economy and organizations should include programs that will explore, experiment, track, investigate, and detail the variety and complexity of technology-based organizational change and their socioeconomic consequences over time. Three arenas of investigation seem particularly important.

Research on the Role of Organizations in the Development of a Digital Economy

This program of research will attempt to document and identify why and how organizations are connecting to the Internet, both quantitatively and qualitatively. That is, we need to collect indicators over time of how many and what types of organizations are connecting to the Internet and how, as well as which organizations are not connecting and why. We also need to examine the social and technical challenges and opportunities that organizations face as they begin to internetwork. And we need to understand, through in-depth field studies, what it means for organizations to be internetworked, that is, what are the consequences—intended and unintended, initial and ongoing—of internetworking, for organizations, members, and communities.

Research on Social Transformations within and across
Internetworked Organizations

This program of research will focus on the kinds of changes being
enacted within and across organizations as they internetwork. Of
particular interest is understanding and classifying the range of
work processes associated with internetworking, and the implications of tighter and looser coupling with stakeholders such as
workers, customers, partners, regulators, suppliers, and citizens.
The example of information overload experienced by the Forest
Service is just one of many difficult issues facing organizations as
they attempt to engage in the digital economy. Others include
whether and how to integrate data, information systems, and local
work practices with those of customers, suppliers, and alliance
partners, all of whom may have different standards, protocols,
traditions, demands, incentives, and work processes, and how
much organizational information to share with various stakeholders and the public. As various social changes are implemented, new
kinds of roles, skills, capabilities, challenges, and processes are
likely to emerge, and these need to be examined along with the
personal, organizational, and economic implications. For example,
what does it mean to work in an internetworked organization?
What are the social, cultural, and personal implications of working
this way? What are the changes in quality of life for people who work
in internetworked organizations? And what are the unintended
institutional consequences of new ways of organizing in the digital
economy?

Research on the Development and Use of Internetworking
Technologies

This program of research would examine the types of
internetworking technologies developed for the digital economy
and consider how they are being used by various organizations. It
would attempt to identify differences in use and outcomes associated with a variety of internetworking technologies, as well as when,
where, and why these technologies are used within and across
organizations. Such new uses will create important new challenges

for the users of internetworking technologies, and we need to understand how and in what ways more or less effective uses emerge and are sustained or modified over time. New internetworking technologies and uses will put new demands on existing technology departments, and these need to be investigated. In addition, we currently have a plethora of yet-to-be-invented component technologies that will need to become part of the internetworked infrastructure of the digital economy. How this multiplicity of internetworking technologies will work together, which (if any) configurations will dominate, which social values will be embedded in them, and how organizations will deal with increased access to their people and systems are all important empirical research questions.

The digital economy is a phenomenon that is embedded in a variety of different social and temporal contexts, that relies on an evolving technological infrastructure, and whose uses are multiple and emergent. As a result, research studies will yield not precise predictions—because that is not possible in an unprecedented and enacted world—but underlying *patterns* of socioeconomic implications of working and organizing in various digital ways in different contexts. Similarly, research studies will offer not crisp prescriptions—because these are unhelpful in a dynamic, variable, and emergent world—but general *principles* to guide our ongoing and collective shaping of a digital world. Influenced by an understanding of patterns and principles, research can help to engage all of us in a dialogue about what future we want to invent.

Conclusion

While an enacted view recognizes that the digital economy, as a complex, emergent phenomenon, is not precisely predictable or completely manipulable, it does not suggest that we are powerless. Quite the contrary. By recognizing how our energies and efforts, interests and innovations, visions and values produce the nature, form, features, and effects of this digital economy, we can see how we might shape this phenomenon in new and effective ways. There is a well-known saying that the best way to predict the future is to invent it. As we invent the digital economy, we also have the opportunity to design experiments, prototypes, and research studies, as well as to engage in discussions and dialogues about our invention and its socioeconomic implications, so that we can continue to learn from and influence the worlds we are creating.

Acknowledgment

Thanks to Brian Kahin and Erik Brynjolfsson for helpful comments. Any opinions, findings, and conclusions or recommendations expressed in this material are those of the authors and do not necessarily reflect the view of the National Science Foundation.

References

Applegate, Lynda M., James I. Cash, Jr., and D. Quinn Mills, 1988. "Information Technology and Tomorrow's Manager." *Harvard Business Review* (November–December): 128–136.

Argyris, C., and D. Schön, 1978. *Organizational Learning: A Theory of Action Perspective*. Reading, MA: Addison-Wesley.

Attewell, P., and J. Rule, 1984. "Computing and Organizations: What We Know and What We Don't Know." *Communications of the ACM* 27(12): 1184–1191.

Bakos, Y., 1998. "The Emerging Role of Electronic Marketplaces on the Internet." *Communications of the ACM* 41(8): 35–42.

Barley, S. R., 1988. "Technology, Power, and the Social Organization of Work." *Research in the Sociology of Organizations* 6: 33–80.

Bijker, W., 1997. *Of Bicycles, Bakelites and Bulbs: Toward a Theory of Sociotechnical Change*. Cambridge, MA: MIT Press.

Bell, D., 1979. "The Social Framework of the Information Society." In Michael Dertouzos and Joel Moses, eds., *The Computer Age: A Twenty-year View* (Cambridge, MA: MIT Press), 163–211.

Berners-Lee, T., 1996. Private communication (May 17).

Blauner, R., 1964. *Alienation and Freedom*. Chicago, IL: University of Chicago Press.

Brody, H., 1992. "Of Bytes and Rights: Freedom of Expression and Electronic Communications." *Technology Review* 95(8): 22.

Brynjolfsson, E., 1993. "The Productivity Paradox of Information Technology: Review and Assessment." *Communications of the ACM* 37(12): 66–77.

Bullen, C. V., and J. L. Bennett, 1991. "Groupware in Practice: An Interpretation of Work Experiences." In R. Kling, ed., *Computerization and Controversy* (San Diego, CA: Academic Press), 257–287.

Button, G., ed., 1993. *Technology in Working Order: Studies in Work, Interaction, and Technology*. London: Routledge.

Cairncross, F., 1997. *The Death of Distance: How the Communications Revolution Will Change Our Lives*. Boston: Harvard Business School Press.

Carley, K. M., 2000. "Organizational Change and the Digital Economy: A Computational Organization Science Perspective." This volume.

Chung, Woo Young, 1998. "Why Do People Use the Internet?" Unpublished Ph.D. dissertation, Boston University School of Management.

Culnan, M., 1999. "Georgetown Internet Privacy Policy Study." McDonough School of Business, Georgetown University. http://www.msb.edu/faculty/culnanm/gippshome.html.

Culnan, M., and S. Milberg, 1999. http://www.msb.edu/faculty/culnanm/home.html.

David, P., 2000. "Understanding Digital Technology's Evolution and the Path of Measured Productivity Growth: Present and Future in the Mirror of the Past." This volume.

Davidow, W. H., and M. S. Malone, 1992. *The Virtual Corporation: Structuring and Revitalizing the Corporation of the 21st Century*. New York: HarperCollins.

Davis, E., 1997. "Spiritual Telegraphs and the Technology of Communications: Tuning into the Electromagnetic Imagination." Series on "Watch Your Language" at Public Netbase Media-Space, April 10. http://www.t0.or.at/davis/davislec1.html.

Demchak, C. C., C. Friis, and T. La Porte, 2000. "Webbing Governance: National Differences in Constructing the Face of Public Organizations." In G. D. Garson, ed., *Handbook of Public Information Systems* (New York: Marcel Dekker).

Denny, M., and M. Fuss, 1983. "The Effects of Factor Prices and Technological Change on the Occupational Demand for Labor: Evidence from Canadian Telecommunications." *Journal of Human Resources* Spring: 161–176.

Dyson, E., G. Gilder, G. Keyworth, and A. Toffler, 1996. "Cyberspace and the American Dream." *The Information Society* 12(3): 295–308.

Elofson, G., and W. N. Robinson, 1998. "Creating a Custom Mass-Production Channel on the Internet." *Communications of the ACM* 41(3): 56–62.

Galegher, J., L. Sproull, and S. Kiesler, 1998. "Legitimacy, Authority, and Community in Electronic Support Groups." *Written Communication* 15(4): 493–530.

Gasser, L., 1986. "The Integration of Computing and Routine Work." *ACM Transactions on Office Information Systems* 4(3): 205–225.

Giddens, A., 1984. *The Constitution of Society: Outline of the Theory of Structure*. Berkeley, CA: University of California Press.

Ginzberg, E., 1982. "The Mechanization of Work." *Scientific American* 247(3): 67–75.

Guice, J., 1998. "Looking Backward and Forward at the Internet." *The Information Society* 14(3): 201–212.

Giuliano, V., 1982. "The Mechanization of Office Work." *Scientific American* 247(3): 148–164.

Gunn, E. P., 1998. "Schwab Puts It All On-line." *Fortune,* December 7: 94.

Handy, C., 1995. "Trust and the Virtual Corporation." *Harvard Business Review* 73 (May–June): 40–50.

Hesse, B. W., L. Sproull, S. Kiesler, and J. P. Walsh, 1993. "Returns to Science: Computer Networks in Oceanography." *Communications of the ACM* 36(8): 90–101.

Hoffman, D., W. Kalsbeek, and T. Novak, 1996. "Internet and Web Use in the U.S." *Communications of the ACM* 39(12): 36–46.

Huber, G. P., 1990. "A Theory of the Effects of Advanced Information Technologies on Organizational Design, Intelligence, and Decision Making." *Academy of Management Review* 15: 47–71.

InterNic, 1999. Internic Domains. http://www.domainstats.com.

Iacono, S., and R. Kling, 1999. "Computerization Movements: The Rise of the Internet and Distant Forms of Work." In J. Yates and J. Van Maanen, eds., *IT and Organizational Transformation: History, Rhetoric, and Practice* (Newbury Park, CA: Sage Publications).

Iyer, P., 1998. "The New Business Class." *The New York Times Magazine,* March 8: 37–40.

Kannan, P. K., A.-M. Chang, and A. B. Whinston, 1998. "Marketing Information on the I-Way." *Communications of the ACM* 41(3): 35–43.

Kling, R., ed., 1996. *Computerization and Controversy,* 2nd ed. San Diego, CA: Academic Press.

Kling, R., and W. Scacchi, 1982. "The Web of Computing: Computer Technology as Social Organization." *Advances in Computers* 21: 1–90.

Kling, R., and R. Lamb, 2000. "IT and Organizational Change in Digital Economies: A Sociotechnical Approach." In this volume.

Kraut, R., S. Koch, and S. Dumais, 1988. "Computerization, Productivity, and Quality of Employment." *Communications of the ACM* 32(2): 220–238.

Kraut, R., W. Scherlis, T. Murkohopadhyay, J. Manning, and S. Kiesler, 1996. "The HomeNet Field Trial of Residential Internet Services." *Communications of the ACM* 39(12): 55–63.

Kraut, R., et al., 1998. "Social Impact of the Internet: What Does It Mean?" *Communications of the ACM* 41(12): 21–22.

Leavitt, H., and T. Whisler, 1958. "Management in the 1980's." *Harvard Business Review* 36: 41–48.

Lyotard, Jean-François,1984. *The Postmodern Condition.* Minneapolis: University of Minnesota Press.

Mackay, W. E., 1988. "Diversity in the Use of Electronic Mail." *ACM Transactions on Office Information Systems* 6(4): 380–397.

Markoff, J., 1999. "Intel Goes to Battle As Its Embedded Serial Number Is Unmasked." *New York Times,* April 29.

Markus, M. L., and D. Robey, 1988. "Information Technology and Organizational Change: Causal Structure in Theory and Research." *Management Science* 34(5): 583–598.

Martin, J., 1996. *Cybercorp: The New Business Revolution.* New York: Amacom.

Marx, L., and M. R. Smith, eds., 1994. *Does Technology Drive History?* Cambridge, MA: MIT Press.

Mowshowitz, A., 1997. "Virtual Organization." *Communications of the ACM* 40(9): 30–37.

National Research Council, 1999. *Funding a Revolution.* Washington, DC: National Academy Press.

Matrix Information and Directory Services, 1997. Internet Growth. http://www.mids.org.

NetNames Ltd., 1999. Domain Names. http://www.domainstats.com.

Network Wizards, 1999. Number of Internet Hosts. http://www.nw.com/zone/host-count-history.

Noble, D., 1984. *Forces of Production: A Social History of Industrial Automation.* New York: Knopf.

NUA Ltd., 1999. How Many Online? May 16. http://www.nua.survey.net/surveys/about/index.html.

Orlikowski, W. J., 1992. "Learning from Notes: Organizational Issues in Groupware Implementation." *Proceedings of the Third Conference on Computer-Supported Cooperative Work,* Toronto, 362–369.

Orlikowski, W. J., 1996. "Improvising Organizational Transformation over Time: A Situated Change Perspective." *Information Systems Research* 7(1): 63–92.

Orlikowski, W. J., and J. D. Hofman, 1997. "An Improvisational Model of Change Management: The Case of Groupware Technologies." *Sloan Management Review* 38(2): 11–21.

Orlikowski, W. J., and J. Yates, 1994. "Genre Repertoire: The Structuring of Communicative Practices in Organizations." *Administrative Science Quarterly* 39(4): 541–574.

Palmer, J. W., and D. A. Griffith, 1998. "An Emerging Model of Web Site Design for Marketing." *Communications of the ACM* 41(3): 44–51.

Pfeffer, J., 1987. "A Resource Dependence Perspective on Intercorporate Relations." In M. Mizruchi and M. Schwartz, eds., *Intercorporate Relations: The Structural Analysis of Business* (New York: Cambridge University Press).

Pinch, T. J., and W. E. Bijker, 1984. "The Social Construction of Facts and

Artefacts; or How the Sociology of Science and the Sociology of Technology Might Benefit Each Other." *Social Studies of Science* 14: 399–441.

Porter, M., and V. Millar, 1985. "How Information Gives You Competitive Advantages." *Harvard Business Review* (July–August): 2–13.

Powell, W. W., 1996. "Trust-Based Forms of Governance." In R. M. Kramer and T. R. Tyler, eds., *Trust in Organizations* (Thousand Oaks, CA: Sage Publications), 51–67.

Rao, H. R., A. F. Salam, and B. DosSantos, 1998. "Introduction (Marketing and the Internet)." *Communications of the ACM* 41(3): 32–34.

Rheingold, H., 1993. *The Virtual Community: Homesteading on the Electronic Frontier.* Reading, MA: Addison-Wesley.

Schryer, C. F., 1993. "Records as Genres." *Written Communication* 10: 200–234.

Shaw, M. J., 1999. "Electronic Commerce: State of the Art." *Conference on E-Commerce in the Global Marketplace,* University of Illinois, Urbana-Champaign, April 15.

Smart, T., 1999. "Delivering Packages, Partnerships." *The Washington Post,* H1: 8.

Smith, M. D., J. Bailey, and E. Brynjolfsson, 2000. "Understanding Digital Markets: Review and Assessment." This volume.

Sproull, L., and S. Kiesler, 1991. *Connections.* Cambridge MA: MIT Press.

Tanriverdi, H., and S. Iacono, 1999. "Diffusion of Telemedicine: A Knowledge Barrier Perspective. *Telemedine Journal* 5(3): 223–243.

Tedeschi, B., 1999. "The Net's Real Business Happens .Com to .Com." *New York Times,* April 19.

Thomas, R. J., 1994. *What Machines Can't Do: Politics and Technology in the Industrial Enterprise.* Berkeley, CA: University of California Press.

Toffler, A., 1980. *The Third Wave.* New York: Morrow.

Turoff, M., 1997. "Virtuality." *Communications of the ACM* 40(9): 38–43.

Von Hippel, E., 1988. *The Sources of Innovation.* New York: Oxford University Press.

Wiener, N., 1954. *The Human Use of Human Beings.* Boston: Houghton Mifflin.

Yates, J., 1999. "The Structuring of Early Computer Use in Life Insurance." *Journal of Design History* 12(1): 5–24.

Yehling, R., 1999. "We've All Got Mail." *The Year in Computing* 3(1): 81–84.

Zimbalist, A., ed., 1979. *Case Studies on the Labor Process.* New York: Monthly Review Press.

Zuboff, S., 1988. *In the Age of the Smart Machine.* New York: Basic Books.

Contributors

Sulin Ba (sulin@rcf-fs.usc.edu, www-rcf.usc.edu/~sulin/) is Assistant Professor of Information Systems and Codirector of the Electronic Economy Research Program (ebizlab) at the Marshall School of Business of the University of Southern California. Her research interests include electronic commerce, knowledge management, and virtual teams. Her current projects involve the design of trusted third parties to help small business overcome online barriers such as security and product quality uncertainty. Her work on the institutional setup to help small business survive and grow in the digital economy has been used as the basis for testimony before the House Committee on Small Business. In the knowledge management area, she investigates how to allocate scarce resources to create knowledge that delivers the most value for organizations.

Joseph Bailey (jbailey@rhsmith.umd.edu, www.rhsmith.umd.edu/tbpp/jbailey/) is Assistant Professor in the Department of Logistics, Business and Public Policy at the University of Maryland. With Lee McKnight, he edited *Internet Economics* (MIT Press, 1997). His research focuses on information infrastructure with respect to pricing and resource distribution, the roles of cybermediaries, Internet economics, and policy analysis.

Erik Brynjolfsson (erikb@mit.edu, ccs.mit.edu/erik/) is Associate Professor at MIT's Sloan School of Management, where he codirects the Program on Electronic Commerce and Marketing. He lectures worldwide on how businesses can effectively use information technology in general and the Internet in particular. His research focuses on three questions: How can information technology transform the structures of markets and firms? What is the impact of information technology investments on productivity and business value? How does the Internet affect commerce in general and information goods in particular?

Kathleen M. Carley (kcarley@ece.cmu.edu, sds.hss.cmu.edu/faculty/carley/carley.htm) is Director of the Center for Computational Analysis of Social and Organizational Systems at Carnegie Mellon University. Her research is in the areas of computational organization theory, social and organizational adaptation and evolution, statistical models for network analysis and network evolution, computational text analysis, and the impact of telecommunication technologies on communication and information diffusion. She founded and coedits, with William A. Wallace, the journal *Computational and Mathematical Organization Theory*.

Paul A. David (paul.david@all-souls.oxford.ac.uk) is Professor of Economics (and by courtesy, Professor of History) at Oxford University. His primary research interest is in the economics of technological change, demographic change, and institutional change, and other areas of theoretical and empirical research on the nature of path-dependence in economic processes in the modern era.

Shane Greenstein (s-greenstein1@nwu.edu, skew2.kellogg.nwu.edu /~greenste/) is Associate Professor in the Management and Strategy Department of the Kellogg Graduate School of Management at Northwestern University. His research interests cover a wide variety of topics in the economics of high technology. He has studied buyer benefits from advances in computing and communication technology, structural change in information technology markets, standardization in electronics markets, growth and investment in digital infrastructure, and government procurement and operation of computing.

John C. Haltiwanger (haltiwan@econ.bsos.umd.edu, www.bsos.umd .edu/econ/haltiwanger), Professor of Economics at the University of Maryland, has recently completed a term as Chief Economist of the U.S. Bureau of the Census. His current research exploits the recently created longitudinal establishment databases that are available at the Bureau of the Census. This research focuses on the process of job creation, job destruction, restructuring, and lumpy investment activity at the plant level and the connection to aggregate fluctuations in employment, investment, and productivity. His book *Job Creation and Destruction* (MIT Press, 1996, coauthored with Steven Davis and Scott Schuh) presents a comprehensive analysis of job creation and destruction in the U.S. manufacturing sector over the last two decades.

Donna Hoffman (hoffman@ecommerce.vanderbilt.edu, www2000 .ogsm.vanderbilt.edu/) co-directs eLab and is Associate Professor of Management at the Owen Graduate School of Management at Vanderbilt University. At eLab, Hoffman studies the commercialization of emerging media. Her current research efforts focus on effective Internet marketing strategies, consumer behavior in online environments, and the policy implications of commercializing the Web.

Heather E. Hudson (hudson@usfca.edu, www.usfca.edu/mclaren/ Admin/Hudson.html) is Director of the Telecommunications Management and Policy Program in the McLaren School of Business at the University of San Francisco. Her books include *Global Connections: International Telecommunications Infrastructure and Policy* (Van Nostrand Reinhold, 1997); *Electronic Byways: State Policies for Rural Development through Telecommunications* (Aspen Institute, 1992, with Edwin Parker), and *Communication Satellites: Their Development and Impact* (Free Press, 1990).

C. Suzanne Iacono (siacono@nsf.gov) is Director, Computation and Social Systems Program, in the Information and Intelligent Systems Division of the Computer and Information Sciences and Engineering Directorate of the National Science Foundation. She is cochair of the Social, Economic and Workforce (SEW) Implications of Information Technology and Information Technology Workforce Development Coordinating Group, which gives policy, program and budget guidance on SEW activities as part of the Interagency Working Group on IT R&D in the executive branch of the federal government. She is also chair of the Social and Economic Implications of IT Working Group for the Information Technology Research initiative at NSF. Recent projects include telemedicine in Boston hospitals, a national study of Internet use in the home, virtual teams, electronic talk, societal implications of nanotechnology, IT and organizational change and computerization movements.

Ron S. Jarmin (rjarmin@ces.census.gov) is a research economist at the Center for Economic Studies of the U.S. Bureau of the Census. He has published papers in the areas of industrial organization, technology and firm performance, industrial classification, and urban economics. He has also done considerable research on the impact of government technology programs on the productivity and survival of manufacturing establishments.

Brian Kahin (kahin@wyoming.com, www.bigfoot.com/~kahin) is currently a fellow of the Internet Policy Institute. He was previously a consultant and senior policy analyst in the White House Office of Science and Technology Policy. Kahin was founding director of the Information Infrastructure Project at Harvard's John F. Kennedy School of Government, where he and Lewis Branscomb initiated the first academic research program to address the social, economic, and policy implications of the Internet. He has been the editor or coeditor of seven books on the information infrastructure and public access to the Internet and has most recently edited (with Hal Varian) *Internet Publishing and Beyond* (MIT Press, 2000).

Lawrence F. Katz (lkatz@harvard.edu, www.economics.harvard.edu /faculty/katz/katz.html) is Professor of Economics at Harvard University and a Research Associate of the National Bureau of Economic Research. His research focuses on issues in the general areas of labor economics and the economics of social problems. His work has examined a wide range of topics including wage and income inequality; unemployment; theories of wage determination; the economics of education; the impact of globalization and technological change on the labor market; and the evaluation of the effectiveness of social and labor market policies. He is currently examining the history of economic inequality in the United States and the roles of technological changes and the pace of educational advance in affecting the wage structure. He served as Chief Economist of the U.S. Department of Labor from January 1993 to August 1994 and was the first Director of the Program on Children at the National Bureau of Economic Research.

Rob Kling (kling@indiana.edu, www.slis.indiana.edu/kling) is Professor of Information Systems and Information Science at the School of Library and Information Science of Indiana University. He is the author of *Computerization and Controversy: Value Conflicts and Social Choices* (Academic Press, 1996). His research focuses on the social consequences of computerization and the social choices that are available to people.

Roberta Lamb (rlamb@hawaii.edu, lamb.cba.hawaii.edu/) is Assistant Professor in the Decision Sciences Department at the University of Hawaii, Manoa, College of Business Administration. Her research interests include CORPS (Computing, Organizations, Policy and Society) and Social and Organizational Informatics.

Josh Lerner (jlerner@hbs.edu, www.people.hbs.edu/jlerner) is Associate Professor at Harvard Business School, with a joint appointment in the Finance and Entrepreneurial Management Units. His research focuses on the structure of venture capital organizations, and their role in transforming scientific discoveries into commercial products. Much of his research is collected in *The Venture Capital Cycle* (MIT Press, 1999). He also examines the impact of intellectual property protection, particularly patents, on the competitive strategies of firms in high-technology industries. He is a co-organizer of the National Bureau of Economic Research's Science and Technology Policy Research Group and is a Faculty Research Fellow in its Corporate Finance and Productivity Programs.

Brent Moulton (brent.moulton@bea.doc.gov) is Associate Director for National Income, Expenditure, and Wealth Accounts at the Department of Commerce's Bureau of Economic Analysis (BEA) and is responsible for producing the national income and product accounts, including gross domestic product. Prior to his appointment to BEA, he spent 13 years at the Bureau of Labor Statistics, where he served as Chief of Price and Index Number Research.

Thomas P. Novak (novak@ecommerce.vanderbilt.edu, www2000 .ogsm.vanderbilt.edu/) is Associate Professor of Management and Codirector of eLab at the Owen Graduate School of Management, Vanderbilt University. He is Director of Owen's MBA program emphasis on electronic commerce. His current research interests include measuring the online consumer experience (flow, consumer control, and the design of compelling online environments); online advertising (Web advertising metrics and modeling online advertising exposure); Internet marketing strategy (business models, new paradigms for electronic commerce); and electronic commerce policy (the "digital divide," privacy, and trust).

Wanda J. Orlikowski (wanda@mit.edu, ccs.mit.edu/wanda.html) is Associate Professor of Information Technologies and Organization Studies at MIT's Sloan School of Management. Her primary research interests focus on the ongoing interaction between organizations and information technology, with particular emphasis on organizing structures, cultures, and work practices. She is currently exploring the organizational and technological aspects of working virtually.

Michael D. Smith, a recent graduate of the Sloan School of Management at MIT, is Assistant Professor at the H. John Heinz III School of Public Policy and Management at Carnegie Mellon University. His research analyzes the nature of structure and competition in electronic markets. His current work addresses retailer pricing strategies and customer choice behavior on the Internet.

Hal R. Varian (hal@SIMS.Berkeley.edu, www.sims.berkeley.edu/ resources/infoecon/) is Dean of the School of Information Management and Systems at the University of California at Berkeley. He is also Professor in the Haas School of Business and in the Department of Economics, and he holds the Class of 1944 Professorship. He is the author of two major economics textbooks, which have been translated into nine languages. His recent work has been concerned with the economics of information technology and the information economy.

Andrew B. Whinston (abw@uts.cc.utexas.edu) is the Hugh Roy Cullen Centennial Chair Professor of Information Systems, Economics, Computer Science, and Library and Information Sciences, IC^2 Fellow, and Director of the Center for Research in Electronic Commerce (http://crec.bus.utexas.edu) at the University of Texas at Austin. He is Editor-in-Chief of the journals *Decision Support Systems* and the *Journal of Organizational Computing and Electronic Commerce*. His recent work focuses on bundle markets in electronic commerce. His books include *The Frontiers of Electronic Commerce* (Addison-Wesley, 1996, with Ravi Kalakota), *Electronic Commerce: A Manager's Guide* (Addison-Wesley, 1997, with Ravi Kalakota), and *The Economics of Electronic Commerce* (Macmillan, 1997, with Dale O. Stahl and Soon-Yong Choi).

Han Zhang is Assistant Professor of Information Technology Management at the DuPree College of Management of Georgia Institute of Technology. He received his doctoral degree in Information Systems from the University of Texas at Austin in summer 2000. His research focuses on online trust issues and the evolution of electronic markets.

Index

DATE DUE

FEB 2 2 2004		
APR 1 8 2004		
FEB 0 8 2005		
FEB 2 7 2005		
MAR 2 1 2005		
APR – 5 2005		
APR 1 2 2005		
	No Longer Property of Mount Allison	

Understanding the Digital Economy